पुरातत्त्व
पुरातत्त्व
PURĀTATTVA

Bulletin of the Indian Archaeological Society

No. 32 2001-02

Editors
K. N. Dikshit and K.S. Ramachandran

D.K. Printworld (P) Ltd.
New Delhi

Cataloging in Publication Data — DK
[Courtesy : D.K. Agencies (P) Ltd. <docinfo@dkagencies.com>]

Purātattva : bulletin of the Indian Archaeological Society, no. 32, 2001-02 / editors, K.N. Dikshit ; K.S. Ramachandran.

p. 29 cm.

Includes bibliographical references.

ISBN 8124603243

1. Archaeology — India — Periodicals. 2. India — Antiquities — Periodicals. 3. India — Civilization — Periodicals. I. Dikshit, K.N. II. Ramachandran, K.S. (Kattalai Sivasubramanium), 1939- III. Indian Archaeological Society.

First Published in 2002
First Reprinted in 2005
ISBN 81-246-0324-3
Price for volume 32 (2001-02): Rs. 1000 US $ 50

Reprint authorised by
Indian Archaeological Society
New Delhi - 110 016

Purātattva is published annually.

Manuscripts (whether in the form of articles or notes or book reviews) offered for publication should be sent to the Editor, Purātattva, Indian Archaeological Society, B-17, Qutab Institutional Area, New Delhi - 110 016.

Published and printed by:
D.K. Printworld (P) Ltd.
'Srikunj,' F-52, Bali Nagar
New Delhi – 110015
Phone : (011) 2545 3975, 2546 6019 Fax : (011) 2546 5926
E-mail : dkprintworld@vsnl.net
www.dkprintworld.com

PURĀTATTVA

CONTENTS

Obituaries

B.P. Sinha
(1919-2002)

Born in 1919 in Bihar Sharif, Bihar, Professor Sinha had a very brilliant academic career, culminating in a first class first at the M. A. examination in History from Patna University. He had more than a dozen books and nearly a hundred papers to his credit. His excavations at Chirand in Bihar will go down as a very significant contribution to the prehistory of Bihar. Likewise, his *magnum opus, The Decline of the Kingdom of Magadh*, will ever continue to show the beacon light on the subject.

As a person, the lean and thin Sinha was all the time bubbling with sweetness and affection, for one and all. Following the name of one of the kings of Bihar, Prof. Sinha was a real Ajatasatru, which means one who never had any enemy.

Sinha was selected for advanced studies abroad in History and joined school of Oriental and African Studies under Prof. L.D. Barnett. He was awarded the Ph.D. Degree on his thesis "Decline of the Kingdom of Magadh circa 455-1000 AD" in 1948 from London University. On his return he rejoined Patna College and when the Post Graduate Department of Ancient Indian History and Culture was started, he joined Patna University and became the Head of the Department in 1958 and Professor in 1959. He went to USA as Visiting Asian Professor and also to Bulgaria and Yugoslavia.

He was also the patron of Indian Archaeological Society and received innumerable academic awards.

In the passing away of Sinha on May 3, 2002, the country has lost a veteran archaeologist and historian. He covered a very wide spectrum of research, right from the stone ages up to the historical times. Not many scholars, living or dead, was a versatile genius as him. The loss is irreparable to the country.

We pray to the Lord to grant peace to the departed soul and to give the necessary courage to Shrimati Sinha and other members of the family to bear this great loss.

K.N. Dikshit

Y.D. Sharma
(1916-2002)

Born on 21st September, 1916 at Gurukul Kangri near Haridwar in Uttaranchal, Y.D. Sharma took his M.A. degree in Sanskrit from St. Stephens College, Delhi University. He won the prestigious Central State Scholarship from Oxford where he completed his B.Litt. and joined Ph.D. on "Civil Law according to Kautilya". He was awarded Ph.D. under Prof. P.W. Thomas before returning to India in 1945.

Sharma, who started work with the Archaeological Survey of India as an Assistant Superintendent in 1946, was initiated into the field work by Sir Mortimer Wheeler. His initial stint was in the south (in Brahmagiri in what is now Karnataka). Following the partition of India, he was posted in Calcutta and worked with Hilary Waddington. While based in Calcutta, he did considerable work in Orissa, particularly in Konarak area which was then quite inaccessible. In an absorbing conversation on a rather chilly October evening at his Kailash Colony residence in south Delhi, he remembered nostalgically how, in those days, he used to go to Konarak in a bullock cart from Puri along the sea coast. He also recounted, as an aside, how once while on a site in Shahjahanpur district in Uttar Pradesh, he and his team members were taken by the villagers to be dacoits having captured a deserted rest house and could be saved with the help of the police with great difficulty: another case of professional hazard of a practising Archaeologist.

Sharma had concentrated on studying sites around Ropar (1952-55) in Punjab and found very useful traces of the heritage of the Harappan Civilization. Studies in these areas had become necessary as following the partition of India the main Harappan sites had fallen in Pakistan and thus to reconstruct the history of the civilization, all potential sites on this side of the border had to be studied. This excavation has unfolded the past patterns hitherto unknown.

Probably the most significant work done by this eminent archaeologist is the study of copper hoards and related discoveries during excavations at Bahadarabad near Haridwar. Another significant work in a nearby site at Alamgirpur in Meerut district was done by Sharma when he studied the pottery excavated by a group of students under the supervision of a teacher. He identified two pieces of the excavated pottery as of Harappan origin and this finding extended the eastern frontier of this civilization to the upper reaches of Ganga valley.

During his professional career, Sharma visited Afghanistan and Mongolia on different assignments. He explored extensively the interior of Afghanistan with Shri T.N. Ramchandran. While posted at Madras, he studied and contributed on the megalithic culture of Kerala specially under ground rock-cut caves.

He retired in 1974 as Deputy Director General. After retirement he joined the Punjab University as Visiting Professor and it was during his stay at the University that he excavated Moharana and noticed Early Harappans as first occupants. The Bara ware was found freely intermingled with them.

He has contributed a number of papers to different books and research journals. His most important contribution was a book entitled *Delhi and its Neighbourhood* in English and Hindi.

Sharma had combined with his profession of Archaeology a passion for trekking and went on many expeditions during his active days. While at Oxford he had cultivated a taste for western classical music but the same was not sustained on his return to India. He used to broadcast frequently on the BBC along with Balraj Sahani and other Indians there.

He passed away on December 21, 2002 and is survived by his wife and a daughter.

K.N. Dikshit

Z.A. Desai
(1925-2002)

Ziauddin A. Desai was born on the 17th May 1925 at Dhanduka, District Ahmedabad, Gujarat. He graduated in 1946 and M.A. (Persian) in 1948 from Bombay University. He obtained first class at both the examinations. He got his D.Litt. in Persian from Tehran University (Iran) in 1959.

He started his career as a Lecturer in Persian (1947-1953). He joined the Archaeological Survey of India as Assistant Superintending Epigraphist in 1953 and was appointed Superintending Epigraphist in 1961. Since 1977 to 1983 he headed the Epigraphy Branch as its Director. After his retirement, he had settled at Ahmedabad where he passed away on March 24, 2002.

While in Survey, he was deputed to the USSR, Afghanisatan, Iran, Bangladesh, Syria, Pakistan and other countries. He had contributed more than two hundered research articles in National and International journals of repute. He also participated in all the conferences relating to history, language and literature, epigraphy art and architecture and manuscripts.

His publications include *Mosques of India, Indo-Islamic Architecture Centres of Islamic learning in India, Life and Work of Faizi, Published Inscriptions of Rajasthan, Athar-i-Qadims-i-Hind and Taj Mahal* (with Begley).

Ziauddin A. Desai was the foremost serving scholar in India in Arabic and Persian Epigraphy, Islamic Art and Architecture. He did pioneering work in the above mentioned fields. He was not only a scholar but also a fine teacher who engaged himself in scholarly pursuits till his death. He had been duly honoured with President's award for his contribution in Arabic and Persian.

Amarendra Nath

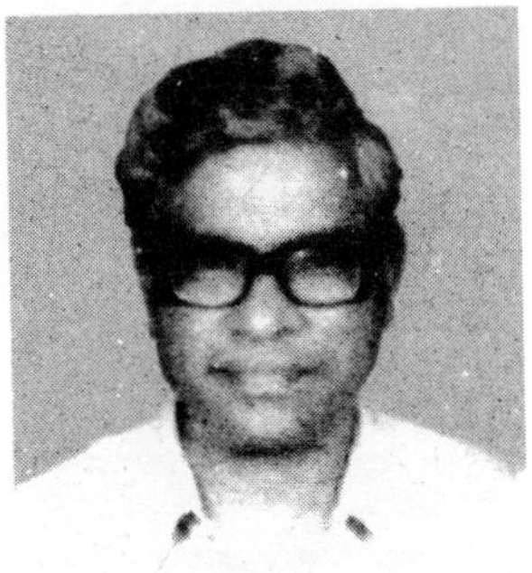

A.M. Shastri
(1934-2002)

Born at Guna in Madhya Pradesh on 5th March, 1934, Ajay Mitra Shastri (originally named Mahendra Kumar) had his early education in the Gurukuls at Rajor (Faizabad) and Ayodhya. It was while being admitted to the Gurukul that he got his name 'Ajay Mitra', He himself choose it from the list of other mitra ending names suggested by his Acharya. The four years that he spent at the Gurukuls inculcated in him a habit of leading a simple hard life, of speaking Sanskrit and a critical approach of accepting nothing without sound reasons. After leaving the Gurukul he joined the Sanskrit *Pathsala* at Baran (Kota district, Rajasthan) where he completed his Madhyama examination and also *Visharad* and *Sahitya* Ratna examinations in Hindi. For his further education, he went to Banaras (Varanasi) where he completed his Shastri examination (1951-53) in first class from the Govt. Sanskrit college. It is this degree that gave him his surname. While doing his Shastri course he also completed his Matriculation and Intermediate examinations. Subsequently he did his Shastri (equivalent to B.A.) in 1953 with Sociology, History and Political Science from Kashi Vidyapeeth and M. A. in Ancient Indian History and Culture from BHU in 1957.

In the same year, he got the job of lecturer in the Dept. of Ancient History and Culture at Nagpur University. It was here that he took up his Ph.D. on *Brihatsamhita* of *Varahamihra*, which he completed in 1962. Dr. Shastri remained with the Nagpur University, first serving as lecturer (1957 to 1965), then as Reader (1965-1977) and finally as Professor (1977-1994) till his retirement.

In his death on 11th Jan 2002, the world of Indology has lost a scholar of great caliber who had great command over various sources and who could write with equal felicity and command on any of the branches of Indological studies.

S.P. Gupta

Shyam Kumar Pandey
(1933-2002)

Shyam Kumar Pandey was born on the 28th June, 1933 at Sagar, Madhya Pradesh. He was educated at Bilaspur and Sagar. After completing M.A. in Ancient Indian History, Culture & Archaeology, he started his career as Assistant Professor in the Department of Ancient Indian History, Culture & Archaeology, University of Sagar, on the 13th November 1961 and was promoted as Reader in the same Department.

His career as an archaeologist started with exploration and excavation of several sites and excavations at Tripuri and Bhimbetka as Assistant Director. Later, he directed the excavations at Malhar and Nandur.

He was the person who had the honour to receive the first Ph.D. on Rock Art.

He was nominated as an Executive Member of the International Foundation of Rock Art organization and Chairman of Indian Rock Art Association. He was Life Member of the Indian Archaeological Society, Indian Society for Prehistoric & Quaternary Studies and Indian History and Culture Society. He was a Fellow of the Indian Council of Historical Research. He visited France and Australia to get acquainted with the rock paintings of the region.

He has published more than fifty research papers and articles in standard journals and contributed a book on *Indian Rock Art*.

He passed away on the 18 August, 2002 and is survived by his wife and two sons.

Manoj Kumar Kurmi

PURĀTATTVA

Number 32 **2001–2002**

Editorial

When Prof. A.K. Narain of Banaras Hindu University founded the Indian Archaeological Society in 1967 at Varanasi, we the archaeologists, never visualized that one day it would attain a height to have its own building and handle several projects. Our dream is achieved. The Society not only established itself in its own building but also entered a new era of activities, creating sister organisations like "Centre for Research and Training in History, Archaeology and Palaeoenvironment" and "The Indraprastha Museum of Art and Archaeology "; the former has been recognized by the University Grants Commission as a centre to conduct Refresher Courses in Archaeology for University and College teachers. The first course (17th June–7th July 2002) was inaugurated by Shri Jagmohan, Hon'ble Minister for Tourism and Culture, Government of India.

The three projects sponsored by the Indian Council of Historical Research, viz. 'Atlas of the Indus-Saraswati Civilization', 'Methodology in Archaeological Research' and 'Growth of Cities in Ancient India' are progressing as per plan. Besides a group of archaeologists and architects are working in Gujarat to complete the report on the earthquake-damaged monuments.

The Society has also undertaken a "Multidisciplinary Scientific Probe into the 'Lost Saraswati': Surface and Sub-surface Investigations". It has been submitted to ISRO for clearance. Different agencies such as the Department of Geology, Delhi University, Physical Research Laboratory, Ahmedabad, IIT Kanpur, Department of Remote Sensing, Shimla and Jodhpur and a few others are involved in this project. A two-day seminar on 'Lost Saraswati' was organized by the Society on the 23rd–24th February 2002 which was chaired by Prof. Yashpal.

The Society also carried out an excavation at Sanjan in Taluka Umargaon, District Valsad, Gujarat, under the direction of Dr. S.P. Gupta, our Chairman, in collaboration with World Zorthusti Cultural Foundation with the financial assistance from the Archaeological Survey of India. This work is also a part of the Indian Council of Historical Research project entitled "Historical and Archaeological Study of Parsi/Zoroastian Religious places of importance in western India with special reference to Bahrot caves" directed by Dr. (Mrs.) Mani Kamerkar. As per oral traditions of the Parsi, a group of Zorastrians who fled the Islamic persecution in Iran in the 7th century A.D., first made landfall on the Indian mainland at a place called Sanjan. It was from here that they spread to other parts of Gujarat and, later to the rest of India. The only semi-historical document is a Persian poem, the *'Kisseh-i-Sanjan'* written in approximately 1600 A.D. regarding this landfall. A report on this excavation is being published here.

Of late, it is realized that the existing Conservation policy of Monuments in India, which started in 1904, completely overlooked peoples' participation in the heritage management since State was considered to be the only instrument which could protect monuments. The Archaeological Survey of India as well as Archaeological Departments of the State Governments so far monopolized this field. To impart training in archaeology and conservation, their efforts could not reach every nook and corner of India where thousands of archaeological monuments, sites and remains are located. We know it is not possible to save all but at least the most important ones should be preserved for posterity. We strongly feel that it is our bounden duty to create awareness among the people about the importance of our cultural heritage through publicity in mass-media, telecasts and other visual. There is a strong need to formulate a 'National Policy on Conservation of Monuments in India'.

We would also like to draw the attention of our readers to the system of holding the annual meetings of the Central Advisory Board of Archaeology under the auspices of Archaeological Survey of India. The Archaeological Survey of India which displayed excavated materials and held meetings among field-workers, provided a forum for discussion of archaeological problems, has long been discontinued. This needs to be revived. The Indian philosophy of conservation, which is also the Asian philosophy, could be also be discussed among field-workers so that conservation of monuments in India may proceed on a set guide lines, and should not be a matter of everybodys concern.

We deeply regret the sad demise of Dr. Y.D. Sharma and Dr. Z.A. Desai both of the Archaeological Survey of India, Prof. B.P. Sinha of Patna University, Prof. Ajay Mitra Shastri of Nagpur University and Dr. S.K. Pandey of Sagar University. May their soul rest in peace. The archaeological fraternity will remember them as exemplary scholars.

The publication of this issue has been financially supported by the Archaeological Survey of India and the Indian Council of Historical Research. We are grateful to them and they are in no way responsible for the views expressed by the authors.

We are thankful to Dr. S.P. Gupta for all the help and encouragement that he gave during the publication of this number. Thanks are also due to our young colleagues in the Society: Shri Manoj Kumar Harbola for preparing the type-script and Sarvashri Tejas Garge, T. Arunraj, M. Rajesh and Ms. Anuja Geetali, Mahua Bhattacharya and Sonali Gupta, and Sarvashri Jassu Ram, M.S. Mani, G. Laxminarayanan and Rakesh Dutta deserve our appreciation.

It is a heartening thing to announce that Shrimati Gayatri Sharma w/o late Dr. Y.D. Sharma and Shri Harish Bhardwaj, her son-in-law provided a corpus of Rupees two lacs to the Society for organizing a memorial lecture to be named after the Late Dr. Sharma called '*Dr. Y.D. Sharma Memorial Lecture*' every year.

We are also thankful to Smt. Anita Mehta and members of her staff for their whole hearted support in bringing out this issue in so short a time and in a fine manner.

K.N. Dikshit

K.S. Ramchandran

The Homeland of Indo-European Languages and Culture: Some Thoughts

B.B. Lal*

I am extremely sorry to find that in its issue dated January 11, the *Indian Express* carried a news story, under the caption 'Aryan Homeland Controversy rages on at History Seminar', which totally misrepresents my views on the subject. I, therefore, feel it is my duty to place before your readers the true picture, by giving below the relevant excerpts from my paper presented at the Seminar. [I am not giving the full text as it is rather long. However, if any reader is inteiested in it, the same may be obtained from me (Tel. 011-26855817)].

When this topic caught the attention of the academic community for the first time, towards the end of the eighteenth century, some Western scholars opined that India, being the home of the earliest extant literature (viz., the Vedas) of the Indo-European group of languages, must have been the original homeland of these languages. However, soon the canvas got enlarged so as not to limit it to India but to include a large part of Central Asia. Thereafter the scenario was taken to Europe and, not surprisingly, almost every part thereof was declared to be the homeland: Scandinavia, Finland, south-west Russia, the Baltic area, Germany, Lithuania, Hungary, the Danube valley and so on. In fact, the rat race was so much that no part of Europe was left out. In a very sarcastic comment Jean-Paul Demoule remarked in 1980 'We have seen that one primarily places the IE's (Indo-Europeans) in the north if one is German, in the east if one is Russian, and in the middle if, being Italian or Spanish, one has no chance of competing for the privilege'.

However, in the course of time this Euro-centric approach began its climb-down and many new regions were upgraded. As of now, the more important claims to the Indo-European homeland pertain, in their geographical locations from west to east, to (1) the Anatolian region of western Asia; (2) the Black Sea-Caspian belt; (3) the steppes of southern Russia; and (4) Sogdiana in south-central Asia.

It is well known that in the case of everyone of these theses, for each proponent there are at least half-a-dozen opponents, and, mind you, all these opponents are Western scholars. Further, the interesting point that emerges from these controversies is that the dispute is not merely between archaeologists on the one hand and linguists on the other, who flaunt their own discipline as being superior that of the other, but amongst archaeologists themselves and similarly amongst linguists, indicating that not even two practitioners of the same discipline see eye to eye. Completely disillusioned with such a scenario, Mallory (1989) rightly observed: 'One does not ask "where is the Indo-European homeland but" *rather where they put it now?'*

On my part, however, I would not like the search to

*Director General (Retd.) Archaeological Survey of India, New Delhi be given up and would only indicate the region to go now. Let us move full circle and try out once again the Indian homeland thesis which was proposed at the end of the eighteenth century, but could not hold the ground then. I am aware that there would be an instantaneous uproar at this proposal, but why be allergic to the very idea itself? The reason for a fresh examination of this proposal is that in those early days there was a total absence of any archaeological data from north-west South Asia, which we now have in abundance. Let me also make it clear that I want the north-west South Asian region as a whole to be re-examined and not merely what is now left over as north-west India. *Let it also be emphasised that the present-day political boundaries did not exist during those ancient days we are dealing with here.*

The recent excavations at Mehrgarh, by J.F. Jarrige, have demonstrated that the north-western part of the Indian subcontinent had reached a Neolithic, i.e., settled agricultural stage, by the seventh millennium BCE. Here it may also be emphasised that the Mehrgarh neolithic complex stands in marked contrast to that of Western Asia. For, example, whereas in the West Asian Neolithic there is the domination of sheep and goat amongst the domesticated animals and of wheat amongst the cultivated cereals, in the Mehrgarh context the cattle dominated over other animals and barley over other cereals. Thus, the Mehrgarh neolithic has its own identity, having no generic relationship with its West Asian counterpart. In other words, the Mehrgarh people were the*'the sons of the soil'*.

Further, there is a continuous story from the succeeding chalcolithic levels onwards, taking us through various evolutionary stages to the Early Harappan from which there emerged the Harappan Civilization itself, around the middle of the third millennium BC.

Again, after a thorough study of the human skeletal remains, Hemphill and his colleagues (1991) have shown that there was a biological continuity right from 4500 BC to 800 BC. A question may now be posed: 'What language did these Chalcolithic-Early Harappan-Mature Harappan people speak'. Though the Harappan script has not yet been deciphered, in spite of so many tall claims, we have yet another way of tackling the issue.

In the *Rigveda*, the River Sarasvati has been stated to be a mighty river flowing from the mountains to the sea (*RV* 7.95.2). By the time of the *Panchvimsa Brahmana* (XXV 10.16) it dried up. When did this drying up of the Sarasvati take place? The answer is provided by the evidence from the excavations at Kalibangan which stood on the bank of the Sarasvati, now going by the name of the Ghaggar. Radiocarbon dates indicate that the Mature Harappan settlement at Kalibangan had to be abandoned around 2000 BC. And, as the hydrological evidence indicates, this abandonment took place on account of the drying up of the Sarasvati. This latter part is duly established by the work of Raikes, an Italian hydrologist, and of his India collaborators (Raikes 1968) has very significantly titled his paper, 'Kalibangan:Death from Natural Causes'. Thus, an in-depth study of the literary-cum-archaeological-*cum*-hydrological-*cum*-radiocarbon evidence duly establishes that the *Rigveda* (which, to recall, speaks of the Sarasvati as a mighty river) *must antedate ca* 2000 BC. By how many centuries, it can be anybody's guess.

We may now take up the geographical evidence yielded by the *Rigveda* itself. The famous *Nadi-stuti* hymn (*RV* 10.75.5&6) refers to the then familiar in a serial order from the east to the west, beginning with the Ganga and ending up with the Indus along with its western tributaries such the Kabul, Kurram, etc., encompassing eastern Afghanistan as well. One might now pose another question: 'Which archaeological culture/civilization was there in this very area during the period preceding 2000 BC? The inescapable answer is: 'The Harappan Civilization'. In other words, the entire circumstantial evidence points to a correlation between the Vedas and the Harappan Civilization. A final seal on this, however, can be put only when the Harappan script is satisfactorily deciphered.

Many objections have been raised from time to time against the Harappan-Vedic equation. These have been fully dealt with in my just-published book, *The Saraswati Flows On*. However, for the benefit of the present readers the same may be briefly summarised here. It is highly misleading to say that the Vedic Aryans were nomads. The *Rigveda* itself throws valuable light on the polity of the times, as indicated by the occurrence in it of such terms as *sabha, samiti, smrat, rajan, rajaka*, etc. The first two terms clearly refer to assemblies that took vital decisions on matters of public interest, while the latter three terms point to a hierarchy of rulers. In *RV* 6.27.8, *Abhyavarti Chayamana is referred to as a Samrat, where-*

as in RV 8.21.18 Chitra is said to be a mere Rajan and the epithet of other still inferior rulers is Rajaka. Does one expect such fine distinction of governance in a nomadic society? That these distinctions are not imaginary, as is likely to be argued by the 'nomad'-theory-protagonists, but real is borne out by the *Shatapatha Brahmana* (V.1.1.12-13) when it clearly states: *avaram hi rajyam param samrajyam,* which means *'the office of Rajan is lower and that of Samrat, the higher'*.

The mention of armours and forts clearly points to the high-level military strategy of the Aryan. Thus, for example, *RV* 10.101.8 mentions:

'Stitch ye (oh gods) the coats of armour, wide and many, make strong forts as of metal, safe from all assailants'.

In Verse *RV* 7.15.14, the devotee further prays that the *fort should have a hundred arms.* Is this the prayer of a nomad?

The Vedic Aryans were well up on the economic front too. As indicated by *RV* 10.33.6, they were engaged in even sea-trade.

'O Soma, from every side pour forth four seas filled with a thousand-fold riches.'

In order to carry out efficiently the sea-trade, the Vedic Aryans used sizeable boats which had as many as a hundred (i.e., a very large number of) oars. This is indicated by *RV* 1.116.5.

The foregoing few examples should leave no doubt in the mind of anyone that, far from being nomads, the Vedic Aryans had reached a very advanced social, political and economic stage. Even the much-touted argument about the absence of the horse from the Harappan Civilization has no validity in the light of the new evidence that is turning up about its presence. The noted international authority on the palaeontology of the horse, Sandor Bokonyi of the Archaeological Institute, Budapest, had declared, as far back as 1993, that 'the domestic nature of the Surkotada horse (a Harappan site in Kuchchh) is undoubtful'. The terracotta model of the horse, found by Mackay in his excavations at Mohenjo--Daro, is displayed in the National Museum, New Delhi, and all are welcome to see it. Lothal, the famous Harappan site is Gujarat, has also yielded a terracotta figure of the horse.

There is yet another argument which is often advanced against an Aryan-Harappan equation. This relates to the spoked wheel which is referred to in the Vedic texts but is stated to be absent during the Harappan times. Sites like Banawali, Kalibangan and Rakhigarhi have yielded ample evidence of spoked wheels from the Mature Harappan levels.

A few scholars, including the Late Sir Mortimer Wheeler, had suggested that the Aryan invaded India around 1500 BC and destroyed the Harappan Civilization. This theory has been shown to be completely wrong by a host of scholars, including Professors George Dales, Mark Kenoyer and Jim Shaffer (all from the USA) and Lord Colin Renfrew from the UK. The last-named states: 'When Wheeler speaks of "the Aryan Invasion of the Land of Seven Rivers, the Panjab", he has no warranty at all, so far as I can see. If one checks the dozen references in the Rigveda to the Seven River, *there is nothing in any of them that to me implies invasion'*.

Thus, putting together the various parts of this jigsaw puzzle, it would mean that if the Vedas reflect the literary counterpart of the Harappan archaeological complex, the Harappans spoke a language called Sanskrit. And since the Harappan Culture had its roots going deep at least into the fifth millennium BC, it would imply that the Sanskrit-speakers were there in this area as early as that. Further, had the Sanskrit-speaking people not been the original inhabitants of this region, we would have got evidence thereof in terms of a substratum language which we really do not have. The presence of a few Dravidian words in the Vedas can be explained by an adstratum and not necessarily by a substratum. As explained elsewhere by the present author (in press), the Harappans came in lateral contact with the Southern Neolithic people who, in all probability, were speakers of the Dravidian language.

We now turn to yet another important piece of evidence. The Boghaz Kuei inscription (in Turkey), dating back to the fourteenth century BC, refers to Indra, Mitra, Nasatya and Varuna as witnesses to a treaty between the Mitanni king Matiwaza and the Hittite king Suppiluliuma. There is also the evidence furnished by a text on the training of horses, which uses typical Sanskrit terms like *ekavartana, trivartana*, etc. Further, there are many Indian names in the region going back to circa seventeenth century BC. After a thorough examination of the entire evidence, the renowned scholar T. Burrow (1955) came to the conclusion: 'The Aryans appear in Mitanni from 1500 BC as the ruling dynasty, which means that *they must have entered the country as conquerors.*' If so, from where could have these conquerors come? *Around 1500* BC *there was no other country in the entire world except India where these above-mentioned gods were worshipped. (As we have shown earlier, the Rigveda is datable to at least to at least 2000* BC, *if not earlier). Putting two and two together, it is clear that the immigrants were from no area other than India*. This movement is likely to have taken place along the belt lying south of the Black and Caspian Seas.

The Ceramic Assemblage in Proto-historic Mewar (Rajasthan) with Special Reference to Gilund and Balathal

Vasant Shinde,* Gregory L. Possehl** and Shweta Sinha Deshpande*

Introduction

Archaeological study in the past included the study and description of pottery in great detail, often to such an extent that reports were no more than a catalogue of ceramic shapes and types without any links to the socio-economic context in which they had existed. In the recent past however, archaeologists have begun to relate ceramics with social archaeology in order to understand better the cultures and their interactions in order to reveal the life of these ancient people who have left us nothing but their broken pottery, structures and tools.

The basin of the Banas River, in Mewar, is one of those regions in India that witnessed the earliest emergence and local development of settled community life based on farming around 3000 B.C. The excavations at Balathal (Udaipur District) have demonstrated the local origins of village life as against the earliest belief that agriculture and village life spread to Central India and the Deccan through the Hapappans. Excavations have similarly shown that the Ahar Culture developed and flourished with growing trade contact with the Harappans after 2600 B.C. In addition, the vertical excavations at Ahar, District Udaipur (Sankalia *et al.* 1969) and the large-scale horizontal excavations at Balathal, District Udaipur (Misra *et al.* 1977) and Gilund, District Rajasthan (Shinde and Possehl in the press) have provided a complete cultural sequence of the region and have thrown light on various aspects including the socio-economic organisation, trade transactions and contacts. Culturally, these include painted and wheel-made ceramic traditions, a specialised blade/flake industry, restricted use of copper and subsistence based on farming, pastoralism and limited hunting.

This paper deals with the ceramic assemblage of the Ahar Culture during the proto-historic between the third and second millennium B.C. Pottery has often been described as the life and blood of archaeology as it is the most common artefact found amongst the sedentary agriculturist and pastoralist communities typical of the period and therefore, this pottery based study has been undertaken to understand the interactions that led to the rise of the Ahar Culture. In this context many case studies have been undertaken in the past by various scholars but were restricted to the typological analysis of various wares, their fabric and similarity or dissimilarity with each other leading to the creation of numerous wares and the description of the various shapes. Few scholars have tried to use the ceramic assemblage to study the origins of the culture, its interactions and trade networks as they existed and this is the essence of this paper. The study will also attempt to conduct a functional analysis of the Chalcolithic pottery where possible, with the help of ethnographic parallels.

*Deccan College, Pune. **University of Pennsylvania Museum, Philadelphia.

Environment

The Mewar region located to the east of the Aravallis comprises the Banas-Berach Basin and geographically is an extension of the Malwa Plateau, which forms a part of Central India. The riverbeds are usually cultivated during the summer months by millet, sorghum, sesame, green grams, black gram, mustard, etc. The region falls in the semi-arid monsoon type environment, characterised by hot and dry summers, cold winters and an unpredictable monsoon with an average rainfall of 900 mm. Maximum temperature varies from 15°C in the winter to 45°C+ in summer. It is currently believed that the climate, geology, physical features, flora and fauna during the Chalcolithic period were similar to those prevalent today. The Aravalli formations around Udaipur are rich in metals and minerals, including copper, lead, zinc, silver and iron and are also rich in fauna such as antelopes, tigers, wild boar and sambhar. Trees such as babul, banyan, tamarind, mango, peepal and neem as well as thorny scrub jungles are common.

The Ahar Culture

The large number of Palaeolithic and Mesolithic sites in south-east Rajasthan testify to the existence of hunting-gathering communities in the region. The changing environment, population pressure and depleting resources are believed to have forced the Mesolithic hunters to adopt an agrarian lifestyle and settle in restricted but congenial environments that provided better resources. Small settlement with an agro-pastoral economy along with hunting and gathering developed in forested areas such as Balathal. With increasing prosperity and surplus, various crafts were necessitated and developed including manufacture of ceramics, building of permanent structures and copper technology. The need for living space led to the development of new settlements and exchange network between them (such as between Ahar, Balathal and Gilund) that facilitated the procurement of goods not available locally in exchange for products locally produced. At Balathal, and Gilund large silo bases, storage bins and structures identified as possible granaries give us a clear indication of the strong agricultural base in the economy. Dietary-bone analysis reveals the predominance of cattle, followed by sheep and goat supplemented by wild animals and fish at the sites. With this shift in subsistence and the development of sedentary settlements, a marked change in social organisation occurred as cultural requirements entailed adaptation to economic and ecological environments and needs. Increasing need for co-operation and organisation of activities relating to subsistence led to division of labour, more efficiency and surpluses required administrative mechanisms for storage, allocation and redistribution. Authority also plays an important role in the administration of pastures, water sources and other collectively held and produced goods. Surpluses allow more time and the ability to support skilled and specialised crafts not possessed by all members of the society thus enhancing trade and exchange. These socio-economic changes led to the development of a chiefdom type society for restructuring and administering these changes. In addition, there seems to have existed a definite relation between the Harappans of Gujarat and Rajasthan with these communities (Misra 1997).

As suggested earlier, based on a number of excavated sites, it is believed that the Chalcolithic cultures worked under a chiefdom organisation with clear evidence of social stratification and economic hierarchy with prominent central authority in the hands of a chief (Sinha 1998, 1999). Scholars have pointed out, the economy of a society forms the base and provides the means for further development. Ratnagar (1991), observed that these economic benefits when exploited by a small group of people leads to the rise of socio-economic differentiation and concentration of economic power in the hands of a few. This eventually gives rise to a chiefdom society followed by organised states. The economic conditions at the Ahar Culture sites were therefore very congenial for an elaborate socio-political organisation or stratified society to evolve.

On the basis of the detailed observation of surrounding ecological condition and the sites, a hierarchy of settlements has been reconstructed. Settlements varied from small hamlets of 0.8 to 1.6 hectares in area to towns like Ahar and regional centres like Gilund sprawling over an area of 5 hectares. The site of Gilund appears to have been the regional centre of the Ahar Culture on account of its strategic location in the centre of the basin and its size. In addition, many settlements located in the proximity of fertile arable land and of medium size have been identified as farming settlements, while settlements like Ahar at the foot of the Aravalli Hills copper ore deposits probably specialised in copper working.

Sites of Ahar Culture

A total of 80 Ahar Culture sites have been located in the Mewar region of Rajasthan and the majority of these settlements are located in areas replete with arable land comprising of large tracts of black cotton soil and perennial supply of water (fig.1). Most of the sites in Mewar are located in the valleys of the Banas, Khari, Berach, Kothari, Gambhiri Rivers and their tributaries. Some are as small as 0.3 hectares (Tarawat), but there is a cluster in the five-hectare range while the largest site, Gilund is approximately 10 hectares in area. Prior to the excavation at Balathal, only two sites, Ahar and Gilund, had been excavated vertically. Deccan College, under late Prof. H.D. Sankalia in 1961-62 excavated the ancient site of Ahar (500 m x 275 m and 15 m thick deposit), located within the city limits of Udaipur in the vicinity of rich copper deposits. Gilund, the largest known Ahar site in Mewar, located on the right bank of the river Banas in Rajasamand District was excavated by the Archaeological Survey of India under the direction of Prof. B.B. Lal in 1959-60 (IAR, 1959-60: 41-46). This site with two prominent mounds spread over an area of 600 m x 350 m and a habitation deposit thickness of 8-15 m is currently being re-excavated by Vasant Shinde and Gregory Possehl. The site of Balathal, 41 km east of Udaipur, has been excavated on large scale by Deccan College and the Institute of Rajasthan Studies, with a view of reconstructing the socio-economic organisation of the early farmers of this region. The site is spread over an area of 2 hectares with a 7 m thick habitation deposit and has good arable land and pastures on the northern side and a huge lake on the southern side of the mound; both factors that may have been the determinant factors that attracted the early farmers. In addition, at Ahar and Balathal a couple of small 'U'shaped fire places with sides and bottoms burnt red have been identified as furnaces for smelting and heating copper and at Balathal two rectangular- pottery kilns, one above the other, have been found.

Ahar, the type-site of the Culture was first excavated on a limited scale by the Department of Archaeology, Rajasthan1954-56 and by the Deccan College in 1961-62. Located on the Ahar river, a tributary of the Banas, the archaeological deposit locally known as *Dhulkot* is about 12.8 m thick and is divided into two periods; Period I Chalcolithic (2580-1500 B.C. or later) with three subphases and Period II Iron Age (Hooja 1988). While no sterile layer was found separating the two periods, there is a gap between the two periods chronologically. The three sub-phases of the Chalcolithic Ahar Culture here are divided on the basis of the ceramic assemblage; Phase Ia (2580-2170 B.C.) is characterised by the presence of Black-and-Red ware especially convex-sided bowls, Buff ware and imitation Buff-slipped ware, Red ware and some Grey ware and the absence of sharply carinated bowls. Phase Ib (2170-2080 B.C.), the Black-and-Red ware continues while the Buff and imitation Buff slipped ware are completely absent and Grey ware, Red ware and cut and ribbed pottery in Red ware are present in increased profusion with some new ceramic types. Phase Ic (2080-1500 B.C.) is characterised by the presence of sharply carinated Black-and Red bowls, absence of sturdy metallic ceramics and dish-on-stands and the presence of Lustrous Red ware similar to that of Rangpur. Pottery from Ahar as described by Sankalia (1969: 18-162) has been the basis for identifying Ahar sites in Rajasthan and Madhya Pradesh, though here one needs to recall Childe (1958:70) and his definition of culture as being 'defined but not constituted by pottery'. Recent excavations at sites like Balathal and Gilund have yielded similar pottery types as at Ahar but with some differences.

No complete house plan was available but from the data recovered it seems that they constructed large houses of stone and mud complete with storage jars and cooking facilities including a couple of 'U'shaped *chulhas* or hearths (Sankalia, 1969; Hooja, 1988). Interestingly, the site yielded only a few microliths mainly blunted-back blades, bores, fluted cores, side scrappers made of chert, chalcedony and quartz and the idea that the culture depended on copper tools to a large extent was put forth by the excavator. The site is identified as a copper smelting and tool manufacturing site based on the finds of copper slag and copper implements like celts, blades, knives, rings, bangles and kohl sticks and the inhabitants are believed to have exploited local copper ore sources (Sankalia 1969, Hooja 1998 and Kashyap 1999). In addition, other artefacts include shell bangles, beads of crystal, terracotta and lapis lazuli, most of which belong to Phase Ib and Ic and terracotta figurines of animals like bulls, elephants and a horse. The people practised agriculture and animal husbandry and cultivated rice and probably legumes and millets like other Chalcolithic cultures.

The rural site of Balathal (24° 43'N and 73° 59'E) is located 42 km east of Udaipur in the Banas basin and is 3 hectares in size (150 m N-S and 135 m E-W) with a deposit of 7 m divisible into two cultural periods. Chalcolithic (2800-1800 B.C.) and Early Historic (200-300 B.C.) with a hiatus of 1600 years (Misra 1997). The proximity of a large freshwater lake and fertile agriculture and pasturelands around the site are believed to have lured the early farming communities to make Balathal their home.

The excavation at the site yielded the earliest evidence of the origin of the 'Early Chalcolithic' (Phase A) farming community in western India. This early society of farmers and herders established their settlement on the bedrock, constructed wattle-and-daub structures and manufactured typical Chalcolithic pottery such as coarse and thick slipped Red ware, thin Red ware, Black-and-Red ware and Reserve Slip ware. Reserve Slipped ware, was introduced by the early settlers and since the earliest known occurrence of this ware in the subcontinent is at Balathal, it may be inferred that the technique of its production was borrowed by the Harappans when they established close contact with the Chalcolithic farmers of Mewar around 2400 B.C. while Black-and-Red ware is believed to be a feature of the Ahar Culture. In this phase however, the majority of the pottery is hand-made, coarse, thick in section and inadequately fired. Shapes such as wide-mouthed deep carinated bowls, small narrow-mouthed jars and storage jars with headed rim, the fossil types of the Chalcolithic phase in this region are present right from the beginning.

Gradual development and technological advancement led to the rise of Phase B (2500-1800 B.C.) or the 'Mature Chalcolithic' at Balathal, and it was this people who established close contacts with the Harappans in Gujarat, resulting in the all round development that is visible in their structures and other material equipment. This phase of Mature Chalcolithic is characterised by three different pottery traditions namely Kayatha in the Chambal Valley, Ahar in the Mewar region and Malwa on the Malwa Plateau. They constructed rectangular or squarish houses, single or double-roomed with elaborate storage and cooking facility. The floors of these structures were made of clay and plastered with cow dung or sometimes lime. The evidence from Balathal indicates that a modicum of planning was introduced and the use of mudbricks and stones for construction of multi-roomed complexes became predominant (Shinde 2000). In the midst of the settlement is located a very impressive stone structure, roughly rectangular on plan and identified as a Fortified Enclosure. It covered an area of 30 m (E-W) by 20 m (N-S) and its function is uncertain. Around this central structure house complexes were laid out in a rectangular plan and were in turn enclosed by a strong outer fortification wall.

The ancient site of Gilund (25° 01' 56" N and 74° 15' 45" E), roughly 100 km to the NE of Udaipur and 1.5 km NE of Gilund village is also known as Madiya Magari and Bhagwanpura. The site was excavated by B.B. Lal and the Archaeological Survey of India in 1959-60 (IAR 1959-60: 41-46) and is currently being re-excavated by Dr. V.S. Shinde of Deccan College, Pune and Dr. G.L. Possehl of the University of Pennsylvania Museum, Philadelphia amongst others. Located just 1 km north of River Banas the site is surrounded by slightly sandy but fertile arable as well pasture lands and leads one to believe that the ancient site was situated to maximise agro-pastoral production. Gilund is the largest site of the Ahar Culture at approximately 10 hectares in extent with two prominent mounds, GLD-1 to the east and 15 m above the plain and GLD-2 to its west and 8 m above the plain. The excavators have identified it as a major population centre, important to the Ahar Culture economic and political imstitutions based on the presence of impressive public architecture made of mudbricks (Shinde and Possehl in press). Both the mounds at the site (GLD-1 and GLD-2) are surrounded by independent mud/mudbrick fortifications with a prepared road between them and a gap observed on the western slope that may have been a gate or an entrance leading to the 'Lower Town' of GLD-2 (Shinde and Possehl in press). GLD-1, the smaller, higher eastern mound recall the elevated areas at some Harappan sites like the Mound of the Great Bath at Mohenjo-Daro, Mound A-B at Harappa, and the 'Bailey-Castle' at Dholavira while GLD-2 resembles the 'lower towns' at these sites (Shinde in press).

The current and ongoing excavations have revealed that the first settlers at Gilund established their occupation on top of a stabilised sand dune and based on preliminary analysis the deposit may be approximately 1.5 m thick. This Early Phase may be comparable to Cultural Phase A at Balathal and is estimated to date between 3000 and 2500 B.C. though the ceramics of the Early Phase at

Gilund generally have fine and well made fabrics, while during the same period at Balathal they were generally coarse grained and crudely made. A burnt area was noticed on top of the dune deposit, though this burning does not appear to be the result of bush clearance since sand dunes do not generally support thick vegetation, nothing conclusive can be said about its nature due to the limited area under excavation. Possibly related sets of pre-fortification Early Phase layers have also been reached on GLD-1.

The Mature Ahar Culture dated 2500-2000 B.C. is the most extensively excavated period at the site. The most spectacular discovery of this period at Gilund includes a structure formed of parallel east-west and north-south running mud brick walls, exposed over an area of 12 m x 12 m. Five, north-south running walls spaced at regular 1 m intervals were found to be joining two east-west running wall spaced 10 m apart. All the walls were plastered as were the gaps between the walls; some of which have yielded working surfaces. It appears at the moment that the parallel and crossing walls were the aboveground foundation courses for a large superstructure probably made primarily of wood and mud and/or other perishable material. The complete extent of this structure has not yet been discerned and the exact function of this structure is not clear, but on the basis of ethnographic parallels it can be identified as a granary (Shinde and Possehl, in press). There is a formal similarity between our 'foundations' and the 'area of the parallel walls' on Mound F at Harappa but it is not certain that the structure at Harappa was a granary but a more general notion of a warehouse might better serve our interpretations (Shinde and Possehl in press). However, the culture, historical relationship between our 'parallel walls' and those of the Harappa warehouse will have to await further excavation at Gilund but if there is a connection it would open up various possibilities about the relationship between the Harappan Civilization and the people on its eastern borderlands (Shinde and Possehl in press). This phase at the site also saw the construction of the large and thick (7.5 m wide) mud and mud brick fortification walls that independently circumscribe the two mounds. The GLD-1 mound also yielded a tandoor from this phase and on GLD-2 a large house complex immediately next to the parallel wall structure, where many mud-lined storage pits, a series of large lime and grass lined pits and a double-hearth were found. It is believed that the occupants of this structure may have been associated with some form of industrial or commercial activity. Several large residential structures complete with silos, storage pits, storage jars, hearths and saddle querns have also been found in this phase and some of these may also be associated with industrial activity.

The Late Phase of Gilund represents a decline in terms of both material and population and this Phase is presently dated to between 2000-1600 B.C. contemporary with the emergence of the post-urban Harappan (Shinde and Possehl in press). Till date, five structures of this phase have been revealed all with the same features. The walls are made of wattle-and-daub and mud-bricks are completely absent, the floors are plastered with clay and silt and contain the same features as the earlier phase except that the size and quality seem to have diminished and the material changed. A radiocarbon date within a hearth of Structure 3, (one of these late structures) is BETA-140702. 1742 B.C. (calibrated) (Shinde and Possehl in press); however, it should be noted that here this level is not the last occupation and at best can be said to the near the end of the Chalcolithic.

The Chalcolithic pottery at Gilund is very similar to the Ahar assemblage, with a predominance of Black-and-Red ware with white painitng, Red Ware and Grey Ware. At Gilund Coarse Red Ware and Coarse Grey Ware are very common, while Black-and-Red Ware is also substantial in amount. A few sherds of Malwa Ware have also been found in the upper levels. The presence of Malwa Ware is especially interesting as Ahar Culture type Black-and-Red Ware has been found at Malwa and this is a good indication of reciprocal trade contacts between the Ahar Culture and the Central Indian and Deccan early farming communities around the second millennium BC. The majority of the pottery at Gilund has not been well fired and has a grey core and the pottery does not generally have the metallic ring that is a feature of the neighbouring Harappan Civilization. Rims were often luted to the body and the lower body portions of larger vessels rusticated. Hand-made pottery is absent and the majority is wheel-made or occasionally moulded. Painting, slipping and decorations are present and were usually done on the rim, neck and shoulder portions of the vessel. The paintings, slip and burnishing were always pre-firing, a characteristic feature of the Ahar Culture. Painting is done in white, red, black or purple and decoration types include;

appliqué, incised, ridged and occasionally rope impressions. Shapes and sizes are diverse ranging from miniature to large pottery and both deluxe and utilitarian ware are present throughout the assemblage. One final observation is that on the basis of the complete pots recovered at Gilund it can be stated that the Rusticated Ware reported from Ahar does not appear to exist here, as rustication is restricted to the lower portions of globular pots with utilitarian bias.

The Ceramic Assemblage

One of the most common and important craft activities of the Chalcolithic Period was pottery manufacture, with various types of wheel-made and in some cases hand-made ceramics divided into fine and coarse wares based on the degree of purity of clay, surface treatment, nature of firing, vessel forms and decoration. Fine pottery is made of refined well-levigated clay, has a thin and highly burnished slip, and is baked at a very high temperature above 700 degrees. Because of these features, it is sturdy, has a reddish core, produces a metallic sound, looks attractive and therefore constitutes deluxe pottery. The common vessel types include dish, globular pot and bowl with or without a stand, in varying sizes. The presence of such high quality pottery suggests the presence of an elite section within the society. The coarse variety is made of unrefined clay, is poorly fired, has grey or black core and is mainly decorated with incised and appliqué designs. The vessel forms in this variety mainly comprise large globular pots of various sizes probably used for storage and cooking.

The Ahar culture is characterised by three basic pottery types Red Ware, Black-and-Red Ware and Grey Ware and these can be further sub-divided into those with fine fabric like Thin Red Ware, Black-and-Red painted in white, Tan Ware and Reserve-Slipped Ware and coarse fabric types such as the Thick Bright-Slipped Red Ware and Grey Ware, which are common to most sites and are often manufactured at the site itself. It has been noticed that the Ahar people appear to be very fond of deep incised patterns which is a feature not seen in the Central Indian or Deccan Chalcolithic Cultures (Sankalia *et al.*, 1969:56). Interestingly a close study of the pottery at Gilund has indicated that Black-and-Red Ware also constituted a major part of the coarse ware as against the earlier belief that it formed the bulk of deluxe pottery or table ware. The various types of wares described by excavators at Ahar and Balathal and as understood by the authors at the site of Gilund are discussed below.

Black-and-Red Ware (B&RW) (fig.1, Plate 1). Black and Red Ware is appropriately named as the interior and the shoulder portion of the outer surface of the vessel is black while the rest of the exterior surface is red or plum red though occasionally it tends to be brownish red, tan or chocolate and this effect is believed to have been achieved through inverted firing technique. Both surfaces are treated with a slip, burnished and the decorations are painted in white pigment, either on the interior or exterior of the pot, possibly pre-firing and, in some cases the paint tends to peel off leaving only a faded image of the design. The motifs include groups of straight or wavy lines, spirals, dots, hatched diamonds, concentric circles and chevrons filled with dots and circles (Sankalia *et al.* 1969:88-98). The shapes in this ware comprise mostly wide-mouthed, convex-sided bowls of varying sizes.

At Ahar Black-and-Red Ware is the predominant ware and in classified into six group in Phase Ia, (Sankalia *et at.* 1969:28); (a) plain unpainted Black-and-Red Ware with one or both sides burnished, (b) Black-and-Red Ware as above but painted in dull white pigment, (c) Black-and-Red Ware with matt surface, (d) Black-and-Red Ware with some portions having a pre-firing brick-red slip mostly on the black portion, (e) entirely black burnished pottery (essentially Black-and-Red Ware of category (a), Sankalia 1969:28, Hooja 1988:56) and (f) Black and Red Ware with gritty core and surface. The shapes include bowls-on-stand, shallow pans and small globular pots or jar/pots with elongated body, while medium and large sized vessels are completely absent. In Phase Ib, all the types described continue and there is an increase in the quantity and a few new shapes are introduced like carinated bowls, convex-sided bowls, deep bowls, bowls with straight sides and lids (Sankalia *et al.* 1969:88-98). Interestingly in this phase there seems to be a tendency to provide a carination bowls. There seems to be a decline in the quantity of Black-and-Red Ware in the last phase and shapes present include miniature globular vessels in addition to those from the earlier levels. Phase Ic also has a few sherds with graffiti on them.

At Balathal Phase A, which brought to light the earliest evidence of the Ahar Culture yielded Black-and-Red

Ware but the fabric was coarse, ill-fired and included painted and unpainted versions. The typical shapes included bowls and dishes. In Phase B the Black-and-Red Ware forms the bulk of the pottery after Thin Red Ware. Almost the entire assemblage of Black-and-Red Ware is fine fabric, well-fired and characterised by shapes like wide-mouthed convex-sided bowls and dishes-on-stands (Shinde 2000; Misra *et al.* 1997).

The excavations at Gilund as studied by the authors has revealed new Black-and-Red Ware data as the site has produced not only small table-ware such as bowls and dishes but also many large and medium size pots of coarse and medium-coarse fabric and appears to be not only a deluxe ware but also a utilitarian ware which is not soa at Balathal or Ahar. The fabric is coarse due to the use of tempering material like tiny grains of stone that makes the pottery gritty and brittle. Black-and-Red Ware at Gilund is representative of typical Ahar Culture Black-and-Red Ware and can be studied under four different varieties: coarse and thick, coarse and thin, fine and thick and fine and thin. The thicker varieties represent vessels like globular pots with wide or narrow mouth, jar/pots and even basins with grooved rims and thin sections, while the thinner varieties are generally medium to small vessels like bowls such as convex-sided deep, shallow bowls, everted rim carinated bowls, featureless convex bowls, globular bowls (seen in the mature phase) basins and small globular pots. As at Ahar where Black-and-Red Ware is even in the washed category, at Gilund two sherds have a wash-like treatment instead of the thick slip that helped hide the coarseness of the fabric. The decorative treatment in case of large vessels used for storage was similar to the Coarse Red Ware pottery where the slip and burnishing was restricted to the shoulder and even incised decorations were used. Very few large and coarse pots seem to be painted in white, a feature restricted to smaller vessels only.

The pre-fortification levels at the site have not yet been excavated sufficiently to reveal the ceramic assemblage, but the middle levels at the site indicate that Black-and-Red Ware was both fine and coarse and large and small vessels were made but were fewer in number than the Grey or Red Wares. In this phase the pottery is less coarse especially when compared to the sites last phase where it becomes coarse with a large amount of tempering including large chunks and dust of mica in the large storage structure on GLD-2, and it can be presumed that this area played an important role in the late phase.

Burnished Black Ware

This ware was encountered in the lower levels of Phase B at Gilund and is uncommon though some sherds were found at Ahar (Sankalia *et al.* 1969). This pottery has fine and coarse varieties with little or no tempering, has a deep black colour core as well as surface and is wheel-made. The surface is black slipped and highly burnished on its entire exterior surface and rim portions. Some of the sherds had white painted decorations done prior to firing on the shoulder portions. Designs included patterns made up of multiple dots, hatched diamonds and chevrons in white paint that is still present and has not peeled of. As very few sherds have been located, the shapes present are still to be determined. But some interesting shapes include an everted rim, straight elongated neck globular small pot (a similar shape has been found in very fine Thin Red Ware), vessels on stands like the bowl on a corrugated elongated stand and other shapes with broad bases. The pottery-context is not yet identifiable but it can be presumed to be either a deluxe ware or a ware meant for special occasions such as rituals. A single sherd of this ware has been found in the late phase from the area around the storage structure, again pointing towards its significant position.

Red Wares

This is the most common ware of the Chalcolithic Ahar and has been divided into sub-varieties based on the fabric and the surface treatment. The Red Wares present include Coarse Red, Thin Red, Tan, Chocolate Slipped and Polychrome Wares. The Coarse Red Ware at these sites is similar to Coarse Grey Ware in fabric, surface treatment and shapes and is of utilitarian purpose like storage and cooking. Of the varieties of Red Ware, Coarse Red is very common and Thin Red while not common is substantial throughout. The other three varieties are rare and in some cases imported from other sites. For example at Ahar, Red Ware forms the bulk of the pottery and has been divided into various sub-groups by the excavator (Sankalia *et al.* 1969: 61-84). In phase Ia, there are six different varieties: (1) thick slipped red ware with a thick fabric and bright red slip sometimes burnished. The interior is heavily scooped, unslipped in most cases and is ill-fired with a grey core. The neck made separately in an old pot mould and is luted to the body. (2) The ware has a red wash, a black gritty core and the exterior is unslipped or rusticated. (3) The ware has a dull brown mechanical slip similar to thick slipped red ware with a gritty core and includes shapes like deep basins, circular pot rests, globular pots with convex sloping shoulders, flared mouth and roughened bases. (4) The ware has a rusticated exterior and a gritty core. The shapes include globular pots and shallow pans probably used for cooking. (5) Red slipped metallic sounding ware (fine) with a gritty core and scooped and unslipped interior. The exterior surface is well burnished, has few decorative elements and common shapes include convex-sided bowls. (6) A drab red variety with gritty core, unslipped and unburnished probably meant for everyday use according to the excavator. In Phase Ib, the Red Ware increases in quantity and there are three main types; Thin Red slipped with a metallic ring made of fine clay and well-fired (Sankalia *et al.* 1969:108). The Coarse Red Ware sees a decrease in quantity in Ib and Red Ware is four to five times more decorated than Grey Ware, which has also reduced in quantity. In phase Ic in Thin Burnished Red Ware carinated bowls are very common and has replaced the convex-sided bowls of Ib. All the three types of Red Ware continue in Ic though Thick Red Slipped Ware is less than the previous phase and shapes like corrugated pots with ribbed designs are absent. The thin variety is present in the same quantities as the Black & Red ware in pahse Ic.

1. Coarse Red Ware

Coarse Red Ware in the Chalcolithic is typically represented by thick bright-slipped Red Ware that is locally produced, primarily used for storage and cooking and in most cases is similar at most sites except for a few shapes. The wares, as described earlier, are made of coarse clay, poorly fired, mainly decorated with incised and appliqué designs. The coarse Red ware is predominated by large narrow-mouthed and wide-mouthed globular jars, small *handis*, storage jars, basins, other utilitarian shapes and dishes-on-stand treated with a highly burnished bright red slip on the upper part or the rim and shoulder of the exterior surface. The body or middle part of the external surface is decorated with two or more parallel raised bands/ridges and a variety of incised designs like multiple wavy lines, chevrons, herringbone patterns, criss-crosses, loops, triangular incisions punctured and appliqué patterns. At Ahar sites in Coarse Red ware, the decoration is either on the shoulder or upper part of the vessel with the rim, neck and base left plain(fig. 2).

At Ahar, Coarse Red Ware is maximum in Phase Ia and decreases in the subsequent phases. At Balathal, the ware formed part of the utilitarian pottery used for cooking and storage in phase A where it was either hand-made or on a slow wheel, made of coarse clay and ill-fired and constituted utilitarian vessels. This continued in Phase B except that now it was wheel-made, probably on a fast wheel and was decorated using the incised, appliqué, cut, punctured designs. In the mature phase the excavator described a ware without any wash, slip, or decoration and the shapes include small narrow mouthed *handis* and jars. At Gilund, as at the other sites, Coarse Red Ware is very common, utilitarian in nature and used for storage and cooking purposes.

It is present throughout and is represented by a wide range of pottery sizes from small to large. The pottery is either wheel-made or moulded. The fabric is gritty and coarse to medium with a lot of tempering material such as granular sand, chopped grass and mica flakes. In the pre-fortification phase of the Early Chalcolithic at Gilund the fabric is coarse and the pottery is wheel-made suggesting that it is later than the earliest phase at Balathal (Phase A) and can be ascribed to the late Phase of the Early Chalcolithic. Here the core tends to be blackish as the pottery is often ill-fired and the slip varies from orange to dark red and is thickly applied mostly on the exterior surface, which is burnished. The interior is either red with no slip or grayish in colour depending on the firing conditions. The Middle Phase at Gilund sees a well-fired Coarse Red Ware assemblage with a finer fabric and has been described as ‘medium Coarse Red Ware’ not seen at any other level. By the Late Phase, the ware has again become much coarser and tempering includes chunks of mica, stone and chopped grass in large quantities. Like in Coarse Grey Ware, the area above and including the shoulder portions is slipped and may also be decorated and burnished, whereas the lower portions are plain or rusticated. Decorations are appliqué, incised, ridged or rope impressed design. Appliqué designs included spirals and circles, similar to those found at the site of Ojiyana. Incised designs include among others, chequered combed, hatched diamonds and diagonal or linear lines. Ridges designs are invariably parallel linear lines on the neck and shoulder portions while rope impressed designs are both true impressions or made to look like them by incising ridges. The decorations are finer and deeper with a careful and meticulous deliberation in the middle or Mature Phase while in the late phase there appears to be a careless frenzy in their execution. Paintings are rare in this variety and the painted versions of Coarse Red have been identified as the imitations or local versions of Malwa Ware, which is present in the Late Chalcolithic Phase at the site. The majority of pottery-shapes in this ware are globular pots with narrow or wide mouths, basins, dishes, lids, pots with handles and very large storage jars.

2. Polychrome Ware

Polychrome Ware as found at Gilund for all practical purposes is a Coarse Red Ware of medium coarse fabric but is classified separately because of its distinctive surface treatment. This surface treatment consists of a combination of white, black and red coloured painted decorations, mostly of single or interlaced diamonds. The shapes are difficult to identify as only a few body-sherds have been found from the middle and lower levels at the site. A similar ware was found at the site Ahar (Sankalia *et al.* 1969), but there too the sherds were limited and shapes unidentifiable.

3. Thin Red Ware

This ware has a thin, highly burnished plum red or occasionally brownish red, tan or chocolate slip on the external surface while the inner surface is without any slip or wash and is generally grayish or tan in colour. The shapes include convex-sided deep bowls of various sizes and occasionally small globular vessels with everted rim, narrow mouth and high neck. They are decorated with a single row of punctured or incised triangles, and occasionally by single or double ridges in low relief on the shoulder. The rim in some cases was made separately and luted to the body(fig. 3).

At Ahar, Sankalia identified a red slipped metallic ceramic with a gritty core and scooped and unslipped interior which though not exactly a Thin Red Ware can be ascribed to this category. The exterior is well-burnished and has few decorative elements and the common shapes include convex-sided bowls. In Phase A at Balathal, Thin Red Ware is present right from the beginning and is made of fine clay, well-fired and are either hand-made or on slow wheel like all the other types in this phase. In Phase B at the site it forms a principal variety unlike at Ahar where it constitutes a small percentage of the pottery. Here it forms part of the deluxe ware assemblage and is plum red to brownish red in colour and is decorated with a single row of punctured or incised triangles or single or double ridges in low relief on the shoulder. The major shapes present include convex-sided deep bowls, globular vessels with everted rims, narrow mouth and high neck jars.

At Gilund, Thin Red Ware has both fine and coarse varieties. The finer variety is uncommon and is present mostly in Phase B and tends to decline by the end of this phase and is completely absent in the Late Chalcolithic Phase. The fabric is very fine with only fine sand as the tempering material and it is both well-fired and thin bodied. The interior surface is generally red and neither burnished nor slipped, while the exterior was slipped in a bright red slip with a highly burnished surface, decorated with single or double parallel ridges on the shoulder, chequered incised decorations or punctured wedge shapes in a line. Shapes include convex-sided deep bowls, wide mouthed globular bowls, flasks, small pots, bowls on flared hollow stands, flared rimmed jars and everted rimmed elongated straight neck globular pots. A few fragments of nail headed rims were also located. Often the rim portions were separately made on the fast wheel and then luted to the body. Made on a fast wheel, the fine variety was clearly meant to be a deluxe ware. The coarser variety of this ware had a fabric similar to the thin coarse variety of Black-and-Red Ware with granular *kankar* used as tempering material. The pottery is ill-fired with a grayish core and the interior is often grey in colour with no surface treatment and the vessels are thin to medium thick in section. The outer surface is slipped and decorated in a manner similar to the finer variety; however, the outer surface often has grey blotches due to poor firing technique and is decorated with white paintings similar to Black-and-Red Ware in a number of cases. The shapes in the coarse variety consisted of narrow or wide mouthed pots and small to large-sized globular pots with everted rims. The pottery appears to be a utilitarian ware used for cooking and serving in the Late Chalcolithic phase and is not common in the mature phase.

An interesting feature observed in Phase B at Gilund (Mature chalcolithic), is the presence of a few sherds of this ware showing combination of black and red effect on the outer surface near the rim portion by the application of slips instead of firing. The pottery is a fine ware typically thin to medium in section, well-fired with a thick slip, highly burnished and without painted decorations, though in some cases it has ridged and punctured designs on the shoulder portion. The red colour of this ware ranges from shades of deep red to light orange to tan and chocolate due to variation in the oxidation during firing and the black colour ranges between black to grey to purple or blue. The shapes include everted rim globular bowls and featureless globular bowls, everted rim straight elongated necked globular small pot (similar shape has been found in Burnished Black Ware also). This technique completely disappears in the late chalcolithic phase and has not been reported from any other chalcolithic site.

4. Tan and chocolate Wares

This ware is of medium thickness, with a thin light orange/tan slip, which in some cases varies to a thick brown or chocolate colour similar to Kayatha Ware. The principal shapes in this ware include the dish, dish-on-stand and bowl-on-stand with considerable variations in size; large convex-sided bowls with thick rims; globular pots with either beaded or flat projecting rims and large basins with ledges on the neck. The prominent ledges were useful to hold vessels while the low ledges may have been purely decorative. With regard to fabric and shape this ware is identical with the sturdy Red Ware of the Gujarat Harappans and the Tan Ware of Gujarat, though unlike the latter, lacks in painted decorations.

At Ahar, in Phase Ia, Tan Ware is of two types one, the metallic with 'beautiful tan-yellow-red slips' and includes shapes like dish-on-stand, ribbed pots, basins and the other, the thick drab tan slipped ware that includes ribbed globular pots and other utilitarian vessels like those in Grey Ware. Another category described by the excavator is the Tan slipped ware with white paintings (40 sherds) and is a variant of Black-and-Red Ware in terms of fabric, shape and painted designs and continues in the next phase Ib without any change and the shapes include stepped dish, hollow stems, deep and large-sized dish-on-stands and hollow flared bases. Tan Ware is divided into seven categories in Ib, though they are all well-formed and of fine fabric with the difference being defined by shades of red; and shapes include stepped dish, shallow dish, corrugated stems, basins, ring stands, globular pots and pot stands. This ware is absent in Phase Ic (Sankalia *et al.* 1969). In addition, another category described by the excavator is a 'chocolate slipped metallic ware' with either a reddish brown or dark chocolate slip and could be a technical extension of the unpainted Tan Ware of Phase Ia. In Phase Ib, the proportion decreases and is described as a separate ware in the 1961-62 excavations while in Phase Ic it is completely absent (Sankalia *et al.* 1969). At Balathal, Phase B yielded fine fabric Tan Ware with a light orange to dark brown or chocolate slip and the variety with dark brown slip resembles Kayatha Ware (Misra *et al.*, 1997). Shapes include the dish, dish-on-stand and bowl-on-stand in various sizes. The site has also yielded two sherds of the base portions of globular pots with ring bases and a few specimens of perforated pots, similar to those used by the Harappans. While Gogte's (1996) view that Tan Ware was imported to the site has been nullified by the finding of a pottery kiln in Phase III and the succeeding Phase IV, apparently designed for firing Tan Ware. However, it is possible that the clay used for making this ware could have been obtained from outside sources. The fact that the kiln seems to have been in continuous use through many generations, provides significant evidence to prove that the inhabitants not only believed in hereditary occupation of craft but also occupied the same structures for residential or workshop with small changes in the structural plan by repairing and reusing the earlier structural configuration (Shinde 2000, Sinha 1998). Unlike the other two sites, at Gilund, Tan Ware is rare and Chocolate Ware has not yet been found. Here the Tan Ware has a fine to medium coarse fabric, is well-fired, has a medium thick body-section and is undecorated. Initially, only a few body fragments were identified; however, in the last season two complete shapes, a beaded rimmed globular pot and a featureless concave carinated shallow bowl have been found.

Grey Ware

This ware has two varieties, a burnished and a plain; while the fabric varies from coarse to fine. At most chalcolithic sites Grey Ware forms a part of coarse utilitarian pottery primarily used for storage and cooking. In the burnished variety the upper part of the exterior is slipped and highly burnished while the plain variety bears a slip but has no burnishing. The lower part of the outer surface of vessels in both varieties are roughened by the application of sand mixed with clay and is often covered with soot, showing that the vessels were used for cooking. The middle portion on the external surface is often decorated with incised, punctured, cut and appliqué designs similar to those of the burnished Red Ware. The most common vessel-forms in both the varieties are wide-mouthed pots, small *handis*, lids with or without handles and hand-made *tavas* used for making *rotis* or unleavened bread.

At Ahar, in Phase Ia, the excavator has divided the Grey Ware into three different categories; (1) outer surface smoothened by a slip, (2) similar to the earlier but slipped and (3) partly burnished and partly coarse. The shapes in all are utilitarian vessels decorated in incised, ribbed and cut designs, lids, dish-on-stands and large storage vessels like basins and storage jars. All three varieties continue in the Phases Ib and Ic but the quantity decreases in each successive phase. In phase Ia a few sherds similar to burnished Grey Ware are painted in white pigment with designs similar those on Black-and-Red Ware. The decorative motifs used in Grey Ware are similar to the Red Ware except that motifs like impressed circles, concentric arcs, combed designs and sharp ridges with cut decorations are absent (Sankalia *et al.* 1969:88). At Ahar, the decorations are on the un-burnished surface (Sankalia *et al.* 1969:125-28), whereas at Gilund they are on the burnished surface. At Balathal in Phase A, Grey Ware is one of the major wares and is made by hand or on a slow wheel, has a coarse fabric and is utilitarian in function. In Phase B it retains its utilitarian nature and the surface treatment, decoration and shapes are similar to that of Coarse Red Ware.

At Gilund, Grey Ware has either a coarse fabric, produced on a fast wheel or moulded with well-levigated clay mixed with fine sand, grass and sometimes tiny mica particles or a finer fabric like that of the fine Thin Slipped Red Ware common in the Mature Chalcolithic Phase(fig. 4). In the case of the coarse ware while the fabric is not the finest and the pots are mostly utilitarian, like storage and cooking pottery is beautifully made as far as the surface treatment and decorative devices are concerned. Sankalia *et al.* (1969) very justifiably stated, 'the Ahar potter, in fact, has demonstrated how a pottery even utilitarian like storage jars can be made beautiful without painting. Also remarkable is his sense, proportion and self-restraint'. The coarse grey ware (Plate 2) as the nomenclature suggests is medium (Mature Phase only a few sherds) to coarse (Mature and Late Phases) in fabric with medium to thick section and blackish or grey in colour due to poor firing and minimum oxidation. In both Coarse and Red and Grey Wares large storage jars and cooking pots were slipped and burnished only up to the shoulder and then decorated by ridging, appliqué, cut and incised designs used singly or in combination don the shoulder whereas the body was bare of any slip, burnish or other decoration based on the large sherds and complete pots found during the excavation showing all these features on the same pot. In the case of large globular pots used for cooking, elongated jars and storage vessels which were buried below the surface level, the body and the base was not only thin and left several plain but also was even rusticated by applying a thin coat of fine sand. Similar treatment of the base is noticed on cooking pots and it is as common practice even today in the region to apply clay and cowdung on the rusticated surface to preserve the beauty of the pot and make it last longer-Some of the important shapes are globular pots with everted rims, carinated jars with everted rim or out-turned rims and large and small basins with thick lugged beaded rim, which served the purpose of handles. Besides these more common types, there are bowl-on-stand with thick stem, dish-on-stand and deep basins with handles and conical lids. An interesting shape, which seems to have a specific purpose, was the small *handi* with red band on the rim, neck, shoulder and the carination. These *handis* are few in number and could have been used for religious purpose.

Recent ethnographic work carried out in the region shows that it was the firing technique of oxygen-reduction or creating a smoky condition within the same kiln, which resulted in the grey colour with blotches of red on the exterior and interior rather the use of any slip other than red ochre. Even today potters make exactly the same ware using the ancient technique to produce wide mouth globular pots for storing and carrying water. A detailed study done on the decoration techniques at Gilund shows that Grey Ware vessels had superficial decorations only the slip, which did not penetrate the clay and often disappears with the fall of the slip and this especially true for combed decorations. This decoration is very common in the Mature Phase at the side and continues into the late Chalcolithic where it is less meticulous and carelessly made. The superficial combed designs perhaps can be traced back to the Sothi culture (*c.* 3000 to 2500 B.C.),which may have influenced the Kayatha combed ware (Wakankar 1967) as the time factor is not as far apart as generally assumed and further study may throw light on this problem.

An interesting feature at Gilund is the presence of a few thin Grey Ware sherds in the middle levels and possible in the lower levels but this needs more research. The fabric of this variety is fine without any gritty tempering, the sherds and pots are thin to medium in section similar to the Thin Slipped Red Ware where the pots are fully slipped and highly burnished on the exterior. Generally this ware is without any decoration and the fine mica particles which gives the vessels a fine sheen; however, in some cases thin ridges on the shoulder portion were present and two sherds were painted in white with horizontal bands and dots like Black-and-Red Ware. The main vessel types present are the convex carinated pot and the everted rimmed convex bowl. Nothing much can be said about the origin or context of this pottery except that it could have been used as a deluxe ware and interestingly it is restricted to the eastern face of GLD-2, which also yielded the Thin Slipped Red Ware of the fine variety.

Buff and Cream Slipped Wares

At Ahar, in Phase Ia, the lower levels yielded a Buff Ware and a buff slipped or cream slipped ware of fine fabric. The former is made of kaolin (Sankalia *et al.* 1969:52), while the later has a cream-coloured slip. Both these types were categorised as Cream Slipped Ware and completely disappear in the following two phases. At Balathal, Phase B yielded Buff Ware of fine fabric that was well-fired and made of well-levigated clay. This ware however, is not made of kaolin and we can possibly relate it to the imitation Buff Ware or Cream Slipped Ware identified in Phase Ia at Ahar. Based on the availability of this ware at both sites it can be presumed and established that the beginnings at Ahar were much later than at Balathal and that Phase Ia Ahar and Phase B of Balathal are contemporary. At Gilund, Buff ware as described above, is completely absent though we do have two sherds of Harappan Buff Ware with paintings in black, from the middle levels of GLD-1; however, the sherds are tiny and shapes cannot be made out.

Reserve Slip Ware

This ware was first recovered in the Ahar Culture at the lowest levels of Balathal Phase A, and now the lower levels of Gilund also yield it, though in limited quantities. The earliest sherds are of the red variety while the typical Harappan veriety is grey on cream. At Balathal this ware comprises two types; an imported fine grey variety and the local red variety of Phase A, which evolved at the site for the first time and was borrowed by the Harappans, who later produced their fine grey Reserve Slipped Ware. The grey variety present in Phase B here may represent the Harappans trading this ware back to the people it originally came from. The local red variety produced by the Early Chalcolithic disappears in the mature phase for reasons that are not known. The imported Reserve Slipped Ware is made from a very fine paste, uniformly fired to a high temperature, treated with a dark grayish slip and has a highly burnished exterior surface. The combed patterns executed on the outer surface are more meticulous as compared to the red variety. The shapes in this variety cannot be made out, since only body sherds have been found. Decorations include a set of eight zigzag lines, a broad band of light grayish colour on the neck, a set of running loops below a horizontal line with double horizontal bands below, a pattern resembling a serrated edge, and horizontal lines at regular intervals filled in with dots(fig. 5).

The coarse Red Reserve Slip Ware is reddish in colour, produced from fine clay to which, fine sand was added as tempering material, is fired uniformly to a high temperature and therefore, the core is brick-red in colour. It was first treated with a red wash over which a thick, dark red slip was applied. When the slip was wet various patterns were executed by scooping out the second slip possibly by a comb-like instrument. The patterns are usually found in sets or groups. Only a shallow dish with a round, slightly incurved rim, cylindrical hollow stem and stand with flared sides and short, out-turned ring is found in this ware. The decoration, mainly on the inner surface, consists of closely spaced horizontal lines and sets of zigzag lines (Misra *et al.* 1995). It is believed that the Reserve slip ware was originally made at Balathal and from their spread to other Harappans. In sharp contrast at Gilund however, only two sherds have been found and they are both from the pre-fortification levels and suggest interesting assumptions on the date of the early levels but further excavations are required before any fixed datum for the origin of Ahar culture at Gilund can be made.

Other Wares

In addition to the typical Ahar pottery available at the sites, we have evidence of foreign ceramic types at all levels. For example in the Early Phase there is Pre-Harappan/Sothi type Combed Ware; Chalcolithic wares from Kayatha such as Cream Slipped Ware and Kayatha red on Red Ware (Balathal and Gilund) and Gujarat Pre-Harappan types from North Gujarat like the Gritty Red Ware (Gilund). In the Mature Phase there is Harappan Buff Ware, sturdy Red Ware in shapes like the constricted neck globular pots/jars (Gilund) and Gujarat Harappan Reserve Slipped Ware (Balathal). In the Late Phase at Ahar (Last Phase) we have Lustrous Red Ware of Rangpur type, thick Red Ware with a bright red slip and paintings in black, thick Red Ware with thick crackled red slip with painting in black with metallic sound, wheel-made Red Ware externally red-slipped and painted in black. A ware with dull red slip un-burnished and painted in black, a ware with dull brown slip painted in black, thin Tan Ware with paintings in white and thick externally red slipped ware with paintings in white are also present.

In addition at Gilund we have the Malwa Ware in the Late Mature and Late Phase and Southern Neolithic Grey Ware especially the channel spouted bowl, which was copied in the Thin Slipped Red Ware of the coarse variety. The site of Gilund like Navdatoli has produced evidence of cup-on-stand, channel-spouted cups and pedastalled goblets, the relationship of which can be traced back to Harappan vessels on stand that seem to have continued into later phases. The site also seems to have made efforts to produce Malwa Ware types locally in the Thin Slipped Red Ware of the coarse variety. All these various ceramic types from the various Chalcolithic cultures and other artefacts indicate a busy trade network, which surely contributed to the development and evolution of these cultures in various parts of western and southern India. This network could have extended throughout the country but we need definite and conclusive data and a more collaborative work among scholars to understand these interactions among cultures that are clearly not isolated and underdeveloped communities.

An interesting and significant aspect gleaned from the study of the pottery of the Ahar culture is the absence of the prolific black painted Red Ware, which is the basis of the Early, Mature and Late Harappan as well as the Malwa, Jorwe and many other Chalcolithic Cultures with the exception of the Neolithic of the south which appears to have had an independent ceramic culture based on Grey Wares. In addition, not only the wares but also the decorative motifs on Ahar ceramics are distinct from those of other cultural assemblages.

Conclusions

Until the excavation at Balathal, in the last decade of the twentieth century, the Ahar Culture was believed to be a post-Harappan culture that arose as a result of the stressed migration of Harappans from their home areas. The earlier levels at Balathal however, revealed an indigenous evolution of the Ahar Culture, which can be labelled as an 'Early Chalcolithic' Phase and dated between 3000-2500 B.C. contemporary with the Early Harappans in Sindh, northern Rajasthan and Gujarat (Shinde 2000). The 'Mature Chalcolithic' Phase of the Ahar dated between 2500-2000 B.C. is visible at Balathal, Gilund and Ahar and is characterised by fortifications, storage structures, sizeable residential structures built of mud-bricks and stones, use of copper and deluxe pottery such as Black and Red Ware, Tan and Reserved Slipped Wares that evolved locally and was copied/manufactured subsequently by the Harappans and other farming communities of Central India and the Deccan. The decline or the 'Late Chalcolithic' Phase of the Ahar Culture can be placed around 2000-1700 B.C. as seen at Gilund, where the ceramic assemblage turns gritty, coarse and ill-finished as far as decorations and surface treatment is concerned. Hence the Ahar people were clearly not distressed Harappans fleeing from their homeland but people of local origin probably locally evolved from the Mesolithic communities of the region as the area has a large number of Mesolithic sites. They developed and flourished initially possibly due to contact with the Harappans of northern Rajasthan and Gujarat and other Chalcolithic cultures of Gujarat and Saurashtra and maintained trade interactions with the Malwa region and areas farther south.

Based on the study of pottery the Chalcolithic in Central India and the Chalcolithic in general can be summarised as follow:

- Early Chalcolithic, Ahar Culture of Phase A Balathal; Anarta culture of Gujarat; pre-Prabhas, lower levels of Padri in Gujarat.
- Middle Chaocolithic characterised by the evolution of the Kayatha culture; Ahar Phase B as seen at Balathal, Ahar and Gilund; Micaceous Red Ware, Padri/Prabhas Patan; Savalda; and the beginning of the Malwa Culture.
- Late Chalcolithic, characterised by flourishing Malwa, Jorwe and Late Jorwe cultures.

As seen from the above discussion of ceramics from the sites of Ahar, Gilund and Balathal we have in recent years related a completely different story of interaction and exchange that is further exemplified by other artefactual evidences followed by lingering socio-religious features which needs to be studied deeply. It is clear that though outside the direct sphere of inclfuence of the Harappan Civilization, these communities maintained a continuous interactive system of exchange in terms of economic, religious and socio-political life. Evidence suggests that the Ahar Culture people extended their contact network not only to the Harappans but also down south via the Tapi and Narmada Rivers to Maharashtra, and east via the Chambal River into Central India and Malwa. Hence a careful study of ceramics has helped to understand the independent origin of this culture in the Mewar region, its gradual development because of internal factors, its blossoming with Harappan influence and trade contacts and finally its decline due to the degeneration of the larger trade network and environmental factors. The study of the ceramic assemblage helps to find the Ahar Culture its rightful place in the development of Indian culture and history as an independent thread and not a shadow of the Harappans.

REFERENCES

Ansarī, Z.D. and M.K. Dhavalikar, 1975, *Excavations at Kayatha*, Poona: Deccan College Research Institute.

Childe, V.G., 1958, 'Retrospect', *Antiquity* 32, p. 70.

Dhavalikar, M.K,. 1970-71, 'Some Aspects of the Chalcolithic Culture of Central India', *Puratattva* (4), pp. 25-30.

Dhavalikar M.K., H.D. Sankalia and Z.D. Ansari (ed.), 1988, *Excavations at Inamgaon*, Deccan College, Pune.

Dhavalikar, M.K., 1994, 'Early Farming Communities of Central India', *Man and Environment*, XIX, pp. 159-68.

Gogte, V.D., 1996, 'Chalcolithic Balathal: a trading centre as revealed by the XRD study of the pottery', *Man and Environment*, XXI (1) pp. 98-100.

Hooja, R., 1988, *The Ahar Culture and Beyond*, BAR International Series 412, England.

IAR 1959-60, *Indian Archaeology Review*, New Delhi: Archaeological Survey of India.

Kashyap, A., 1999, *Harppan Impact on the Chalcolithic Culture of Central India*, Unpublished MA Dissertation, Deccan College, Pune.

Misra, V.N., V. Shinde, R. Mohanty, Kurush Dalal, Anup Misra, Lalit Pandey and Jeevan Kharakwas, 1995, 'The Excavations at Balathal: their contributions to the Chalcolithic and Iron Age Cultures of Mewar, Rajasthan', *Man and Environment*, XX (1) pp. 57-80.

Misra, V.N., 1997, 'Balathal: A Chalcolithic settlement in Mewar, Rajasthan, India: Results of First Three Seasons Excavation', *South Asian Studies* (13), pp. 251-73.

Misra, V.N., V. Shinde, R.K. Mohanty, Lalit Pandey and Jeevan Kharakwal, 1997, 'The Excavations at Balathal, Udaipur District of Rajasthan with Special Reference to Chalcolithic Architecture', *Man and Environment*, XXI, pp. 35-59.

Ratnagar, S., 1991., *Inquiries into the Political Organization of Harappan Society*, Ravish Publishers, Pune.

Sankalia H.D., S.B. Deo and Z.D. Ansari, 1969, *Excavations at Ahar*, Deccan College Research Institute, Pune.

Shinde, V. S., 1991, 'Craft Specialization and Social Organization in the Deccan India, *Anitiquity*, (65), pp. 796-807.

Shinde, V.S., 2000, 'Origin and Development of Chalcolithic Phase in Central India, *Bulletin of Indo-Pacific Prehistory Association* 19 (volume 3): 125-36.

Shinde, V.S. (in press), 'Development of Urbanisation in Mewar, India in the Middle of Third Millenium B.C.', *Journal of Indian Archaeological Society*, Tokyo.

Shinde, V.S. and G.L., Possehl (in press), 'A Report on the Excavations At Gilund 1999-2001, *South Asian Archaeology 2001*, C. Jarrige, ed., Paris.

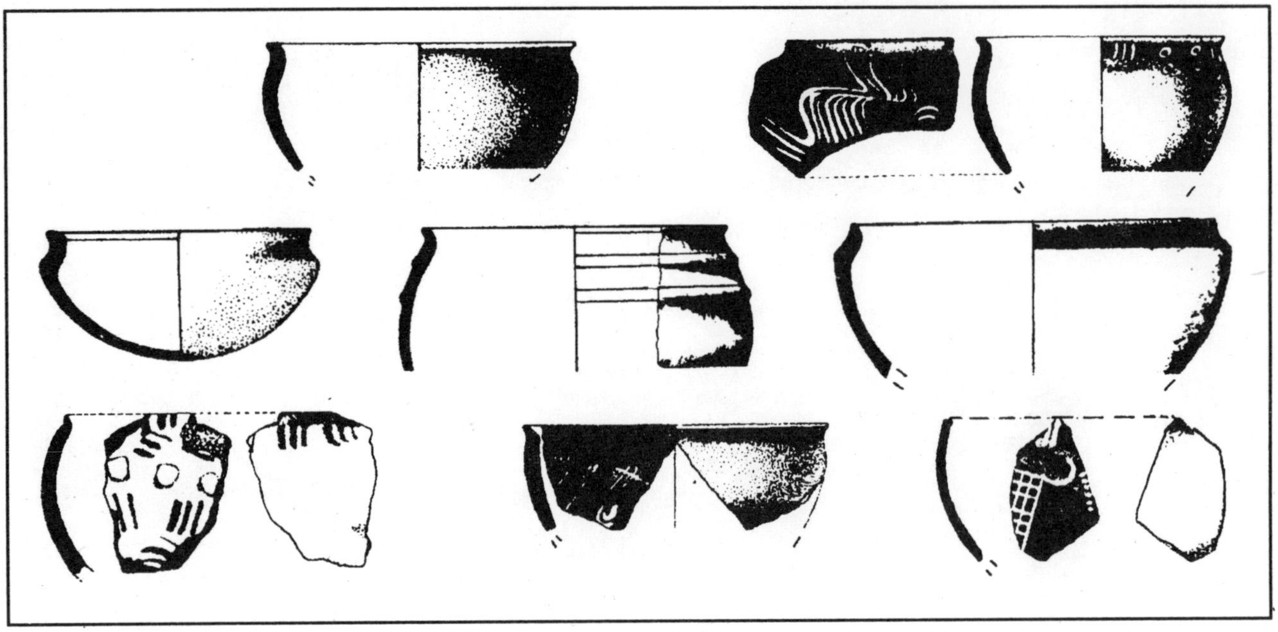

Fig. 1. Black and Red Ware, Ahar Culture

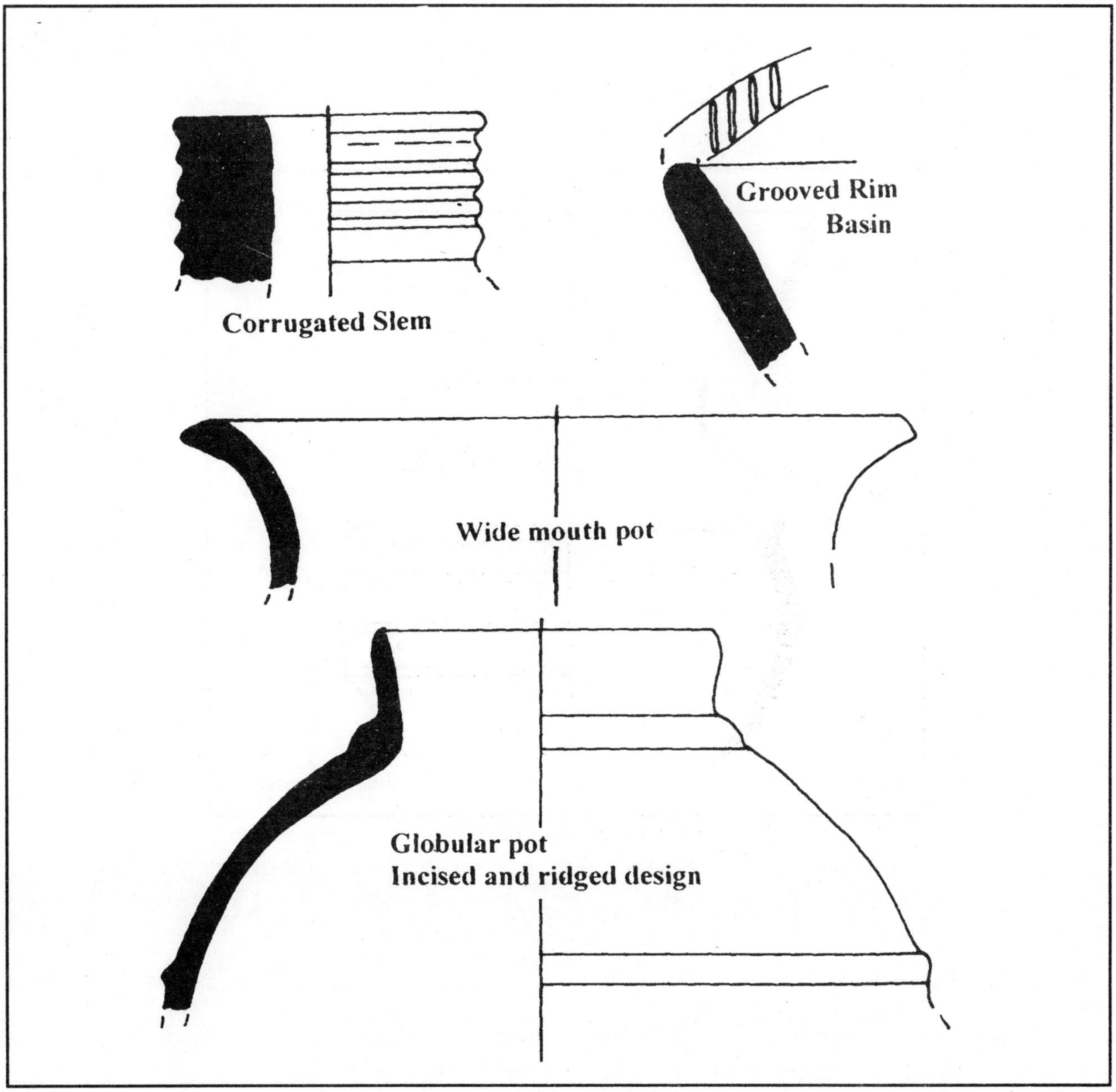

Fig. 2. Coarse red ware

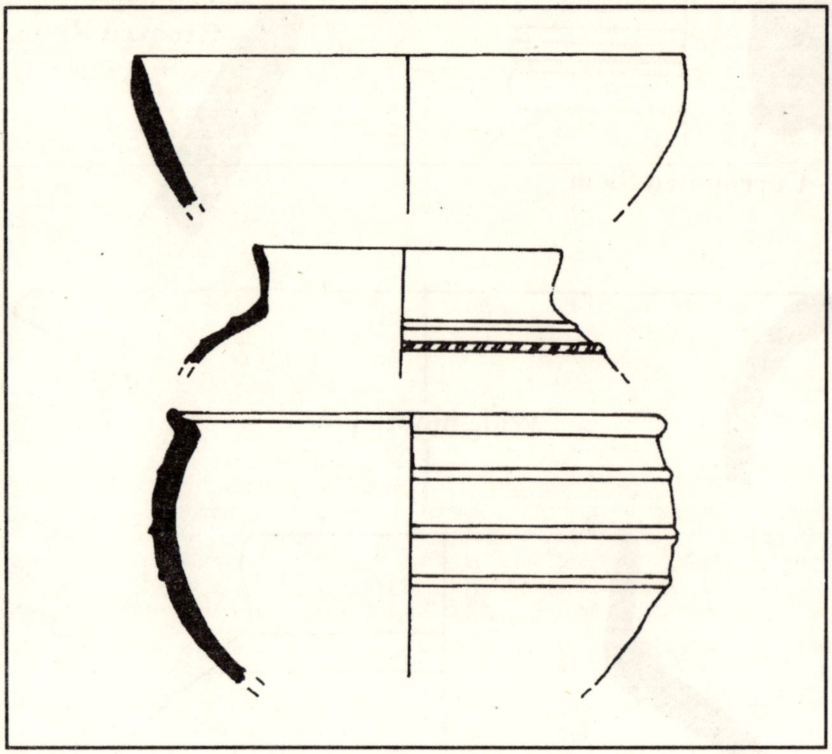

Fig. 3. Thin Red Ware, Ahar Culture

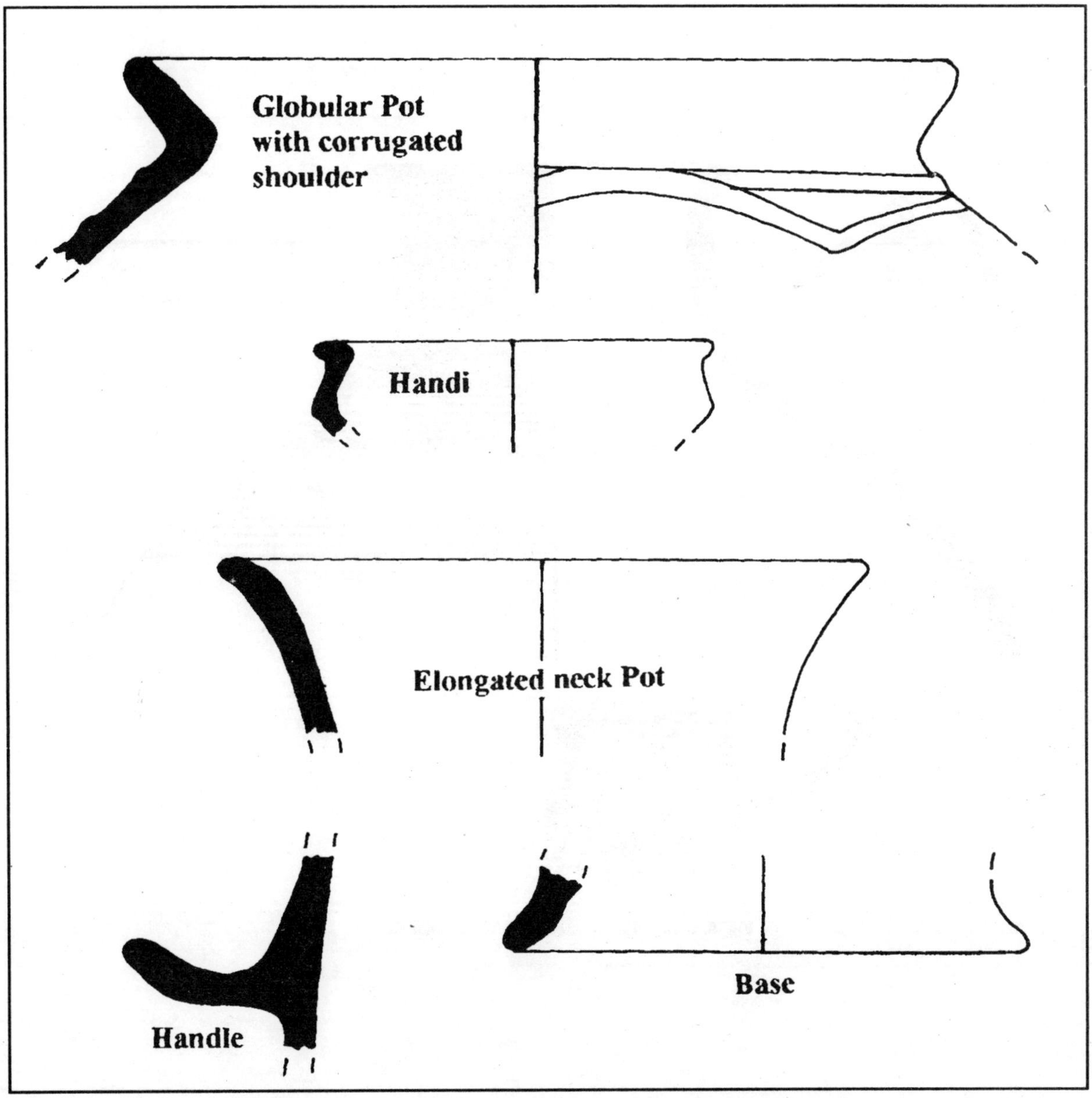

Fig. 4. Coarse Grey Ware Globular Pot, Gilund (Photo Enclosed Separately)

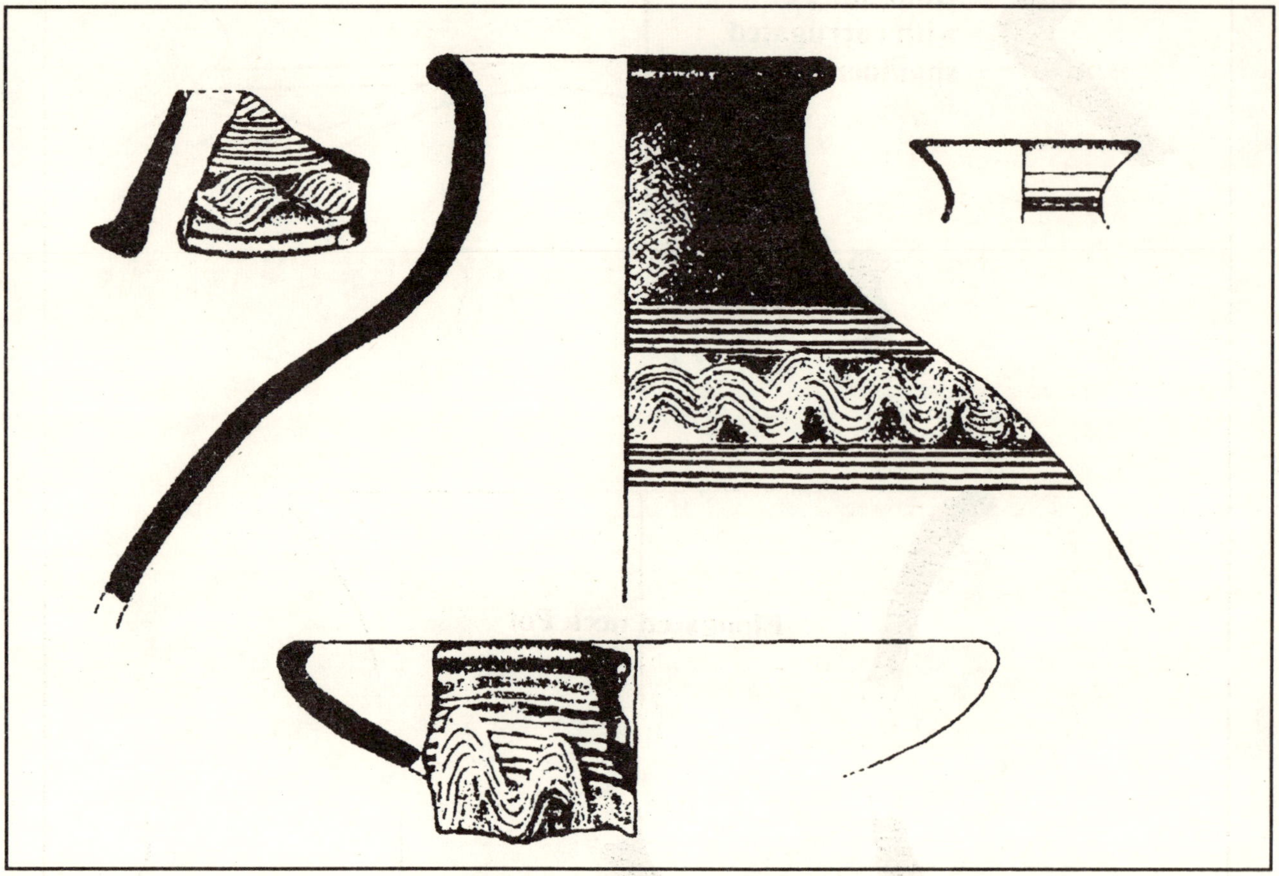

Fig. 5. Coarse Red Reserve Slip Ware, Ahar Culture

Is Every Circular Fire-Pit in Harappan Levels—a *'Tandoor'*?

TEJAS GARGE*

The function of circular fire-pits found in many Harappan sites needs to be re-examined. These are generally called ovens, hearths, furnaces, kilns and altars. These can be examined under three broad categories: domestic ovens, industrial kilns or furnaces and fire-altars associated with religious activities.

Recent ethnographic study at Rakhigarhi village, Haryana leads to another possible interpretation i.e., some of the circular fire-pits which were regarded as the *'tandoors'* and 'fire-altars' may have been special ovens exclusively used for boiling milk.

Archaeological data from the excavated sites suggests that these fire-pits served different functions based on the physical features of the fire-pit and related findings from vicinity. First category is domestic ovens, as they primarily served for cooking. Most of them were circular ovens, but there were also parallel brick channels reported from Mohenjo-daro which were possibly used for cooking (Mackey 1938:16). Other domestic ovens from Mohenjodaro were circular in shape with average diameter of 3.5 ft. These pits had inward sloping walls and flat base with average diameter of 3 ft and maximum depth of 4 ft. Most of them were above surface without any mouth except one in which had opening door in the wall and it is called as the only 'bread-oven' (plate XXXV, f) from Mohenjo-daro (Mackey, 1938:48). Most of them were built in wedged-shaped bricks laid with mud mortar, and their walls had been carefully plastered with mud. The mud-lined walls are highly vitrified and the white ashes are found. No objects were found near them to aid determine their use (Mackay 1938:49-50).

Kalibangan is the first Harappan site where proper attention was paid to the circular ovens. A series of ovens found in a room belonging to the middle phase- Period I. They were both over-ground and underground varieties. They had mud walls periodically plastered (IAR- 1962-63:20). B.B. Lal was the first scholar who thought of functional interpretation of the circular ovens from Kalibangan. In his words, *"The houses usually had a courtyard with rooms on the sides. Within the courtyard were noted wide circular pits, plastered with lime and mud. These appear to have been used for storage of grains, though no actual cereals were found. Cooking was also done in the courtyard as evidenced by the presence of tandoors. These were of both over ground and underground varieties (fig.2.3). This discovery throws the antiquity of modern tandoors back into the first half of the third millennium BC"* (1998:14-15). Thus, function of the circular fire-pits reported from the Early Harappan levels at Kalibangan was possibly for baking rotis or cooking. A community oven (Pl. XXXV) is reported from the Early-Mature transition level or Period IC of Surkotda. Exact location and the description of this oven is not

*Research Scholar, Indian Archaeological Society

given in the report. The diameter of this oven is around one metre, and depth is around 50-60 cm. This oval oven had mud walls and it contained ashes (Joshi 1990:65). A circular brick-lined hearth (dia.1m) was noticed in one of the cells (RGR-6, Early Harappan) at Rakhigarhi. Similar hearth was also found in a cell located on the northern side of the street (Nath, 2001: 44).

Several kilns were noticed in a row, partly underground and partly jutting out of the surface at Kotla-Nihang Khan. Similar kiln is noticed at Bara (Sharma 1976:12). Oval structures of burnt earth are reported from Late Harappan period at Bhagawanpura (Joshi 1978). Oval-shaped kilns were reported from Hulas, Uttar Pradesh, belonging to Late Harappan period. These were plastered with fine clay paste (Dikshit 1981). At Daulatpur the existence of the walled structures, round to oval in shape and burnt inside, were most probably designed as ovens or *bhattis*. Ash, pottery and animal bones were found in these enclosures belonging to the Late Harappan period (Singh 1977). A circular hearth, 50 cm in diameter and 10 cm deep containing ash and charred animal bone-fragments was found in House 16 (Fig.14, Pl. LXXXVI.B, Pl. LIII.A) assignable to Late Harappan period at Daimabad (Sali 1982:181).

Another category of fire-pits reported from Harappan sites is fire-altars. Most of them were rectangular in shape and were built in burnt as well as mud-bricks. Often they contain ash, charcoal, fragments of terracotta cakes and a mud or brick stele in the centre. On an average these fire-pits measured up to a metre in length and half-a-metre in width. These were not overground but sunk into the floor to a depth of about 25 cm. The sides were lined with clay. These types are reported from Kalibangan (IAR-1968-69:31, Lal 1997:227) and Lothal (Rao 1979:83-84, 89, 111, 121). There is another variety of fire-altars, which is oblong or circular in shape. These are also plastered with fine clay and contain deposit of ash, charcoal; sometimes with fragments of animal bones and terracotta cakes. This kind of fire-altar is noticed at Lothal, Banawali (Bisht 1984:95) and Rakhigarhi (Nath 1999:48).

Industrial Kilns or furnaces is the third variety of fire-pits found at the Harappan sites. These were reported from major sites representing Harappan culture- Mohenjo-daro, Harappa, Chaunho-daro, Lothal, Kuntasi, Rakhigarhi, Banawali, Allahdino, Amri, Tarkhanwala-dera, Kunal, Sanghol etc. Circular potter's kiln, rectangular and oval kilns used by lapidary and coppersmiths clearly indicate their function by the potsherds, finished and unfinished objects of semi-precious stones and metal objects found nearby. Here, in this category the function of the fire-pits is clearly defined.

Function of circular ovens - a fresh look

Ethno-archaeology, theoretically, is effective in providing a reasonable degree of hypothetical probability as opposed to subjective speculation and romanticizing about the past. The ethno-archaeological approach has to be rigorously and critically applied to specific problems or areas of research.

Harappan Society appears to be a homogenous composition of people engaged in various different economic activities. A very biased picture of Harappans being only engaged in manufacturing and trade is been projected and emphasised so far. Agricultural economy was the real base in Harappan trade, manufacturing and industrial economy. Similarly pastoral activities also played an important role in the economic life of the Harappan people. Though manufacturing activities are reflected prominently in the material remains, it is difficult to interpret the structures associated with the agricultural and pastoral activities in urban context.

The circular ovens in the Harappan context are interpreted differently by different excavators. But still it remains a fact that they were not given proper attention by excavators in term of publishing their proper location, its measurements etc., except Kalibangan, these circular ovens are interpreted as the *tandoors*. A fresh approach leads to another possible interpretation of this feature which is based on the ethnographic evidence.

The modern village of Rakhigarhi offers an excellent opportunity to study the local culture and how it helps to interpret some aspects of the Harappan culture. The past can be better understood, by describing part of the contemporary experience of the present villagers. The population of Rakhigarhi village is approximately around 3,500. It is a mixed population dominated by *Jat* community followed by *Banias, Brahmins* and other backward castes. The main occupation of the villagers is agriculture, dairy and related activities. The village settlement today has its origin in the medieval and British times. Earlier village was confined to the top of ancient mound-RGR-4 and has many medieval structures in this area. Most of the houses in Rakhigarhi are single storeyed modest houses. Very few cases are double-storeyed buildings and very rarely three-storeyed buildings are seen. Most of the houses are made of burnt bricks; roof is mostly flat made of wooden beams and planks. The floors are either of stone slabs, cement or cow dung. In case of house plans, elaborate houses have an open courtyard in the middle, surrounded by square or rectangular rooms built for storage and dwelling purpose (fig.1). In some cases, verandah is incorporated between courtyard and rooms. At some places verandah is seen on the outer face of the house, adjoining to the street. Other type of common plan seen at Rakhigarhi is, a courtyard in front, with hearth or *chulha* and *harha*. Two to five-roomed housing-complex followed by a small courtyard in front is slightly raised from the level of street. This platform of courtyard is either built of burnt bricks or rammed mud plastered with cow-dung. Often this courtyard is enclosed with a low wall of burnt bricks. In some houses, this enclosure is made of thorny bushes. This enclosure or outer courtyard is a very important part of every household, as they are multifunctional. These courtyards are used for tying domesticated animals like buffalo, cow, sheep and goat. Cooking activity is also carried out in the courtyard; water is stored in *matkas*, placed on a small platform raised along with the wall of house on the floor of the courtyard. Craftsmen like potters also work in the courtyard. Now a days many courtyards are converted into shops. The inner or back side courtyards are also used for storage purposes - storage of fodder and fuel. They also consist of bathing or washing platform.

Here *harhas* or ovens made on the floor deserve special attention (fig. 2). The *chulha* and *harha* are the common elements of every courtyard at Rakhigarhi village. First type the regular U-shaped *chulha* where routine cooking activities are carried out and the other is *harha*, a kind of oven where special cooking activities are carried out which need slow heating - like boiling milk. Sometimes other food items are also prepared here, but the main function of *harha* is to boil milk. The U-shaped ones have single opening for inserting fuel and cleaning. But the *harha* which is completely circular in shape does not have any opening. Fuel used for this is essentially charcoal and cow dung cakes. This *harha* is found in three different varieties. First is circular made in a shallow pit within the floor of courtyard (fig. 3). This circular pit is well plastered with cow dung and fine clay. Fuel - coal or cow dung cakes are kept inside this pit and it is lit which gives slow heating. On top of this pot is kept filled with milk. This whole pit is covered by a lid made of fine clay mixed with horse-dung and cow-dung. In this way milk is boiled for a long time without overflowing out of the vase unlike in normal *chulha* The other types of *harhas* are either placed on a raised platform or mobile ones.

The second type of *harha* is also a circular pit, but these pits are made on a rectangular platform roughly averaging 125 x 45cm in size, raised 30 cm above the ground (fig.4). Depth of these pits varies between 25 and 30 cm. This *harha* is also provided with a lid made of fine clay.

The third type of *harha* looks like thick unbaked clay pot (fig. 5). This is also made of fine clay, horse-dung and cow dung with average height 30 to 40 cm. This *harha* is also provided lid made of same material of 10 cm thickness. Lids of all types of *harhas* are known as *belan* in local language; all these *belans* have perforations on top so that the smoke is let off the *harha*.

The first and second types of *harhas*- underground and over ground with platform - are quite important from archaeological point of view. Similar type of circular fire-pits without any opening or mouth are reported from Early Harappan levels of Rakhigarhi and Banawali as well from the Late Harappan levels of Hulas, Bhagawanpura, Daimabad and Daulatpur. The *tandoors* reported from Early Harappan levels at Kalibangan are quite similar to that of *harhas* of underground as wel' overground types with platform. Another noticeable thing about these circular domestic ovens is that they are reported from either Early or Late Harappan levels. The fire-altars, industrial kilns, furnaces and domestic hearths and bread ovens are reported from the Mature Harappan levels. This fact signifies the functional difference of the circular ovens and its connection with pastoral activities. During Early and Late Harappan times pastoral economy was quite dominant. The circular ovens reported from these levels are comparable to those of modern *harhas*, not only on the basis of shape and dimensions but their function could have been the same.

Regional environment is the most dominant factoring influencing the culture of people controlling their behaviour patterns and eventually evolving traditional practices, which sometimes, continues for thousands of years. Today we see animal husbandry is common in Haryana-Punjab region. Almost every household in villages, towns and cities keep cattle. This trend must have been the legacy of the Neolithic people. However, in the Saraswati basin this is perhaps, from the Early Harappan times. Today also, the area covered by the Harappan Civilization - Haryana, Punjab, and Gujarat and to an extent UP - is known for its milk production and milk products. Milk is a perishable item; processing is needed for production of curds and ghee, which is long lasting. For this process one has to boil milk on slow heat. If, this has to be done in large quantity and that too with traditional methods keeping in mind the conditions that prevailed during the Harappan times oven like *harha* is the most suitable apparatus. This could have been used on both domestic as well commercial levels.

Can we postulate that a separate class of people was engaged in the production of milk and milk products? Further study only can confirm this and also to our knowledge of the Harappan Society. We need to study the role of pastoral economy of the Harappans which is a neglected factor particularly in urban areas. It is here ethno-archaeology has its role to play. Archaeologists, would do well to adopt this method also in their future studies.

REFERENCES

Bisht R.S. 1984. Structural Remains and Town Planning at Banawali in Lal, B.B. and S.P. Gupta Lal,(eds) *Frontiers of the Indus Civilization*, Books and Books, New Delhi, p.95.

Dales G.F and Kenoyer J.M. 1989. Excavations at Harappa-1988 *Pakistan Archaeology*, vol. II, Department of Archaeology and Museums, Karachi, p. 114-16.

Dikshit K.N. 1981. The Excavations at Hulas and Further Exploration of the Upper Ganga-Yamuna Doab, *Man and Environment*, V, ISPQS, Pune.

Ghosh A. (Ed.) 1989, *An Encyclopedia of Indian Archaeology*, ICHR, New Delhi, p.183.

Indian Archaeology - A Review 1962-63, p.20

Joshi J.P. 1990, Excavations at Surkotda 1971-72 and Explorations in Kutch, *Memoirs of Archaeological Survey of India, No. 87, Archaeological Survey of India*, New Delhi, p.65.

Lal B.B. 1997. *The Earliest Civilization of South Asia (Rise, Maturity and Decline)*, Aryan Books International, New Delhi, p. 227.

Lal B.B. 1998. India 1947-1997: *New Light on the Indus Civilization*, Aryan Books International, New Delhi, pp.14, 15.

Mackay E.J.H. 1938, *Further Excavations at Mohenjo-daro*, Indological Book Corporation, New Delhi, vol. I & II, pp. 16, 48, 49-50, 154, 172, 177.

Nath Amarendra, 2001. Rakhigarhi: 1999-2000 *Purattatva* No.31, Indian Archaeological Society, New Delhi, p.44.

Rao S. R. 1979. Lothal - A Harappan Port Town. vol. I, *Memoirs of the Archaeological Survey of India*, No.78, p.83-84, 89, 111, 121.

Sali S.A. 1982. Harappans at Daimabad in Possehl G.L. (ed) *Harappan Civilization, A Contemporary Perspective*, Oxford & IBH Publishing Co. New Delhi, p.181.

Sharma D.V. 1979. Harappan Furnaces Purattatva, No. 11, New Delhi, pp.125-27.

Sharma Y.D. 1982. Harappan Complex on Sutlej (India) in Gregory Possehl (ed) *Harappn Civilization- A Contemporary Perspective*, New Delhi.

Vats, M.S. 1974. *Excavations at Harappa*, Bharatiya Publishing House (Reprint),Varanasi, vols. I, II, p.470-3.

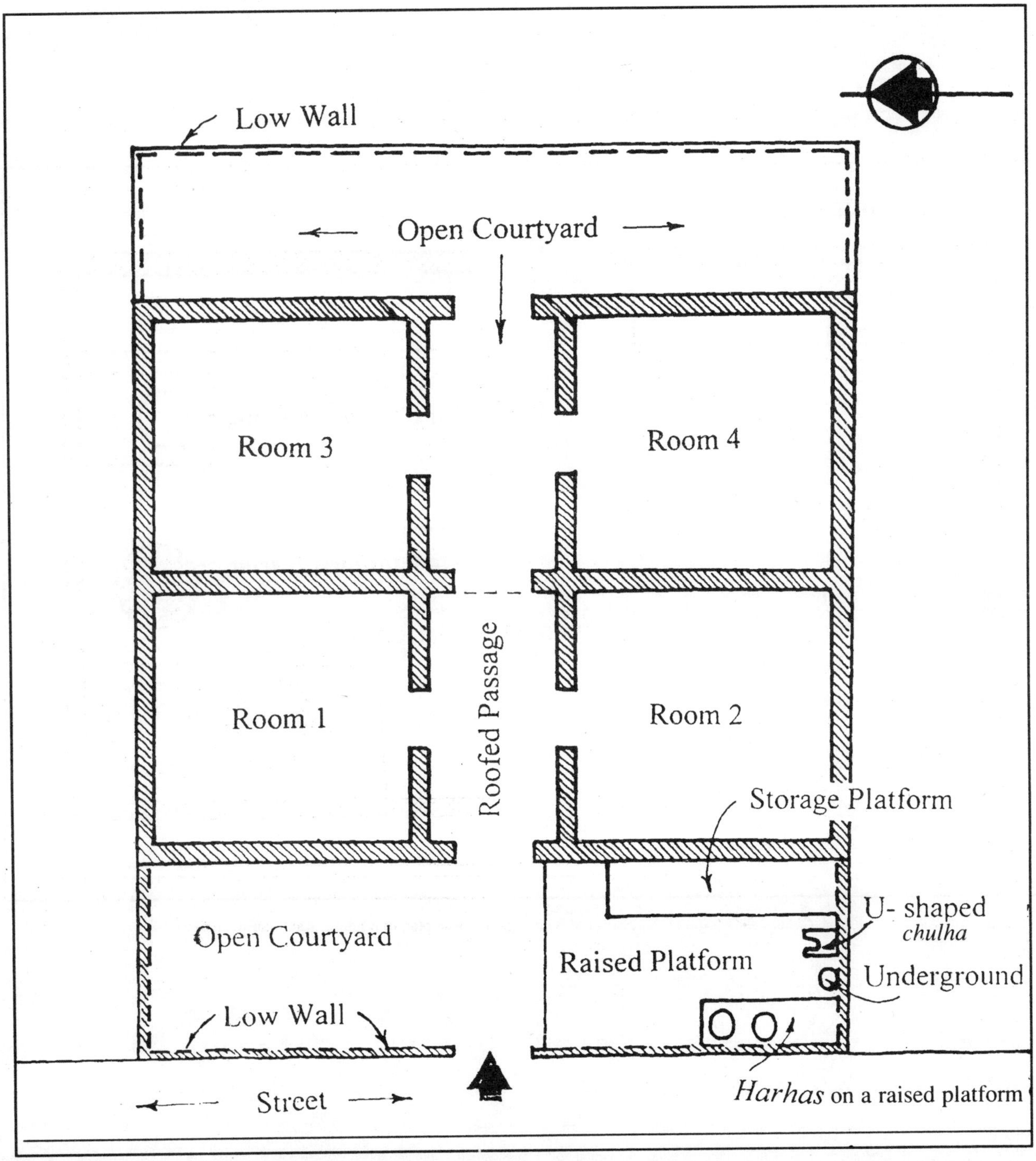

Fig. 1. Typical House plan of the modern houses in village Rakhigarhi

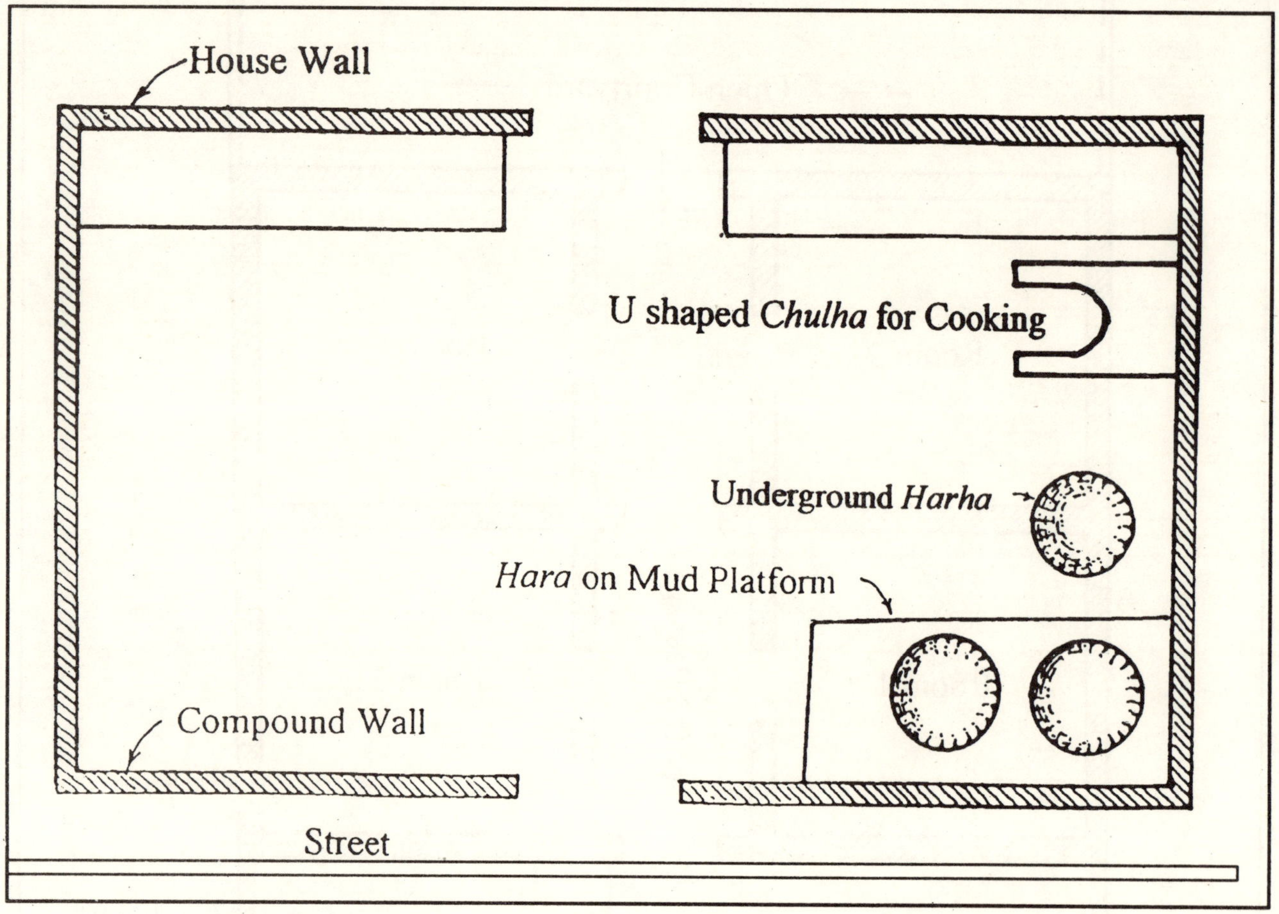

Fig. 2. *Chulha* and *Harha* in the courtyard with typical house plan of a house, Rakhigarhi Village

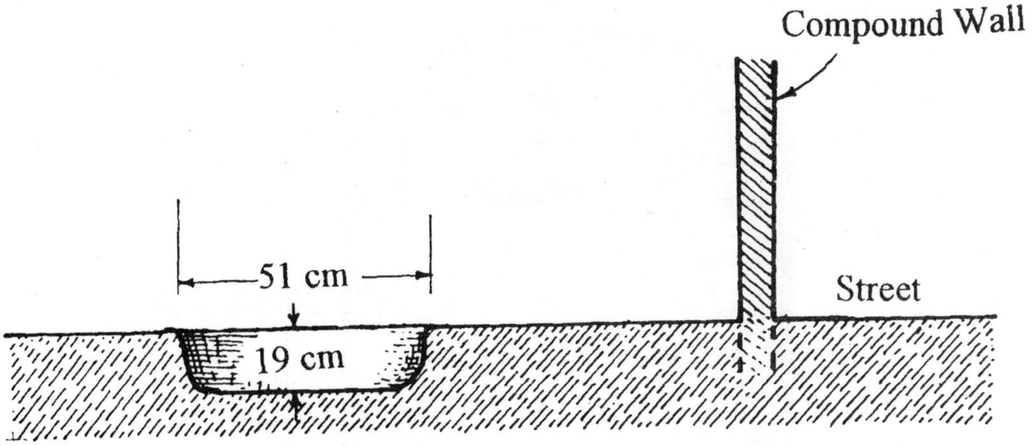

Fig. 3. Underground *Harha*

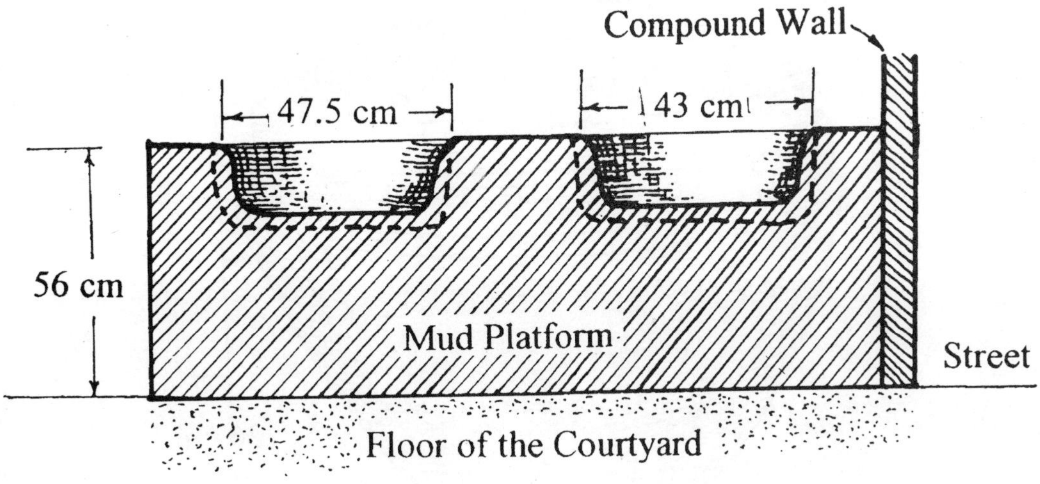

Fig. 4. *Harha* on Platform (section)

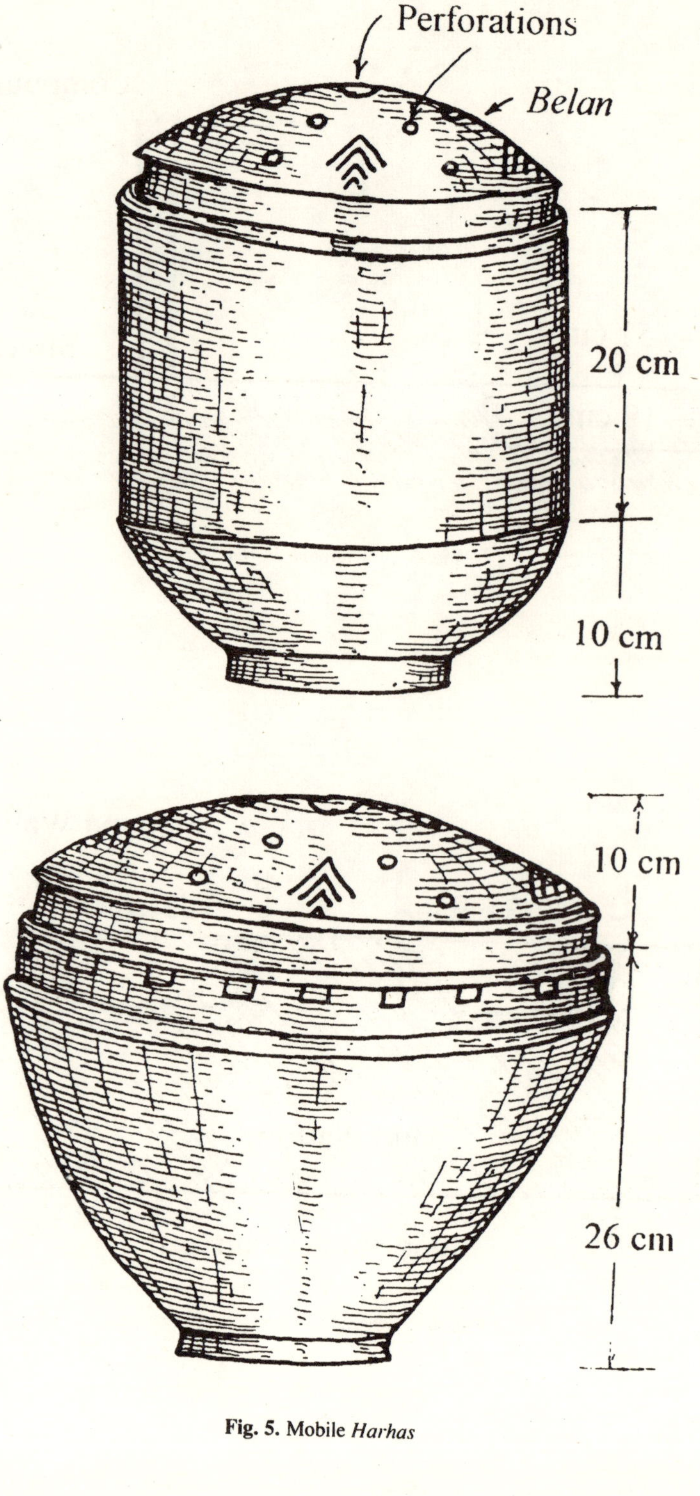

Fig. 5. Mobile *Harhas*

A Report on Excavation at Madarpur, A Copper Hoard Site

D.V. Sharma*, A. Pradhan**, V.N. Prabhakar***, A.K. Bhargav****, K.A. Kabui**

Introduction

In January 2000, the first author received information about a chance discovery of some copper objects from a village near Thakurdvara, district Moradabad, U.P. Subsequently, a team of archaeologist headed by the author visited the site to substantiate reported finds and met the district authorities in police station. Thakurdvara. A hoard of 31 copper anthropomorphic figures was recovered by the local police. The in-charge, police station narrated in detail the sequence of events about this unique discovery and how recovery was made from the labour. Shri V. N. Prabhakar, Assistant Archeologist, documented the 31 anthropomorphic figures. Next morning, a police constable accompanied us to the find spot located near a brick kiln in village Madarpur which was surveyed thoroughly. This hoard could be rescued solely owing to prompt action of the local police.

This discovery not only provided fresh material for study of copper hoards but also opened a new chapter to understand the settlement pattern and human habitation in the Upper Ganga doab during 2nd millennium B.C. The chance discovery at Madarpur may throw light on OCP - related problems after its find at Hastinapur and Lothal.

Location and Approach to the Site

The Ochre Coloured Pottery (OCP) site/find spot of Copper Hoard near village Madarpur (78° 48' N and 29° 12' 38" E) is situated in tehsil Thakurdvara, District Moradabad, Uttar Pradesh, at a distance of 50 km from district headquarters. It is approachable from Moradabad via Thakurdvara and is located towards east on the right side of Thakurdvara-Surjanagar mettalled Road, at a distance of 8km from Thakurdvara (fig 1). The find spot lies approximately 100m north-east of a brick kiln of Haji Sirajuddin of Ramnagar Khaguwala village. A seasonal rivulet locally known as Japti-Nala/Jabdi Nala, a tributary of Ram-ganga flows near by to east of the site and down stream joins Repi or Repti nala flowing at a distance of 8 km and the combined waters flow down stream for 12 km to meet the Ramganga near Karanpura. By train nearest station is Moradabad on the Delhi-Kathgodam railway line.

Discovery and Inspection of Site

The anthropomorphic figures were discovered from the site Madarpur. The find spot falls under the revenue boundary of village Bhaipur in the Patwari's record. The height (2.3cm) of agricultural find spot area was compar-

*Superintending Archaeologist, Archaeological Survey of India, Excavation Br.-II, New Delhi
**Archaeological Survey of India, Agra Circle, 22 The Mall, Agra
***Archaeological Survey of India, Aurangabad Circle, Aurangabad
****Archaeological Survey of India, Janpath, New Delhi

atively higher then the present level. On 7th January 2000, Shamsuddin labour engaged by the Haji was digging soil to prepare mud-bricks. He found a stack of 31 copper anthropomorphic figures placed over one above other *in situ*. Initially, the labour concealed these all and distributed among two groups. Intentionally out of curiosity one arm portion of a figure was broken by them to ascertain its metal contents as they presumed it to be gold. But some how police got information and recovered a lot of 31 copper figures from both groups and confiscated them. On 10th January, 2000, the author examined this copper hoard in the police station and visited find spot also. In total, 31 anthropomorphic figures were examined, out of which five were found with one hand broken. The size and shape of each figures is different from other (Table-1). Stylistically, two anthropomorphic figures in relation to arm and leg posture depict a distinct feature hither to unknown. One hand in each case is found turned upward while foot portion is less conspicuous and concave-shaped (Pls. 4 and 5). The legs have been shown merely symbolic in form of two projections at bottom. This posture suggests depiction of a seated crossed-legged *(padmasana)* human being. The hand posture of both figures having one arm upraised also suggests them to be a deity. Both these figures are unique and significant for the following reasons: (a) such form and shape of anthropomorphic figures have not been reported so far from any known site; (b) these figures could be religious icons but in the absence of adequate data it would be conjectural. To some extent both appears to be seated in yogic posture and (c) the other noteworthy feature of Madarpur copper hoard is that all are dwarfish and bear visible oblique hammer marks on both sides. That Madarpur site has yielded a big copper hoard that too only anthropomorphic figures is also interesting phenomenon. Last but not least the OCP pottery and its associated coarse red ware have been found in contemporary deposit. Thus on circumstantial evidence the two appear to be associated. The entire copper hoard was found at a depth of approximately 1.8 m below present surface level. The soil composition was compact in nature, very hard and difficult to dig. The colour of the soil varies from yellowish brown to very light brown. The OCP occurs in sediments of a few metres thick, brown in colour, sandy and silt in texture and detritus appearance. None of them has the character of a normal habitation deposit. These sediments could arise either because of a huge deluge of floods that engulfed the doab. Originally these were derived from glacial environments which were subsequently deposited by floods (Agarwal 1982:198).

A large portion of the original level of the field had already been dug out adjoining the find spot before this discovery. A regular layer containing Ochre Coloured Pottery (OCP) deposit was visible in exposed section at site. The OCP sherds were found scattered all around within an area approximately 100 m x 75 m adjoining find spot. It was decided to undertake a small trial pit measuring 2m x 2m for excavation to discover remaining objects, if any. The OCP was found from a layer of 25 cm thickness but no more copper objects were found, although on surface OCP pottery was available in this agricultural field all over. The discovery of such a large hoard from the levels of OCP deposit *in situ* is significant. To prevent any attempt of digging by the villagers till regular excavation is undertaken for further research, the local police was requested to deploy police guard at site. The team of archaeologist took possession of 31 anthropomorphic figures from local police and brought them to Agra Circle for research and study purpose. Three of them are presently in the National Museum, New Delhi on display. Immediate systematic excavation is essential to discover more copper objects and OCP to asses the potentiality of the site. It was also necessary to ascertain the cultural sequence at Madarpur site owing to its location below foot hills of Kumaun region on alluvial plains of the Ramganga.

Table showing size of Copper Anthropomorphic figures, Madarpur

Sr. No. 1	Maximum length in cm. 'Head' to 'Foot' at centre. 2	Maximum width ('arm') to ('ar') in cm. 3	Width of bottom (foot side) in cm. 4	Maximum thickness in cm. 5	Descritpion/Remarks 6
1	22.3	28.0	14.3	0.5	Blunt edged head and foot portion

1	2	3	4	5	6
2	17.0	22.2	12.1	0.5	One side of foot portion is sharp edged
3	17.7	25.6	13.2	0.5	Blunt edged head and foot portion
4	22.4	27.4	15.0	0.8	One hand found upraised
5	17.0	23.0	11.1	0.7	The foot portion is slightly angular in shape with sharp edge
6	19.2	25.2	14.6	0.8	The foot portion is with blunt edge
7	20.9	20.7	12.8	0.8	The right arm is broken. The foot portion has blunt edge
8	18.5	23.2	11.5	0.7	The foot portion has blunt edge
9	26.8	21.5	15.0	0.8	The left arm was found broken during recovery and broken piece is available and could be joined together. A little copper sample was taken from this broken arm to analyze its metal content. The foot portion is slightly angular in shape
10	17.8	24.2	11.9	0.7	The foot portion has blunt edge
11	14.5	18.5	9.7	0.6	The left arm has sharp edge
12	18.2	20.6	11.5	0.6	The left hand of the figurine was found broken originally and remaining portion of the arm could not be discovered
13	17.2	22.4	11.6	0.6	Left side of foot portion has sharp edge
14	17.3	24.5	11.6	0.8	Foot portion has slight curve at corners and middle portion is blunt
15	17.7	22.9	8.9	1.0	Both corners of foot portion are sharp edged
16	18.3	25.9	11.1	0.8	Foot portion is blunting edged and slightly concave
17	17.1	22.2	9.7	0.7	Foot portion has sharp corners at edge
18.	17.8	24.5	13.5	0.8	Foot portion is sharp at both corners and lower portion of left arm has sharp edge
19	19.6	28.9	12.0	0.8	Foot portion is blunt, both arms are sharp edged at elbow portion and a circular chip appears chopped off originally. Probably this happened during annealing process
20	21.2	29.0	15.8	0.7	Foot portion is slightly angular at either corner. Foot portion edge is blunt
21	16.9	23.6	13.8	0.7	Foot portion has very slight curve at base and left side of foot and arm is sharp edged
22	21.8	25.8	13.6	0.6	Both foot corners are angular in shape and are slightly sharp edged
23	15.8	22.8	13.1	0.6	Foot portion is concave and left portion of leg appears to be broken originally as patina has been deposited in core. Elbow portion of

1	2	3	4	5	6
					left arm is slightly sharp and right corner of foot is also sharp edged
24	18.2	25.3	12.7	0.6	The foot portion is blunt edged
25	17.5	23.9	12.6	0.8	Foot portion is blunt edged and slightly curved at both corners
26	20.3	28.2	13.8	0.6	Foot portion is blunt edged and leg portion is slightly curved with concave shaped base
27		22.7	12.6	1.0	Concave-shaped foot portion with edge. Leg portions are angular. Left hand was found broken and arm portion could not be discovered
28	20.6	28.7	11.5	0.9	Foot portion bottom side is blunt and left corner has sharp edge
29	22.5	26.4	12.6	0.6	Foot and head portions are blunt?
30	19.0	26.3	12.3	0.7	Foot and head portions are blunt. Left leg corner is sharp edged
31	21.0	20.8	12.2	0.8	Left hand found broken and could not b discovered

Note: Head portion of 31 anthropomorphic figures are found blunt, more or less in each case prominently projected and semi-circular in shape. The leg portion of all the figures is dwarfish and conspicuous. The arms are also prominently found stretched in some cases while a few specimens depict disproportionate size and shape of arms. All figures have oblique hammering marks on obverse and reverse side. One arm portion of a figure was broken freshly by labour while one arm portion of remaining four figures in each case was missing. This suggests that above four figures were stacked by OCP- users with one hand in broken condition. This signifies their importance ritualistically or functionally.

Excavation at Madarpur Site

As stated above excavation at Madarpur site was undertaken the Archaeological Survey of India (ASI) from 3rd January 2001 to 24th February 2001 under the direction of the first author, then Superintending Archaeologist, Agra Circle assisted by Arakhita Pradhan, V.N. Prabhakar, Atul Bhargava, Assistant Archaeologist; Shri Chiranji Lal, Draftsman-I and Shri Y.P. Agrawal, Surveyor-I. The site was thoroughly explored and studied before digging. Broadly, surface exploration indicated a concentration of pottery around the find spot of copper hoard area and north-western portion of the site. The area towards west and south-west of find spot was already disturbed even up to natural soil due to brick manufacturing activities. The habitation area near find spot measuring 20x20m was undertaken for excavation. The trenches were numbered as ZA6, Qdt 2, ZE 2, ZE 2 Qdt 2, A6 Qdt 4, and A1 Qdt 1 and laid out within a radius of 120 metres from the find spot towards south-east, east and north east direction (Fig.2). It was necessary to ascertain the extension of habitation area and settlement pattern. The excavation revealed that habitation area was occupied within 120m x 120m circumference approximately. Trench YJ1,Qdt 2 and 3 was laid to ascertain the total height of the original site.

Cultural Sequence

Madarpur is single culture site having a total OCP habitation deposit of 35-48cm above natural soil, after which the site was deserted as no habitation deposit was found. A sterile deposit of 1.8m was found over OCP deposit which is again a striking feature at Madarpur and has also been observed at other OCP sites. This deposit is clearly perceptible and distinct in colour and composition suggesting some flood activities over OCP settlements at least on two or three occasions. Madarpur is the only site where anthropomorphic figures from a single culture site have been found. This suggests contemporaneity of copper hoard with OCP pottery without any ambiguity. Radiocarbon dates of charcoal samples, soil analysis, seed samples and copper analysis data from Madarpur would throw ample light on various aspects of OCP-users and their settlement pattern.

Section Scraping and Excavation of YJ 1 Qdts. 2and 3

A 1.8m sterile soil deposit was revealed in trench YJ1, Qdts. 2 and 3. The composition of layer (1) was sand and silt of 45cm thick and brownish in colour. Layer (2) measures 28cm thickness, compact in nature and containing deposit of black colour clay. Layer (3) was again silt deposit 64cm thick, loose in composition with brownish colour. Layers (4) and (5) were again different in colour and compact in composition having thickness of 55cm. These layers (1) to (5)were sterile This may perhaps to floods: more evidence is necessary to confirm this. Layer (6) measures 33cm, comparatively less compact in nature with yellowish brown colour has yielded Ochre Colour Pottery above the natural soil (Fig. 3).

Excavation of Square XG-1

In XG-1 a trench measuring 10x10m was laid including the find spot. No copper objects/figures in adjoining area to find spot were found *in situ* during excavation, although OCP pottery and its associated coarse red ware was available from the level contemporary to copper hoard. This fact was also confirmed from excavated area in Qd. 2 and 3 of XG-1. Layers (1) and (2) of both these quadrants are also 18cm in thickness sterile soil deposit. Layers (3) and (4) with thickness of 41cm have yielded OCP pottery, its associated red ware and antiquities (Fig. 4). The evidence of a mud floor was noticed in this trench and neck portion of a vase having flaring-out rim also found lying over it. The percentage of pottery was comparatively higher in these quadrants and suggests that probably this area was densely inhabited. Beside this, fragments of stone pestles were also found. Charcoal sample in good quantity were fond in good quantity were carefully collected and preserved for scientific analysis to determine carbon 14 dating. These samples have been sent to the Birbal Sahni Institute of Palaeobotany, Lucknow for examination and results are awaited. The remaining area of this square in the above cited quadrant 4 was completely disturbed. The soil composition of layer (3) was compact in nature and of yellowish brown colour with light reddish spots. Layer (4) was comparatively less compact than layer (3) with yellowish brown colour. This is one more point in respect of colour and composition of soil from many excavated sites of OCP and Madarpur confirms this which is found at all OCP sites. This again suggests some flood activity, particularly in the Upper Ganga-Yamuna region. Furthe evidence is required to substantiate this point. (fig. 4)

Excavation of Square XF-1

As mentioned above quadrants 3 and 4 of this square have already been partly damaged by the labourers while remaining quadrant 1 and 2 were intact. Four layers up to 82cm depth were brought to in these quadrants. The total thickness of layer (1) and (2) was 37cms. Layer (1) is yellowish brown in colour and comparatively less compact and soil composition is clay, silt and sand and has been broadly differentiated on the basis of colour and soil composition. Layer (2) was more compact in nature, blackish grey in colour and mixed with black *kankars*. Both the layers are sterile. Layer (3) was of yellowish brown colour mixed with red spots, compact and 8cm thick and comprises more percentage of clay than silt. Availability of pottery was fairly good and a few brick bats were also found. *Kankars* of black colour were also found in this besides sherds of the OCP and its associated coarse red ware. A significant discovery from here was a terracotta toy cart frame and this will be described in detail separately. The total thickness of layer (4) is 40cm and is composed of light yellowish brown coloured soil with black kankars and comparatively less compact in nature. Apart from the ceramics, three stone fragments, probably pestles and one fragment of a terracotta sling ball were found from here. The total thickness of habitation deposit in this square is 48cm.

The stratigraphical position in all 4 quadrants of above square was more or less similar but pottery percentage remained higher in layer (4) in than layer (3).

Excavation of Square YG-1

Soil composition and colour of layers in all the four quadrants of this square was more or less similar to that of XF-1. Layer (1) in all the four quadrants has more or less same thickness (7 to 8cm) with yellowish brown colour soil and compact in hardness. A few black kankars were also found mixed in this layer. Similarly layer (2) was blackish in colour and compact in hardness with black *kankars* and 12cm in thickness; both are sterile. The thickness of layer (3) is 13cms comprising yellowish brown colour soil with reddish spots and compact in hardness. OCP and its associated red ware, fragments of stone pestles and one broken terracotta wheel were found from this level. The thickness of habitation deposit of layer (4) is 27cm and the soil was comparatively less compact with yellowish brown colour having a greyish tinge besides containing black *kankars*. Pottry from here consisted of OCP and its associated red ware besides fragment of a terracotta wheel, fragments of stone pestles, brick-bats, charcoal, charred seed. An oval-shaped hearth is a unique discovery in this deposit. The important pottery shapes viz. miniature pot; *lota* and a vase having flared out rim with long neck were noteworthy. The *lota* was found lying near the hearth which suggests that this area was probably used as kitchen by the OCP-users (Plates 13 and 14). The total habitation deposit of OCP in layers (3) and (4) was 40cms and stratigraphically more and less similar in composition to that found in other squares so far excavated.

Excavation of Square YF1

The excavation of the four quadrants here revealed soil composition similar to that found in the above described squares (Plates 15 and 15A). The maximum thickness of layer (1) was 13cm which comprises yellowish brown coloured compact, hard soil. Layer (2) was blackish, compact hard soil containing a few black *kankars*. The maximum thickness of this layer was 37cm. Evidence of water action was observed in layers (1) and (2). Both the layers were sloping in northern direction suggesting that flow of water from south to north. Layer (3) was 17cm thick (max), yellowish brown in colour and compact in hardness also containing black *kankars*. OCP pottery and its associated coarse red ware were found from this layer. The important antiquity from this layer was a fragment of a stone pestle. Layer (4) has greyish with yellowish brown colour, comparatively less compact and containing black *kankars*. The maximum thickness of this layer was 27cm. There was a 14cm slope in this layer. Besides OCP and its associated coarse red ware, important finds from this level were evidence of ash from a open burnt place, charcoal, chunks of burnt clay, fragments of stone pestles, ochre colour slipped miniature pot which was clearly visible on plan, an OCP potsherd with three perforation, base portion of a pot with engraved 'tectiform' design on its base, base portion of a pot (probably goblet) depicting a design in bas-relief, a potsherd with graffiti mark on inner side of a pot, a fragment of a terracotta toy cart wheel with a hole in centre were some of the significant discoveries from this level. The shapes and design on OCP pottery found from Madarpur site are quite interesting. Two perforated pot sherds, graffiti mark in bas-relief, 'tectiform' designs on base portion of a pot has not been reported so far from any excavated OCP site. Such traits are only visible in Harappan pottery and Madarpur pottery designs seem to have some affinity with them.

Apart from above, square A1 Qdt1, ZA6 Qdt2, ZE2 Qdt2, A6 Qdt4, YH1 Qdts 2 and 3 were also taken up for excavation.

Five layers of square A1 Qdt1 were exposed up to the depth of 123cm. Layers (1) to (3) were sterile deposit of 57cm. Layer (4) was 10cm thick, yellowish brown in colour and comparatively less compact. In this layer black *kankar* and white calcareous nodules were also found. Except a rim portion of a bowl, no other pottery types were found and pottery percentage was comparatively meagre. A small piece, probably of river shell was an interesting find from layer (4) at the depth of 85 cm. Layer (5) was 32cm thick, light greyish in colour and comparatively less compact; black *kankars* and white calcareous nodules were also found deposited in the level. The percentage of pottery was higher in this layer as compared to layer (4).

ZA6 Qdt2 was excavated up to the depth of 123cm. Layers (1) to (4) 81cm thick, were sterile. The colour of layer (1) was brownish mixed with greyish patches and loose in nature. This is washed material and unreliable for stratigraphy. Layer (2) yellowish brown, compact soil contained black *kankars*. Layer (3) black compact deposit also contained black *kankars*. Layer (4) yellowish brown soil with reddish spots mixed with black *kankars* was less compact. Layer (5) was 40cm thick, yellowish brown, compact deposit, contained black and white *kankars*. Layer (6) was 22cm thick, light greyish, less compact soil with black as well as white kankars. Layers (5) and (6) are habitation layers. OCP and its associated pottery were found in these deposits.

ZE2 Qdt2 was up to a depth of 163cm.where layers (1) to (5) turned out to be sterile. Layer (1) 11cm thick yellowish brown compact soil contained black kankars. Layer (2) 36cm thick blackish compact soil with black kankars layer (4), 37cm thick blackish compact deposit contained white calcareous *kankar*s besides black ones. Layer (6) 31cm thick blackish compact soil with comparatively large amount of white calcareous *kankars* as also black ones, though in lesser percent. Twenty OCP sherds were picked up in this layer.

A6 Qdt 4 was excavated upto the depth of 70cm. Layesr (1) to (3) was sterile deposit. Layer (1) 8cm thick, yellowish brown in colour, less compact in nature contained black kankar. Layer (2) was 22cm thick; blackish in colour, compact in, nature also contained black *kankar*. Layer (3) 12cm thick, yellowish brown with reddish spot deposit contained black *kankars*. The nature and colour composition of this layer was similar to layer (3) of XF 1, XG1, YG1 and YF1. All the above trenches yielded high percentage of OCP pottery from layer (3) but pottery was not found in layer (3) here. Layer (4) 20cm thick, light yellowish brown, less compact soil contained black kankars. The OCP pottery and its associated coarse red ware was available from this level but in less quantity.

YH1 Qdt 2 and 3 were excavated from layer (1) to (4) up to the depth of 73cm. Layer (1) was 10cm thick, yellowish brown compact soil contained black kankars. Layer (2) was 20cm thick, blackish compact deposit also contained black kankars. Layer (3) 8cm thick yellowish brown compact soil contained black *kankars*. This layer (3) had yielded OCP pottery, fragment of a stone pestle and fragment of a toy cart wheel. Layer (4) was 35cm thick, yellowish brown in colour, comparatively less compact in nature and mixed with black kankars. This had also yielded OCP pottery and its associated coarse red wares. From layer (1) and (2) up to depth of 30cm was sterile while layers (3) and layer (4) are habitation strata.

Settlement Pattern

At present 2.3m a maximum height of the mound is available in square YJ1 Qdts 2 and 3. Total six layers were exposed in this square to reach natural soil. As evident from the data available from squares XG1, F1, YG1, YF1, YH1 Qdts 2 and 3, A1 Qdt 1, ZA6 Qdt 2, ZE2 Qdt 2, A6 Qdt 4 and YJ1 Qdts 2 and 3 we can reconstruct that total the area of habitation. It was was approximately 140m long from east to west and 120m wide towards north-south.. The maximum thickness of cultural deposit at Madarpur site is 48cm. An oval shaped open hearth measuring 40cm in diameter was found in YG1 Qdt2. The hearth contained ash and charcoal in good quantity. Baked clay chunks of brown colour were found lying near this hearth. A complete *lota* was also found lying near it at a distance of 0.6m. Apart from this, rim portion of some pots were found *in situ* near the hearth. There evidence of a large size shallow pit cut into natural soil at a distance of approximately 1.25m towards north-west of the hearth. This, almost circular pit measured 2.35m north-south and 2.4m east-west. OCP and its associated coarse red ware pot sherds were found from this pit in large number including a partly broken fragile miniature pot was also lying in it.

All these unequivocally suggest that in all probably this area was used as a kitchen-complex. Another evidence recorded carefully during excavation was the remains of an open fire; ash was found on the ground at this place. This suggests lighting fire in the open place as is the practice even today in winter season. Some pot sherds were also found lying near this place. To the north-west of this another pit measuring approximately 1.65m x 1.50m diameter was also found cut into natural soil in trench YF1 Qdts1 and 4. This pit contained broken pot sherds in lesser quantity. Such evidences and remains of human activity being concentrated at a particular place suggest that this complex was an area preferred for human habitation at Madarpur.

Trench XG1 Qdt 2 had also revealed evidence of a mud floor. A flared out rim portion of a vase with long neck and partly broken pieces of coarse red ware pots in different colour were found lying on this floor. A post-hole measuring 9 cm diameter was visible on plan near the vase. Two more post-holes measuring 7.5 cm and 7.0 cm in diameter were also found in the vicinity of it. The distance between these two post holes was 20cm and 16cm respectively.

Some more evidence of post-holes and discovery of brick bats from the site suggest construction of some kind of structure of mud or wattle and daub with thatched roof. Be it as it may, habitation at Madarpur was restricted to an area at a higher place due to the closeness of river in close vicinity. This suggests availability of water supply throughout the year.

Antiquities and other finds

A total of 45 antiquities were found from the site during excavation. These antiquities are divided broadly into two categories viz. terracotta and stone objects.

Terracotta Objects:

Four fragments of terracotta toy cart wheels of various sizes were found in different trenches. One fragment of terracotta toy cart frame and one wheel has holes for inserting axle.

i) Terracotta toy cart frame: The frame is made of well-levigated clay, adequately fired, having smooth surface and fine texture. It has two holes horizontally and three vertically. The fragment measures 6.2 cm x 3.9 cm x 3 3 cm. Such fine specimen has not been reported so far from OCP levels any where else.

ii) Fragments of toy cart wheels: Four fragments of terracotta toy cart wheels of different size were found in different trenches. The biggest one measures 13cm diameter and has a hole in the centre. The small one is 8cm in diameter (Plate-1 and Fig. 5: 1-3). Both fragments are made of fine clay, well-fired with smooth surface and texture. Their cores are thick in centre and thin towards the edge. The remaining two other pieces of wheel are also partly broken and measures in diameter ranging between 9 cm to 12 cm approximately. Both these fragments are also baked ranging with fine texture and has smooth surface.

iii) Broken piece of a sling ball: A partly broken piece of a sling ball measuring 3cm in diameter is the sole example from Madarpur. It is well-fired and has smooth surface.

iv) Specimens with graffiti mark: One broken piece of a goblet (?) base has graffiti marks in bas-relief (fig. 5:4). One more piece of a bowl base has incised graffiti marks at the bottom (Fig. 5:5 and Plate-2). These marks perhaps similar to Harappan script. But this is purely a conjecture. The third pot sherd has also incised graffiti mark on inner side of a pot (fig. 5:6).

Stone Objects:

Thirty-seven stone objects of different shape and size were found during excavation. Out of these twenty-seven are broken fragments of stone pestles. The remaining pieces also probably are different parts of grinders and pestles. The functional portion of pestles in some cases has become very smooth. These stone objects are of grey and white in colour and the stone used is granite and quartzite.

Pottery

The ceramic industry at Madarpur unearthed from excavation includes OCP and its associated coarse red ware. It is basically wheel turned but in case of a knobbed lid applique technique has been used to fix the knob. The OCP sherds are made of well-levigated clay with fine fabric and smooth core and adequately fired. The ochre colour wash of the OCP has a tendency to peel off easily. Four sherds have incised decoration with geometrical designs, criss-cross pattern and oblique lines on the exterior of pot. The associated coarse red ware is sturdy in nature with coarse fabric and medium to thick core. Sand has also been used and mixed with clay for preparation of this pottery. Cord impressed designs are visible on exterior portion of the pottery. Important shapes in OCP includes dish, bowl, basin, *handi* (Fig. 6), vase, storage jar, miniature pot (fig. 7), *lota*, lid, bowl with ring base and dish-on-stand (figs. 8-10). Two of OCP have perforations which is noteworthy. Both these pot sherds resemble Harappan perforated jars and has not been reported so far from any OCP sites. Large number of rim portion of vases having flaring rims and S-shaped neck were also found from the site. Some bowls have featureless rim, out turned rim and have carinated body with convex side. The important shapes in associated coarse red ware include vase, dish, bowl, *handi* and jar (fig.11).

Samples for technical report

Soil samples from different layer and levels were collected from Madarpur. These samples were sent to IIT, Kanpur for chemical analysis of soil deposit and other cognate examination. The report on charcoal and seed samples sent to the Birbal Sahni Institute of Palaeobotany, Lucknow for radiocarbon dating is awaited. Some samples for Thermoluminiscence (TL) dating of pottery were also collected from site.

One sample from copper hoard was sent to IIT, Kanpur for analysis and micrographic study of copper structure. The scientific report on copper from Madarpur has shown that composition of the metal was almost pure Cu (Copper) with minor impurities of C and Sb. The major elements identified in the second phase particles were Cu, Bb and S, which indicated that these particles were sulfides. The presence of these sulfides has been related to the probably Cu extraction process (Balusubramaniam, 2001).

Summary

The excavation at Madarpur is important from different standpoints.

A. Anthropomorphic figures and that too, in such a large quantity have not been reported so far from any excavated/explored site of OCP (Pl. 3). Out of these, two pieces are unique in shape and discovered for first time from OCP levels (Pl. 4–5). These two anthropomorphs appears to be for religious use or 8 for primitive form of *Srivatsa* symbol.

B. Some new features in OCP pottery type such as perforated potsherds akin to Harappan perforated jars has also been reported first time from this site. The Madarpur ceramic industry has some affinity with Harappan pottery found in western Uttar Pradesh.

C. Terracotta toy cart frame and wheels also suggests affinity with Harappan terracottas of similar nature from excavated sites of western Uttar Pradesh.

D. Graffitti mark with incised design and in bas-relief on pot sherd from Madarpur resemble the technique used for Harappan sealing.

E. Settlement pattern of the site suggest some kind of semi-permanent nature. It appears that the OCP-users were traders in copper and were carrying business particularly with Upper Ganga-Yamuna region. Kumaon hill region is the known source since time immemorial and famous for extracting copper from ores. The *Agri* Communities of Kumaon region are still engaged in extracting copper from these ores. *Roorkee* term in Kumaon regional language denotes this as a centre for copper smelting. The entire exercise of this process is practiced at Roorkee. The authors are of the opinion that in all probability Kumaon region were exploited by these proto-historic nomadic traders for supply of copper to the plains and fertile regions of western Uttar Pradesh.

On the basis of above discussion it is tentatively surmised that OCP users inhabited in Upper Ganga valley and were contemporary to the Harappans. However, more evidences are required to confirm this assumption.

Acknowledgements

The authors acknowledge their thanks to S/Shri Chiranji Lal, Draftsman-I, Y.P. Agrawal, Surveyor-Grade II and Ramesh S. Mulimani, Assistant Archaeologist of Agra Circle of ASI for preparation of pottery drawings, preparation of contour plan and helped in taking measurements of the anthropomorphic figures respectively. We are thankful to Shri Vishnu Kant, Assistant Archaeologist, ASI, Excavation Branch-II, New Delhi suggesting ways to improve data presentation. We also thank to S/Shri V.P. Verma, Draftsman-I, Ram Kumar, Surveyor and Shri Vinod Kumar, Photographer of Excavation Branch-II of ASI; and Shri Baldev, Draftsman, Headqarter, ASI for improvement of some drawings. Last but not least we are beholden to express our deep appreciation for Shri Haji Shirajuddin and his son Shri Iqbal Ahmad of Ram Nagar Khaguwal, Thaurdwara who rendered all possible assistance to the ASI staff during the course of excavation at the site.

REFERENCES

1. On earlier occasions also as usually happened in case of copper hoards discovery

Agrawal, D.P. 1982. *The Archaeology of India.*

Balusubramaniam, R et al 2001. Some Metallurgical Aspects of an OCP period Copper Hoard, *Man and Environment*, XXVI (2): 89-97.

Dikshit, K.N. 1979. The Ochre Coloured Ware Settlements in the Ganga-Yamuna Doab, in (D. P. Agrawal and D.K. Chakraborty Eds) *Essays in Indian Protohistory* 285-299, New Delhi: Munshiram Manoharlal.

Ghosh,A. 1989. Copper Hoard, *Encyclopaedia of Indian Archaeology*, Vol. I, New Delhi: Munshiram Manoharlal.

Lal, B.B. 1951. Further Copper Hoards from the Gangetic Basin and a Review of the Problems, *Ancient India*, 7:20-39.

——————1971-72. A Note on the Excavation at Saipai, *Puratattva* 5: 46-49.

Sahi, M.D.N. 2001. Ochre Coloured Pottery: Its Genetic Relationship with Harappan Ware, *Man And Environment* XXVI(2): 74-88.

Sharma, D.P. 2002. *Newly Discovered Copper Hoard Weapons of South Asia*, New Delhi: Bharatiya Kala Prakashan.

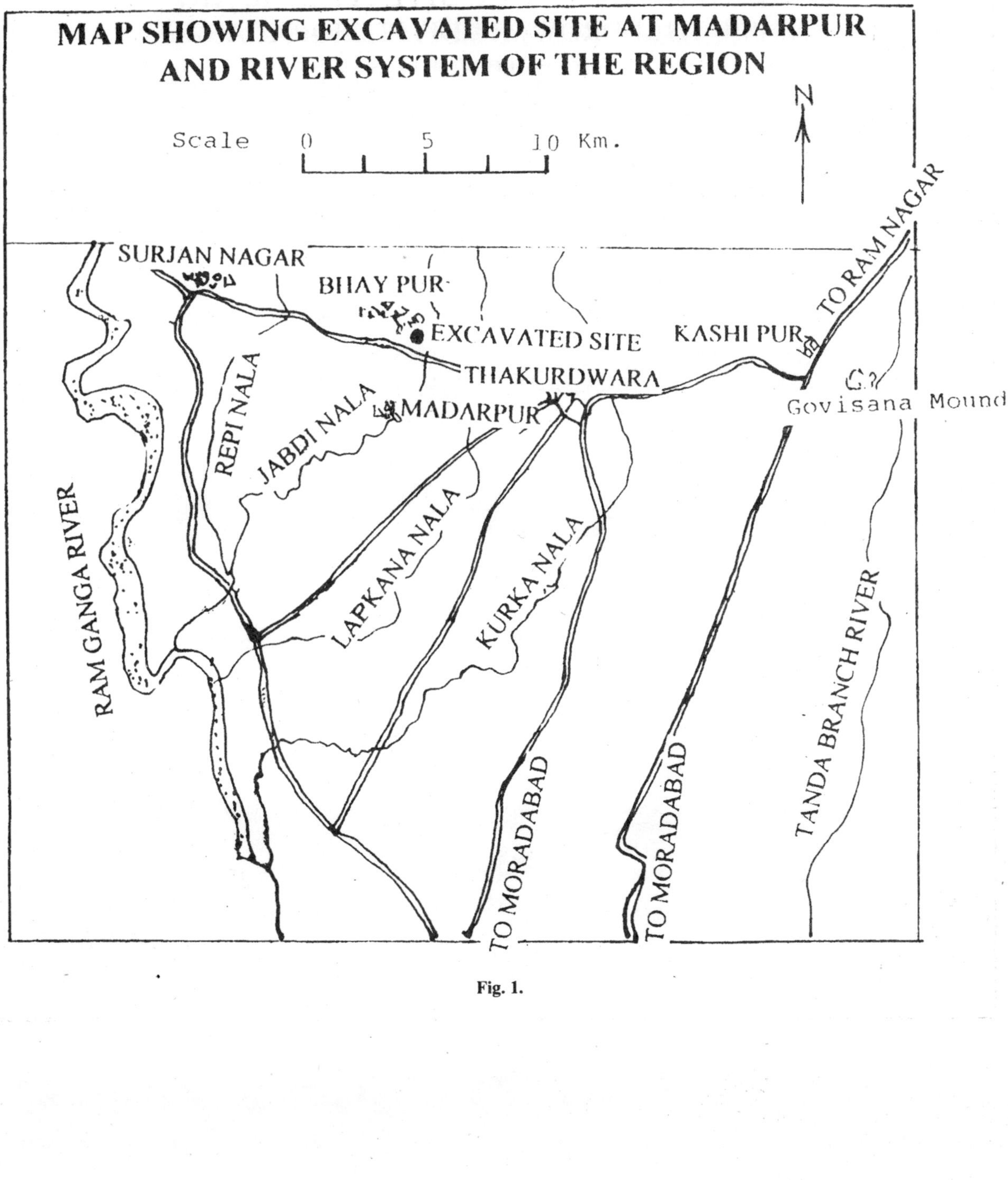
MAP SHOWING EXCAVATED SITE AT MADARPUR AND RIVER SYSTEM OF THE REGION
Scale 0 5 10 Km.
N
SURJAN NAGAR
BHAY PUR
EXCAVATED SITE
KASHI PUR
TO RAM NAGAR
THAKURDWARA
Govisana Mound
MADARPUR
REPI NALA
JABDI NALA
LAPKANA NALA
KURKA NALA
RAM GANGA RIVER
TANDA BRANCH RIVER
TO MORADABAD
TO MORADABAD

Fig. 1.

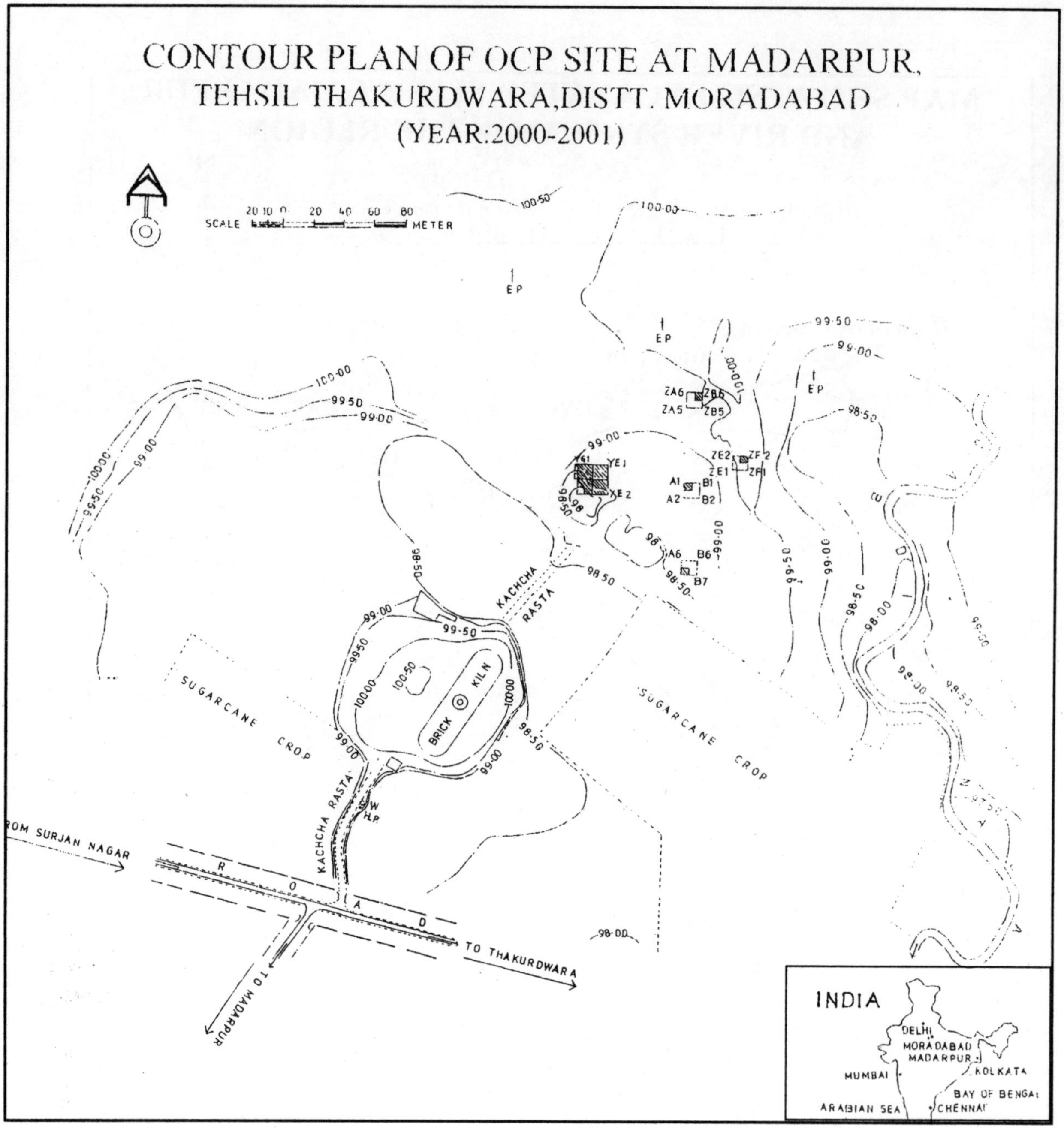
CONTOUR PLAN OF OCP SITE AT MADARPUR,
TEHSIL THAKURDWARA,DISTT. MORADABAD
(YEAR:2000-2001)
SCALE
METER
EP
KACHCHA RASTA
BRICK KILN
SUGARCANE CROP
FROM SURJAN NAGAR
ROAD
TO THAKURDWARA
TO MADARPUR
H.P.
INDIA
DELHI
MORADABAD
MADARPUR
MUMBAI
KOLKATA
BAY OF BENGAL
ARABIAN SEA
CHENNAI

Fig. 2.

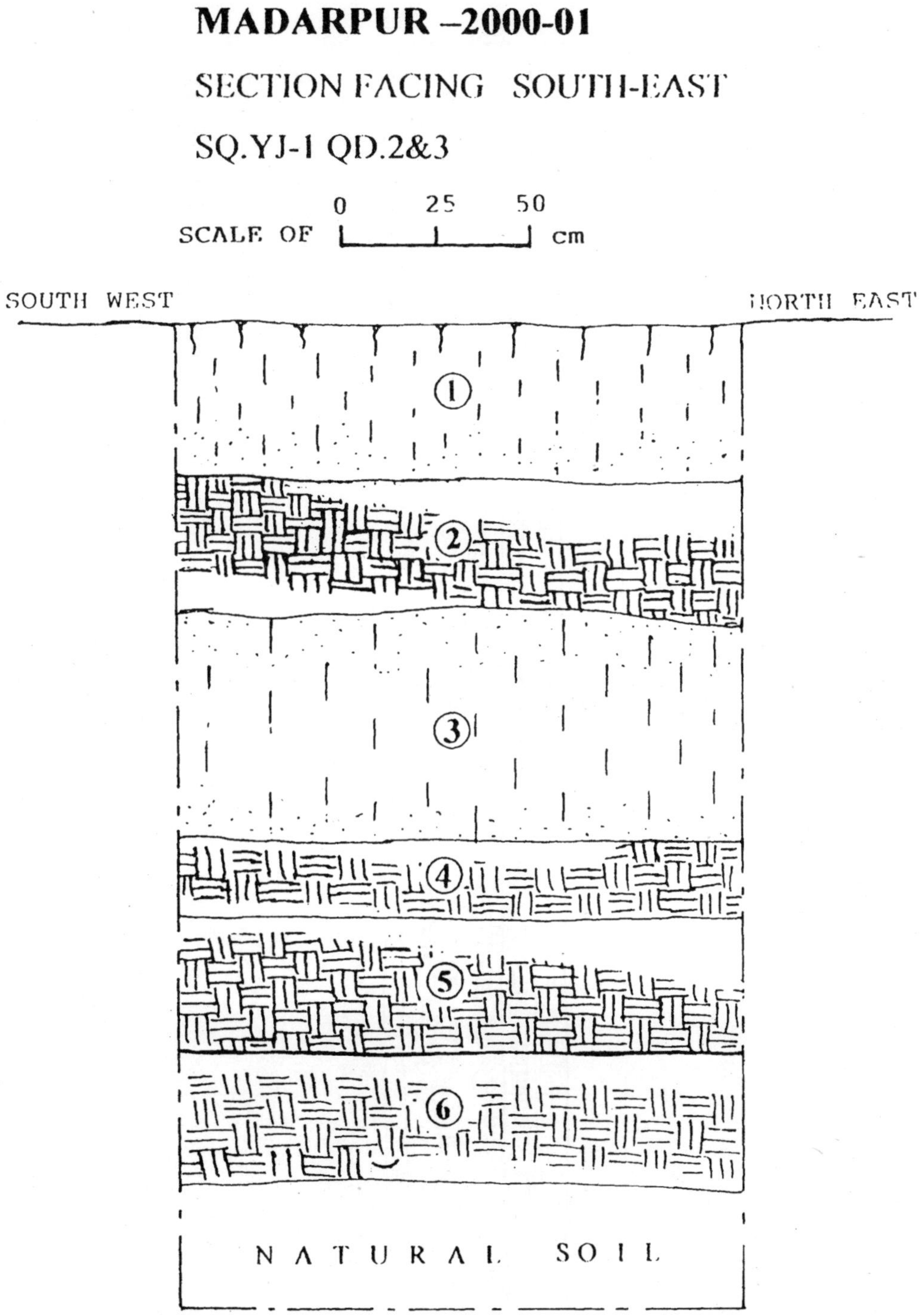
MADARPUR –2000-01
SECTION FACING SOUTH-EAST
SQ.YJ-1 QD.2&3
0 25 50
SCALE OF cm
SOUTH WEST
NORTH EAST
1
2
3
4
5
6
NATURAL SOIL

Fig. 3.

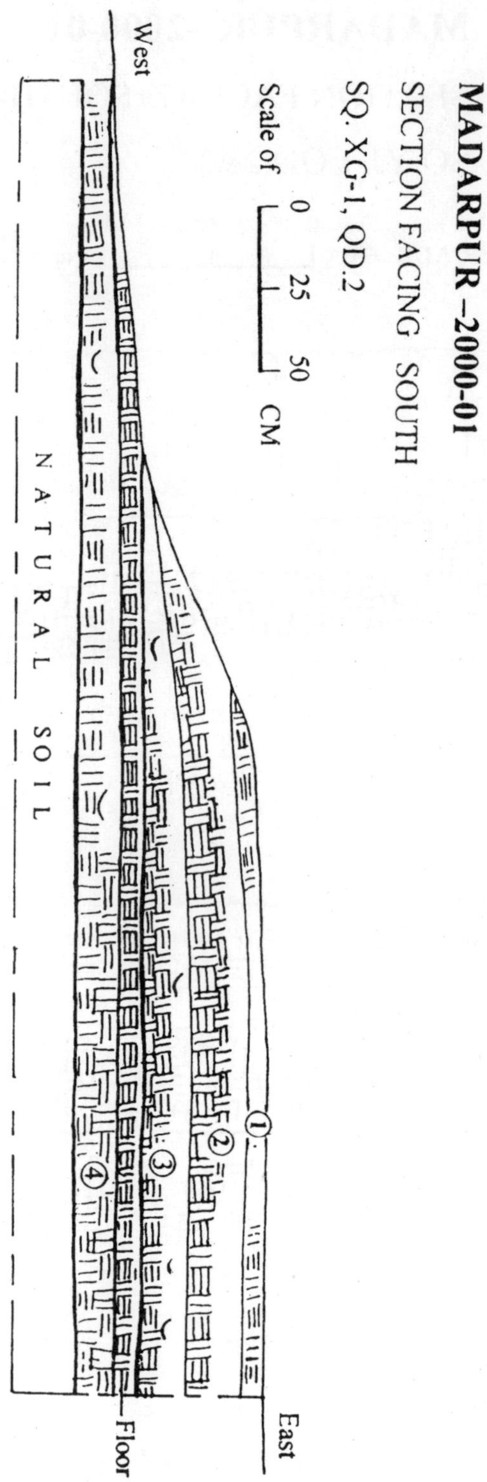
MADARPUR –2000-01
SECTION FACING SOUTH
SQ. XG-1, QD.2
Scale of 0 25 50 CM
West
East
Floor
NATURAL SOIL
1
2
3
4

Fig. 4.

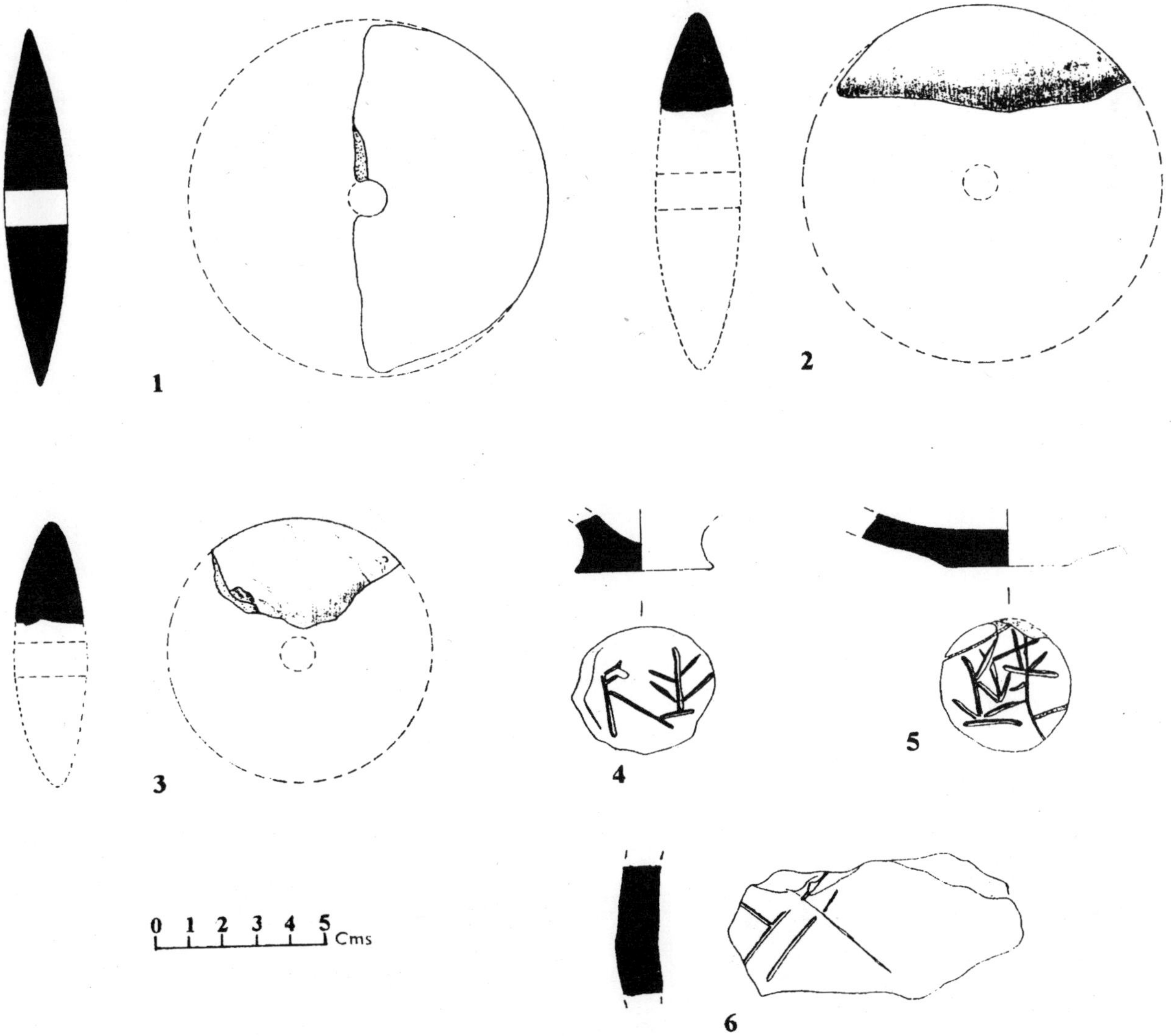

Fig. 5. 1–3- fragments of toy cart wheels; 4- graffiti mark in bas -relief; 5–6 graffiti marks

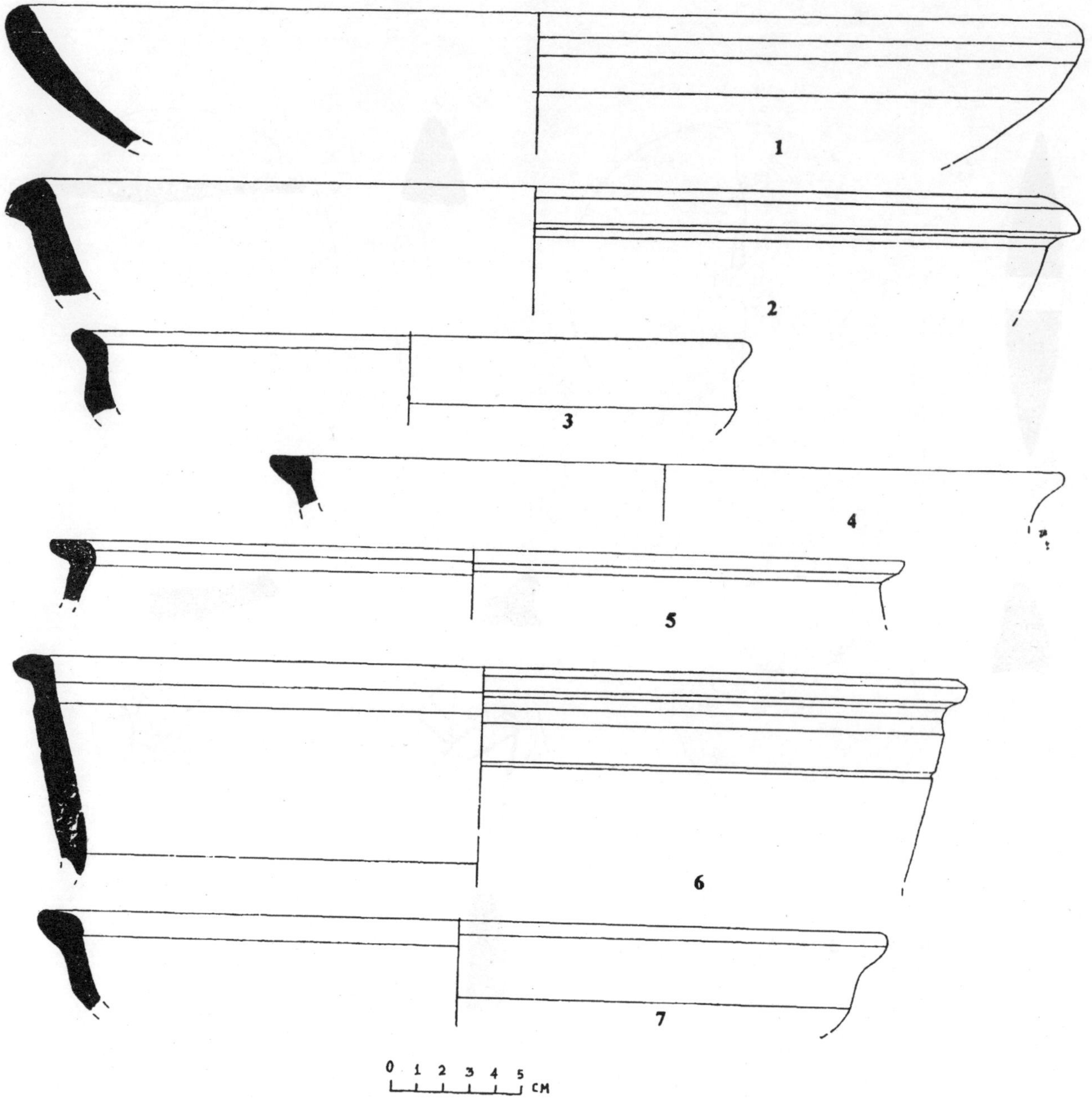

Fig. 6. Madarpur, Ochre Coloured pottery shaes; Basins and Handi

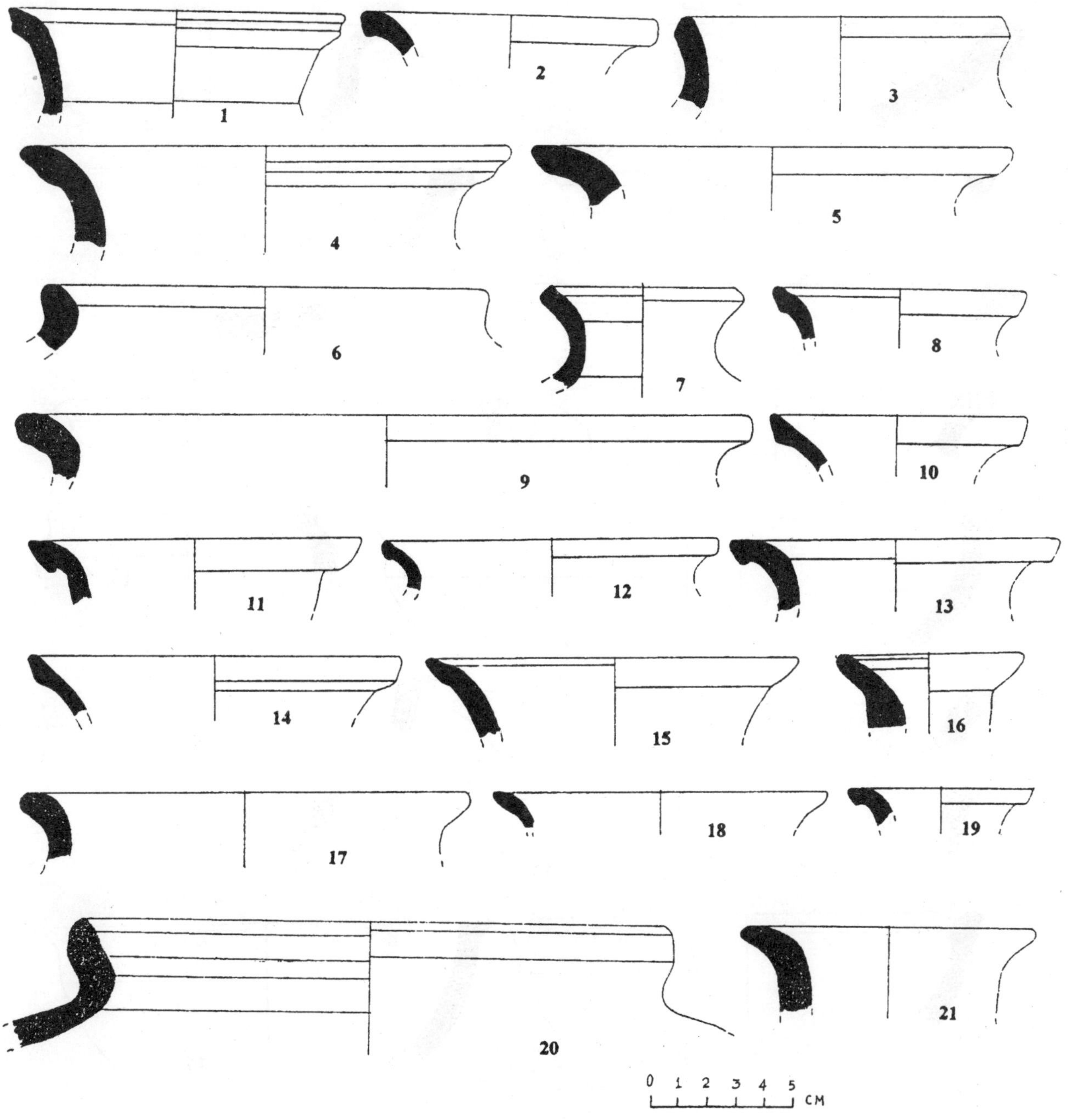

Fig. 7. Madarpur, Ochre Coloured Pottery shapes; Jars, vases and miniature pots

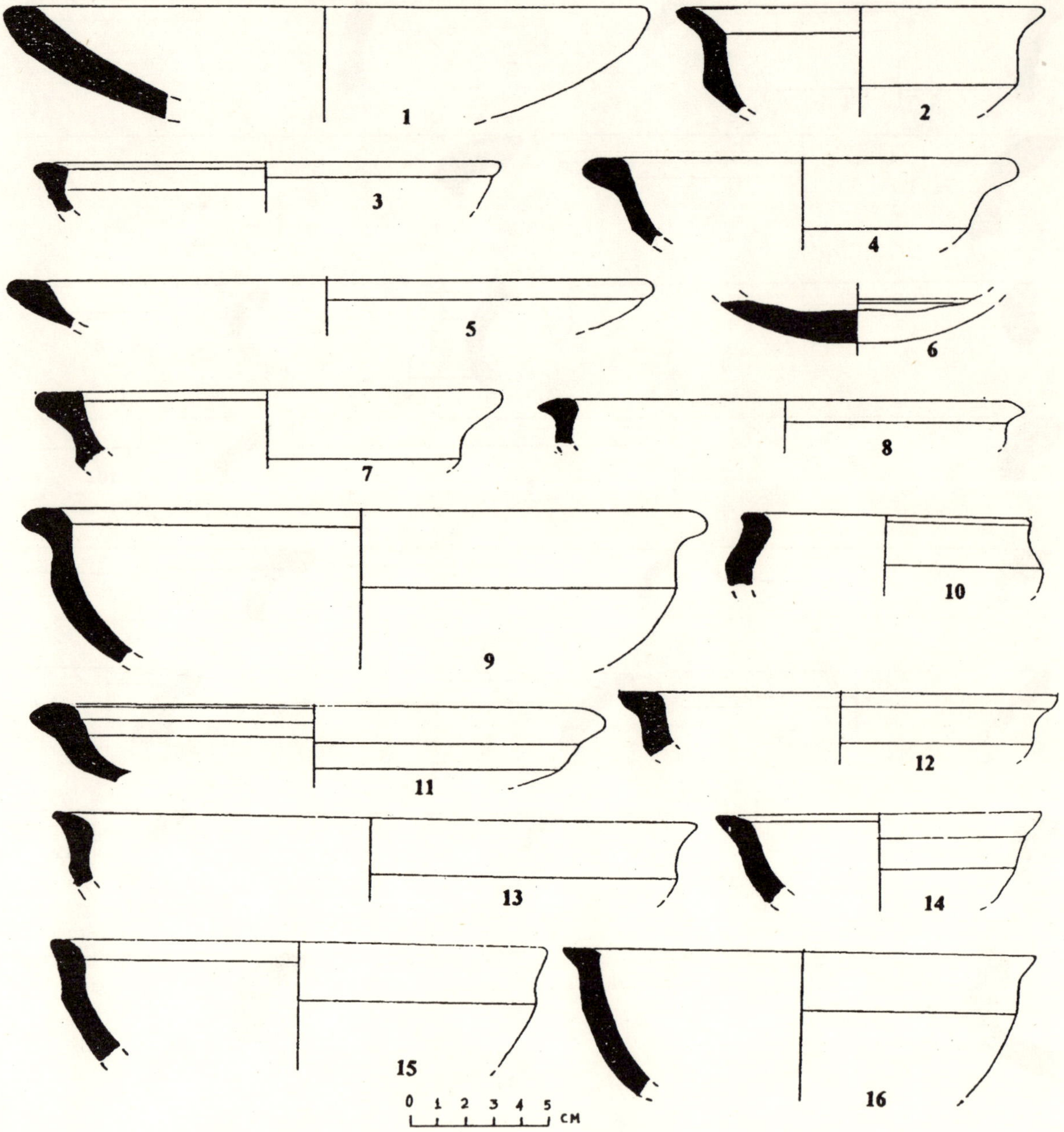

Fig. 8. Madarpur, Ochre Coloured Pottery shapes: Bowls and dishes

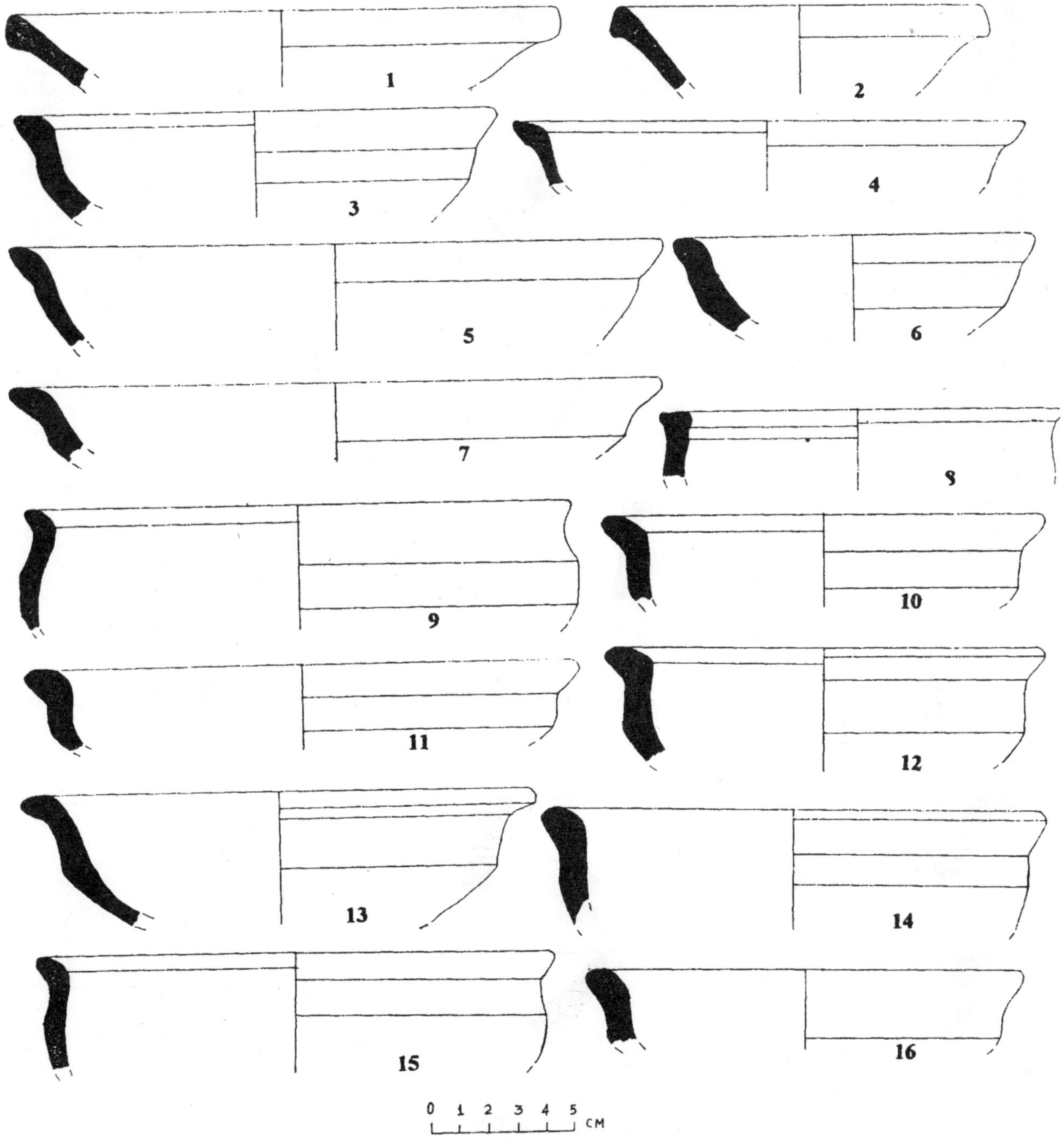

Fig. 9. Madarpur, Ochre Coloured Pottery shapes: Bowls and dishes

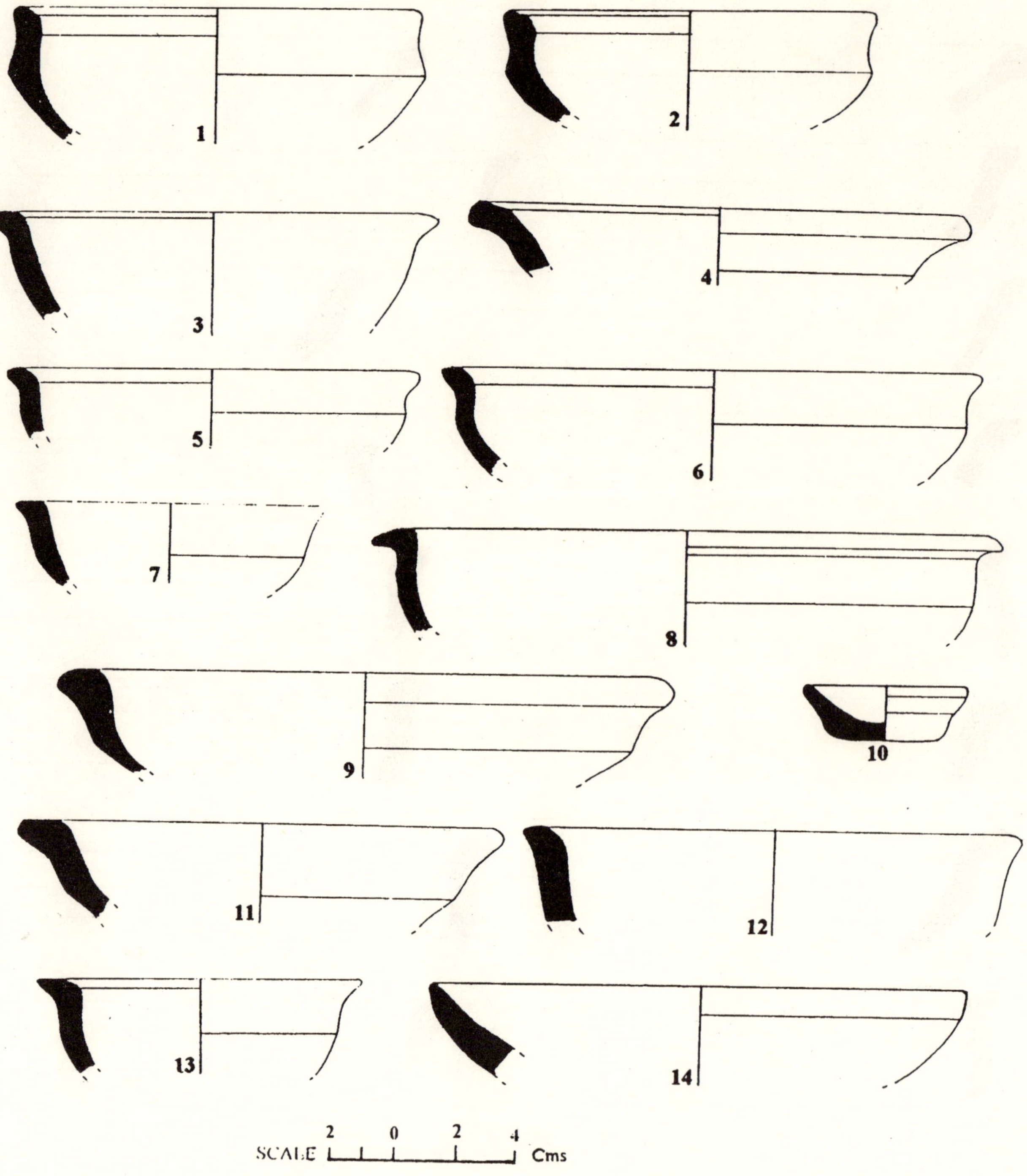

Fig. 10. Madarpur, Bowls & Dishes, Ochre Coloured Pottery (OCP)

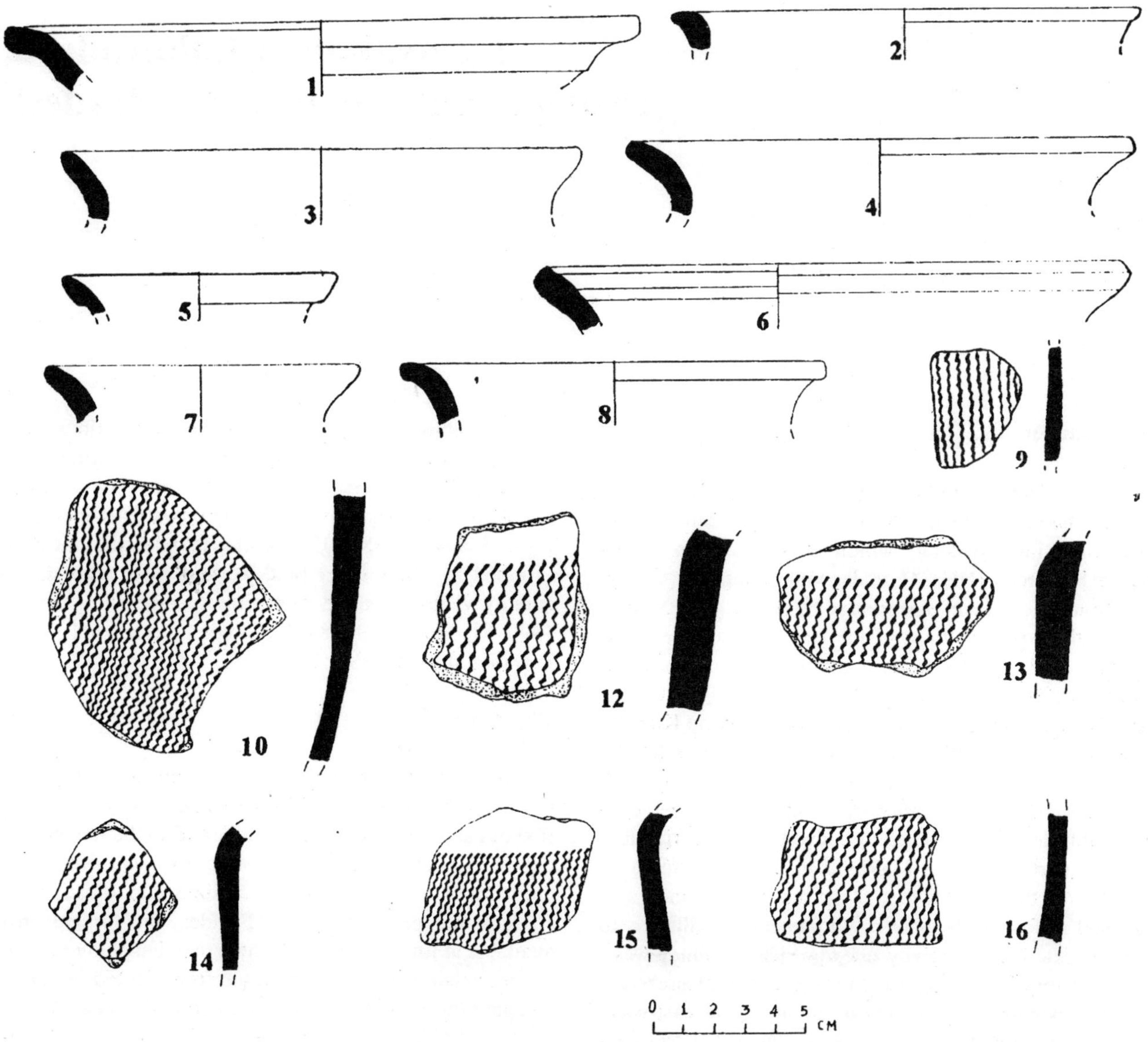

Fig. 11. Madarpur: Pottery shapes & decorative motifs of associated red ware of OCP

Excavation at Lahuradeva, District Sant Nagar, Uttar Pradesh

RAKESH TEWARI,* R.K. SRIVASTAVA,* K.K. SINGH*

Introduction

The mound of Lohradeva or Lahuradeva (26° 46' N; 82° 57' E) is located at a distance of about 5 km south to the Bhujaini Crossing, which is situated on Basti-Gorakhpur road (NH 28), under village Jagdishpur (fig. 1). Earlier, a lake surrounded it from three sides. Presently, however, most of the lake-area is under agriculture, and only its western portion still retains water round the year. Its excess water spills over into a small river called Katnahia, which is a tributary of the Kuwano and flows about 500 m away to the west of this lake in summers. During the rainy season it almost merges with the lake. The eastern portion of the mound has been considerably levelled in order to convert it into agriculture field. Courtesy 'Samai Mai-ka-than' (a local temple)—located on the western part of the mound, that the grace as well as fear of its deity could prevent the villagers to further extend their activity, due to which remaining western portion of the mound is in a good state of preservation. It extends over an area of about 220 m east-west, 140 m north-south, and is about 4 m elevated from the surrounding levels.

The adjoining village of this site, Jagdishpur, happens to be the native place of Krishna Nand Tripathi of the Gorakhpur University, and obviously he noticed this site for the first time. The archaeological significance of this site along with the details of its surface finds were published by S.N. Chaturvedi of the Department of Ancient Indian History, Culture and Archaeology, Gorakhpur University in 1980, and onwards (Chaturvedi 1980: 339-40; 1985: 105). Further its potential has been assessed by many other field-workers also, who subsequently visited this site from time to time (Singh *et al.* 1990: 81; Singh 1990: 89-93; Singh and Kumar 1994: 9; Tewari and Mani 1996: 159).

Objectives

It is notable here that though the deposits of pre-copper phase had been found in the earlier excavations carried out at Sohgaura and Imlidih Khurd in the neighbouring district of Gorakhpur, their antiquity was surmised on the basis of comparative considerations due to paucity of charcoal samples for dating. Besides, the limited area available at lower levels prevented detailed study regarding the other aspects of the culture represented by them. Keeping these points in view limited early habitation at deposit of Lahuradeva appeared ideal for such investigations. The objectives of the excavation of the first season were to ascertain the cultural sequence of the site and to have an idea regarding the prospects of further work particularly about the early farming community settled here. The site was subjected to excavation in the auspices of the U.P. State Archaeological Department, between

*U.P. State Archaeological Department, Roshanud-daula Kothi, Kaisarbagh, Lucknow (U.P.)

November 2001 and March 2002. The excavation was carried out under the direction of first two authors, assisted by Ram Vinay, G.C. Singh, Rajiv Trivedi, B.K. Srivastava, R.G. Mishra and M.M. Dimri, besides, the third author of this paper.

Culture Sequence

The entire site was divided into standard zones A, X, Y, and Z starting roughly from the central area of the mound. Three locations in central, eastern, and south-eastern portions of the site were selected for probing. The excavations carried out in the trenches measuring 10 x 10 m, further divided into quadrants of 5.0 x 5.0 m, covered total area of 235 square meters. The habitation deposits revealed in the excavations collectively represent following five-fold tentative culture sequence:

Period V	Early centuries BC/AD
Period IV	Marked by NBPW
Period III	Early Iron Age
Period II	Copper Age
Period I	Early Farming Phase

On the basis of the nature of deposits, radiocarbon dates and culture material Period I is sub-divided into two sub-periods—IA and IB. Remains of Period IA have been found in lower most kankar mixed layers of trench nos. YA 2 Qdt.1 (layer No. 6) & 4 (layer No. 12, 13 & 14), YA1 Qdt.1 (layer No. 13, 14). Thickness of this deposit is about 45 cm. The cultural remains of this deposit are represented by a considerable quantity of potsherds, a few charred and un-charred bones, scattered small pieces of charcoal, small burnt chunks of clay, a small piece of stone and tortoise-shell.

Ceramic industries of Period IA are consisting of mainly red ware and black-and-red ware, which include mostly hand made varieties. The proportion of black-and-red ware sherds is as high as about 50 per cent of the pottery assemblage. More than two-third of the thickness of their inner core is generally black, while a thin portion of the exterior core is red. The thickness of the outer red surface is, however, more than that of red wash and slip. Some of the black-and-red ware and red ware potsherds bear black and red slips respectively on their interior and exterior surfaces. Burnishing is also evident, in addition to slip-treatment in quite many examples. Red slip is very fine in a few cases.

Generally the pottery is ill-fired having coarse and porous surface and uneven core. The clay used for pottery making comprises husk and straw marks and is not well levigated. A good number of potsherds are decorated with cord impressions. Applied decoration showing rope pattern is also found. The main shapes include convex-sided bowls, pedestal bowls knobbed vessel, miniature bowl and vases. Some of the important shapes are illustrated under fig. 2. The high proportion of coarse variety of black-and-red ware is worth noting.

The structural remains of this sub-period are represented by burnt clay chunks and nodules bearing reed and straw marks, which indicate that the houses of this period were made of wattle and daub. Another important feature of this period is probably an irregular channel running through all the three Qdts. mentioned above. It has been traced for a length of 12 m, which is about 23 to 53 cm broad. It's depth, however, could not be determined during this season's work.

Carbonised material of Period IA, collected by flotation-method is very significant because according to K.S. Saraswat of the Birbal Sahni Institute of Palaeobotany, Lucknow, it contains grains of cultivated rice (Oryza sativa) along with a few wild grasses. Apart from that, the husk-marks of rice are also evident embedded in the core of a number of potsherds of this sub-period. The presence of stone piece, mentioned above, is also important because it appears to be of Himalayan origin, indicating thereby direct and indirect interaction between the people inhabiting here and those of Himalayan area during Period IA.

Above evidences show that the area, which has revealed the remains of Period IA, would have been, in all probability either a peripheral region or an activity area having no permanent structures on that very spot.

Two radiocarbon dates, mentioned below, are available for the charcoal samples collected from the trench nos. YA2 and YA1.

1. BS-1951: BP 5320 ± 90 (cal. BC 4220, 4196, 4161)

2. BS-1966: BP 6290 ± 160 (cal. BC 5298)

Above dates indicate that the remains related to the earliest human activities of Period I at Lahuradeva may be placed in late sixth and fifth millennium B.C. A radicarbon age determination is also available for the calcrete, collected form the unit comprising the layers representing Period IA, and that of natural soil. This date, BS-1965: BP 4440 ±140 (cal. BC 3358 - 2902), according to I.B. Singh (Personal communication), gives an idea about a dry phase around 5000 yr. BP, because of which *kankar* formation occurred in the concerned unit. Therefore, this climatic phase, around 3000 B.C., contributed to the formation of calcrete, which consequently consolidated the cultural deposit formed earlier in the sixth and fifth millennium BC. Period IB is represented by layers 11 (YA-2, Qdt. 4) and 12 (YA-1, Qdt.1). It is notable that the deposit of this phase is consisting of compact yellowish earth, while that of IA contained small to large-sized *kankar* nodules. As far ceramic industries are concerned the tradition of earlier phase, i.e. coarse variety of red ware and black-and-red ware (Pl. 1), besides, a few sherds of grey ware continued to occur in almost same proportions and variations. Quantity of burnished pottery increased. The quality of black-and-red ware of medium fabric also shows comparative improvement. Appearance of a broken sherd, which bears painted linear design over fine dark red slip on the exterior in creamy white colour, is significant. Worth mentioning new shapes include beaker, perforated and legged vessels, spouts, and knobbed vessel. Some of the important shapes are illustrated under fig. 3.

Associated materials include terracotta bead, a terracotta sling ball, a bone arrowhead, a small chunk of dried steatite, and small charcoal pieces. Charred and uncharred bones, and large quantity of carbonised material have also been recovered. Some of the bones show cutmarks and a few of them appear to be used as implements. Structural remains are represented by some post-holes, burnt clay chunks—some of which bear reed and straw marks indicating thereby construction of wattle and daub houses, two successive floors prepared with clay—bearing an armed clay hearth based on each of them.

A radiocarbon date for the charcoal sample collected from layer no. 11. (YA-2 Qdt.4) is BS-1950: BP 3750 ± 90 (cal. BC 2135, 2079, 2056). Another radiocarbon date, for the charcoal sample collected from Qdt.1 (YA-2) - BS-1938: BP 3180 ± 70 (cal. BC 1519 (1435) 1399), is also available. It is, however, not reliable because a deep pit is cut in this quadrant almost from the surface down into the natural soil to construct a brick-well of a considerable size in Period V, due to which mixing of the later material is quite possible.

Period II is characterised by the appearance of black slipped ware in a considerable proportion, painted potteries, and copper objects. Deposits of this period have been found at all the three locations (Tr. nos. YA2, YA1, YK1 & J6). Collectively its maximum thickness is about 1.60 m. All the ceramic industries of the preceding period continued to occur. Paintings have been found on the sherds of all the ceramic industries in general, and of black slipped ware, and black-and-red ware in particular. The colours used are mostly white to creamy white (Pl. 2) and some times black and ochre. Incised (Pl. 3) and appliqué decorations continued in small proportion. Corded pattern of decoration also continued. Its proportion, however, in comparison to Period I, is reduced. Quantity of slipped and burnished pottery, besides certain shapes such as dish-on-stand, bowl-on-stand, pedestal bowl, perforated legged vessel, lipped vessel, disc based bowl, button based lids and spouts increased in a good proportion. One of the spouts, treated with red slip, decorated with linear design in black pigment is important to note. This variety of painted spout is not known so far from any other site of the Ganga Valley. Near absence of convex- sided dish is also notable. Thick red ware sherds showing bold perforations across the core on their body remind Harappan tradition. Associated material consisting of beads of terracotta, semi-precious stones and steatite, bone-points, -awls, and -arrowheads, stone-chips, a broken stone-celt of black basalt, stone-hammer, stone-ball, large quantity of charred and un-charred bones, antlers and archaeo-botanical remains, etc. Some of the worked bones showing cutmarks appear to have been used as implements. Copper objects, represented in small quantity, notably include fishing hook, antimony rod, and nail cutter. Some of the very well made, ground, polished and decorated bone arrowheads, of tanged, barbed and socketed varieties, often bearing punctured circlets, are worth mentioning for their superb workmanship. Some curious looking terracotta objects, which appear like legs or pedestals of some indeterminate object, are also notable finds of this period. Such objects have also been found in the nearby area from Sikridih and Imlidih in Gorakhpur district (Singh 1993:32). Structural activities of this period are mainly represented by post-holes, rammed earthen floors, a mud wall, burnt clay chunks often bearing reed-marks and hearths. A few notable structures, almost circular in plan, found to have been excavated in the surface soil. Their internal surface is coated with clay-plaster of about 8 cm thickness. These structures seem to have been used as grain silos or bins and are comparable to similar structures found in the excavations at Imlidih in district Gorakhpur (Singh 1993: 30) and Chechar Kutubpur in district Vaishali in Bihar (IAR 1977-78: 17-18). Period III is represented at ZK1 by layer nos. 3 to 6 having about 80 cm thick deposits. This period is characterised by the appearance of iron artefacts. Ceramic industries, shapes of the potteries and patterns of decoration are almost the same as of Period II. Important iron objects include sickle (?), knife and nails, etc. Bone arrowheads, terracotta beads, beads of semi-precious stones, steatite beads are the notable finds amongst the associated materials. Two earthen floors, with a thickness of about 10 to 15 cm, have been found in the excavations. Burning activities are observed on one of them. A radiocarbon date for the charcoal sample, collected from the layer from which iron artefacts were found, is BS-1939: BP 2940 + 100 (cal. 1205, 1205, 1188 BC).

Period IV is mainly represented in trench nos. J6 and J7. Thickness of its occupational deposit is about 1.20 m. This period is characterised by the presence of NBPW. Ceramic industries of the preceding periods continued to occur. Sherds of coarse variety of black-and-red ware and red ware, however, are comparatively in a small proportion. Potsherds, found in lower levels, show continuity in decorative patterns. Quality of NBPW is very fine having, golden, silvery, and bi-chrome varieties. Some of the NBPW sherds are also decorated with painted patterns generally executed in black colour. Interestingly a few red ware sherds appearing to represent the vessels with perforated body with some variations continue to occur even in this period. Presence of iron slags in the excavated material shows the smelting activity going on at this site during Period IV. Successive floor levels, found in the deposits of this period, are prepared with rammed mud mixed with small potsherds. Their thickness ranges between 8 to 10 cm. Burnt clay nodules and clay-chunks with reed and straw impressions are also present in the assemblage. A good proportion of bone pieces with cut-marks, and charred bones indicate that the meat was an important component of the dietary system. Numerous steatite beads, beads of semi-precious stones, terracotta beads, bone arrowheads, awls and points, besides, iron and copper artefacts are the other important finds.

Occupational remains of Period V have been found in the Trench No. YA2 only. Potsherds of this period, however, were also recovered in the pits and mixed deposits of Trench Nos. J6 and J7. Amongst the notable structural remains a portion of a multi-roomed house having well-laid walls made of burnt bricks and a deep brick well are worth mentioning. Red ware is the most dominant pottery of this period. Absence of other ceramic industries, such as black slipped ware, NBPW, black-and-red ware, and paintings is remarkable. Important shapes in red ware include carinated bowls with in-turned rim, inkpot type lids, sprinklers and high-necked water vessels. Vase-shaped and pear-shaped terracotta beads, besides, terracotta human figures are the other notable finds of this period.

Preliminary Observations

First season's work at Lahuradeva has fulfilled its objectives of revealing the cultural sequence of the site, and to have an idea about the early farming settlement. Besides, it has provided significant information regarding the other aspects of the respective cultures. The presence of a cultural phase in the lowest levels characterised by the appearance of coarse variety of red ware and black-and-red ware (often comprising cord impressions on their exterior) is comparable with those earlier observed at Sohgaura and Imlidih in district Gorakhpur (Chaturvedi 1985: 103; Singh 1993). It is to be noted again that no C^{14} dates could be determined for this phase at Sohgaura and Imlidih for want of required charcoal samples. Therefore, the dates available for Period IA of Lahuradeva may be useful to assess the antiquity of these sites also. These dates, cal. *circa* sixth and fifth millennium BC, are hitherto earliest indicators of human activity in the Sarayupar area of the mid-Ganga Valley. The presence of cultivated rice in such an early context reminds the early dates proposed for the cultivation of rice at Koldihwa (Misra 1977: 116-17; Sharma 1980: 198-200) in the Vindhyan Region of district Allahabad. Further excavations at Lahuradeva to be continued in the next season may reveal more details regarding the activities of this period.

The appearance of black-and-red ware sherds in a large proportion, right from Period IA, is worth noting, regarding the origin of this type of pottery in the Indian Subcontinent. On the basis of its presence in the Neolithic context at Brahmagiri, Sangankallu, Tekkalakota, Maski, Prakash, Bahal, etc., and other considerations Kumar suggested indigenous Neolithic origin for black-and-red ware in 1975 (Kumar 1975; Singh 1982: xxii). This suggestion was, however, rejected considering the then available evidences and it was observed that 'chalcolithic Lothal enjoys the parental position so far as the origin of BRW in India is concerned and the Egyptian BRW most probably appears to be the lineal progenitor of the Lothal BRW' (Singh 1982: xxxi). In view of the above-mentioned new evidence revealed at Lahuradeva these views need a fresh review.

Another important aspect, to be underlined here regarding the first season's outcome of the Lahuradeva excavation, is an early C^{14} date, i.e. cal. *circa* 1200 B.C. for the iron-bearing layer. This date further corroborates our conclusions, arrived at, about the antiquity of the early use of iron in mid Ganga Valley, on the basis of the evidences revealed in the excavations carried out at Raja Nala-ka-tila in district Sonbhadra, Malhar in district Chandauli, Dadupur in district Lucknow (Tewari *et al.* 1996: 75-95; 1997: 99-105; 2000: 69-98; 2002: 99-116) and at Jhusi in district Allahabad (Misra *et al.* 2000: 28-29).

Acknowledgements

The authors would like to express their gratitude to the Director General, Archaeological Survey of India (ASI) for granting the permission to excavate at Lahuradeva mound. Our grateful thanks are especially due to Shri R.S. Bisht, Director, ASI for the encouragement he provided by taking keen interest in our work. We express our grateful thanks to Dr. K.S. Saraswat of the Birbal Sahni Institute of Palaeobotany, Lucknow who stayed with us in our camp regarding the collection of archaeo-botanical remains and benefited us by his illuminating discussions as also by his cheerful presence. We extend our grateful thanks to Dr. Rajagopalan and Dr. Sekar of the same institution C^{14} dates for our charcoal samples could be determinated on priority basis in a very short duration. Prof. I.B. Singh, Head of the Geology Department, Lucknow University, took pains to be instrumental for the C^{14} dating of the *kankar* collected from the deposits of Period I of Lahuradeva, and readily provided his observations regarding the process and probable reasons of its formation. We are extremely thankful to him. We would like to put on record here that Dr. P.C. Pant, Dr. P. Singh and Dr. R.N. Singh of BHU, spared their valuable time to come over to our site and stayed for a considerable time with us. Dr. V.D. Misra and Dr. Dwivedi from Allahabad University and Dr. Sitaram Dube from Vikram University, Ujjain also visited our site during the excavations. Their views and discussions have immensely benefited us for which we are short of appropriate words to express our grateful thanks to them.

REFERENCES

Chaturvedi, S.N., 1980, 'Excavations at Sathiaon-Fajilnagar, District Deoria and Explorations in the Districts of Gorakhpur and Basti of Uttar Pradesh', *History and Archaeology*, I: 333-340.

——— 1985, 'Advance of Vindhyan Neolithic and Chalcolithic Cultures to the Himalayan Tarai: Excavation and Explorations in Sarayupara Region of Uttar Pradesh', *Man and Environment*, IX: 101-108.

Kumar, A., 1974, 'The Protohistoric Black-and-Red Ware—A plea for Neolithic origin', *Indica*, XI, March 1974, No.1: 13-15, 17. (as quoted by Singh 1982: XLV.)

Misra, V.D., 1977, *Some Aspects of Indian Archaeology*, Prabhat Prakashan, Allahabad.

Misra, V.D., J.N. Pal and M.C. Gupta, 2000,'Further Excavations at Jhusi, *Pragdhara* 10: 23-30.

Sharma, G.R., V.D. Misra, D. Mandal, B.B. Misra, J.N. Pal, 1980, *Beginning of Agriculture*, Abhinav Prakashan, Allahabad.

Singh, B.P., 1990, Gulrihwaghat and Lohra Dewa: Chalcolithic Settlements in District Basti, Uttar Pradesh', *Pragdhara* 1: 89-93.

Singh, B.P. and R. Kumar, 1994, 'Explorations in districts Basti and

Sidharthnagar in the Saryupar Plains of Eastern Uttar Pradesh', *Pragdhara* 4: 1-12.

Singh, H.N., 1982, *History and Archaeology of Black-and-Red Ware (Chalcolithic Period)*, Sundip Prakashan, Delhi.

Singh, P., 1993, 'Archaeological Excavations at Imlidih Khurd - 1992', *Pragdhara* 3: 21-35.

Singh, P., A.K. Singh and I.J. Singh, 1990, 'Explorations along the Kuwana River in Districts Gorakhpur and Basti', *Pragdhara* 1: 69-82.

Tewari, Rakesh; B.R. Mani, 1996, 'Further Archaeological Investigations in Sarayupar Area', *Pragdhara* 6: 149-68

Tewari, R., R.K. Srivastava, 1997, 'Excavations at Raja Nala Ka Tila (1995-96), District Sonbhadra (U.P.): Preliminary Observations', *Pragdhara* 7: 77-95;

———, 1998, 'Excavations at Raja Nala Ka Tila (1996-97), District Sonbhadra (U.P.): Preliminary Observations', *Pragdhara* 8: 99-105.

Tewari, R., R.K. Srivastava, K.S. Sarasvat and K.K. Singh, 2000, 'Excavations at Malhar 1999: A Preliminary Report, District Chandauli (U.P.)', *Pragdhara* 10: 69-98.

Tewari, R., R.K. Srivastava, and K.K. Singh, 2002, 'Dadupur Excavations 1999–2000–2002, District Lucknow, Uttar Pradesh Preliminary Report, *Pragdhara* 12: 99-116.

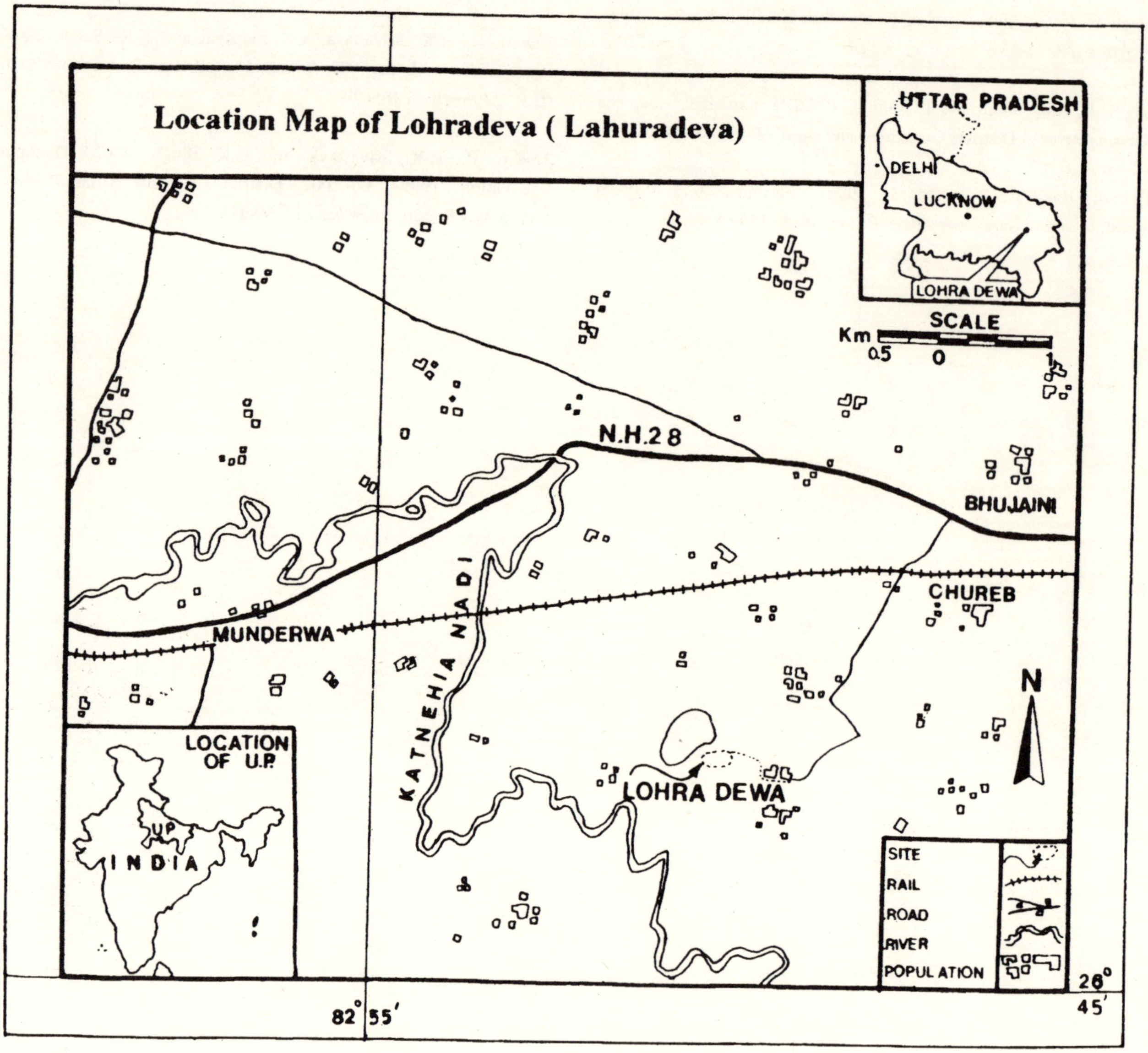

Fig.1. Location Map of Lohradeva (Lahuradeva).

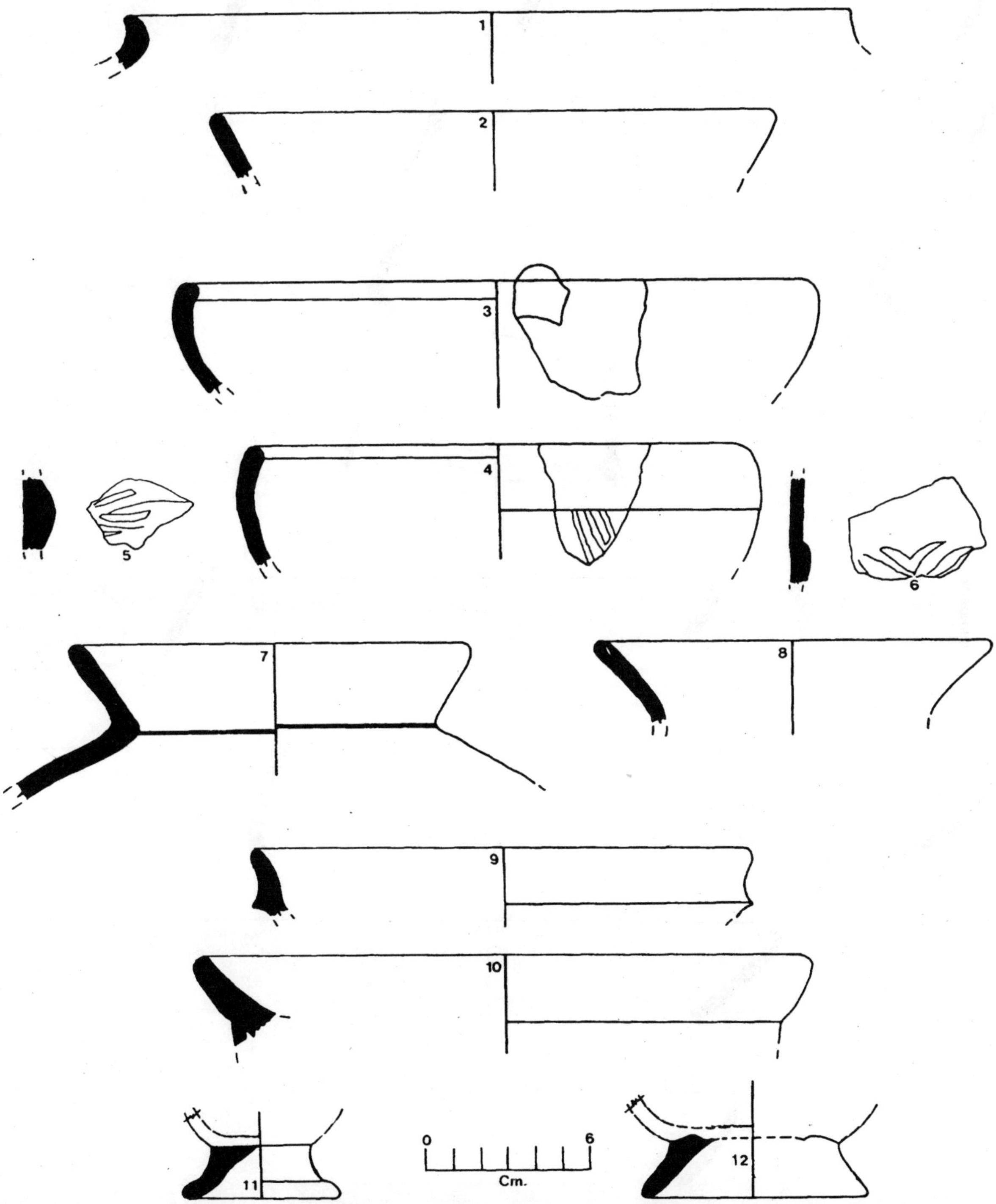

Fig. 2. Shapes of the representative potsherds of Period IA.

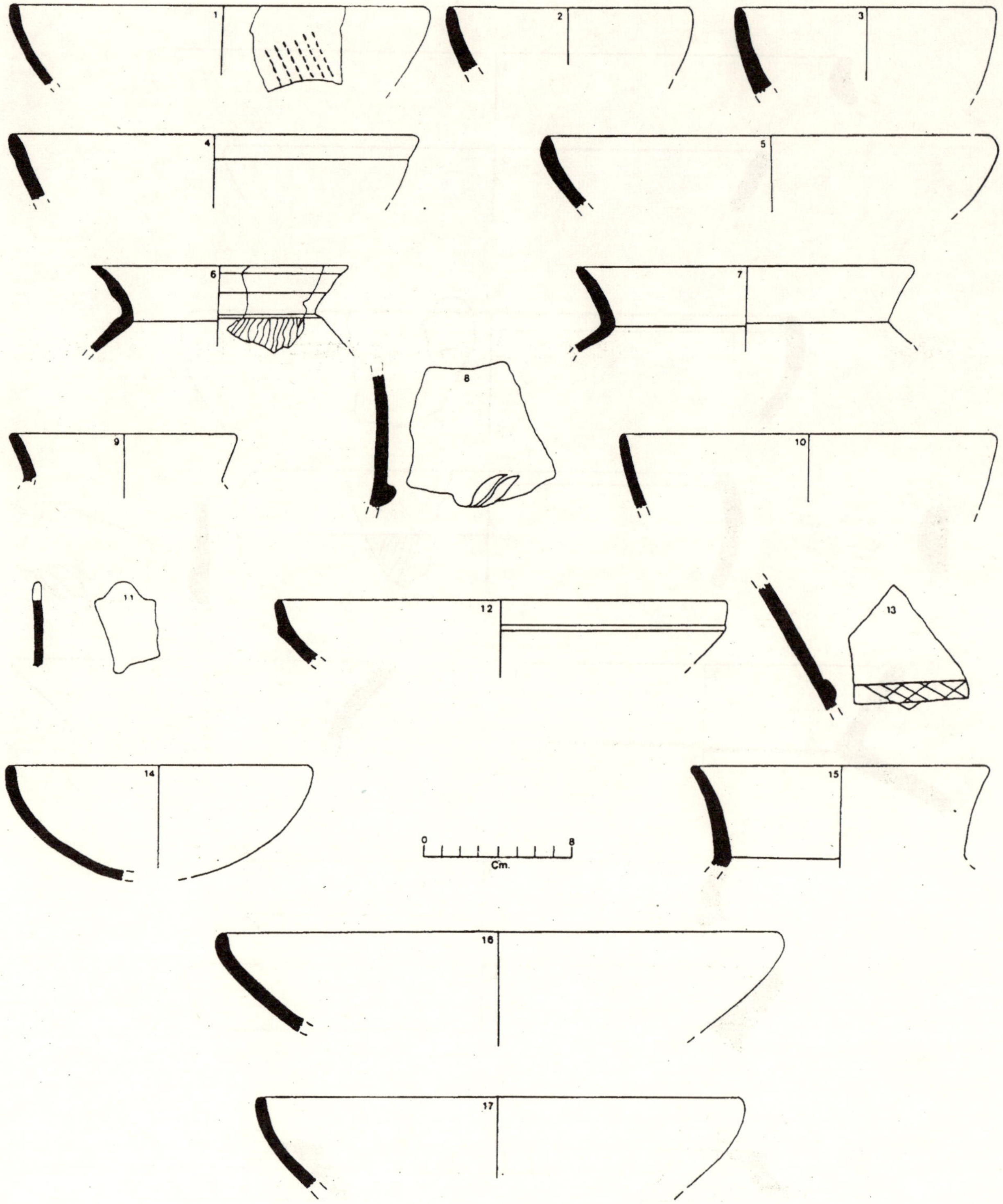

Fig. 3. Shapes of the representative potsherds of Period IB.

Archaeological Investigation at Kelshi, District Ratnagiri, Maharashtra

P.P. JOGLEKAR*, SUSHAMA DEO*, ARATI DESHPANDE-MUKHERJEE* AND SAVITA GHATE*

Introduction

At Kelshi, District Ratnagiri, Maharashtra (fig.1) two sand dunes are found; of these, one located on the estuarir.e waterfront is at present inactive. Based on the archaeological material found in the sand, at Kelshi, Karlekar (1999-2000) conducted studies based on topographic map and IRS 1B image. He reported significant changes in the morphology of the Kelshi creek system. It was thought that the dune is lithified. However, occurrence of archceological material on the dune suggested that it might be an occupation site. Joshi (2001) suggested that the sea level during the medieval period was lower than today. Faunal remains collected earlier from the surface of the dune showed presence of domestic animals, fish and molluscan shells, and a few human remains (Joglekar *et al.* 1996-97). Fresh geomorphological studies conducted in 2000-2001 revealed that the dune is not as old as it was thought to be earlier (Ghatpande 1993) since it has preserved an archaeological site within it (Deo *et al.* 2001).

It was noticed that the old sand dune that has preserved archaeological material is getting destroyed at a fast rate. Since it is not solidified, the material above is falling down and tidal action also adds to this destruction. Every year, the dune is subjected to destruction because of human activity also particularly during a local fair in early summer when several hundred people assemble on the dune and play. Thus, it is feared that the site may get completely damaged within a couple of years. Hence, in the year 2001-2002, preliminary field observations were made at Kelshi with three aims: (i) to find out the relationship of the old (inactive) and active sand dune (ii) understanding the nature and extent of archaeological occupation over the old (now inactive) sand dune; and (iii) to collect cultural material necessary for understanding the relative chronology of the site.

The northern face of the dune is eroded due to the wave action. The dune-section is approachable from this face. A pole erected by some highway construction company surveyors is present here that marks the height of the eroded dune surface from the present-day sea level. This pole has been a great help to get to datum line. Hence, stratigraphy of the dune section is described in terms of the height above the present-day sea level instead of conventional method of depth below the datum line. Section scrapping was done in order to collect archaeological material from stratified contexts.

Dune Characteristics

Kelshi (73° 3' N; 17° 6' E) is situated in taluka Dapoli, District Ratnagiri. It is located on the mouth of a very small estuary Bharja. The stream is swift and non-perennial. This estuary covers an area of about 6 sq km. It runs

*Departmet of Archaeology, Deccan College, Pune-6

for a distance of 3 km inland. There are a number of small streams running for less than 1 Km of which more join the estuary on its northern bank as compared to the southern bank. Narrow and elongated terraces border the estuary. The tidal environment is of mesotidal type. Semi-diurnal types of tides are recorded and waves are generally moderate to low on this coast. Only during the monsoon season are waves high and destructive. There is a small pocket beach on the coast of Kelshi, located between two rocky headlands. The northern side is bounded by the Dighi hill (highest altitude of 190 m AMSL). The old dune is 150 m away from the presently active dune formed on the present pocket beach.

The old dune at Kelshi is triangular in shape and stretches 560 m in north-south direction. The average height is 18 m and the highest point (32.4 m) is located on the northern part of the dune. The western face of the dune has a convex slope and the landward face is a steeply sloping. Ripple marks are present over most of the dune surface. Vegetation is more abundant on the southern side compared to the northern side. The eastern face is devoid of any vegetation. The eastern slope directly merges with the flat terrace on the landward side. At many places sand fans created by moving sand are seen. The location of Kelshi dune is such that at present it is away from the open sea environment. This dune is isolated from the active dunes by a tidal channel. During high tide, this old dune can only be approached from its landward side because the active dunes are completely under water. As a result of this, the old dune is completely cut off from the present beach. The old beach facing the dune has preserved a shell lag. The base of the dune is sand flat with perfectly horizontal bedding. The sand flat is characterised by a smooth surface having a low gradient. The sand flat over which dune is located is very interesting as the sand flat occurs where waves get weakened. It indicates a sluggish water environment. Normally it is found in the heads of open bays, behind islands, or at the inner margins of extensive shallows on which waves die out. The loss of energy enables the sand to be deposited in the shallows.

Occupational Phases

Habitation layers are visible on the northern face of the dune. This section facing the estuary on north was scrapped. Archaeological material was collected by scrapping horizontally from one metre wide band. Although the dune is 18-32 m in height, since it was not possible to approach the top, scrapping was restricted to a height of 8 m from the present-day sea level. The deposit was sieved so that no cultural material is lost. Stratigraphy of the dune seems to be highly complex. Field observations suggest that the dune has preserved record of human occupation over a long period of time.

The basal part of the dune up to 2.15 m is devoid of any habitation deposit. Sedimentological analysis of this part revealed that this is made up of fine sand (3 to 3.3 m). The cultural material starts occurring at about 2.15 m above the present-day sea level. The section marked up to the height of 8 m revealed three major phases of occupations that are based on the nature and size of the pottery assemblage (fig. 2). At Kelshi, a major component of the pottery assemblage b5elongs to Red Ware and Grey ware. These two types have been found in variable amounts in all three phases. Glazed ware and Celadon ware are found only in Phase III.

Phase I (2.15-4.0 m above base level)

The pottery is highly fragmented which consists of thin Red ware and thin Grey ware. No slip was applied in case of both the varieties. Some of the potsherds are so fragmented that it is not possible to recognise the shapes. A few fragments of micaceous red ware were found from 2.3-2.5 m collection unit. A floor level is visible at 2.72 m level. A large number of pottery pieces (about 75) were found on this floor level. A platform-like structure made of laterite slabs is present at 4.00 m level. The slabs are about 10 cm in thickness and are found spread over a large area in the section. These laterite slabs seem to have been brought in the site from time to time, perhaps to start a new house-building activity.

Phase II (4.0-6.0 m above base level)

Occupation layers have lesser ceramic fragments than that of the earlier phase. Pottery found in these layers is also fragmented. A few Red ware and Grey ware sherds are better preserved. A few sherds are described below:

Red Ware (Fig. 3-4)

Red ware sherds belong to storage jars with projecting triangular rim, globular pots with externally everted rim, pots with blunt carination and corrugation at neck, spouts of jar, carinated bowls and dishes. All the jars and bowls have slip on the outer side. The Red ware sherds are both of thick and thin varieties. A dish (KLS 106) has slip only on the inner side. The designs include small corrugation (e.g., KLS 10 and 105).

Grey Ware (Fig. 4)

A number of Grey ware sherds have been found. However, rim sherds useful for shape diagnosis are few. The pots are mainly medium-sized and made of medium coarse fabric. A number of Grey and Red ware sherds are without slip (fig. 5). These include impressions of various patterns-square (KLS 50), vertical lines (KLS 70) and oblique lines on the shoulder (KLS 46). A Grey ware sherd (KLS 75) has an appliqué band with a pinched design. Shapes include pot with short neck and flaring rim, handis, pot with constricted neck, etc.

Gap between Phae II and III

Phase II ends with a laterite platform located at 6.0 m. Another laterite platform is visible at 7.0 m above ground. In between these two platforms, one metre thick deposit of sand is seen. This sand is completely devoid of any cultural material.

Phase III (7.0-8.0 m above base level)

Occupation layers have lesser number of potsherds. The Red ware and Grey ware forms like globular pots, bowls and dishes continue in this phase. Cultural material (mainly pottery and fish bones) is seen scattered above 8 m from the ground level. However, it has not been collected. A number of Glazed ware (fig. 5) and celadon ware fragments were found between 7 and 8 m above ground level.

Glazed ware sherds, are with thick core of dull yellowish colour. The glaze is of three types: olive green, pale cream and grey. Glass coating has been seen only on one surface in most of the cases. Most of the Glazed ware sherds have thick yellowish or brown core and are olive green in colour. These sherds are similar to those found at Nevasa during Period VI (Muslim-Maratha) (Sankalia *et al.* 1960) and Daulatabad (fourteenth-eighteenth century A.D.) (Mate, M.S. 1992). One fragment of cream coloured dish/bowl (KLS 33) has black painting on the inner side. Field observation revealed that the Glazed ware fragments are mostly above 6.0 m level. However, isolated occurrence of green Glazed ware sherds within the deposit of Phase I is noticed from 2.9-3.1 m level. There is a possibility of contamination from the upper strata. However, such green glazed ware has been found from pre-Muslim layers at Nevasa and Maheshwar. Also such Glazed ware fragments belonging to the early Local imitations of imported pottery are known from Muslim period layers at Daulatabad—a medieval fort near Aurangabad. At present, it is neither possible to comment on the chronological context of these Glazed ware nor their origin (local/foreign).

The celadon ware exhibits thin and compact white core. Most of these sherds show coating of pale blue on both the surfaces. There are many decorations executed in bright blue colour. One sherd showed pale green coating on both the surfaces (KLS 28), while another (KLS 17) has a plain white coating on both surfaces. Both these sherds are without any decoration. These sherds are similar to those found on China ware from Daulatabad.

Glass objects

A number of glass objects have been found from Phase II (5.3-5.6 m level). These objects include drinking cups or small globular pots and four bangle pieces (both monochrome and polychrome). Most of the fragments of three drinking cups have been found from 5.3-5.6 m level except one turquoise blue fragment found in 5.6-6.0 m level. The cups are made of translucent green glass. Visual inspection reveals that it is similar to the glass found at Nevasa from Period V and VI (Muslim-Maratha Period). The bangles are emerald green in colour and are not translucent. One bangle of polychrome type is found from 5.3-5.5 m level, and it is similar in colour scheme to one found at Nevasa (No. 817) from Period VI and Brahmapuri (Bhamani context) (Sankalia *et al.* 1952). This broad bangle has yellow base band and two pale green bands. The circumference is beaded like the Bhamani period specimen found at Brahmapuri.

Faunal Material

During a visit to the site in 1996 faunal material was

collected from the surface of the dune. It showed presence of domestic animals, fish and molluscan shells, and a few human remains (1996-97). A number of animal skeletal elements have been found both on the dune surface and within the stratified contexts in 2001-02 field investigations. All the three occupation phases yielded remains of both vertebrate and invertebrate animals. The invertebrate mainly those of marine molluscan shells outnumber the vertebrates. The overall faunal assemblage recovered has shown fairly good preservation. Most characteristic taphonomic feature visible it that of post-depositional activity of bio-eroders such as barnacles on the bones and shells washed down from the mound.

Mammals

Following eight mammalian bone fragments were found within the stratified contexts (Pl. 1).

KLS 1: A distal portion of metatarsal of *Bos/Bubalus* sp. The bone is in good condition but shows encrustation with barnacles.

KLS 2: A broken calcaneum belonging to *Bos/Bubalus* sp. The tuber calcis is broken and surface has gnawing and cut marks.

KLS 3: Portion of distal humerus of *Bos/Bubalus* sp. This fragment is calcified and shows shopping marks.

KLS 4: Portion of distal humerus (right side) belonging to *Bos/Bubalus*.

KLS 5: Fragment of a carpal bone of *Bos/Bubalus*.

KLS 6: Fragment of a mandible of *Bos/Bubalus*.

KLS 7: Fragment of rib of *Bos/Babalus*.

KLS 8: Fragment of a long bone of a small reminant (Sheep/goat)

Fish

Fish bones (NISP=113) consist of very small unidentifiable fragments. Most commonly represented parts are those of vertebrae and spines (Pl. 2). All these fish bones are of marine fish. Species identification has been carried out due to want of standard comparative reference collection. A few of th fish vertebrae were measured (Table 1).

Molluscs

Molluscan shells are seen in all the three occupation phases (Pl. 3–4). These are also scattered on the dune surface as well as on a narrow strip of sandbar created by the estuary at the base of the dune. Molluscan shells were

Table 1: Measurements of fish vertebrae (in mm)

Serial No.	Context	Lateral diameter	Dorso-ventral diameter
KLS 71	2.5-2.7 m	09.88	08.09
KLS 72	2.5-2.7 m	12.32	11.87
KLS 73	2.9-3.1 m	22.44	7.68
KLS 74	2.9-3.1 m	24.86	07.20
KLS 75	Dune Surface	29.08	13.37
KLS 76	Dune Surface	24.31	08.26
KLS 77	Dune Surface	26.31	–
KLS 78	Dune Surface	34.10	45.54

found in all the collection units.

Molluscan shells dominate the faunal assemblage at Kelshi. A total of 17 species have been identified (Table 2). No freshwater species are represented at the site Except an estuarine species of bivalve (*Gelonia* sp.), all are of marine habitat.

The shells in general exhibit good preservation but have a chalky appearance due to exposure to varied climate factors. A majority of the species present are characteristic of an open coast with rocky inter-tidal areas and estuarine sand/mud flats. The most commonly represented shells are those of *Meretrix meretrix, tapes sp., Paphia sp., Crassostrea cucullata and Umbonium vestarium.* All these excepting *Umbonium vestarium* had been intentionally brought to the site for dietary use. Similar species continue to be exploited even today on the Konkan coast. In the case of small gastropod *Umbonium vestarium,* it was naturally introduced into the deposit. Those tiny shells are found in abundance on sandy beaches below the high tide mark.

Good quality molluscs appear to have been procured as observed from the fairly large-sized shells. No evidence for sheel working has been observed like shell debitage or shell objects. Hence molluscan utilisation had been strictly for dietary reasons. An all year round exploitation is visualised, as these species are easily available throught out the year. Taking into consideration the large quantity of shells present, molluscs had probably served as an important food resources for the site inhabitants along with other food such as fish and mammals.

Concluding Remarks

Kelshi was a minor port with a very little trade during early nineteenth century and has been a place of not much significance. In sixteenth century, Portuguese Dom

Table 2: Molluscan taxa identified at Kelshi

No	Species	Family	Bivalve/Gastropod
1.	*Meretrix meretrix*	Veneridae	Bivalve
2.	*Paphia sp.*	Veneridae	Bivalve
3.	*Tapes sp.*	Veneridae	Bivalve
4.	*Acanthocardia lata*	Cardiidae	Bivalve
5.	*Perna viridis*	Mytilidae	Bivalve
6.	*Gelonia sp.*	Corbiculidae	Bivalve
7.	*Placuna placenta*	Anomiidae	Bivalve
8.	*Crassostrea cucullata*	Ostreidae	Bivalve
9.	*Crassostrea gryphoides*	Ostreidae	Bivalve
10.	*Anadara sp.*	Arcidae	Bivalve
11.	*Umbonium vestiarium*	Trochidae	Gastropod
12.	*Conus sp.*	Cornidae	Gastropod
13.	*Natica didyma*	Naticidae	Gastropod
14.	*Natica picta*	Naticidae	Gastropod
15.	*Turritella duplicate*	Turritellidae	Gastropod
16.	*Thais sp.*	Muricidae	Gastropod
17.	*Cerithidae sp.*	Cerithiidae	Gastropod

Joao de Castro in AD 1538 mentions it to be a place of mosques. De La Valle (1624) anchored here but did not go on the shore of Kelshi (Ratnagiri District 1962).

Chronology of occupation at Kelshi is not clear at present. Based on the occurrence of Glazed ware and Celadon ware, it can be assumed that Phase III perhaps represents Muslim-Maratha period. The pottery assemblage shows mainly the types required for routine domestic activities. A few sherds of decorated Celadon ware are of fine make. Kelshi was a minor port till the late nineteenth century. Glazed ware and glass objects indicate that the site could have been a trading port. More intensive investigations here would reveal importance of Kelshi in the larger context of trade and trade-related activities. Evidence for such activities is noticed in field observations conducted in 2002. On the opposite bank of the Bharja estuary, an old jetty-like structure was noticed. At this site a few medieval pottery pieces were found. Prehistoric archaeological sites are known from Konkan and literary records also show that during the early historic period Konkan had several ports and port-towns. However, material evidence for historical human habitation is so far missing. For the first time a long historical occupation is documented at Kelshi. It is not possible to answer many interesting questions about the occupation of the sand dune at Kelshi. Yet this preliminary attempt in itself is a significant step towards understanding medieval archaeology of Konkan coast.

Acknowledgements

This work was carried out using the Departmental Grant (2001-02) given to P.P. Joglekar, who is thankful to the authorities of the Deccan College. Prof. M.S. Mate gave valuable guidance about various aspects of medieval archaeology and Mr. Abhijit Dandekar helped in pottery diagnosis. Mr. Bharat Dighe and Shrikant Pradhan prepared pottery drawings and Mr. Sunil Jadhav did black and white photography.

REFERENCES

Deo, S.G., Savita Ghate, Arati Deshpande-Mukherjee and P.P. Joglekar, 2001, 'Geomorphological Observations at and around Kelshi Region, Konkan Coast, Maharashtra', *Man and Environment* 26 (1): 69-74.

Deshpande-Mukherjee, Arati, 2000, 'An Ethnographic Account of Contemporary Shellfish Garhering on the Konkan Coast, Maharashtra', *Man and Environment 25(2)*: pp. 79-92.

Ghatpande, Jyoti, 1993, 'Lithified Eoliam Coastal Sand Dune at Kelshi, in *Coastal Geomorphology* (S.N. Karlekar ed.), pp. 182-95, Pune: Aparna Publications.

Joglekar, P.P., Arati Deshpande-Mukherjee and Sharmila Joshi, 1996-97, 'Report on the Faunal Remains from Keshi, District Ratnagiri, Maharashtra', *Puratattavai 27*: pp. 91-95.

Joshi, Sharmila, 2001, 'Monsoon Generated Environmental Crisis in Konkan (Coastal Maharashtra) during Medieval Period', in *Monsson and Civilization* (Y. Yasuda and V. Shinde eds.), pp. 127-28, Kyoto: International Research Centre for Japanese Studies.

Karlekar, S.N., 1999-2000 'Respon,se of Kelshi Creek to a Rising Sea Level on Maharashtra Coast as Indicated by a Satellite Image', *Maeer's MIT Pune Journal, Special* Issue, pp. 42-47.

Maharashtra State Gazetteer, Ratnagiri District, 1962, Revised Edition, Mumbai: Government of Maharashtra.

Mate, M.S. and T.V. Pathy, 1992, *Daulatabad: A Report*, Pune: Deccan College.

Rahman, S.S.M., 2000, 'A Study of Glazed Ware from Maharashtra Citadel: An Implication for External Contact', *Journal of Bengal Art* 5: 189-94.

Sankalia, H.D., S.B. Deo, Z.D. Ansari and S. Ehrhardt, 1960., *From History to Prehistory at Nevasa (1954-56)*, Pune: Deccan College.

Sankalia, H.D. and M.G. Dikshit, 1952, *Excavations at Brajmapuri (Kolhapur) 1945-46*, Pune: Deccan College.

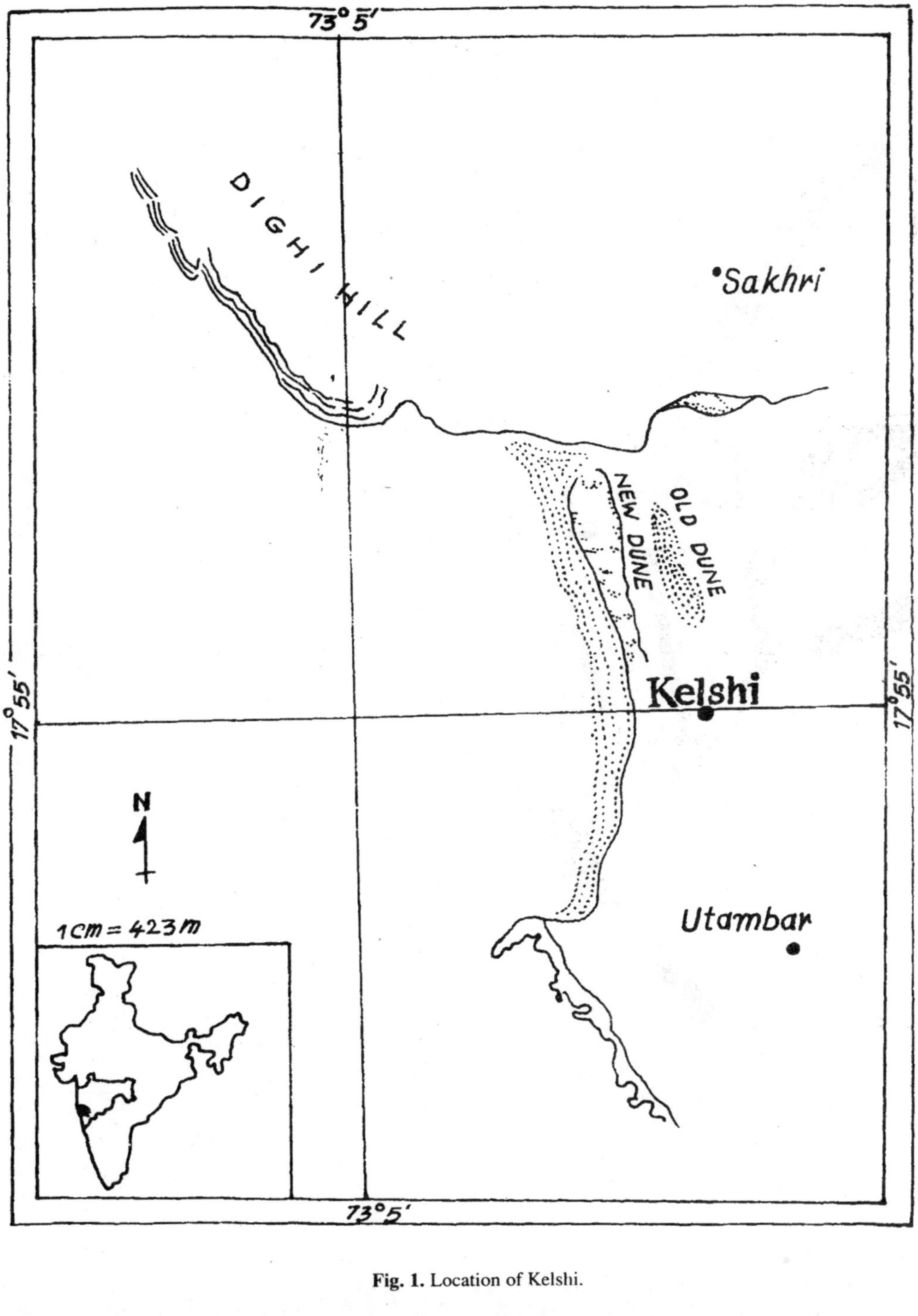

Fig. 1. Location of Kelshi.

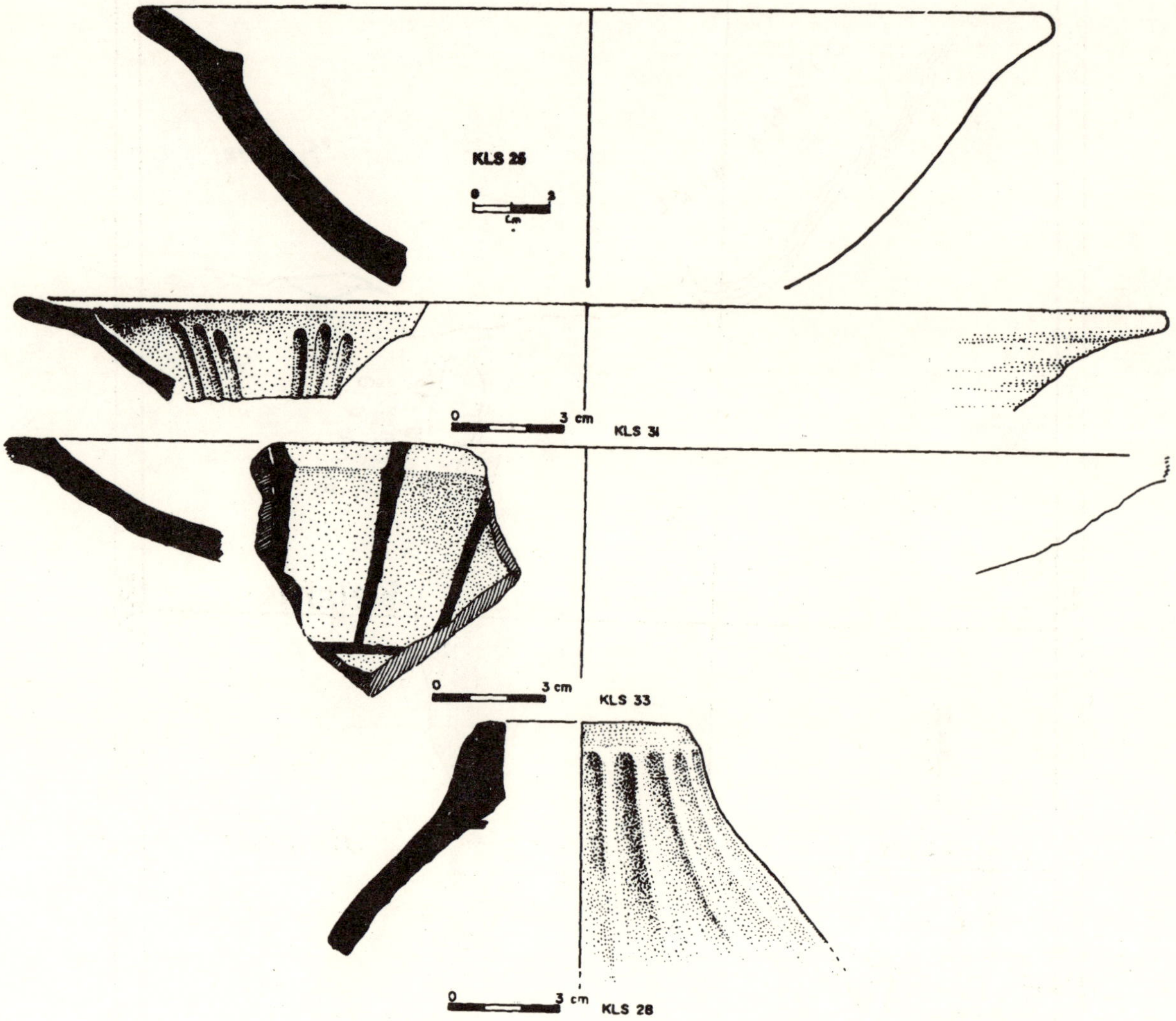
KLS 25
0 3 cm KLS 31
0 3 cm KLS 33
0 3 cm KLS 28

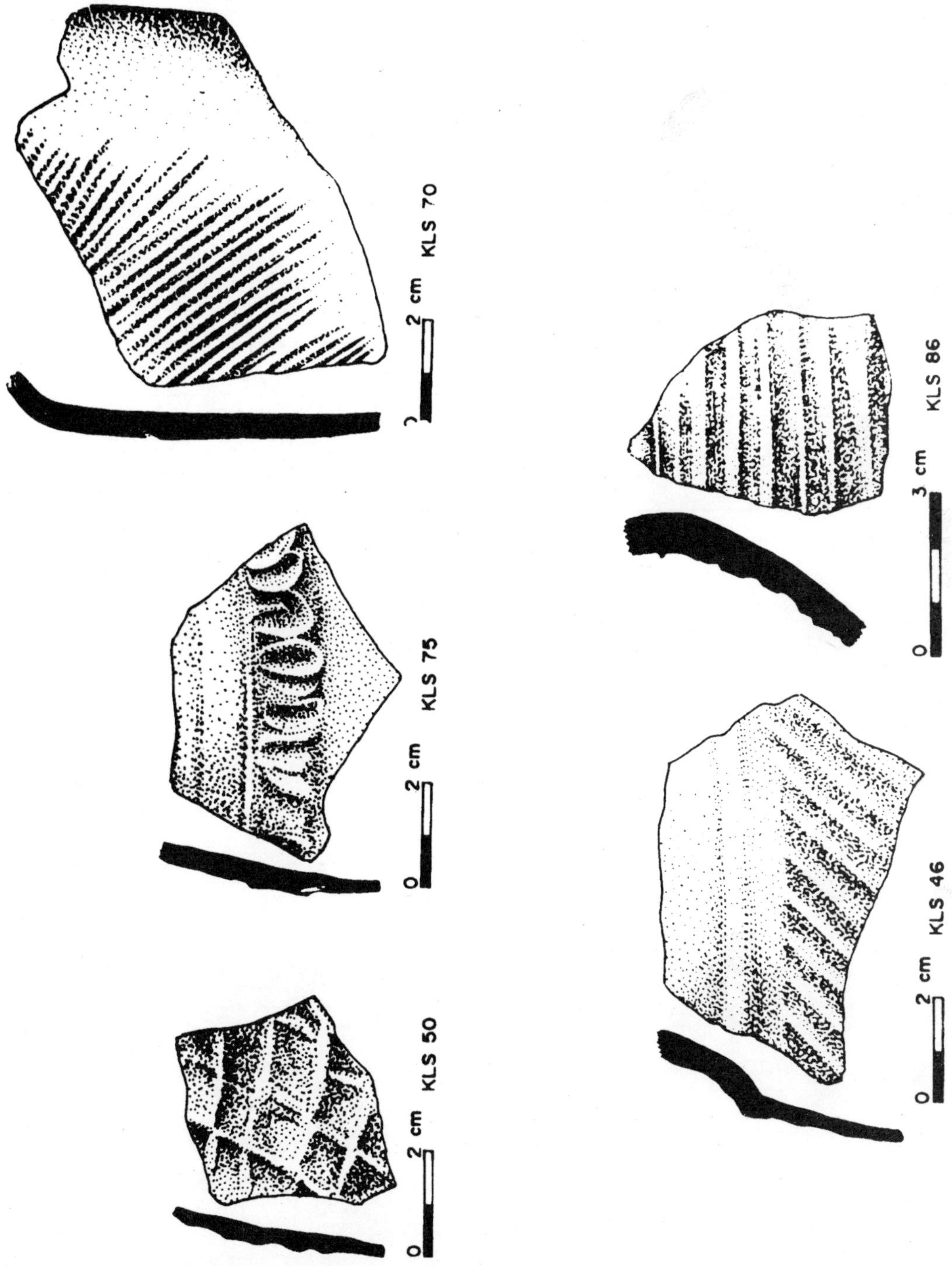

Fig. 3.

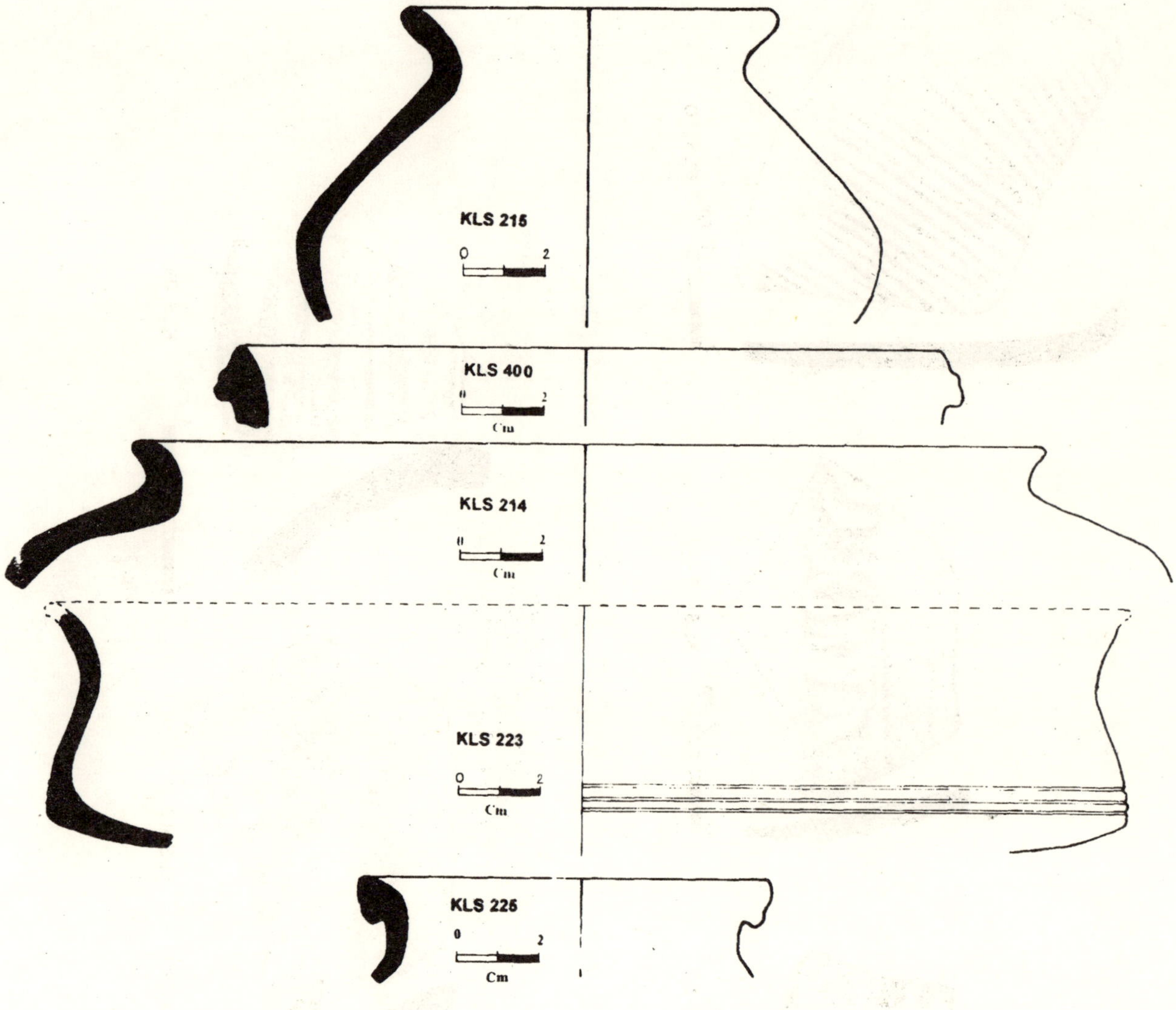

Fig. 4.

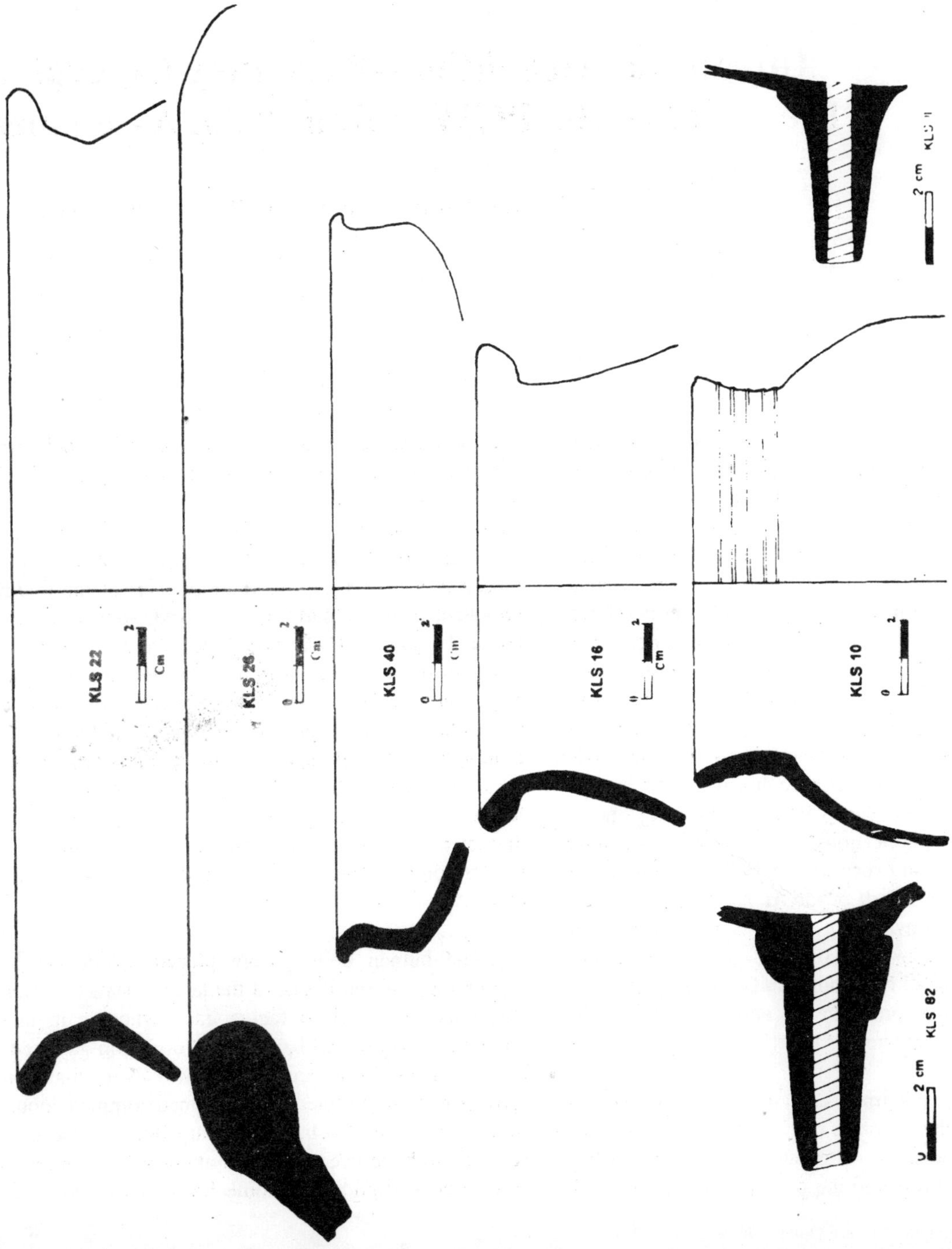

Fig. 5.

Uttranchal Megaliths—Were they Co-eval or Precursor of the PGW Culture? An Assessment

K.P. NAUTIYAL,* RAKESH C. BHATT,** M.S.CHAUHAN***

During the last one decade sustained archaeological investigations in the central Himalaya, (fig. 1), comprising mainly the two divisions of Garhwal and Kumaon in the present newly-created state of Uttaranchal, have brought to light a few important and epoch-making cultural vestiges spanning a time range between the second to the first millenniuim B.C. The two discoveries pertained to the megaliths and the Painted Grey Ware culture. It was in 1964 S.P. Dabral reported, for the first time, the existence of a few pit-burials at Malari (3800 m. MSL) in Chamoli district, 61 km north-west beyond Joshimath on the bank of Dhauliganga (Dabral 1964: 223-35). His information was based on a chance discovery of a human skeleton along with potsherds in a road-building operation. In one of his publications D.P. Agrawal also claims to have carried out an expedition in 1950 to examine the graves at Malari on behalf of the Archaeological Survey of India (ASI) (Agrawal *et al.* 1991). It was however, in the 1980s that the Department of History and Archaeology of the H.N. Bahuguna, Garhwal University put up an extensive probe in the entire Niti Valley in which lies the present site of Malari.

Consequently, few trial excavations revealed that the ancient users of these graves dug out horizontal pits by cutting the soft calcareous rock and interred therein the skeletal remains. From top the pits appeared to be oval with an entrance on the western face of the rock (Bhatt and Nautiyal 1987-88 and Nautiyal *et al.* 1986). The entrance was subsequently blocked by heavy boulders. One of the burials gave evidence of a complete skeleton of a horse oriented in east-west direction. The animal was placed in a flexed posture reminding us of the tradition prevalent in many parts of the world, such as at Sialk, Giyan, Hissar, etc. (Grishman 1952).The associated material with the horse-skeleton included red and black ware pots. Out of them two black ware pots were notable with spouts having rich engraved designs on the bulbous portion of the body and the neck with zigzag flowing vertical broad bands in black. A variety of grooved designs formed the repertoire. A few dishes with five centimeter diameter were the other notable finds. A red ware jar with handles on both the sides was another important discovery.

The human bodies were placed upside down in crouching position. In one of the large burials two human skeletons were noticed facing each other again in the crouching posture. AS based on information gathered by him from the local people, Agrawal avers that a few 'graves were stone-lined and contained complete inhumations, and some also had secondary burials'. He is also reported to have been informed about the discovery of a 'few bronze tripods and some horse harnessing equip-

* Fellow, Indian Institute of Advanced Study, Shimla
** Reader, Deptt. of History & Archaeology, H.N. Bahuguna, Garhwal University, Srinagar (Uttaranchal)
*** Deputy Superintending Archaeologist, ASI, Mini Circle, Shimla

ment' (Agrawal *et al.* 1998).

A recent exploration in the Niti valley by the Archaeology Department of Garhwal University has again brought to light more burials at Malari along with funerary materials consisting of pottery and one gold face-mask which speaks for the use of gold by these people, besides bronze and iron.

Western Ramganga Megaliths

The Ramganga, rising from the forests and mountains of Kodiya Bagar and Binsar, a part of the Higher Himalayan mountain chain, covers a catchments area of about a 100 km up to the foothill town of Ramnagar in Uttaranchal. Below the initial stage of the source region, the river valley was explored over a considerably long stretch of 32 km with very fruitful results proving the existence of a multiple burials consisting of cist chambers and urn burials.

These burials, noticed at Sanana-Baseri, Jainal-Naula, Srikot, etc., situated on the bank of the river along its course, besides Koorman near Ganai, a small township situated on the confluence of the Ramganga and Kauravgad rivers; Ladyura in Almora district and Gagrigol situated on the left bank of the Gomati, again in Almora district and reported by Agrawal and his team (1998), were some of the important sites of Uttaranchal giving us a homogeneous materials relating to the megalithic culture, which so far had remained alien to the Himalayan region.

Out of the above-mentioned sites Sanana-Baseri, Jainal-Naula and Srikot were taken up for excavation by the Garhwal University, while Ladyura was excavated by A.K. Sharma under the auspices of the A.S.I. Rest of the sites were probed by D.P. Agrawal, J.S. Kharakwal, etc., either through intensive exploration or by scrapping the exposed section.

The burials in all these sites the dead bodies were found to have been interred in various directions and orientation was not meticulously observed. For example, most of the cist burials at Sanana were oriented in east-west direction, but a few of them were also in north-north-east, south-south-west and even in the north-south directions. Before interring the dead body almost all the graves were dug into the hard alluvial deposit reaching to a depth of 1 m and 1.50 m from the top surface. On the basis of the nature of the soil which shows only gravel, sand and stone and no habitational material, it is inferred that the dead was interred away from the habitation and subsequently the post-exposure remains were preserved for secondary interment (Khanduri, V. Nautiyal, Bhatt and Farswan 1997).

Similarly, the urn burials found in a group at Sanana and Baseri was separated by a stone wall in between the cist and the urn burials. The urns were of large-sized hand-made jars with mat impressions and ripple marks ranging in size between 48 to 56 cm in diameter. The urns were of a sturdy or coarse red and black wares and were invariably used for interment.

Comparison between the Uttaranchal burials and burials in the rest of the country

Without going much into the architectural framework these burials, it is very pertinent to take notice of the comparison brought out by Sharma between the Uttaranchal megaliths and those in the rest of the country (Sharma 1997:74). According to him most of the characteristic features in both of these groups show some sort of a striking resemblance. Those which go along with it are the Konnur groups (Karnataka), Chatnali (Bhairavanapada and Rajawala, Dharwar area in Karnataka), Pudukkotai in Tamil Nadu, Leh Valley in N.W. Himalaya, Chunar in Mirzapur district in U.P., etc. The characteristics of the megaliths in India rightly presented by Sharma obviously leads us to conclude that the culture with its minor geographical variations and different cultural groups became a landmark between the first half of the second and first millennium B.C.

Funerary material and the pottery

(a) Malari

As indicated, the burials at Malari provided evidence of a variety of funerary goods consisting of the beads of semi-precious stones and of white paste, highly rusted iron implements, such as arrow-heads and knives with a provision of hafting. Interestingly, there were some bone arrow-heads and bronze tripods as reported by Agrawal. Gold was not scarce as evidenced by the latest discovery of a gold mask from one of the burials at Malari (Personal communication from Prof. Vinod Nautiyal).

(b) Ramganga Valley

The story of the Ramganga valley burials is quite different. Most of them did not contain any significant funerary goods excepting fragments of human bones and at times only the teeth numbering as much as twenty or more. But the grave goods consist of pots and scarcely beads of agate or carnelian. The presence of iron is evidenced by two fragmentary iron pins and a nail along with a broken piece of a sickle. This lone evidence was collected from one of the burials at Baseri, but rest of the excavated burials did not furnish any evidence of the use of any kind of metal. From Ladyura Sharma (1997) reported the discovery of iron 'objects of indeterminate shape' from one of the cists. This shows sparing use of iron as is indicated by a few scattered and stray recordings from Malari and the Sanana-Baseri megaliths. This is indeed surprising as most of the megalithic remains from other parts of the north and particularly from the south represent a complete know-how of a full-fledged iron technology.

Why was iron meagre in the central Himalaya is really baffling as iron ores are known to have existed along with the copper mines since the most ancient past and there are indications that mining was already known enterprise (Atkinson 1989; Agrawal *et al.* 1998). However, in the present state of our knowledge, it can be surmised that the people of the megalithic culture in Himalaya were probably less knowledgeable regarding exploitation of ores and technology. And therefore, this might be the reason for the great scarcity of iron in almost all the sites connected with the megaliths in Uttaranchal.

Pottery

Pottery (fig. 2) forms a larger part of the recovered material. This is invariably wheel-made and includes a variety consisting of medium-sized bowls, dishes, globular goblets, pedestalled-bowl and bowl with flattened base. More or less intact pots were about eighty, besides a large number of pot-sherds from both Sanana and Baseri. The fabric and wares range from the coarse red to a fine wheel-made red and grey ware. Most of the pots were kept on flat schist stone slabs and invariably occupied the western flank of the dead body. The larger pots in coarse red ware representing urns show ripple marks on the outer surface. From Ladyura, the pottery is mostly wheel-made coarse red ware with a thick section. In few cases red slip is noticed on the outer surface. Grey ware was also recovered in the excavation (Sharma 1997). Surface finds at Ladyura brought out an interesting black ware bowl with three knobs, convex sides and a featureless rim with a diameter of 23 cm (Agrawal 1991). This three legged bowl is notable from Ladyura is totally a new feature from those of the Sanana and Baseri assemblage.

On the whole, the study of pottery shows a variety in fabric, shape, design and colour-scheme. Unlike the characteristic features of the south Indian megalithic culture, the Uttaranchal megaliths are totally devoid of the Black-and-Red ware as also the micaceous red ware.

The most important aspect to be noted about the main pottery group is its prolific painted designs, which brings it nearer the Painted Grey Ware tradition of the Ganga-Yamuna Doab, which is generally light grey in colour but sometimes reddish and has an ashy-grey core (Dhavalikar 1999: 124). From these megalithic burials also grey and red wares and having a grey core recovered. Similar to the PGW it has mainly linear motifs consisting of horizontal, vertical and oblique thick strokes, like both in the inner and outer surfaces. In contrast to the PG ware, the pots from the Ramganga valley burials show a black rim-band, besides ripple marks in a few red-polished ware pots.

Not only the painted designs, which carry a great similarity, but the forms are intrinsically the same with a predominance of the bowls and dishes of different sizes. Most of the bowls are either concave or convex with splayed-out rim and carinated to a rounded base or eleptical shape and also a vertical sharpened rim and rounded sides. In one case there is a flared rim with a ledge on the body and slight depression on the shoulder and an elliptical base. Interestingly, there is one miniature vase of grey ware with horizontally splayed out rim and concave side carinated to a rounded base with a variety of thick strokes in the inner and outer surfaces and also on the bottom. Similarly the dishes are closely akin to the forms of the PGW dish with the same painted designs consisting of a variety of strokes.

Almost all the shapes of the dishes and the bowls are comparable with the shapes of the Painted Grey Ware earlier found at Hastinapur (Lal 1954-55), Ahichchhatra (Ghosh and Panigrahi 1946), Thapli (Nautiyal and Khanduri 1991), Jakhera (Sahi 1994) and other sites in the Ganga-Yamuna Daob. A few pots bearing common features in the form of ripple marks with resemblance in variety and shapes of the form at Jakhera are interesting. According to Sahi, ripple-marked pottery and the PGW paintings are found from Period IIA at Jakhera and he puts it as a proto-PG ware or a forerunner of the PGW. Though geographically two are far-flung areas, yet the views propounded by Sahi seem to be cogent (Sahi 1994) and as such it can be safely surmised that megalithic people at Sanana-Baseri and in the entire Ramganga Valley and in its peripheral regions were anterior to the PGW culture.

Pedestalled bowl and its Parallel

Pedestalled bowl is an important discovery form the cist burials at Baseri and Koorman which exhibit several 'morphological parallels' with chalcolithic pottery from elsewhere (Agrawal 1998). It is found in Phase III at Navadatoli in central India. Sankalia has drawn parallel between the Navadatoli find and that from the Kherai graves in Pakistan (Sankalia 1963). He has discussed various sub-types of this bowl pointing out the similarity of the type at Sialk, Giyan and Hissar Period II. Besides it is also present at Loebnar and several other Gandhara grave cultural assemblage (Stacul 1987, 1992 and Gupta 1994: 51). From India once again, it is reported in coarse grey ware from Ahar in Rajasthan. On the basis of such parallels Sankalia has suggested that various cultural streams had indirect contacts with India around the beginning of the second millennium B.C. Agrawal and Kharakwal have drawn similarity of the Kumaon type with the Kherai and Swat Pd IV types (Agrawal 1998) which according to Stacul (1987) have been assigned to the mid-second millennium B.C. Another grey ware flaring bowl from Koorman burial according to Agrawal (1998) has an exact parallel at Bir-Kot-Ghwandi in Swat Valley Pd IV as shown by Stacul in fig. 31 f.p. 84 (1987).

Summing up, it may be noted that the pottery from the Uttaranchal megalithic burial is highly enigmatic, but interesting taking us back to about *circa* second millennium B.C. the period when the area was witnessing a great inward movement of people from the central Asian steppes to the north-western and northern part of the Indian sub-continent traversing the greater part of the Tibetan plateau and reaching to Leh-Laddakh, Himachal Pradesh and to Uttaranchal through its Niti, Mana and several other passes. During the course of this journey Malari must have been the first stage of their sojourn as attested by a series of graves and other antiquities found here.

REFERENCES

Agrawal, D.P., D. Bhatt, S. Malviya, J.S. Kharakwal, 1991, 'Archaeology of Kumaun: Problems and Prospects', *Man and Environment* 16 (1): 59-63.

Agrawal, D.P., Kharakwal, J.S., 1998, *Central Himalayas: An Archaeological, Linguistic and Cultural Synthesis*, New Delhi.

Agrawal, D.P. Sheela Kusumgar, M.G. Yadav, V.D. Gogte, Jeevan Kharakwal and Manju Pant, 1995, 'Was Kumaon the Source of Early Iron in North India?' *Man and Environment* 20 (1): 81-85.

Atkinson, E.T., 1884, *The Himalayan Districts of North-Western Provinces of India*, vol. 2, 3, Allahabad.

Atkinson, E.T., 1889, *The Himalayan Gazetteer, New Delhi*, Cosmo Publishers (Reprint).

Bhatt, R.C., Nautiyal, K.P., 1987-88, 'Trans-Himalayan Burials vis-a-vis Malari: An Assessment', *JOHSARD*, 11 & 12, pp. 95-101.

Dabral, S.P., 1964, *Uttarakhand Ke Bhotantik*, Dogadda, Garhwal 223-35.

Dhavalikar, M.K., 1999, *Historical Archaeology of India*, New Delhi, Books & Books.

Ghosh, A., K.C. Panigrahi, 1946, 'The Pottery of Ahichchhatra, District Bareilly, U.P.', *Ancient India*, No. 1, 37-59.

Grishman, R., 1952, *Iran*, Middlesex.

Gupta, S.P., 1979, *Archaeology of Soviet Central Asia*, B.R. Publications. New Delhi.

Gupta, S.P., 1994, 'Gandhara Grave Culture: Its Bearing on the problems of Painted Grey ware and Aryan Megration,' *Painted Grey Ware*, ed. R.C. Gaur, Jaipur, 46-64.

Khanduri, B.M., Vinod Nautiyal, R.C. Bhatt, Y.S. Farswan, 1997, 'Megalithic Burial Complexes in Mid-central Himalaya; New Discoveries and Results', *Him Kanti*, ed. B.M. Khanduri, Vinod Nautiyal (Archaeology, Art and History, Prof. K.P. Nautiyal Felicitation Volume). Book India Publishing Co., Delhi.

Lal, B.B., 1954-55, 'Excavation of Hastinapur and other Explorations in the upper Ganga and Sutlej Basins, 1950-52: New Light on the Dark Age between the end of Harappan culture and the early historical period', *Ancient India*, No. 10-11.

Nautiyal, K.P., 1969, *The Archaeology of Kumaon (Including Dehradun)*, Chowkhamab Sanskrit Series, Varanasi.

Nautiyal, K.P., B.M. Khanduri, 1986, 'A New Cultural Dimension in the Central Himalayan Region of Uttarakhand: An Archaeological Assessment', *ANNALI*, vol. 46: pp. 77-100.

Nautiyal, K.P., B.M. Khanduri, V. Nautiyal, D.L. Rajput, R.C. Bhatt, 1987, 'Painted Grey Ware culture in Garhwal Himalaya: New Evidence and Interpretation', *Puratattva* 11-14 (17).

Nautiyal, K.P., 1989, *Protohistoric India*, Agam Kala Prakashan, Delhi.

Nautiyal, K.P., B.M. Khanduri, 1991, *Emergence of Early Culture in Garhwal Central Himalaya (A Study based on Excavations at Thapli and Ranihat)*, University Museum Srinagar, Garhwal.

Sahi, M.D.N. 1994, *Aspects of Indian Archaeology*, Delhi.

Sankalia, H.D., 1963, 'New Light on Indo-Iranian or Western Asiatic Relations Between 1700-12 B.C.,' *Artibus Asiae* 26,(34) 312-32.

Sharma, A.K., 1997, 'Excavàtion at Ladyura, Kumaon Himalaya, *Him Kanti* (Archaeology, Art & History); 71-76. (Prof. K.P. Nautiyal Felicitation Volume), ed. B.M. Khanduri, Vinod Nauṭiyal, Book India Publishing Co., Delhi.

Sircar, D.C., 1960, *Studies in the Geography of Ancient and Mediaeval India*, Banaras.

Stacul, G. 1987, 'Prehistoric and Protohistoric Swat, Pakistan', *East & West*, vol. 27, 1967-68.

Tucci, G. 1977, 'On Swat: The Dards and connected Problems', *East and West*, New Series, vol. 27, pp. 9-103.

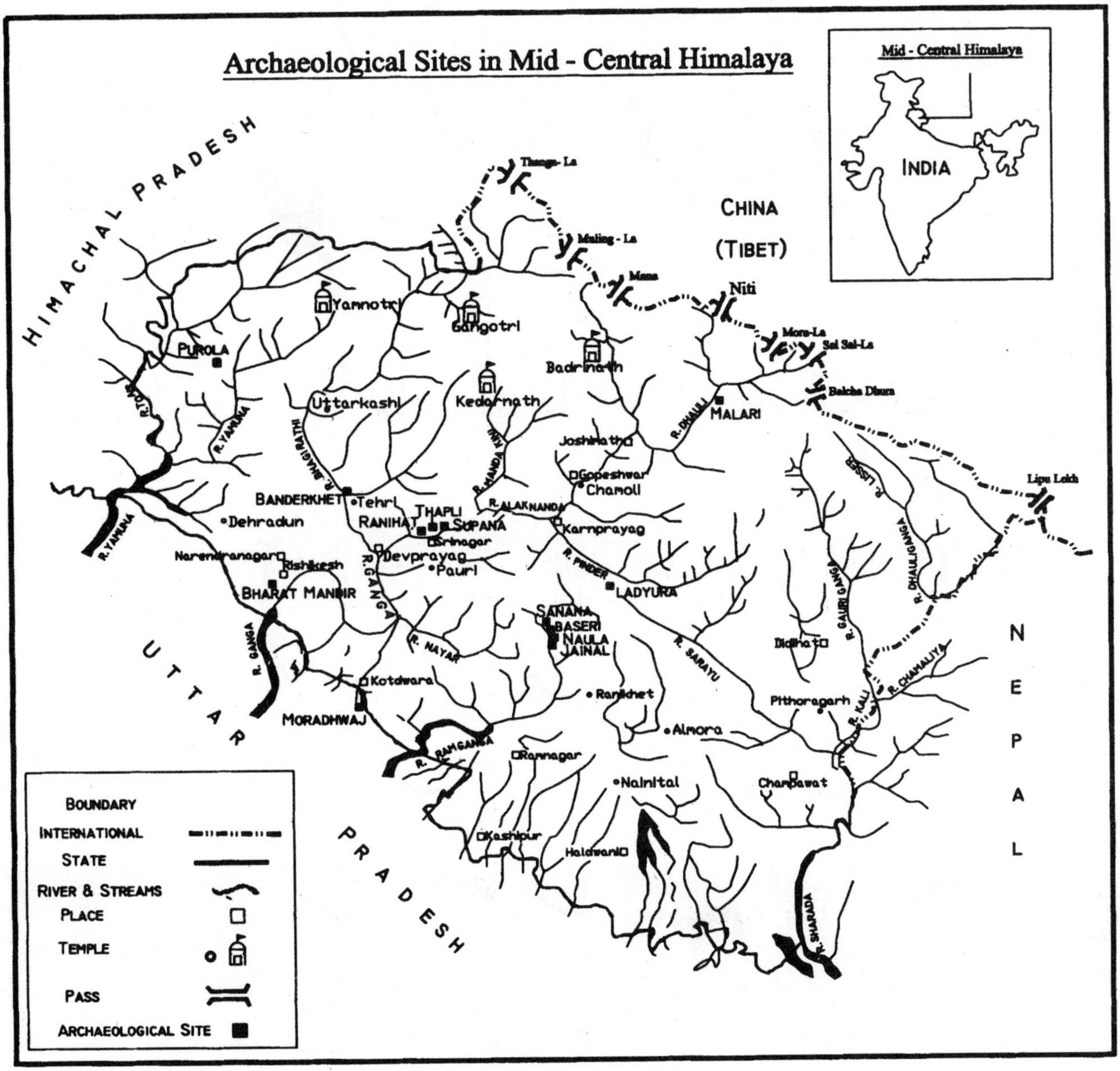
Archaeological Sites in Mid - Central Himalaya
Mid - Central Himalaya
INDIA
CHINA
(TIBET)
HIMACHAL PRADESH
UTTAR PRADESH
NEPAL
Thanga- La
Maling - La
Mana
Niti
Mora-La
Sal Sal-La
Balcha Dhura
Lipu Lekh
Yamnotri
Gangotri
Badrinath
Kedarnath
Uttarkashi
PUROLA
MALARI
Joshimath
Gopeshwar
Chamoli
BANDERKHET
Tehri
THAPLI
RANIHAT
SUPANA
Srinagar
Devprayag
Pauri
Karnprayag
Dehradun
Narendranagar
Rishikesh
BHARAT MANDIR
LADYURA
SANANA
BASERI
NAULA
JAINAL
Kotdwara
MORADHWAJ
Ranikhet
Almora
Pithoragarh
Champawat
Ramnagar
Nainital
Kashipur
Haldwani
R. YAMUNA
R. TONS
R. BHAGIRATHI
R. ALAKNANDA
R. MANDAKINI
R. DHAULI
R. GANGA
R. NAYAR
R. PINDER
R. SARAYU
R. RAMGANGA
R. GAURI GANGA
R. DHAULIGANGA
R. CHAMALIYA
R. KALI
R. SHARADA
R. LASSER
BOUNDARY
INTERNATIONAL
STATE
RIVER & STREAMS
PLACE
TEMPLE
PASS
ARCHAEOLOGICAL SITE

Fig. 1.

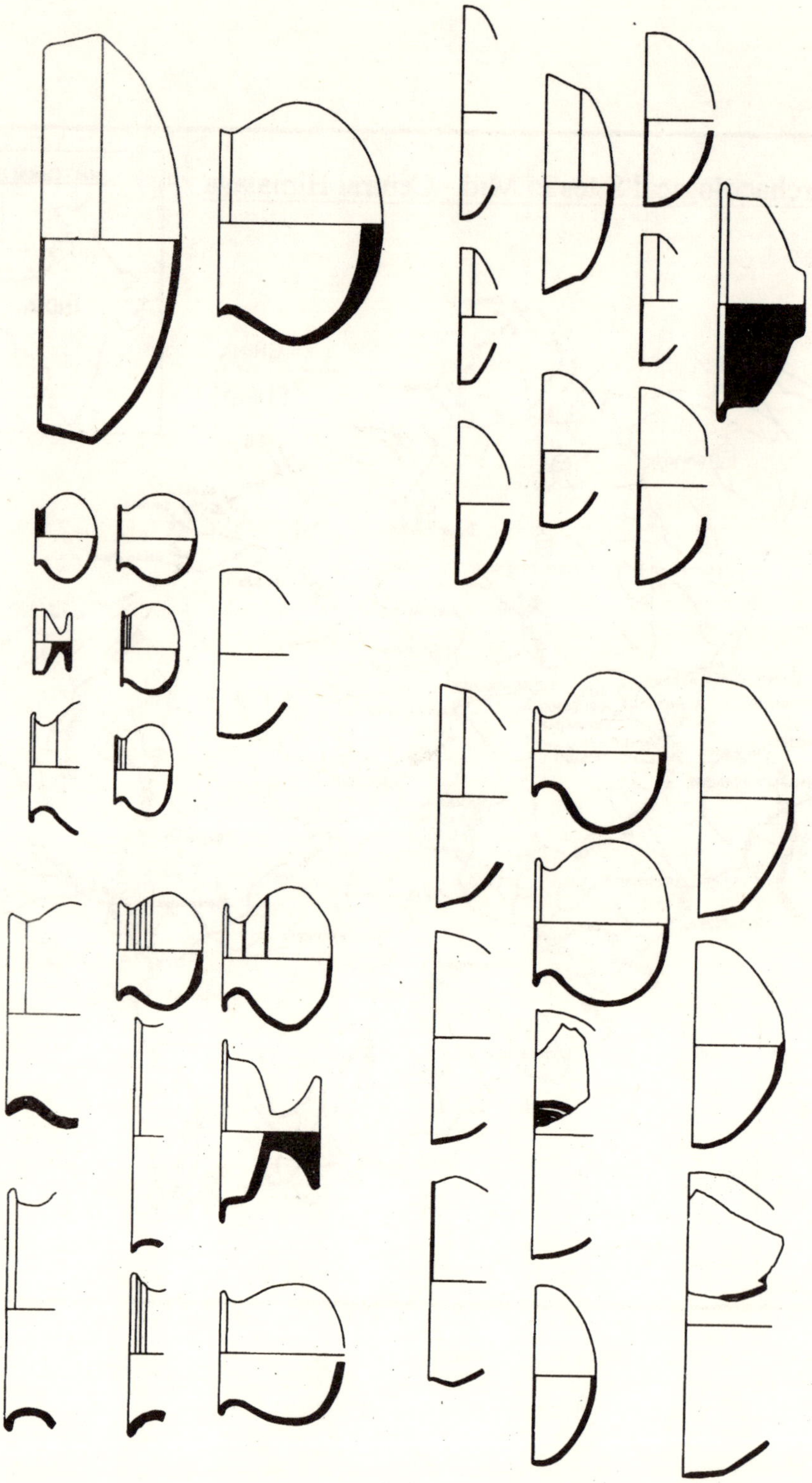

Fig. 2. Megalithic Pottery from Burials, Sannan, and Baseri, Almora

Excavation at Pachkheri: A Megalithic Habitation Site

AMARENDRA NATH*

Pachkheri (20° 55' E; 79° 30' N) lies slightly over 60 km south by south-east of Nagpur, approachable via Kuhi-Mandhal road leading to Ambhora. There is a regular state bus service connecting this place besides rail link up to its tahsil, Kuhi, on the Nagpur-Nagbhir section. Earlier the site was explored by the author[1] which reported a rare combination of ancient habitation (PKD-1) associated with the remains of menhirs (PKD-2) and pit-circle with cairn (PKD-3).

In all four cuttings, one each at PKD-1, and PKD-3 and two at PKD-2, were laid out in order to ascertain the sequence of culture and chronology of the site and the nature and formation of the menhirs and pit-circle with cairn, besides its cprrelation with the habitation strata (fig.1). It afforded evidence of five distinct occupational deposits (fig. 2).

Period I being Mesolithic in character was noticed in the cuttings of PKD-2, while both the types of burials assigned to Period II were coeval with the lowermost horizon of the iron using folk noted at the habitation site (PKD-1). The remaining three successive occupational period identified were Mauryan (Period III), Satavahana (Period IV) and Medieval (Period V).

At PKD-2 in Period I, the trench laid on the south side of the main road yielded microlithic assemblage, free from pottery, from layer (2) while the other cutting laid on the north side of the same road has reported it from layer (3) (fig. 3). It may be clarified here cuttings are along the south-western slope, but due to its ruthless cutting to form artificial terraces for paddy cultivation, its primary soil coverage has undergone drastic change in the recent past. It has caused denudation of primary sediments in the southern cutting area living a thin deposit over the microlithic later while in the northern cutting secondary deposition led to thick accumulation over the said layer. However, the composition of the sediments yielding microlithic tools has remained homogeneous. The deposit 25 to 30 cm thick, composed of poor clay content of compact dull brown colour, mixed with coarse lateritic gravel, rests over the consolidated matrix of Deccan trap. The microlithic assemblage essentially non-geometric in character comprise mostly simple artefacts such as flakes, chips, blades, flake and blade cores, apart from a few specimens of points and a backed blade.

Period II attributed to Megalithic culture of Vidarbha, revealed occupational layers of painted and plain pottery supported by iron technology, in the cutting of PKD-1 which was laid on a resasonobly flat land at 253 m contour elevation. The deposit overlying the natural black cotton soil mixed gravelly material was homogeneous deposit of grayish soil of semi-compact nature, represented by three layers, namely (9) to (7). The ceramic

*Director, Archaeological Survey of India, New Delhi.

industry of the period were mainly Black-and-Red ware, Red ware with and without paintings and black-slipped ware. The shapes met with were vases, bowls and dishes. Some of the shapes of red and Black-and-Red wares bore black paintings on rim and shoulder portions. The design-elements included latticed diamonds, comb pattern over the shoulder and group of vertical strokes covering both inner and outer surfaces of the rim.

Apart from patches of mud-floors, a kiln of U-shape was noticed. It was contemporary to layer (8) and its chamber was cut into layer (9) while its base was resting over the natural soil. It measured 85 x 75 x 10 cm.

An iron rod (PKD-1) and a ring fastener of plano-convex shape and a copper bowl (PKD-3) are some of the important finds of this horizon.

Period III, represented by layers (6) and (5), attributed to the Mauryan period, did not reveal the diagnostic pottery types, however, it brought to light a few associated red wares showing vases of Ahichchhatra 10A type[2] and Black-and-Red ware bowls generally occurring in the NBPW horizon in the Gangetic plains. The deposit was comprised of semi-compact brownish soil mixed with ash, charcoal and bones. The ceramic traditions were of a coarse dull red ware and micaceous red ware. A mud-floor pf uneven type (4 x 4 m) with irregular post-holes was recorded from this horizon. Among the finds animal bones of the *Bos* species predominated over other species. Important antiquities included iron sickle and ring-fastener, terracotta annular bead and an ear-stud.

Layers (4) and (3) of the habitation in Period IV were attributed to the Satavahana. The deposit comprised a semi-compact light brown soil mixed with stone rubble. Earlier pottery types decreased in frequency and medium fabric of red and brown-slipped ware made its appearance. Important shapes consitituted typical multi-lipped vases, storage jars, basins and lid-cum-bowls. Some of the characteristic stamped pottery showed *tri-ratna* occurring at regular intervals on the shoulders of vases while a group of rosettes figured below a thick rim (Pl. 1). The deposit was much disturbed due to a later pit activity.

Among the antiquities arrowheads, knives and U-shaped clamp of iron, polisher and grinder of stone, votive tanks, spindle-whorls of terracotta, and beads of semi-precious stone and terracotta deserve special mention.

In Period V, layers (2) and (1) composed of grey to black soil mixed with brick-bats were assigned to medieval period. The distinguishing ceramic industry included grey and red ware of medium to coarse fabric. The frequency of antiquities found from this horizon were higher than the rest of the cultural levels. It included couple of gold objects namely a tiny rectangular fragment of a bangle (?) and a disc, copper objects in the form of bangles and rings, iron objects like knife, arrowhead, chisel, spatula, spoon, needles, nails and clamp, terracotta objects like mother goddess, animal figurines, wheel and spindles, skin rubber, crucible, etc., beads of semi-precious stones, glass and terracotta were also reported. Dating evidence was provided by a copper coin issued by Muhammad Shah I of Bahmani dynasty (*circa* fourteenth century AD).

Reverting to the excavations of menhirs at PKD-2 it may be noted that these menhirs are one of the unique group of monuments ever reported from any of the Megalithic site situated in the Wainganga valley (Pl. 2). Here, Menhirs 1 to 4 basically aligned in the north-south direction, fall in the cutting of north side of the road (Fig. 3) while the remaining two at south (fig. 4). Menhirs of these two cutting need not be separated into two group as the laying of road across the alignment is a recent phenomenon, it is quite likely that in the process of laying road some of the intermediary menhirs were got uprooted.

The cuttings reaveled a departure in the mode of erection of Menhirs noted earlier in the excavations at Maski where the excavated ones revealed that it was raised on the existing ground itself without any pit and was propped up all round by a ring of rubble packing[3]. In contrast, here these were all found raised in pits of various shapes and size, dug into the natural soil. Like Maski, no sepulchral association was observed either in the respective pits or within the excavated area. But some of the pits showed some special features.

Menhir 1 consists of an undressed monolith showing sub-rectangular cross-section. Tilted towards south, it measures 125 x 90 x 35 cm. For erecting a pit of approximately 40 m deep and 120 cm in diameter was dug. After erection it was filled with dug up soil from all the sides, however, from the western side it was strengthened by heavy duty stones, one of the upright stone packing was even visible above the ground level.

Menhir 2 slightly deviated towards west from the alignment, was raised at a distance of approximately 180 cm from the former. It consisted of barely worked slab of conical form and irregular section. Tilted towards east it measured 95 x 60 x 25 cm. The circular pit (dia 85 cm) up to a depth of 45 cm bore some special features. Along the pit line it had ring of stone-work forming an enclosure, an unusual phenomenon never reported before. Inner part of it was given a dressing of fine levigated clay at the base and was pitched with not only with uneven stones but also by two split stones of triangular shape. Above it the pit was filled with usual packing of stone mixed soil.

Almost in the same alignment of the former was found another Menhir of rectangular shape (70 x 40 x 15 cm). This Menhir 3 was laid horizontally in an oblong pit (80 x 45 x 20 cm) with a tilt towards south. After laying the partially dressed slab the sides of the pit were meticulousely pitched with stones.

Further deviated towards east, from the alignment of the fomer two, Menhir 4 was one of the largest Menhirs erected at the site. Tilted towards south, it measured 215 x 100 x 40 cm. Barely worked boulder damaged from the top was fixed in U-shaped tapering pit (170 x 100 cm).

Menhirs 5 was erected on the south side of the road at a distance of approximately 25 m from the former. Of this menhir only the ghost pit of conical shape was noticed in the cutting of Menhir 6. Its removal, in recent past, for domestic purpose was verified from the villagers.

Pit-circle with cairn (PKD-3) consisted of a circle of undressed Deccan trap boulders with an external diameter of 16 m (fig. 5). The circle stones of south-western side were dislodged while some of the stones in westerń side were virtually removed in recent days. The centre of the circle entombed a near oval pit burial measuring 380 x 300 x 80 cm. The upper section of the pit showed a deposit of the gravel mixed brownish red soil which formed the contemporary working level (layer 3), while the lower section had natural gravel deposit. Towards the eastern base of the pit a stone slab (170 x 45 cm) of Menhir-6 (PKD-2) type was found placed in north-south orientation. No other material of funerary rights was found at the base, however, a battered copper bowl was placed at the upper portion of the northern inner edge of the pit. Further, say 120 cm west of the pit were noticed red ware vases having typical flared or near funnel type rims, in a battered condition immediately above the contemporary working-level. Apparently, the grave goods were placed at all levels, without any regular order, having evidently been placed simultaneousely with the throwing in of the filling earth. The first 55 cm of the pit (layer-5) was filled with fine brown clayey earth brought from elsewhere while its remaining upper portion was piled up to a height of 60 cm with uneven local stone chips (layer 4), forming an hemispherical heap above the contemporary working level (i.e., ancient humus, layer 3). After the completion of interment process the circumference of the circle was sealed by two successive layers of earth acquiring the shape of the hemispherical tumulus. The penultimate layer (2) was dump of say 80 cm in height of lacally available earth of dark brown colour occasionally mixed with stone chips. Above it, layer (1) was the deposit of cairn and brownish earth sustematically served as dressing to the tumulus. Its concentration on the southern half was more than on the northern half of the circle. Such an uneven scattering of cairn was mainly due to the lack of uniform serwing system, it had nothing to do perhaps with the disposal practice.

The excavation carried out at the site was trial in nature but has provided sufficient date to add our knowledge especially on the archaeology of the mentions of the region.

REFERENCES

1. *Indian Archaeology, 1987-88-A Review*, pp. 85-87, fig. 19.

2. A. Ghosh and K.C. Panigrahi, 'Pottery of Ahichchhatra (U.P.)', *Ancient India*, No. 1, pp. 42-43.

3. B.K. Thapar, 'Maski 1954: A Chalcolithic Site of the Southern Deccan', *Ancient India*, No. 13, pp. 35-37, Pl. XV, XVI.

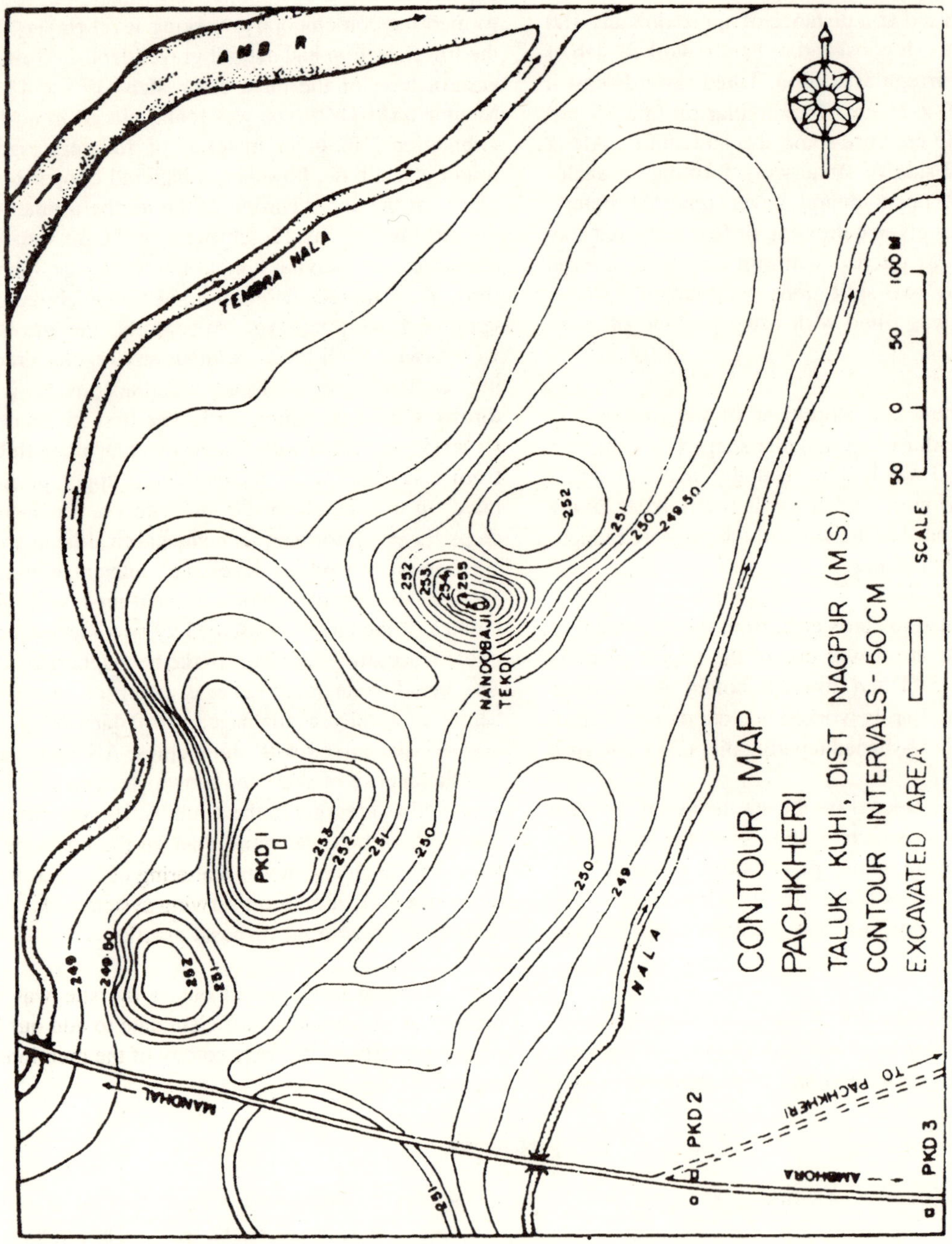
CONTOUR MAP
PACHKHERI
TALUK KUHI, DIST NAGPUR (M S)
CONTOUR INTERVALS - 50 CM
EXCAVATED AREA
SCALE
50 0 50 100 M
NANDOBAJI TEKDI
TEMBRA NALA
NALA
PKD 1
PKD 2
PKD 3
TO PACHKHERI
MANDHAL
AMBHORA

Fig. 1.

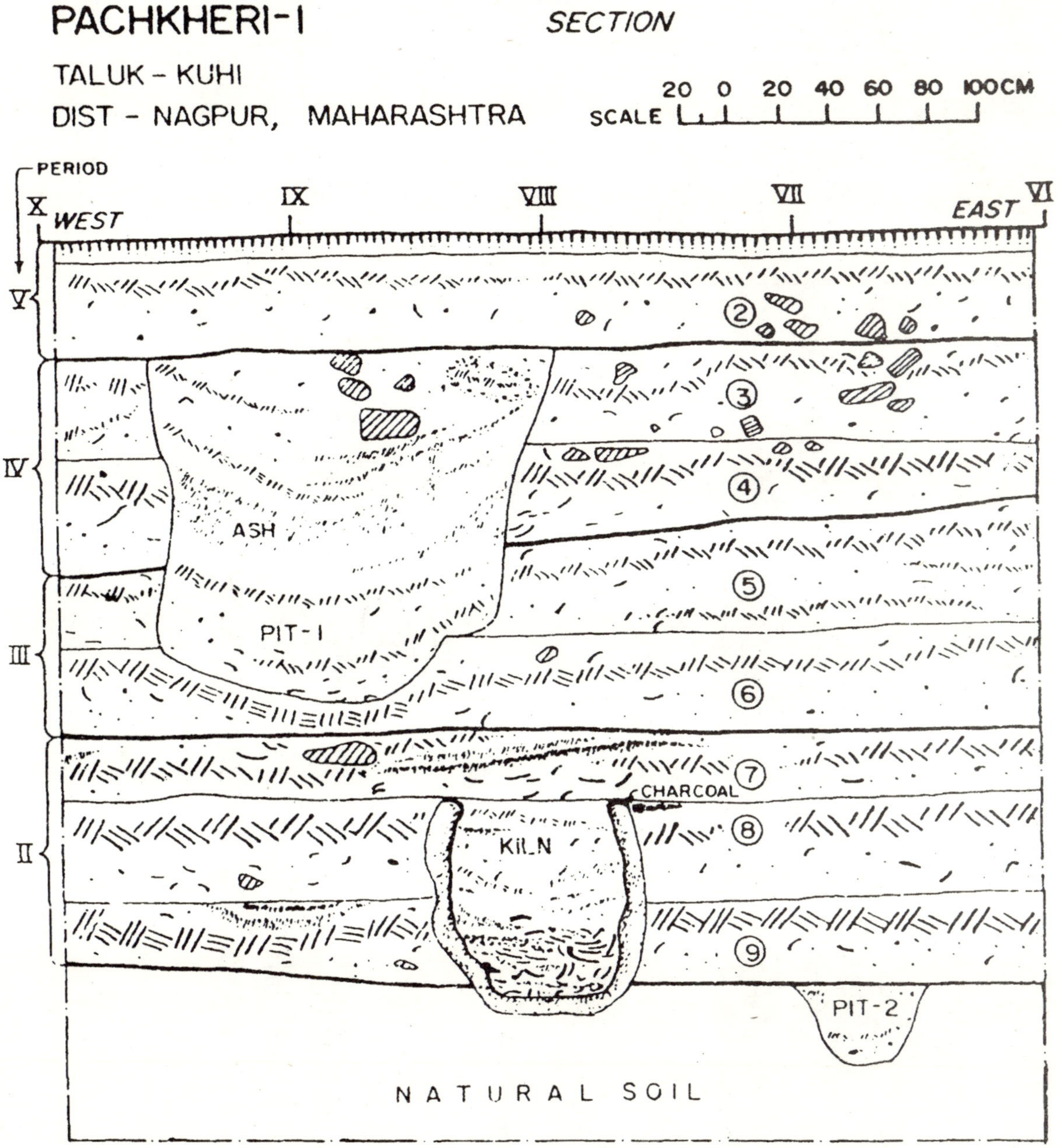
PACHKHERI-1
SECTION
TALUK - KUHI
DIST - NAGPUR, MAHARASHTRA
20 0 20 40 60 80 100CM
SCALE
PERIOD
X
IX
VIII
VII
VI
WEST
EAST
V
IV
III
II
2
3
4
5
6
7
8
9
ASH
PIT-1
KILN
CHARCOAL
PIT-2
NATURAL SOIL

Fig. 2.

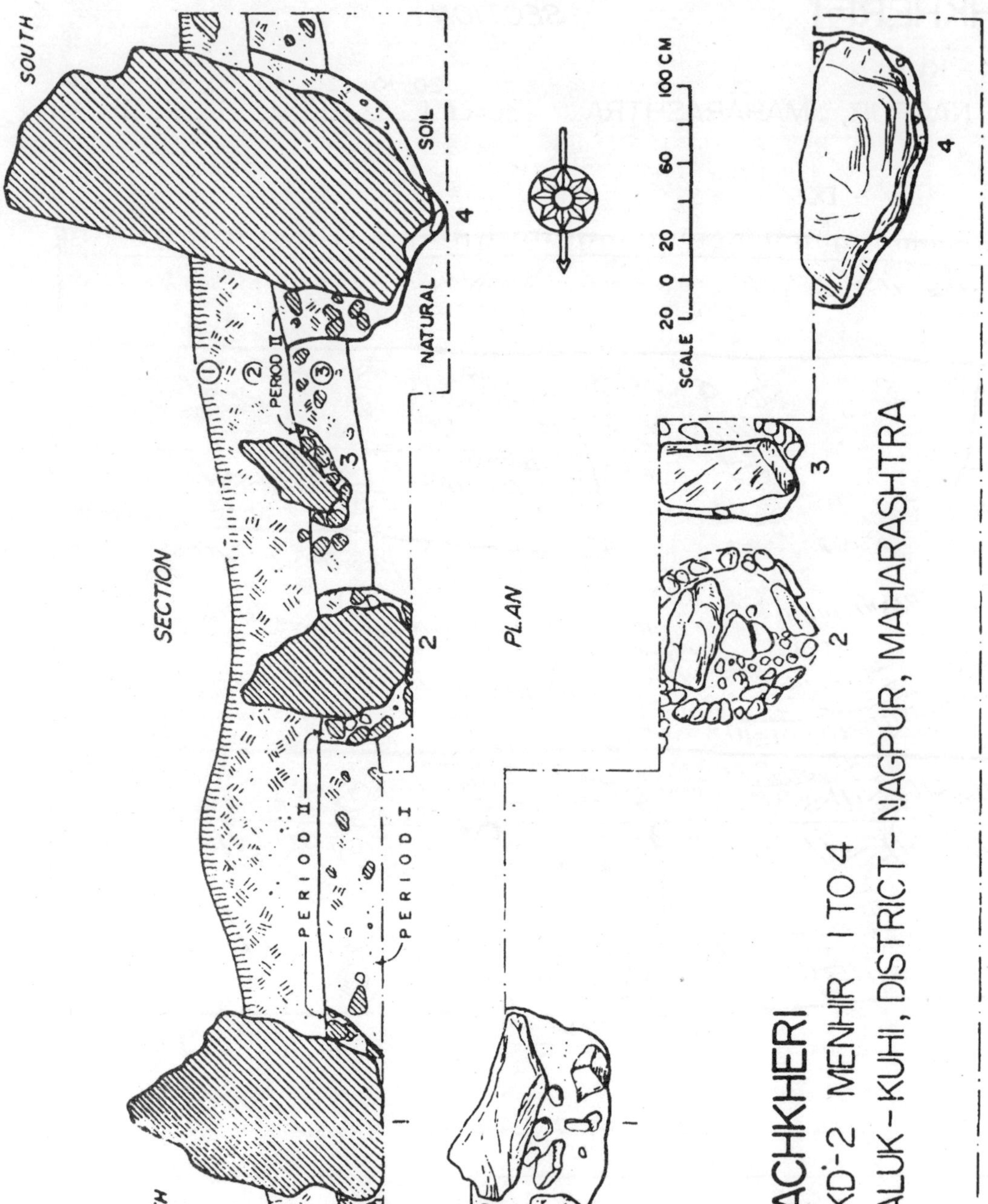
NORTH
SECTION
SOUTH
PERIOD II
PERIOD I
NATURAL SOIL
PLAN
SCALE 20 0 20 60 100 CM
PACHKHERI
PKD-2 MENHIR 1 TO 4
TALUK - KUHI, DISTRICT - NAGPUR, MAHARASHTRA

Fig. 3.

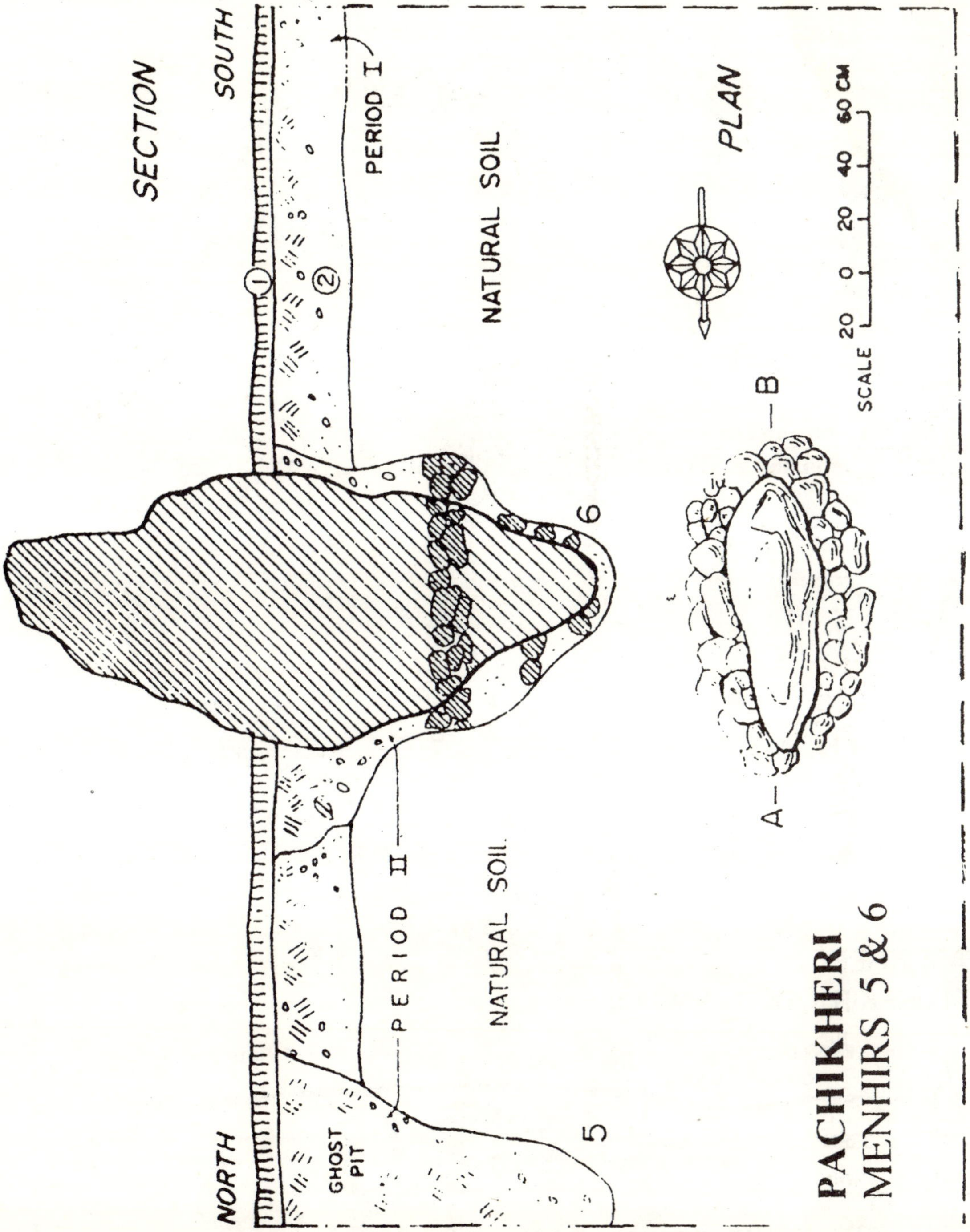
SECTION
NORTH
SOUTH
1
2
GHOST PIT
PERIOD I
PERIOD II
NATURAL SOIL
NATURAL SOIL
5
6
PLAN
A
B
SCALE
20 0 20 40 60 CM
PACHIKHERI
MENHIRS 5 & 6

Fig. 4.

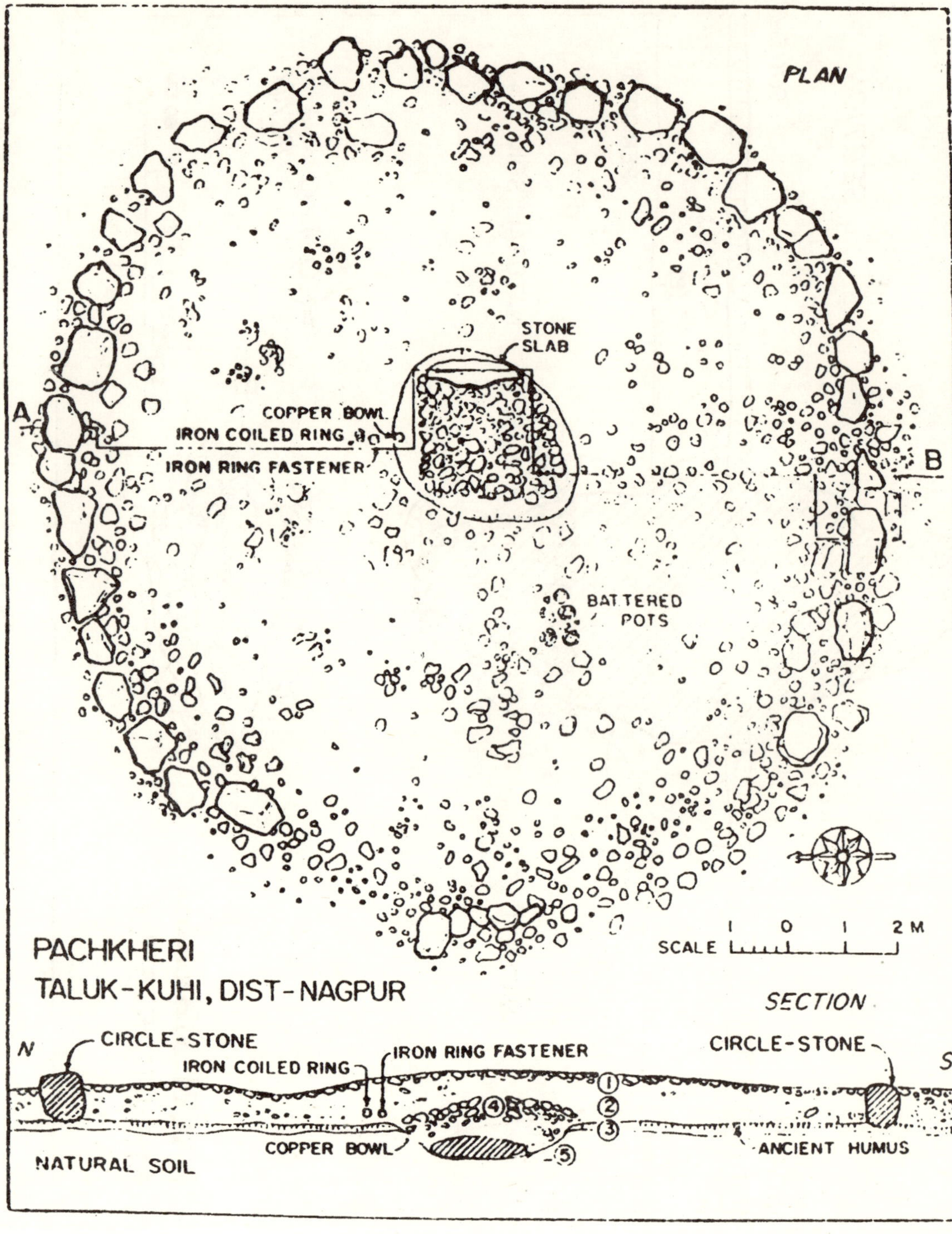
PLAN
STONE SLAB
COPPER BOWL
IRON COILED RING
IRON RING FASTENER
A
B
BATTERED POTS
PACHKHERI
TALUK-KUHI, DIST-NAGPUR
SCALE
1 0 1 2 M
SECTION
N
S
CIRCLE-STONE
IRON COILED RING
IRON RING FASTENER
CIRCLE-STONE
COPPER BOWL
NATURAL SOIL
ANCIENT HUMUS

Fig. 5.

Living Megalithic Practices Amongst the Madia Gonds of Bhamragad, District Gadchiroli, Maharashtra

ANUJA GEETALI*

Megalithism in peninsular India includes a variety of sepulchral and commemorative monuments which are either built of large stones, rude or chiselled and generally associated with a somewhat homogeneous group of the Black-and-Red ware and an equally homogeneous group of iron tools and weapons (Ghosh 1989). Megalithism in some form or the other is still in vogue in India among the tribal population of different regions such as the Kurumbars, the Gadabas, the Bodos, the Mundas, etc. The north-eastern states are rich in megalithic tradition. The *Lotha Nagas*, the *Kaccha Nagas* and the *Khasis* in Assam erect memorial stones over the burials.

One such survival of megalithism is observed amongst the Madia Gonds of Bhamragad, District Gadchiroli. In the present work an attempt has been made to highlight the tradition of erecting memorial stones prevalent among this tribe and also to provide a deeper insight into the culture of this living tradition, its socio-economic and religious settings and its persistence in the present times. A brief comparative analysis of the ancient megalithic stone-circles of Vidarbha and modern monuments of the Madias has been made. In all four villages, Hemalkasa, Gollaguda, Zareguda and Lahiri were selected for the present study and they have yielded very interesting information.

The Madia Gonds

In Maharashtra, Madias are located in Chandrapur and Godchiroli districts and are chiefly concentrated in the Bhamragad region. Of the total 128 villages in Bhamragad tehsil Madias inhabit one hundred and eleven. Bhamragad became an independent tehsil on 14 March, 1997 of the Gadchiroli district. The main rivers here are Indravati, Palam Gautami and Parl-Kotta. The whole area is surrounded by hills spreading up to the border touching Bastar. The soil is alluvial loam, gravely coarse and somewhat sandy.

Madia means, 'forest-dwellers' (Deogaonkar 1982) and they do not like to abandon their wild habitat. The Madias can be subdivided into two groups. The *Bada* and the *Chota Madia*, depending upon their traditional places of domicile. The *Bada Madias* live in the far off forest tracts on hills and in relatively more primitive condition. The *Chota Madias* are more modernised and have migrated from the forests to the plains. Though the subsistence economy of the Madias is cultivation, it is often supplemented by hunting, fishing and gathering. Collection of honey, gum and *mahua* flowers, plucking of *tendu* leaves, cutting bamboos for paper mill is common among them. Their religion can be described as animism because they have a tendency to give a form to every object, animate or inanimate. The *Perma,* i.e., *pujari* has great significance

*Research Scholar, Deccan College, Pune

in their society. He performs all religious rites. Traditionally, he is the medicine man and inherits the knowledge of herbal medicines. The chief deities of the Madias are *Farasapen, Bada Deo, Tadoba* and *Mariai*. *Ghotuls* are common among the Madias. This is a large house near the village where unmarried youths and maidens get together to sing and dance at night. It is an interesting and useful social institution.

The Memorial Stones

The monuments erected by the tribal people include menhirs, stone-seats, cromlechs, dolmens and stone-circles. These monuments are either sepulchral or commemorative in nature. The Madia Gonds of Bhamragad erect two varieties of memorial stones of, *viz*., menhirs and dolmens. Menhirs are the vertically standing, dressed or undressed stones. It neither encloses a burial nor protects it. In the Gondi it is called *Uraskal* from the words *'Urasna'*, to bury and *'kal'* a stone (Deogaonkar) Menhirs are erected for men and usually stand in long rows by the roadside near the village boundary but sometimes found in the village also. They are broader at the base and narrow towards the top. It is not polished on either side and is hewn from a big rock. One can see menhirs of two types: (a) wooden and (b) stone. The wooden-one cannot be termed as megalithic monument; it is rather a memorial pillar. The stone menhirs are generally of granite. Dolmens are stone-slabs or boulders arranged in a square or a rectangular plan supporting a capstone. The whole construction is above the ground. The function of dolmen is two-fold. If they are found isolated and without any association of menhir then they are erected for a woman. But if dolmens are found at the foot of menhir then they serve as a seat for the dead person. The Madias believe that their ancestors stand in the form of menhirs and dolmens are erected as seats for the dead when they are tired.

Funerary Rites

When a person dies the whole village assemble and the village headman announces mourning period for three days, which is called *Polava* (Deogoankar: 25). Certain things, such as raw rice grains, water in a small pot and the cloths, mirror, comb and turban of the dead person are kept near the burial; since the Madias believe that the dead person would need these things in his after life. The earthen pots are not specially made for funerary use but those which were used daily by the dead person. Holes are made on all the things which were left for the dead so that nobody can use them again.

The Madias practice two types of burials. In the first one, the dead person is buried and then covered with soil. Big stones are then properly placed in rectangular shape by using clay as binding material so that these stones stick together. It is the most economic type of burial. Poor people who cannot afford to spend much money follow this type. The other type is, constructing a tomb (*samadhi*). The tombs are of different types and are generally built of cement.

Erection of the Memorial Stones

The menhirs and dolmens are not erected in one single spot in the burial ground, but are found in clusters. Since the Madia society is an egalitarian society, the burials and the memorial stones are not according to any class-wise or caste-wise division. However, clusters are mainly family clusters The Madias generally bury their dead near the place where the other relatives are also buried. But no specific place is allotted to a specific family.

The memorial stones can be constructed anytime within the period of one month to one year after the death of a person. The whole village participates in collecting the stone for the memorial. If a reputed person dies, the stone is brought in a bullock-cart. As the whole village participates stone is decided according to convenience rather than by an auspicious period (*muhurta*). According to one informant, *Gibba* the stone is cut by an axe and is tied by a string. The stone is then brought in a procession with dancing and singing to the accompaniment of beating of drums. Women are also allowed to participate in procession. The stone is brought to the burial ground and then the *Perma* erects the memorial stone. In the absence of the *Perma* any male villager or relative can erect the memorial stone. The *Perma* sacrifices raw rice grains and a chicken. The day on which the memorial stone is erected is called *'Teravi'*. The memorial stone is not worshipped regularly. On occasions such as *Diwali* and *Pandum* the relatives of dead person visit the memorial stone. They do not perform *puja* at the stone but offer some raw rice grains. A newly-married couple generally visits the memorial stone and they also offer raw rice to beget the blessings of the dead person. Traditionally, the Madias do not erect memorial stone for an infant (whose teeth have not grown and who are breast-fed). In case of an unmarried woman her parents can erect a dolmen for her. If a woman dies in pregnancy or childbirth, no memorial stone is erected and she is buried on the other side of the nulla. A person who dies because of some digestive diseases is cremated and not buried but his memorial stone can be erected.

The memorial stones are constructed on the outskirts of the village. Some are also found inside the village, e.g., in the village, Karempally, not less than thirty are erected in the heart of village. So there is no specific place where the menhirs and dolmens are erected but generally they are located on the communal land of the village. The length of the menhirs varies between 60 cm to 170 cm. The biggest menhir is in the village Kandodi near Bhamragad town. The more important or famous a man the taller is the stone. The height of the menhir also depends upon the age of the dead person. If the person who has died is elderly then the stone is greater in height. The stone used for menhir is granite and it is brought from the adjoining mountains but sometimes the Madias bring the stone from riverbeds. The stone is properly dressed before erection. The menhirs can also be made of wood. The *Gond-Gowaries* (skilled in carpentry) are hired to make the wooden menhirs out of the wood of silk cotton tree (*sawari*). It costs around Rs. 500 to Rs. 1000/ to carve the wood and to decorate. People who can afford this amount order wooden menhirs. They are sometimes painted with colours like blue and are shown with horns and 10 paise coins are stuck in place of eyes. The *Bada Madia* sacrifice a bull after erecting a menhir. It may be due to this practice that bovine decorations are sometimes carved on the wooden pillar. The stone menhirs too are sometimes decorated with wooden motifs such as peacock, guns, deer-heads and buffalo or bison-horns, all placed on a wooden platform fixed on the top portion of the menhir. These are often the objects liked by the dead person. The dolmens are always made of stone. Wood is not used in dolmens. The length of the dolmens varies between 40 cm to 12 cm. And the capstone is sometimes very high measuring 90 cm in width. Unlike the menhirs, the height of the dolmen does not indicate status or age of the woman.

Ancient Megalithic Monuments of Vidarbha

The north-eastern region of Maharashtra, i.e., Vidarbha is best known for its megalithic remains on a large scale. The Nagpur University and the Deccan College, Pune have excavated most of the megalithic sites in Vidarbha. Sites like Takalghat-Khapa, Kharwada, Raipur, Junapani, Mahurjhari, Naikund and Borgaon have produced remarkable data for better understanding of the megalithic culture in Maharashtra. After studying the burials, it is apparent that death was an important event in the life of megalithic community. The elaborate way in which the stone-circles were made or the cist and chambers were arranged and executed indicates that it must have involved the united effort of a fairly large section of the community (Deo, S.B. 1983). Though the ancient stone-circles and the Madia memorial stones, though superficially, seem typologically very different as also chronologically wide apart, it is felt that the cultural study of the living practice of megalithism in the vicinity of ancient megalithic circles might be able to provide some valuable ethnographic insights of the cultural settings of the ancient monuments. Hence, a brief comparative analysis of the ancient and modern monuments shows the following points:

The megalithic practices of Madias suggest some important aspects of their life such as their social and religious practices, their superstitions, their beliefs, their economic conditions and their emotions regarding the dead.

Variations in the ancient stone-circles such as size, number of builders, quantum of filling cist or boulder chamber within, funerary goods, presence or absence of horse remains and presence or absence of skeletal remains indicate social differentiation. Whether this reflects a hierarchical society with sharply defined powers, roles and functions is difficult to surmise. Madia evidence shows that variation in megalithic construction indicates social differentiation, particularly, economic differentiation but not necessarily any sharp hierarchical strata of the society. Clusters of megaliths occur in both, the ancient and the present Madia contexts. The Madia analogy suggests that they could be family or clan clusters spanning over some generations.

The Madias deposit an interesting variety of funerary goods for the use of the dead. They are mainly personal goods of daily and personal use; more often specific objects of the dead are also be interred in the grave. In the ancient megaliths too one regularly encounters earthen pots, nail parers, craft-tools and adzes. These in fact are the minimum repertoire encountered practically in all megaliths. Besides these other larger craft-tools and in some case heavy weapons are encountered. The Madias of present day, place guns carved of wood over a menhir to indicate the person's preference for modern weapons of hunting but has nothing to do with any special or warrior status.

The ancient megaliths do not contain child burials. Very few female skeletons have been identified. The Madias, on the other hand, have a separate variety, the dolmens constructed for women while the men are represented by the vertically standing menhirs. Small children and infants are disposed off without the memorial construction. The Madia analogy also suggest that age and experience, with which comes the headship and responsibility of the family or the clan, earned greater respect which is mirrored in the funerary practices.

Sacrificing a chicken is a normal practice as a part of the funerary ritual, but to ward off the ill effects of magic and witchcraft, sacrificial offering a bull is considered more prestigious. The wooden menhirs with a bullhead perhaps implies that the ancestors were thought to be possessing bovine powers. The occasional presence of the horse in the ancient graves may have similar implications.

The memorial stones are raised much after the actual event of the death and primary disposal of the body. The desire to honour and remember the dead to interact socially through feasts to the entire family or community seems to suggest that the memorials had relevance to the family to cultivate the continued social support-structure and to bring all the family and members together periodically. Similar ancient context cannot be ruled out.

Given the number of memorials, it does not appear that the Madias are inclined to raise memorials for every person dying. The gender and age preferences are obvious as also the economic status of the person and the families are concerned. This hypothesis can be projected backwards to the ancient megaliths also.

Construction and erection of memorials is a community effort amongst the Madias. Voluntary community help is organised and was forthcoming. This strengthens the social bonds as well as within the community, which prevents the isolation of kin-groups in calamities and helps to gather together. The large stone-circles of ancient times may also have required community help and the compulsion could also have been similar. The Madia practices indicate that the influence from other cultures can be absorbed without giving up the original and traditional practices. The new influences may alter the extraneous features of the memorials but not necessarily the inner emotions and psycho-religious world. The variations in ancient megaliths may also reflect cross-cultural influences.

Belief in life-after-death is common to both. Probably also common is the proactive role of ancestors as 'guardian angels' of the community, standing guard on the outskirts of the settlement. The absence of habitation sites in case of ancient megaliths also indicate that they were constructed away from the settlements.

The paper has tried to facilitate understanding the behavioural pattern of the Madia-funerary practices.

REFERENCES

Deo, S.B., 1983, 'Personality of Vidarbha Megaliths', in Dhavalikar, M.K. and Deo, S.B.(eds), *Studies in Indian Archaeology*, p.23.

Deogaonkar, S.G., 1982, *The Madia of Bhamragad*, Inter-Indian Publication., New Delhi, pp.11 and 25.

Ghosh, A., 1989, *Encyclopedia of Indian Archaeology*, Munshiram Manoharlal Pvt., New Delhi, p.110.

The Underwater Exploration of Mahabalipuram in Bay of Bengal

ALOK TRIPATHI*

Introduction

Mahabalipuram (12°37' N, 80°12' E) is a coastal town famous for ancient temples of the Pallava period. It is located nearly 60 km south of Chennai, the capital of Tamil Nadu. It was also famous as an ancient sea-port on the Coromandel Coast. By the time of Narasimha Varman I (A.D. 630-68) this port-town had become an important entrepot for local and foreign trade, especially with China and South-East Asian countries. The coastal area south of Chennai has long sandy beaches. The area around Mahabalipuram also has granite outcrops running parallel to and beyond the shore. Pallavas utilised these outcrops for carving out cave-temples, *rathas* and large *bas-reliefs*. Some low rocky outcrops are also seen in the sea near Mahabalipuram. Accounts of early European travellers make it clear that the drifting sand affected many monuments located on the seashore. Besides the changes in shoreline also has affected the monuments on the coast. It is believed that some of the monuments on the coast at Mahabalipuram had submerged in sea.

Systematic underwater archaeological exploration of Mahabalipuram was felt necessary to examine the veracity of such a belief. Underwater studies also generate data of scientific, cultural and educational value. The results of such study may also be of immense help for protection of coastal monuments, which are threatened by the incursion of the sea. The Underwater Archaeology Wing of the Archaeological Survey of India carried out onshore exploration from Saluvankuppam in the north to Sadras in the south and offshore explorations off Mahabalipuram in Bay of Bengal in November 2001 and March 2002[1].

History

The antiquity of Mahabalipuram is not certain. Presence of megalithic pottery in the early levels of some of the excavations in this region and megalithic monuments located nearby suggest that the area was inhabited during megalithic period. *Melange* mentioned by Ptolemy, to the north of Poduke, could be identified with Mamallapuram. Discovery of two Roman coins of Theodosius (*circa* AD 326-395) at Mahabalipuram (Ramaswami 1989: 23-24) indicates that the site might have been a trading centre visited by the Romans during that period. The Chinese had regular maritime exchange with south India and particularly with the kingdom of Kanchi and Mahabalipuram could have been a Pallava port. *Perumpanarruppadai* by Rudran Kannanar, describes a port-city near Kanchipuram as 'Nirpeyaru', which is identified with Kadanmallai of Thirumangai Alvar (Venkkayya 1909:233; Iyengar 1928). One of the early Alvars namely Puthattalvar was born at Mallai or Mamallapuram. He says that Vishnu has nine abodes and Mallai is one amongst them. Thirumangai Alvar, a

*Underwater Archaeological Wing, Archaeological Survey of India, New Delhi-110011

renowned Vaishnava saint has devoted 26 verses to Mallai in his *Periya Tirumoli.*

From the Pallava times onwards there are regular references to Mahabalipuram as a port-town. It gained prominence after Mamalla started carving rock-cut caves.

He also despatched a naval expedition to Sri Lanka from Mahabalipuram in aid of Manavarman, the prince of Ceylon. *Chulavamsa* one of Sri Lanka's chronicles also confirms the Pallava naval expedition to Sri Lanka. The Kasakudi copper plates of Nandivarman Pallavamalla (A.D. 731-96) record this naval expedition sent by Narasimhavarman (Hiultzsch, *SII*, vol. II). An inscription in the Adivaraha temple dated in the last year of the reign of Nandivarman Pallavamalla (A.D. 796) mentions a guild at Mamallapuram. *Nandikalambakam* by Perundevanar, a Tamil work written in praise of Nandivarman III (A.D. 846-69) mentions Mallai and Mylai as two major ports on the Tondaimandalam coast.

The port town remained in prominence during later periods also. Four Chola inscriptions of Rajaraja I in the Shore temple and another in the Adiranchanda *mandapa* in Saluvankuppam bear witness to this. These inscriptions also mention the presence of foreign merchants at Mamallapuram. The nature and importance of Mahabalipuram could have declined after the fourteenth century A.D.

Previous Studies

Chambers visited Mamallapuram in 1772 and described a few monuments. He does not mention the five *rathas*, which were perhaps covered entirely by sand. In 1871 Alexander Hunter removed the sand and exposed the Adiranchanda *mandapa* in Saluvankuppam, which had already been exposed by Colin Mackenzie in 1816. Thus it is certain that the drifting sand was affecting many monuments located on the seashore. The important monuments were exposed from time to time but many other contemporary structures might be lying buried under the thick cover of sand. Excavations conducted earlier have also unearthed some important structures of different periods.

In 1990-91 the Madras Circle of the Archaeological Survey of India unearthed an elliptical structure having a monolithic standing varaha, a miniature shrine, an ancient well and a number of inscriptions, belonging to early Pallava period, in the Shore-temple complex [2]. A massive stepped structure was also unearthed during clearing of the sand dune in the Shore temple-complex (Narsimhaiah 2000: 100-109; Narasimhan 1995: 199-204). The excavation conducted during 1998-99 and 1999-2000 revealed that the stepped structure continues on the north side also almost parallel to the coastline. Besides, two brick structures were also exposed to the west of Shore temple.

In 1995 the Geological Survey of India in collaboration with the Archaeological Survey of India had carried out bathymetric survey off Mahabalipuram. Results of the survey revealed that the area of Mahabalipuram has potential archaeological materials and needs to be explored systematically.

The Seven Pagodas

Mahabalipuram was also popularly known as 'Seven Pagodas' to European travellers. The very title of the article of William Chambers published in 1788 in the first volume of *Asiatic Researches* makes it very clear. Scholars differ widely regarding the origin of this name and there are several theories based upon various references and their interpretations. It is generally believed that the term Seven Pagodas originated from seven temples (*pagodas*), which once stood on the shore and were visible from the sea.

The *Carta Catalana*, a world map prepared in Catalonia, Spain in 1375 mentions 'Setemelti' on east coast of India. Scholars identified Setemelti with Mahabalipuram, which is presumed to be the corrupt form of Italian 'Sette Templi', meaning seven temples or Seven Pagodas (Ramaswami 1989: 364-66). The earliest reference to 'Seven Pagodas' is found in the travel records of an Italian traveller Gasparo Balbi (1590). Balbi also mentioned to have seen *'eight pleasant hillocks not very high'*. With such description it seems possible that these low hillocks might have also appeared like Pagodas from a distance and vice versa.

Mention of Seven Pagodas by Charles Gubbins in 1708 (Gubbins 1853), M. Sonnerat in 1782 (Sonnerat 1788), and John Goldingham in 1798 besides a host of other travellers and writers (Goldingham 1798) indicate the popularity of this name during eighteenth century. Equating Mahabalipuram with Seven Pagodas continued in the nineteenth (Milburn 1825) as well as twentieth century (Fyson 1949).

Scholars are divided about the identification of these seven temples. Some believe that these seven temples are monolithic *rathas* and the Shore temple while some others say that there were seven temples on the shore out of which five or six have been destroyed by the sea or have since been submerged and only the Shore temple survived. These views are conjectures and the interpretations of the records of early travellers.

Maria Graham writing about the origin of the place says that, 'There is a tradition that five magnificent pagodas have been swallowed up at this place by the sea, the ruined temple I have mentioned (Shore temple) and one still entire in the village making the seven pagodas whence the place had its name' (Graham 1813). However, William Hamilton could not find any logic behind this name. He wrote 'In the vicinity of this town are the celebrated ruins of ancient Hindoo temples dedicated to Vishnu, generally called the 7 Pagodas, but it is not known for what reason, as no such number exist here' (Hamilton 1815; 1820). In 1835 an article, appeared in *The Asiatic Journal* questioning of the name. It mentions, 'There were formerly several other temples in the neighbourhood of these ruins (Shore temple), now literally covered by the sea, and from these the place has taken its name of Seven Pagodas, as an appellation given it by the navigators of the coast'.

These above-mentioned descriptions recorded by travellers over the centuries probably indicate the existence of seven temples which gave the name Seven Pagodas was very popular till the last century (Fyson 1949). This tradition needs to be investigated scientifically and the only way to do this was to resort to underwater archaeological exploration.

Submerged Remains

William Chambers who visited Mahabalipuram in 1772 and 1776 was the first to publish a detailed account of ancient monuments and the site in 1788. He says, 'And the natives of the place declared to the writer of this account, that the more aged people among them, remembered to have seen the tops of several Pagodas far out in the sea, which being covered with copper were particularly visible at sun rise, as their shining surface used then to reflect the sun's rays but, that now that effect was no longer produced, as the copper had since become incrusted with mould and verde grease' (Chambers, 1788:153-54). Maria Graham writes, 'There is a tradition that a large city and five magnificent pagodas have been swallowed up at this place by the sea' (Graham 1813). An article appeared in *The Asiatic Journal* in 1835 giving very useful information which says that, 'on the extremity of the beach there is, or was, for its situation might not always be tenable, a stone pagoda, of very peculiar construction, put together without cement; immense masses of fragments lie around it. The surf dashing against them with a degree of violence, which seems to threaten instantaneous destruction. There were formerly several other temples in the neighbourhood of these ruins, now literally covered by the sea'. These early accounts of Mahabalipuram by European travellers indicate that there has been a strong tradition of submerged temples.

Recent Underwater Investigations

The Underwater Archaeology Wing of the Archaeological Survey of India (hereafter the Wing) decided to undertake its first underwater exploration in the Bay of Bengal off Tamil Nadu. In November 2001 the Wing carried out its first offshore investigation (Tripathi2002a). It also included onshore exploration from Saluvankuppam in the north to Sadras in the south and exploration along the backwaters (Tripathi 2002b: 145-46).

The Wing has a small team comprising archaeologists and photographer headed by a trained underwater archaeologist. Besides, young archaeologists holding Post Graduate Diploma in Archaeology from the Institute of Archaeology also joined the team. The author carried out diving in Area I and underwater exploration in Area II, east of Shore temple in the Bay of Bengal. Records of onshore exploration, preparation of drawings of the archaeological remains discovered during the exploration, maintaining dive-records, log books, filling the data sheets, marking the finds, retrieval, packing and transportation of archaeological materials, were meticulously carried out. Photographic documentation of coastal features, activities of the team, techniques employed and artefacts recovered were also made.

Methodology used and Techniques employed

Systematic investigations with a well-defined, simple but effective methodology in the Inter-tidal zone at the low tide were the first step. The area exposed during the low tide was studied to select the probable search-area off-shore. A detailed plan for exploration was prepared on the site. The entire area was divided in groups—Area I and Area II—depending upon the bathymetry of the area. Since the depth near shore is very less it was decided to carry out systematic swim-line survey. Safety of the team members and the equipments was given top priority. All possible precautions were taken for the safety and security of the staff during offshore exploration. Life jackets were provided on board. Diver was provided with a line to have some sort of communication and attachment with the boat. While diving no movement was allowed on the surface. A vehicle was always kept ready on shore.

A well-planned documentation programme was followed on the site. Every activity, recovery, use of techniques, instrumentation was documented through various means of photography. Drawings were also prepared of the important objects. The location of the remains and other important details were also drawn with the help of available means.

Coastal Exploration

Before venturing into the sea it was necessary to study the coastal region. To study coastal features and ancient sites around Mahabalipuram an area from Saluvankuppam, in the north, to Sadras in the south was selected. The entire area was covered by vehicles and also on foot. Near shore features were examined minutely. Geomorphology of the area was also observed and documented. Nearby villages, settlements of fishermen and temples were studied. The team also visited known archaeological sites in this region, excavated area and old temples. Thorough interaction was kept with fishermen of the area. Experiences of particularly old fishermen were documented with the help of an interpreter. These discussions were very fruitful and provided valuable information about traditional boat building, navigation and potential areas in the sea.

While exploring the area around Mahabalipuram the row of tanks to the west of hillock, and a channel probably connecting it to the sea were found to be of great interest. This channel south of Shore temple is about 35 m wide. The sea sand has blocked the mouth of this channel. Due to continuous rain it was filled with water and easily traceable to a length of more than 150 m. The channel running east to west in a straight line is clearly visible on the high-resolution satellite imagery.

Offshore Exploration

Though the sea was rough but it was necessary to examine the submerged rocks and supposed submerged structures east of the Shore temple. Local fishermen were persuaded to assist the team in offshore exploration. As soon as the weather improved underwater exploration started. A 8.70 m long mechanised boat named Kadiravan was hired for conducting dives and offshore investigations. Sea was still rough and diving cylinder and luggage bags on the open deck had to be tied with ropes to prevent them from falling in the sea. Waves near shore were very high and strong. Besides motor, oars were also used to tide over these high waves.

Submerged Rocks

There are several submerged rocks off Mahabalipuram. During the low tide tops of these rocks are visible above the water. Local fishermen have assigned specific names to seven prominent rocks. These rocks are—Setakal parai, Vengal parai, Korali parai, Pinna parai, Kolim parai, Ratta parai and Tundu parai. The names of these rocks are based on their shape, size or on the availability of a particular type of fish near these rocks (Tripathi 2001).

High waves hitting these rocks and whirling water were making it impossible to take the boat very close to these rocks. The boat was anchored near a submerged rock to carryout diving. Due to heavy movement and tying of the cylinder on board one of its valve developed problem. Diving was a must for studying the submerged features and it was decided to dive to examine the submerged rocks. Since the director of the exploration was the only diver, a line was provided for to keep contact with the boat. Due to rough weather and continuous rains sea was very rough and the visibility was very poor. The entire submerged rocks are covered with flora and fauna growing over them. Shape and size of many rocks and stones were very interesting. Removal of overgrowth and close observation of the surfaces of the rocks were necessary to find out whether they are natural or man-made. But due to high waves hitting the rocks it was not possible to stay close to these rocks and clear the surface of these submerged rocks.

Later on underwater exploration was shifted to Area II. This area, between Area I and Shore Temple is comparatively shallow. Depth in this area varies from 6 to 8 m. However the waves were stronger being nearer to shore. Underwater exploration here revealed that the submarine conditions were almost similar at both the places. The offshore investigation made it clear that both the areas are important for underwater archaeological exploration and need to be examined in more detail.

Fieldwork - March 2002

In March 2002 the Wing undertook further investigation off Mahabalipuram. Now the area of study was limited to the north of Shore Temple where sea had encroached upon a large area due to seasonal shift of sand. More emphasis was given to the documentation of submerged structures in Area III, north of Shore Temple. Systematic study of the area, to the north of the Mahishasura rock brought to light submerged remains of archaeological interest. Among these, three walls and a number of carved architectural members belonging to ancient temples are noteworthy.

These walls starting from the shore goes into the sea. Parts of these submerged walls get exposed during the low tide. These are of thick slabs of granite. And run north-south and east-west. The one, which runs east to west, is well preserved and the longest among all the structures found so far. Other two walls running north to south are fragmentary and much damaged. Two long stone slabs, each having two vertical slits to receive two other stone slabs were planted upright. Two shorter stone slabs, which were also having two similar slits, were inserted between these upright stones to make a box-like structure. Several such blocks arranged in a row formed a wall. A series of such blocks was recorded running east to west, perpendicular to the shoreline north of Shore Temple. Some such blocks, in a series or isolated, were parts of the walls running north to south. This technique of construction on shore is so effective that still these structures are *in situ* despite violent sea and high-energy waves (Pl. 1 & 2).

Area III is very important for the study of submergence of coastal structures. Structural remains found in this area suggest change in coastline or sea level fluctuation during historic period. The entire area was found strewn with a number of architectural members of various shapes and sizes. Some of these architectural members are of very big in size and could not have been transported by the waves from elsewhere. These architectural members found here are well-dressed and a few are tastefully decorated and seem to be the parts of some ancient temple. Some lying in shallow waters could be seen during low tide. Due to regular exposure and submergence, there is overgrowth of seaweeds. This overgrowth of marine flora not only changes their appearance but also hides the surface features and carvings. Some others lying in deeper water get exposed partially. A variety of thick, square, long and rectangular slabs, parts of brackets, parts of mouldings, bases of pillars, a single-holed stone anchor or a rectangular slab with a hole, granite slab with grooves to hold two vertical slabs together, etc., were documented. Some were drawn to measurement. Orientation of the submerged remains are studied to understand their layout and purpose. Locations of important remains were also marked.

Structures unearthed to the north of Shore Temple earlier were dated to early Pallava period (Narsimhaiah 2000:100-09; Narasimhan 1995:199-204). The long-stepped structure to the west of Shore Temple has also been dated to Pallava period. No datable artefact is found, so far, to assign any date to the presently detected submerged remains. On the basis of construction-technique they can be compared with stepped structures that were unearthed to the west of Shore Temple. Keeping their relative levels of construction in mind these structures may also be asigned, tentatively, to the Pallava period 3, if not earlier. The exact date of these structures and their relation with existing ones can only be determined after excavation and thorough systematic study.

Post-fieldwork Analysis

To study the area scientifically help of modern tools are also being taken. The Wing obtained High Resolution

Satellite Imagery to define and study the archaeological features. The False Colour Composite of PAN and LISS III data obtained on the 12 February 2001 on the 12,500 scale was used to study important features. It is interesting to note that one of the submerged rocks east of Shore Temple is also visible on the imagery. Study of multi-date and multi-band data is always more useful for defining the features and better interpretation of imagery. A copy of another set of data of different period on a different scale is also being studied for comparison. The data gathered from the study of Satellite imagery will be examined and put to use during the next field season.

Old Records

The findings in the sea need to be corroborated with other literary or datable archaeological evidence. Attempts are being made to collect information about the old records; particularly old maps of the area would be of great help to study the changes in shoreline. Besides, these maps also show several other natural as well as man-made features which have either changed or lost, over a long period of time. A sketch-map of 1949 shows a series of tanks south-west of hillock, which is not seen now. The area has largely been occupied by stone carvers and covered under modern constructions. Available records are being studied to compare these offshore finds. A number of old drawings and photographs of Mahabalipuram are also available. These illustrations are valuable source of information. Efforts are being made to collect old drawings and photographs preserved in various archives, museums and other institutions in India and abroad.

Conclusion

Mahabalipuram is known world over for its monuments and no volume on Indian art and architecture can be completed without the mention of monuments of Mahabalipuram. Scholars, from India and abroad, have done a lot of work on the history, development, art and architecture of these Pallava monuments (Kennedy 1898; Longhurzt 1924; 1928; 1930; Rabe 2001; Ramaswami 1980; 1989; Sastri 1926; Sivarama-murti 1992; Srinivasan 1975; Vogel 1914) but at the same time very little is done about the archaeology of this place. Mahabalipuram is said to be an ancient port and a flourishing town but we do not have convincing material evidence to corroborate the graphic descriptions given in various ancient literatures. We still do not know where the ancient port was located? How the place came to be known as 'Seven Pagodas'? Which are those seven temples? Whether there is a submerged city off the coast as strongly believed by locals and referred by travellers for several centuries? Where was the ancient town and how it was planned?

Offshore Investigations at Mahabalipuram indicate that some more structures existed near Shore Temple. Perhaps the change in shoreline destroyed these structures and their remains lay submerged in the Bay of Bengal. Results of the two brief fieldworks in 2001 and 2002 are very rewarding. Planning and selection of search area based upon the field study have proved very effective. The important areas have been identified and the buried remains need to be exposed for further study to determine the exact nature, extension, date and purpose of these submerged structures. Ongoing underwater archaeological investigations, would hopefully solve the mystery of these sunken remains off Mahabalipuram.

Acknowledgements

The author is grateful to Smt. Komal Anand, the then Director General, Archaeological Survey of India (ASI) for deciding to start the Wing in the Archaeological Survey of India. Thanks are also due to Smt. Kasturi Gupta Menon, the present Director General, ASI for her support and encouragement to the development of this nascent branch of archaeology in the country. Thanks are alsodue to Dr. R.S. Bisht, Director, ASI for his guidance, the Superintending Archaeologist, Chennai Circle and the staff of the Sub-Circle, Mahabalipuram for the support provided by them. Author is also thankful to Shri Sanjay Sharma for excellent photographic documentation, to Shri Arun Raj for his help in fieldwork and particularly to have meaningful interactions with local fishermen and also to Shri Manoj Sharma, Assistant Archaeologist.

NOTES

Soon after the second fieldwork of the Wing, a few Indian and foreign divers visited the site in April 2002 (Report on the Completion of the Joint SES/NIO Expedition to south-east India originally posted by Graham Hancock on the Message Board of this site, 6 April 2002, *The Official Graham Hancock Website: Underworld*) and claimed in newspapers to have discovered the submerged remains for the first time at Maha-balipuram. Not only that both the partners are claiming credit for this discovery ('Preliminary Underwater Archaeological Explorations of Mahabalipuram Statement by National Institute of Oceanography, 9 April 2002' and Who Discovered the Underwater Ruins at Mahabalipuram? And Who is Claiming What? Originally posted on the Massage Board, 13 April 2002, *The Official Graham Hancock Website: Underworld*). However, systematic fieldwork was going on as per the provisions of the Ancient Monuments and Archaeological Sites and Remains Act, 1958, since long.

2. Rabe mentions about excavation of a treasury crypt in 1990 and finding of a bronze sword at Mahabalipuram (Rabe 2001: 16). Author had long personal discussions with the then Superintending Archaeologist of the Archaeological Survey of India who exposed the structures of the Pallava period in 1990-91. He informed that there was neither any such excavation nor any such find (Narasinhaiah 2000: 100-09).

3. Dr. Glenn Milne from university of Durham, UK writes that the area where the structures exist ~~would~~ have been submerged around six thousand years ago. (Dr. Glenn Milne Dates Submergence of Mahabalipuram Structures to 6000 BP First Posted by Graham Hancock on the Message Board of This Site, 10 April 2002, *The Official Graham Hancock Website: Underworld*). This date has not been accepted even by the members of Graham Hancock's Joint Expedition team, i.e., the archaeologists of the National Institute of Oceanography.

REFERENCES

Anon, 1835, 'Cave Temples of India', *The Asiatic Journal*, London.

Chambers, William, 1788, 'Some Account of the Sculptures and Ruins at Mavalipuram, a Place a few Miles North of Sadras, and Known to Seamen by the Name of Seven Pagodas', *Asiatic Resesarches*, vol. I, Calcutta.

Fyson, D.R.,1949, *Mahabalipuram or Seven Pagodas*, Madras.

Balbi,Gasparo, 1590, *Viaggio dell' Indie Orientali*, Venice.

Goldingham, John, 1798, 'Some Account of the Sculptures at Mahabalipuram, usually called the Seven Pagodas', *Asiatic Researches*, vol. V, Calcutta.

Graham, Maria, 1813, *Journal of a Residence in India.*

Gubbins, Charles, 1853, 'Notes on the Ruins at Mahabalipuram on the Coromandel Coast', *Journal of the Asiatic Society of Bengal*, vol. XXII, Calcutta.

Hamilton, William, 1815, *East India Gazetteer*, London.

Hamilton, William, 1820, *A Geographical, Statistical and Historical Description of Hindostan and Adjacent Countries*, I.

Hultzch, E. (ed), *South Indian Inscriptions*, vol. II.

Iyengar, M. Raghava, 1928, *Journal of Oriental Research*, Madras.

Jouveau-Dubreuil, G., (1916-18), *The Pallava Antiquities*, Pondicherry.

Longhurst, A.H., 1924, *The Pallava Architecture*, MASI, No. 17, 33 and 40, ASI, Calcutta.

Milburn, William, 1825, *Oriental Commerce or The East India Trader's Complete Guide*, London.

Narasimhaaiah, B., 2000, 'Significance of Recently Discovered Structures at Mamallapuram. Mahabalipuram),' *Journal of Mythic Society, Vol. XCI, No. 3.*

Narasimhan, K.T., 1995, 'Recently Discovered Pallava Monolithic and Structural Remains at Mamallapuram', *Sri Nagabhinandanam*, eds. L.K. Srinivasan and S. Nagaraju), Bangalore.

Rabe, Michael D., 2001, *The Great Penance at Mamallapuram*, Institute of Asian Studies, Chennai.

Ramaswami, N.S., 1980, *Mamallapuram: An Annotated Bibliograpy,* New Era Publications, Madras.

———, 1989, *2000 Years of Mamallapuram,* vol. I, Navrang, New Delhi.

Rao, S.R.,T.S.S. Rao and H.N. Siddiquie, 1981, *Marine Archaeological studies in Indian waters,* Project report, National Institute of Oceanography, Dona Paula.

Sastri, H. Krishna, 'The Vayalur Pillar Inscription of Rajasimha II', *Epigraphia Indica,* XVII.

Sivaramamurti, C., 1992., *Mahabalipuram,* V edition, ASI, New Delhi.

Srinivasan, K.R., 1975, *Dharmarajaratha and its Sculptures Mahabalipuram,* Abhinav Publications, New Delhi.

Sennerat, M., 1978, *A voyage to the East-Indies and China', Performed by Order of Lewis XV, between theYears 1774 and 1781,* (tr. by Francis Magus), Calcutta.

Tripathi, Alok, 2001, 'Underwater Exploration Off Mahabalipuram', Paper presented during the Annual Conference of the Indian Archaeological Society, Vadodara.

———, 2002a, *Exploration Off Mahabalipuram in Bay of Bengal,* Archaeological Survey of India, New Delhi (Unpublished Report).

———, 2002b, Underwater Exploration Off Mahabalipuram and Arikamedu, Avanam', *Journal of the Tamil Nadu Archaeological Society,* vol. 13, Thanjavur.

Venkayya, V., 1909, 'The Pallavas Annual Report', *Archaeological Survey of India,* 1906-07, ASI, Calcutta.

Vogel, J. Ph., 1914, 'Iconographic notes on the Seven Pagodas', *Annual Report, Archaeological Surve of India,* 1910-11 ASI, Calcutta.

In Search of High Tin-Bronze in Eastern India

Ashok Kumar Singh,* Pranab Chattopadhyay**

Introduction

The recent discovery of copper-bronze objects at four sites have enriched metallurgical heritage of eastern India. The terminology of eastern India in this paper roughly represents an area east of Allahabad, comprising Eastern Uttar Pradesh, Bihar, West Bengal and Bangladesh. In this vast area only a few sites are known where high tin-bronze artefacts are obtained. The sites are Wari-Bateswar, district Narshingadi, Chandraketu-garh, district North 24-Parganas, West Bengal, Agiabir, district Mirzapur, Uttar Pradesh and Mahasthan, district Bogra of Bangladesh. The copper-bronze objects discovered in these four sites are of varying nature but for a specific reason two items, *viz*., mirrors and knobbed vessels have been identified and comparative studies are being made which will throw some light on the problematic high tin-bronze vessels of South-East Asia.

The objective of the present paper is to re-evaluate the use of high tin-bronze in eastern India and to discuss the justification of their import from South-East Asian neighbourhood. At the same time the manufacturing technique of this proto-historic object was also investigated.

Copper-Bronze

Use of copper is known from prehistoric times and that was native copper. Simple forging techniques may be used with native copper. In the Chalcolithic period, all over the subcontinent, evidences of making and shaping of copper from ore minerals are noted. The application of poling was evidenced later, which is an improvement in pyrometallurgy. Pure copper is found difficult to use. Man has discovered alloying it with the addition of tin and other elements. The ore minerals in connection with copper-bronze are very much known in eastern India. Copper is available in plenty in Singhbhum district of Jharkhand. Activities of mining, smelting and manufacturing of copper are known from Rakha mines. Small pockets of copper ores are known in Medinipur, Bankura and Purulia districts of West Bengal. Copper is also known from Manipur. All those sites yielded material remains pertaining to smelting of copper. The export of copper to South-East Asia was also known from Tamralipti port in Medinipur district. It is known that a basic raw material for manufacturing bronze is tin, which is normally obtained from the mineral cassiterite. However, the source of tin is scanty in eastern India. The known deposits of tin are from Chapatand and Nurungo in Hazaribagh district, Paharsingh of Ranchi district and small amount of tin are also reported from Gaya, Giridih and Purulia districts. All these sites bear pre-industrial evidences of tin (Chakrabarti 1997). There are enough evidences of continuity of tin in India throughout the ages. However, the sources of tin clearly indicate that it

* Department of Ancient Indian History, Culture & Archaeology, Banaras Hindu University, Varanasi-221005
**Centre for Archaeological Studies and Training, Eastern India, 43 Shakespeare Sarani, Kolkata-700017

could not satisfy the need of domestic market. It is, therefore, presumed that, tin was also imported to eastern India like silver from South-East Asia.

Alloying is noted from the very beginning. Till now there is not enough evidence of the use of pure metal in case of Chalcolithic copper objects of eastern India. The only use of pure copper was noted in an object from Dhuliapur, district Medinipur. It was perhaps contemporary to chalcolithic period or earlier. Through spectrographic analysis, presence of trace amount of other elements cannot be accepted as an alloy. However, the use of alloying is noted from the analysis of the late chalcolithic. During the chalcolithic period, the copper objects were manufactured by casting and subsequent forging practices. Alloying with tin was known but the knowledge relating to its proper composition was perhaps not adequate (Chattopadhyay 2002A). The objects mostly found are bangles, beads, earrings, finger rings, fishhook, etc. Evidence of bronze was found in the chalcolithic Bengal from the analysed bronze specimens from Bahiri, Bhartpur, Dihor, Mangalkot and Pandurajar Dhibi contain more or less 9-11 per cent tin. In metallurgical terminology this variety of bronze is known as *alpha-bronze*.

Advancement in bronze making was observed with the increase in alloying content and its difference in manufacturing. Subsequently in the early historic period, the most noted use of this alloy, popularly known as *kansha* highlights the use of high tin bronze. This alloy with tin of around 22.5 per cent is known as *beta-bronze*, depending on the cooling characteristic. The microstructure expected in high tin-bronze objects is composed normally of acicular martensitic needles in quenched form. This quenched beta bronze appears to be golden in colour after polishing. In metallurgical explanations indicated through the copper-tin equilibrium system of binary alloys, the alloy formed up to 11 per cent tin is known as *alpha-bronze*. In case of high tin-bronzes of around 22.5 per cent is known as *beta-bronze* in a temperature between 586°-755° Celsius. The high tin-bronze vessels were made by casting in *cire perdue* or lost wax process followed with quenching and polishing. Some of them were finished with bands of fine incised decorations.

Harappan copper-bronze objects

One may recall the constituents of Harappan copper-bronze artefacts. Agrawal (1971) has given the analysis of the same as follows. Seventy per cent tools found at Harappan sites were unalloyed, indicating the scarcity of tin. Tin content varied widely indicating the lack of proper knowledge of alloying. The content of tin was in the range of 8 to 12 per cent in the total of 14 per cent of tools. Only less than 8 per cent of tools indicated arsenic, lead or nickel alloying. At Lothal, the contents of alloying elements, such as arsenic, are different from Mohenjo-Daro. The latter site perhaps utilised copper ore of Rajasthan. On the other hand, copper-bronze objects of Lothal were perhaps imported from Oman; alternately it may surmised that the smiths learnt to remove the arsenic. The range of tin of 2.27 to 13.80 per cent indicates the use of both low and high tin-bronzes (Biswas 1996).

Use of mirror in old world

Mirrors made of copper-bronze alloy are known from different parts of pre- and early historic times. This, one of the most popular household objects was known from Kulli culture of Baluchistan, Lothal and Taxila and also from the Hahn dynasties of China. Lothal smiths made mirror with low tin-bronze. For manufacturing of mirror in the Old World, bronze constituting 20-30 per cent tins was used and simply made by casting. This high tin alloy was selected for manufacturing polished surface so that it appears almost similar to glass mirrors in reflecting properties. Even in the present day, traditional bronze mirror is continuing in south India (Srinivasan 1998).

Copper mirrors in Indian context

Mirrors in the shape of circular metal discs, originally polished on one side and plain or with a design on the other, have been found in a limited number at many sites. Copper mirrors with a long handle are reported from Harappa (Vats 1940:391). The diameters of these mirrors are 16 cm and 17.50 cm respectively. The finest example of copper mirrors (nineteen in number) came from Taxila where they were found in the Saka-Parthian levels at Sirkap datable to first century B.C. (Marshall 1951: 215, 584-85, Pl. 182. Nos. 208-211). They are circular in shape and vary between 5.55 and 16.5 cm in diameter. Three specimens have been found in the Kundangar hoard at Brahmapuri (District Kolhapur, Maharashtra) from the Satavahana period datable to first-third A.D. (Khandalvala 1960: 27-95). One copper mirror was recovered from Ter

(District Osmanabad, Maharashtra) in the later Satavahana period. Two copper mirrors were reported from Masan Dih district Ghazipur, U.P., one in the NBP levels and the other in the Gupta levels (Ghosh 1989: I:348). Two handled circular bronze mirrors with recessed face have been reported from Rairh (Puri 1940:343).

Mirrors of eastern India

As mentioned earlier, recent archaeological findings of high tin-bronze objects and knobbed vessel from Wari-Bateswar region of district Narshingdi of Bangladesh (Basa and Rahaman 1998, Jahan 1999, Haque *et al.* 2000) deserve mentioning. The sensational discovery of bronze mirror from Mahasthangarh period II (200 B.C. 200 A.D. level) further highlights the use of high tin-bronze (Salles 1999). Excavation during 1995 had revealed a disc mirror 18.5 cm in diameter (Pl. 1). The tang handle is 6.4 cm long and 2 cm wide at its fastening to the disc. The mirroring face is flat. The recent addition of a high tin-bronze mirror from Chandraketugarh, in the collection of the State Archaeological Museum, Calcutta (Chattopad-hyay 2002) has further enlarged the use of it in eastern India. (Pl. 2) This was a chance find. Analysis of the mirror has revealed its alloy contents further. The fragmentary mirror was originally 132 mm in diameter, designed with a flat rim of 11 mm thick outside and attached with a handle 44 mm in length. The visual appearance indicates that it was a cast one. Until metallographical analysis is made it cannot be said whether any thermomechanical treatment had been performed.

Similar types of copper mirror, along with knobbed vessel and large cooking vessels were obtained in excavation at Agiabir, district Mirzapur, Uttar Pradesh recently, from mid level of N.B. P. 4th–5th century BC (Singh & Singh 1999-2000, 2002) (Pl. 3–4).

The discovery of knobbed vessel at Wari-Bateswar (Pathan 1989, Basa and Rahaman 1998, Jahan 1999, Haque et. al. 2000) also reminds similar bowls at Ban Don Ta Phet. One of the bowl bears a knob and the second one is a broken. A rim like circle surrounds both the specimens.

Knobbed vessel

It is known that a few bronze bowls of Wari-Bateswar was unearthed which further melted down. Amongst the fragments of knobbed bowls two of them included circular base. The specimens from Wari-Bateswar were studied were studied by Basa and Rahman (1998). It is known that one of them is with a knob at centre. No analysis or measurement accompanied the report.

Chemical analysis

Chemical analysis of the mirror of Chandraketugarh was done through the Hilger-Watts Emission spectrograph. The semi-quantitative analysis of trace elements

Table 1: Mirror

Site	Diameter	Thickness-Rim	Length of Handle
Agiabir	14	0.57	6.0
Chandraketugarh	13.2	1.1	4.4
Mahasthan	18.5	---	6.4

Table 2: Knobbed vessel

Site	Diameter mouth Centimeter	Diameter body Centimeter	Thickness of rim Centimeter	Height Centimeter
Agiabir	27.6	33.6	0.57	3.2
Wari-Bateswar Only fragments,—no measurement has been referred by the author.				

was carried out with RU standard with the wavelength chosen between 2700-4400 A. The result showing major elements only are incorporated in Table: 3.

Table 3: Analysis of Bronze mirror of Chandraketugarh

Copper	Tin	Zinc	Lead	Silver	Iron	Arsenic
Base	19.0	0.2	0.5	1.0	0.8	0.2

Presence of high tin-bronzes are not brown in Chalcolithic context in eastern India. Tentatively it may be conclude that use of high tin bronze began in early historic period. The mirror from Chandraketugarh highlights the stages of the metal craft of the early historic period in Eastern India. The copper bronze objects of Agiabir on the other hand, highlight the stage of copper-bronze objects during fifth to sixth century B.C.

Two fragments of knobbed vessel from Agiabir were selected for analysis. Visually the surface was observed through a microscope. It was found fully converted into malachite $CuCO_3.Cu(OH)_2$. In case of copper-bronze objects this is a common feature (Chase 1979). One of the fragments weighing 0.8371 grams was analysed with the help of Atomic absorption spectroscope, shown in Table 4, where copper, tin, lead and zinc searched more precisely.

Table 4: Atomic Absorption Analysis of Knobbed vessel of Agiabir

Copper	Tin	Zinc	Lead
35.83	17.98	not traceable	not traceable

Metallography

Another fragment was selected for metallographic studies whose cross section was about 2 mm. The specimen was polished across its cross-section and solid metallic core was revealed with heavily corroded outside surface. The specimen was observed through metallographic microscope. Subsequently it was etched with ferric chloride, ammonium hydroxide and hydrogen peroxide, to reveal its manufacturing technique.

The etched side, across-section was thoroughly scanned with a JEOL, JSM 5200 Electron microscope at a magnification 1000X at 20 KV, 436 PMT. The specimen clearly, indicated that it was made up a single phase and no evidence of dendritic cast structure or no evidence of twins representing evidence of annealing. On the other hand, the election photomicrograph revealed the internal structure of martensite showing random dislocations and stacking faults (Pl. 5). Authors have referred similarity in structure plate no 3295 (*Metals Handbook* 1973). One thing should be considered that due to long corrosions and ageing the needle like structures have modified a bit.

South-East Asian Connection

There are enough evidence that India and South-East Asia was closely connected, and both these areas witnessed developed agriculture and metallurgy. Through close connection in trade, commerce and religion both the regions benefited. Through archaeological excavations the material remains have been unearthed from different sites of South-East Asia.

The most important site of the region is Ban Don Ta Phet, which is located at West Central Thailand in the Kanchanaburi Province. The C14 dates indicate within a range of 360-390 B.C. and 15 B.C. to A.D. 430. This is contemporary to Mahasthan and some other sites of Indian subcontinent. However, Agiabirs periodisation pertaining copper-bronze objects is earlier to the sites of South-East Asian sites. The most of the discovered objects have been obtained from different funerals, which have been excavated here. The most important of the objects recovered are beads, bronze vessels and jewellery. The later were made with bronze, bone, ivory, glass and semi-precious stones. The bronze vessels recovered from this site were made of high tin bronze (Rajpitak and Seeley 1979). XRF analyses indicated the presence of about 23 per cent tin in those objects.

Excavation have revealed the fragmentary incised high tin cast bronze vessels with the scene of people, animals, etc., which clearly indicates Indian connections. It was further known vessels of Bengal origin (Glover 1985; Rajpitak and Seeley 1979). The water bowls made of this material were brittle but its golden appearance (golden colour when freshly polished) was highly esteemed in the society.

There are few more sites in Thailand. The excavated objects from Wat Khlong Thom (referred by Glover 1996: 135) indicate expatriate Indian artisans worked under the protection of local ruler. Evidences farther include the remains of tin smelting and to export-tin-short India.

A number of similar bronze mirror and vessels made of high tin-bronze from the South-East and near East Asia is known. Example may be cited of the bowls discovered at Than Hoa province of Vietnam, now exhibited at Musee Guimet.

The thickness of bronze bowls of Ban Don Ta Phet and also Wari-Bateswar are extremely thin whereas the same from Agiabir are thicker and less sophisticated. From this angle it may be accepted as a crude product and likely to have been made earlier.

Use of knobbed vessels

According to Glover (1989) the knobbed vessels were not of everyday use. He considers its rituals and funerary use only. In Buddhist concept he has equated with the *'Mandala'*—a schematic cosmological symbol, representing Mount Meru and the surrounding ocean. This clearly represents the penetration of Buddhist cosmology to South-East Asia. Perhaps Glover's equation of all the bronze bowls from South-East Asian as grave goods was related to the findings only. However, the similar object of Agiabir would perhaps change the assumption of earlier scholars. The finds from Agiabir is definitely a knobbed vessels. It undoubtedly establishes that the bronzes of Agiabir exclusively used as domestic objects and not for funerary use.

Conclusion

From the present finding it was only proved the connection of eastern India and South-East Asia both as commercial and religious ground. High tin-bronze artefacts, knobbed vessels, etc., are only indications or carriers. Early copper specimens from Non Nok Tha are made of low tin bronzes like eastern India. The high tin bronze artefacts from Mahasthan, Chandraketugarh, Wari-Bateswar and Agiabir were never identified as manufactured in South-East Asia. The objects with decorations discovered there have not proved as manufactured in South-East Asia. In historic and subsequent period tons of high tin-bronze artefacts and utensils have been made in eastern India as well as down up to Kerala. If Tamraliptis copper export was accepted then it may be presumed was with an exchange of tin. Only in-depth studies of those objects with trace elements and isotopic analysis can solve the enigma. The future analysis of copper bronze specimens of Agiabir will highlight the beginning of high tin bronze in eastern India. Thus, the finds of South-East Asia at least indicates the close contact with India but does not satisfactorily identify that it originated South-East Asia.

So far Agiabir is concerned, presently this is the earliest site in eastern India. Technologically the analysed specimen indicates the crude or better beginning of quenching techniques. Further analyses will highlight the intensities of it'.

Acknowledgements

We are very thankful to Prof. Purushottam Singh, Banaras Hindu University for providing the material for chemical analysis and giving fruitful suggestions. Authors acknowledge the supports provided by Dr. Gautam Sengupta, Mr. Pratip Kumar Mitra and Ms Sutapa Roy of CASTEI, Kolkata, Mr. M.L. Dutta of CMERI, Durgapur. Prof. Bimal Chaudhuri, Mr. R. Bhar (USIC) and Dr. B. Bhattacharya of Department of Metallurgy, Jadavpur University have extended analytical supports. We are also thankful to Dr. J.F. Salles of France-Bangladesh joint project for giving permission to use the photography of mirror from Mahasthangarh excavation.

REFERENCES

Agrawal, D.P., 1971., *Copper Bronze Age in India*, Munshiram Manoharlal, Delhi, pp. 168.

Basa, K.K. and S.S.M. Rahaman, 1998, 'Bronze knobbed bowls from Wari, Bangladesh: Implication for Trade, *Journal of Bengal Art*, 3, 291-98.

Biswas, A.K., 1996, *Minerals and Metal of Ancient India*, New Delhi:

D.K. Printworld, New Delhi, pp. 109, 124 and 129.

Chase, W.T., 1979, 'Solid samples from metallic antiquities and their examination', *Proc. 2nd ISCRP, Cultural Property and Analytical Chemistry*, pp. 73-109.

Chattopadhyay, P.K., 2002A., *Archaeometallurgy in India: Studies on Technoculture in early copper and Iron Ages in Bihar, Jharkhand and West Bengal*, Patna: K.P. Jayaswal Research Institute.

Chattopathyay, P.K., 2002, 'Metal finds from Chandraketugarh, West Bengal: *Archaeotechnical studies*', *in Archaeology of Eastern India: New Perspectives*, Kolkata: CASTEI.

Deo, S.B., 1990, 'Alexandrian copper mirror from Ter, Maharashtra', *Archaeology & Art*, Sri Krishna Deva Felicitation Volume, New Delhi, pp. 134-37.

Ghosh, A., (ed.), 1989, *An Encyclopedia of Indian Archaeology*, New Delhi: Munshiram Manoharlal.

Glover, I.C., 1985, 'Indian-Thai exchanges in the protohistoric period, paper presented at Research Conference Early South East Asia'.

Glover, I.C., 1989, *Early Trade between India and Southeast Asia, a link in the development of a world trading system*, University of Hull, pp. 143.

Glover, I.C., 1998, 'Recent archaeological evidence for early maritime contacts between India and South East Asia', in *Tradition and Archaeology*, edited by H.P. Ray and J.F. Salles, Delhi: Manohar Publishers and Distirbutors, pp. 129-58.

Haque, E., S.S. Mustafizur Rahaman and S.M. Kamrul Ahsan, 2000, 'A preliminary report on Wari-Bateswar trial excavation by ICSBA', *Journal of Bengal Art*, 5, 283-315.

Jahan, Shanaj Husne, 1999, 'Wari Bateswar; an important Centre of maritime activities in Ancient Bengal', *Journal of Bengal Art*, 4, 207-16.

Khandalvala, Karl, 1960, 'Brahmpuri—A consideration of the metal objects found in the Kundangar Hoard', *Lalitkala*, No. 7, pp. 27-95, New Delhi: Lalitkala Academy.

Marshall, John, 1951, (reprinted 1975), *Taxila*, vol. I-III, Delhi: Motilal Banarasidas.

Margabandhu, C., 1976-77, 'Ancient Indian Hand-mirrors and their importance', *Journal of Oriental Institute, Baroda*, XXVI, No.4, pp. 432-36.

Pathan, H., 1989, *Pratnatawick Nidarshan Wari Bateswar Narshingdi*, Granth Suhrid Prakasani (in Bangla).

Puri, K.N., 1940, *Excavations at Rairh*, pp. 43, Pl.XX.15; Pl. XXI.14.

Rajpitak, W. and Neigel J. Seeley, 1979, 'The bronze bowls from Ban Don Ta Phet, Thailand: an enigma of prehistoric metallurgy', *World Archaeology*, 11 (1) 26-31.

Salles, J.F., 1999, 'Excavations of Mahasthangarh: New evidence of contacts with the Ganges valley', *Journal of Bengal Art*, 4, 25-32.

Metals Hanbook, 1973, vol. 8, Ohio: American Society of Metals, pp. 200-201.

Singh, P. and Ashok K. Singh, 1999-2000, 'Excavations at Agiabir, district Mirzapur, Uttar Pradesh', *Pragdhara* No. 10, 31-55.

Singh, P. and Ashok K. Singh, 2002, *Agiabir a protohistoric settlement of the Mid-Ganga valley*, Shimla: Indian Institute of Advanced Studies.

Srinivasan, S., 1998, 'High tin bronze working in India: the bowl makers of Kerala', in *Archaeometallurgy in India*, ed. V. Tripathi, Delhi: Sharada Publishing House, pp. 241-50.

Srinivasan, S. and Ian C. Glover, 1998, 'High tin bronze mirrors of Kerala, South India', *IAMS*, vol. 20, p. 15.

Vats, Madhu Sarup, 1940, (reprinted 1997), *Excavations at Harappa*, vol. I & II, New Delhi: Munshiram Manoharlal.

Deplastering and Conservation of Lord Jagannath Temple, Puri (Orissa): A Case Study

K.N. DIKSHIT*

Introduction

The paper deals with the results of the conservation work carried out on the Lord Jagannath temple, Puri, by the Archaeological Survey of India (ASI) in the last three decades during 1973-2002. The author who was asked to direct this project faced a variety of problems which have been projected for the information of other experts, as such type of deplastering work was not attempted earlier in any part of the world. The Jagannath temple was the first monument in India followed by Sher Shah Suri's tomb at Gaya, Bihar where epoxy was used in the historic buildings. The conservation status of the main temple, structural preservation of the various temples in the complex and the chemical treatment carried out on them is discussed in detail. The provision of a stainless steel Truss more as a major of security rather than conservation and studies by the scientists of ASI on the grouting of ashlar stone rubble masonry with polymer modified cementitious (PMC) for sealing of cracks and joints are the other information of this project. In this work Asian philosophy of conservation by not allowing any reconstruction for structural strengthening has been strictly followed by the Indian conservators.

In the Puri Gazetteer, O'Malley stresses "the all-Indian primarily Buddhist background of Jagannath, alludes shortly to the tribal origin of his 'crude image' and finally at least concedes that not unnaturally Jagannath has a secure place in the affections of the Oriyas". (O'Malley, 1929).

Puri, the famous pilgrim centre of Orissa, with its great cultural tradition is known by various names, Puri, Nilachal, Purshottam, Srikshetra, Sankhashetra, etc. It derives its importance from the famous temple of Lord Jagannath.(Fig.1) In this temple, are installed images of Krishṇa, the paramount deity, his elder brother Balabhadra, and their sister, Subhadra. The *Puranas* have devoted a considerable portion to the sanctity of the place and its presiding deity with some differences in degrees. The *Utakal khanda* of the *Skanda Purana* contains elaborate description about the *Purshottam Kshetra*.

In the quest for the history of Orissa and the temple chronicle *Mạdalapanji*, Eschmann, Kulke and Tripathi have propounded a new interpretation for better understanding of the history of Orissa and have published their *magnum opus, The Cult of Jagannath and the Regional Tradition of Orissa* in 1978. Their contributions to the volume highlight some new aspects for understanding the various dimensions of Orissan history.

The Temple

The Jagannath temple was constructed during the

*B-17, Qutab Institutional Area, New Delhi

reign of Chodagangadeva in the 12th century and flourished under the royal patronage of the Gajapati kings of Orissa who were the guardians of the temple tradition and instrumental in disseminating the Jagannath cult all over the country (Pl.1. The Muslim invasion tolled the death knell to the Gajapati rule and the Kalinga empire fell into decay.

About 300 years back the body of the temple was plastered in order to protect the temple from saline climate. In 1954, the Government of Orissa passed a special, Act known as Lord Jagannath Temple Act 1954 under which the State Government took over the charge of temple administration and management. The Gajapati Maharaja of Puri became the Chairman of the Committee. In1987 for the proper conduct and safety of people and car the Govt. of Orissa passed a Code for the annual car festival when Jagannath and his siblings visit their aunt besides the numerous devotees of the Lord.

In 1974 the Archaeological Survey of India took up conservation of the Jagannath Temple complex. During the last 28 years, a major portion of the temple complex has been preserved, but still a lot of work remains to be done. The total area of the temple complex is 9.75 acres. Besides conservation, the surroundings were also improved by removing the encroachments near the main entrance of the temple.

As per the recommendations of the Expert Committee (EC), appointed by the Government of India in 1973, a preliminary survey of the Jagannath Temple complex was undertaken. For the proper assessment of the problem of repairs, it was found necessary to know the historical development and the archaeological potentiality of the temple. As a consequence, it was found necessary to examine the structure by removing the coats of plaster covering at various places so that the nature of the stone and the extent of decay it had undergone during the centuries past. Removal of plaster would enable us to undertake remedial measures affecting the fabric of the temple structure.

Work could not progress as desired. Stay orders by the High Court of Orissa to stop the conservation work were got vacated by the Government of India as the Judges were satisfied that the steps taken by the Archaeological Survey of India were in the interest of the structural stability of the temple. However, in the fifth meeting of the EC held on 4th February 1985 a Technical Committee (TC) was recommended with experts from the Central Building Research Institute, Roorkee, Structural Engineering Research Centre, Ghaziabad, Departmentof Roads and Buildings, Govt. of Orissa (Dikshit, 1998, 30-34).

Main Temple

The Jagannath temple which stands on a raised platform approachable from ground level by a flight of 22 steps has four gates and two compound walls known as Meghanada Prachir and Kurma Prachir(Fig.2). The outer wall has serrated battlements on the top for defensive purpose. The gates are ornately decorated. The *deul* of this temple is rising to a height of about 65 metres, thus making it the tallest temple in Orissa (Fig. 3). In style, it is the duplicate of the Lingaraj Temple of Bhubaneswar. It is *panchrath* on plan with its *jangha* divided into two storeys. The sculptures on the walls are covered with protective coats of heavy lime plaster. The first such coat according to the *Madalapanji*, a temple chronicle was done during the reign of Prataparudra (1504-1532). This plastering was repeated by Narsinghadev in 1647. As the temple was destroyed by the Muslim, it was again thoroughly repaired in the time of Krishna Deva Raya (1713-1718). After 50 years, the Queen of Virakishoradeva again got the walls plastered. The *jagamohana* of the temple having the principal segments of a *rekha deul* follows the pattern of the Lingaraj temple. The *natamandir* was added later on whereas the *bhogmandapa* is smaller than the other structures.

Among the important temples inside the complex, mention may be made of *muktimandapa,* Narsimha temple, Bimla Devi temple, Bhubaneswari temple, Surya Mandir and the temple of Lakshmi. Besides one can see Kaibalya Baikuntha, the flower gardens, the Ananda Bazaar and Snan Vedi where the deities are given ceremonial bath.

Before taking up the conservation of the main temple, it was decided to remove the plaster from the Lakshmi temple situated in the same complex with common problems of the main temple, so as to develop necessary expertise for tackling the problem.

Case Study of the Lakshmi Temple

The Archaeological Survey of India (ASI) took up the preservation of the Lakshmi temple located inside the Jagannath temple-complex in the first instance. The survey of Lakshmi temple revealed leakage at the junction of the *Mukhasala* and *Vimana* as in the case of the Lord Jagannath temple. It was stopped by removing the decayed stones and injecting cement mortar. The plaster on the walls of the temple was removed and the damaged stones were replaced.

While removing the plaster from the walls of the Lakshmi temple, it was noticed that the coats of plaster were not applied directly on the friezes but potsherds covered them and then plaster was applied. Where the cavities were deep, brickbats were also used in order to provide a base for plastering. It may be added that this kind of intensive conservation work by the ASI Survey brought to light the magnificent details of ancient, sculptures and carvings decorating the walls of the Lakshmi temple (Pl. 3–6). All the loose sculptures and disintegrated stones were reset in position after proper documentation and numbering and removing the rusted and worn out dowels. Joints of vertical walls of the entire temple having wide cracks at several places were conserved with epoxy resin mortar and combination mortar. The surface has been treated chemically to remove all injurious salts and treated with preservative layers.

Damaged condition of the Main Temple

The general condition of the main temple at the time of protection was far from satisfactory. The available ancient records show that in order to protect the stones from the actions of salt and rain water, the temple was plastered over four times between the sixteenth and eighteenth centuries and as a result, the thickness of plaster cover over the damaged stones increased to about 30 centimetres. The temple was also damaged by vandals. This might have been a contributory factor in developing fissures in the facing masonry,the other reason being oxidization of iron wires, dowels and clamps used in the original construction.

Crack Pattern

During the conservation of the main temple of Lord Jagannath a typical crack pattern was noticed in exposed portion of the structure such as:

(i) vertical cracks which may cause slipping of a portion of the structure;

(ii) vertical cracks which are not very deep but at the same time dangerous;

(iii) horizontal or vertical cracks which are not structural in nature but should be repaired in the interest of strengthening the structure; and

(iv) cracks of local nature which is not dangerous but should be closed to prevent further deterioration and ingress of rain water.

In respect of category (i) epoxy resin grouting together with the use of copper dowels for stiching the masonry was suggested, whereas for category (ii) the suggested treatment was grouting with conventional materials for the interior preparation and resin grouting on the periphery and sealing of joints or cracks by resin putty. For category (iii), grouting with conventional material with resin pointing was suggested. For the last category (iv), resin coupled with copper dowels would suffice. The removal of plaster alone could undertake remedial measures to the fabric of the temple structure.

In the main temple removal of old plaster was taken up first to find out the nature and extent of damage and the causes of the flaking of stones. The dead load of the plaster was adding to the total load of the structure causing additional strain. There are as many as nine plaster layers. The plaster has lost its binding property and has become porous. During the rains absorption of moisture containing salt is high and the dead weight of plaster increases considerably.

Masonry consolidation

In the main temple, a portion at the junction of the *Mukhasala* and the *Vimana* was found leaking in the rainy season. The dead plaster at the junction was removed and cracks and fissures were carefully grouted with conventional material and water-tightened with suitable mortar mixed with a water proofing compound. It was felt necessary to remove the plaster along the vertical side of the junction of the *Vimana* and the *Mukhasala* so as to study in what way the two parts of the structure were integrated. The slope of the covering, plaster was so aligned as to facilitate easy drainage of water away from the joints.

The stone masonry, which was covered with thick lime plaster all over the walls of *bada-deul* was badly shattered. The de-plastering work was limited to the springing level of spire. It was taken up at the corners first and then extended towards the middle portion. After major portion of de-plastering work was done, consolidation of the northern side was taken up first. This portion was thoroughly stabilized by grouting fissures and voids, resetting broken dislodged members and replacing missing members.

The process of consolidation up to the end of upper *jangha* was continued and the eastern, northern and western sides were consolidated. All the projecting members were further reinforced by inserting stainless steel round bars with resin mortar. At this point, measures were taken to arrest further decay of the recently exposed and consolidated stone masonry by means of chemical or other stone preservatives (Pl. 7 and 8).

The southern side of the upper *jangha* was found badly damaged due to multiple cracks and missing architectural members. This was anticipated as the additional corbel masonry supports were provided to heavy *amla*-stone on this side of *sikhara*. This work was also attended to, but it was modified in 1996 by introducing stainless steel pillars around the beki, each supported by horizontal connecting bars.

As the de-plastering work was taken up beyond the level of the springing of the spire, further work was slow. A wooden platform was constructed above the scaffolding to give support to the falling debris and with the help of specially designed channel made of zinc sheets, the loose mortar was brought down to avoid floating of dust and dirt in the temple premises.

Apart from the main shrine, subsidiary shrines like *Muktimandapa*, which was in danger, has been consolidated by strengthening the weathered columns and broken stone beams, aftc grouting fissures and voids with resin mortar. Capitals of all the columns were also strengthened by epoxy resin, duly strengthened by inserting non-corrosive metal pins, and missing stones were replaced with new ones. The de-plastering work of Narasimha, Surya temple and Vimla temples was also taken up from 1987 onwards. In some places, the khondalite stone had deteriorated, and so it was replaced.

Attempt was also made to save the carved portion by fixing it with the help of epoxy resin on a new stone of the same size making it a monoblock. But at some places it looked out of place and should be discouraged. The worn out carved portion was strengthened by injecting PMC through drilled holes. The same technique may also be used by the ASI in future for conserving the carved portion at Konarak and elsewhere in Orissa

Removal of some plaster from the door-jams of Narasimha temple brought to light an ancient inscription.

The western and northern parts of *kurmabeda* were also attended to for structural repairs.

Falling of a stone from *Amla Bedha*

The Puri town was seized with panic when on the 14 June, 1990 a stone weighing about five tonnes fell down from the *amla bedha* i.e. from the top of the main temple. Fortunately it did not damage the structure but it created in the minds of the citizens and the Government great concern as the structure showed worrying cracks and signs of degradation. This incident also provided an opportunity to understand and assess the process of deterioration and safety levels of the temple. The ASI immediately called an Expert Committee meeting on 15-16 July, 1990 to consider the possible causes of the unexpected collapse of the *amalaka* stone and the remedial steps to be taken and to consider whether the temple is sound and also to formulate further programme of work for immediate and long term measures for the safety and proper preservation of the temple. Many scientific institutions were involved and their experiments and analytical tests strengthened the view that the plaster has lost its physical and chemical characteristics. The binding strength of the mortar has been impaired through centuries of exposure and other climatic factors, especially salt laden winds. At present the plaster has become more porous allowing retention of moisture and, therefore, the structure is now loaded with a plaster which does not serve any further purpose. The complete de-plastering has to continue so that hidden defects are identified and rectified.

In the subsequent meeting held on 18 May 1992, it was reported that de-plastering was completed and fallen portion of the *amalaka* restored by substituting new ones as per the original along with sealing of the cracks and fissures and grouting wherever necessary (Pls. 9, 10 and 11).

Garbhagriha: falling of stone inside

On the 13 August 1992 at about 16.00 hours a mishap again occurred. Two pieces of corbelled stone weighing about one tonne with lime, detached from the south-east corner of the *garbhagriha* fell down inside the temple at a distance of about four metres from the *'Ratna Singhasan,'* that is the seat of Lord Balabhadra. This falling of stone made public demand more vocal, although it was a known fact that during the last years, stones had fallen from *garbha-griha* roof and also from *amla* and other places at frequent intervals. However, this incident of collapse without warning created a state of panic about the stability of the structure. A Technical Group appointed by the ASI with experts from CBRI Roorkee, SERC Ghaziabad, IIT Kharagpur and Caltech, Calcutta met and discussed possible conservation measures-short term as well as long term, and suggested finalization of the work within a specified time.

Condition of the *garbhagriha*

It was noticed by experts that several veneer stones had cracked almost in the centre along the full length and were lying loose and prone to falling off. These cracks at some places were not visible from the front but were noticed after the removal from their seats. The continuous cracks which are about two metres long were also noticed at the corners of walls on the ground floor and also in the first floor. The southern face of the corridor was considerably bulging out on the first floor, whereas on the northern side, a couple of stone bulged out. The steel joists supporting the first floor slab were seen heavily rusted. The cantilever stone slabs on the outside were badly cracked. It was in all probability due to the projection of supporting decorative sculptures.

The walls are about 5.3 metres thick and are made up of veneer stones joined together with clamps forming the two outer wall skins. Inside these outer skins, there was stone rubble of roughly dressed unconnected stones with large gaps leaving continuous vertical joints at places. There seemed to be no interlocking between the outside veneer stones and the inner stones constituting the rubble (Trikha, 1993). Still there may be large voids in the rubble masonry. Condensed moisture has seeped through the plaster in the rubble masonry. As there is no bonding between the two walls and rubble stones, they must have affected the pattern of load distribution. The bulging of a few stones on the northern side may be due to this fact. However, no wall of the temple was opened and examined.

The greatest damage was done to the temple by the iron clamps used to connect the adjacent stones. The work of de-plastering should continue and suitable chemical preservative be used for holding the adjacent stones in the veneer together. Epoxy sand mortar may be used to fix these stones in position. The visible cracks both on the inside and outside should be sealed by epoxy injection. It was essential to grout such materials by injection technique which will not solidify the structure fully and alter its structural behaviour.

Appointment of a Core Committee by the Govt. of Orissa

Seeing the gravity of the situation, the Government of Orissa also constituted a core committee for examining measures to be taken for preservation of the temple. Experts from the ASI, SAIL, RRL, Bhubaneshwar, Civil Engineering Department., IIT Kharagpur, representatives of chemical firms-Caltech, Cico and Sika Qualcrete, all based in Calcutta, and PWD engineers of Orissa were invited for a workshop on 25-26 December, 1992 (Recommendation of the working group, Govt. of Orissa). The experts, agreed to the suggestion of the ASI for a provision of a Truss of stainless steel, 304 for the exposed members and stainless steel 316 for bearings, etc. which will be embedded in the wall instead of vertical column like structure with cantilever brackets.

Stainless Steel Truss

The Truss, in the shape of a Frustrum of a trapezium of 4.42 x 4.40 metres at the top and 8.85 x 8.85 metres at the bottom with a height of 4 metres, was designed by IIT

Kharghpur for a total load of 300 tonnes against a total incumbent load of 480 tonnes. The rest of the load was transferred through chemical bonding of stones to the main temple walls at 1.5 metres below the lowest corbel. Six purlins run below each of the layers of corbel stones. The base runner was fixed in the temple with care and embedding and cutting of chases proceeded in a phased manner. The Truss with horizontal ties to reduce lateral displacement was found meeting the requirements. The ASI agreed to entrust the fabrication of the Truss to Orissa Small Scale Industries Corporation. However, it was also opined that it should not be supported on the walls but rest on the newly constructed pillars. The work was completed in time. (Pl. 12).

Remedial strategy

The ASI, which took over the maintenance and supervision of the temple after the First Expert Committee meeting in 1973, continued conservation and preservation work by removing the outside plaster, cleaning the stone surface by a light acytic acid and thereafter applying methyle-methacrylate 2% to the stone for preserving and protecting them. This procedure was followed by the ASI i.e. extraction of injurious soluble salts from the fabric of the monument, cleaning of the surface by harmless chemicals, consolidation of fragile stones followed by the fungicidal treatment to eradicate micro-organisms and preservation with a thermo-plastic used internationally by experts. The treatment was considered necessary because of its proximity of the monument to the sea (Minutes of the Expert Committee Meetings from 1973 to 1992).

After the fall of *amalaka* and corbel stones, structural renovation measures were taken for grouting the ashlar stone rubble masonry with PMC (Polymer Modified Cementations) for sealing of cracks and joints on all the three floors after making grooves and pinning the corbel and other stones with stainless steel pins with epoxy resin formulation. The adhesion of the ashlar masonry surface with the grout mix is an important requirement for structural strength and durability. It is evident that the polymer loading with addition of plasticizers and retarders helps to secure adequate adhesion.(Sharma and Maiti, 1996). Since the polymer emulsion has 40 percent solid content, the work was entrusted to Caltech India Ltd. Calcutta who prepared the samples from the ordinary Portland cement with polymer loadings of 5% and 10%. The cracks and joints were sealed by PMC of required consistency mixed with stone dust and strengthened by fixing stainless steel 'L' shaped strips. About eighty corbels were pinned by drilling holes and inserting 1m to 1.5m long stainless steel rods. Only air curing was allowed. The bond strength of all PMC mortars was more than that of the cement mortar. The different grout mix formulations were used first in plan scheme and setting times were determined by using Vicat Apparatus by fixing water content. The grouting was performed under pressure inside and outside through a perforated pipe about 2.5 to 3.00 metres long and then inserted into drilled holes at a space of 1.00 - 1.50 metre. The consolidation of vertical inner walls of the ground floor by drilling holes and injecting cement polymer mixture was carried out. The eastern arched corridor of the first floor inside the walls and corbels and the second floor were also grouted for strengthening the core (IAR 93-94, 168). As the walls are very thick, care was taken to limit the initial grout intake by reducing the pressure. The grouting from outside was done in parallel bands to avoid excessive consolidation (Pl. 13).

Acknowledgements

I am grateful to Shri M.N. Deshpande, former Director General, and Shri R. Sengupta, Director Conservation, Archaeological Survey of India, who are responsible for formulating the conservation policy of this temple. In this project Dr. B.B. Lal, Shri B.N. Tandon and Shri R.K. Sharma directed the scientific operations and Dr. S. Maiti worked meticulously in the field. Drs. S.S. Biswas and G.C. Chauley also carried out conservation of this temple. Special thanks are also due to Shri A.N. Tiwari, who was instrumental on behalf of the Govt. of Orissa, under the then Chief Minister Smt. Nandini Satapathy to start this work. Prof. A.P. Gupta, Shri G.C. Mitra, Shri A.C. Grover, Prof. D.N. Trikha, Shri B.K. Goel and Shri M.P. Jaisingh contributed in their own way to strengthening the structural stability of this temple. Shri S.B. Choudhary, S. Upadhyay and Mihir Sarkar carried out structural conservation at the site. Shri Bishwadip Sen of Caltech India Ltd. extended grouting facilities, including supply of material. The photographs are by the courtesy of the Archaeological Survey of India.

REFERENCES

Dikshit, K.N. 1988, Conservation of Lord Jagannath temple, *Journal of Conservati Property in India*, vol. 21, New Delhi, pp. 30-34.

Government of Orissa 1992, *Recommendation of the Working Group for the Preservation of ShriJagannath Temple,* Puri (Cyclostyled copy).

Indian Archaeology-A Review, 1975-76 to 1994-95.

Minutes of the Expert Committee Meeting on Lord Jagannath temple appointed by the Archaeological Survey of India from First meeting (24-25 September 1973) to Tenth meeting (18 May 1992), including minutes of the Technical Expert Committee. The author was Member Secretary of most of these committee meetings since 1973 and participated as Superintending Archaeologist, Director and Joint Director General Archaeological Survey of India till his retirement in 1994.

O' Malley, L.S.S., 1929. *Puri* (Bihar and Orissa Gazetteers), Patna.

Sharma, R.K.and S.Maity 1996, Grouts for Structural Strengthening of Ashlar Masonry Structures, *Journal of Conservation of Cultural Property in India*, vol. 29, New Delhi, pp. 28-38.

Trikha, D.N., 1993, *Report of the visit to Lord Jagannath Temple at Puri* (Director, SERC, Ghaziabad, (Typed Note).

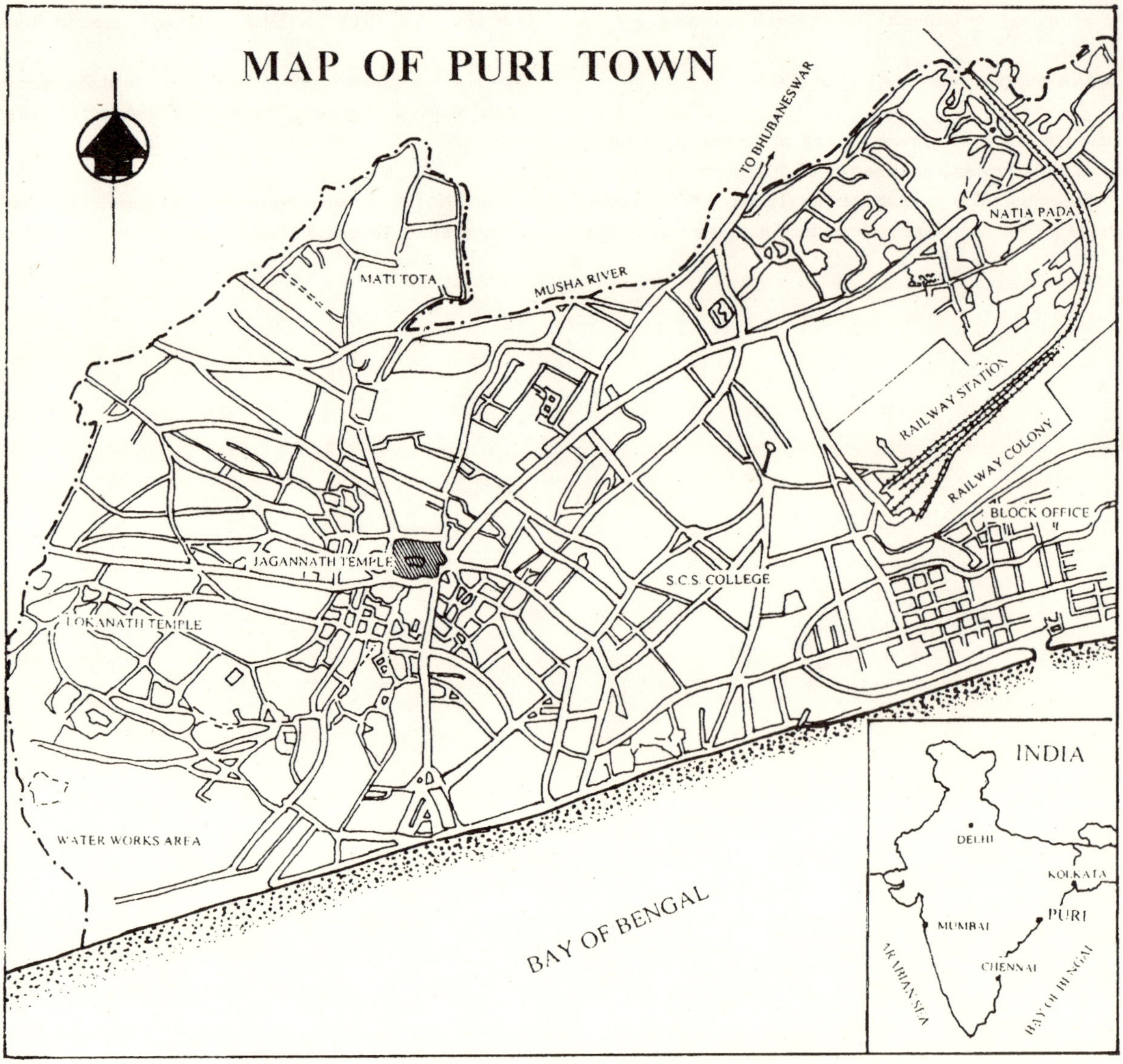
MAP OF PURI TOWN
TO BHUBANESWAR
NATIA PADA
MATI TOTA
MUSHA RIVER
RAILWAY STATION
RAILWAY COLONY
BLOCK OFFICE
JAGANNATH TEMPLE
S.C.S. COLLEGE
LOKANATH TEMPLE
WATER WORKS AREA
BAY OF BENGAL
INDIA
DELHI
KOLKATA
PURI
MUMBAI
CHENNAI

Fig. 1.

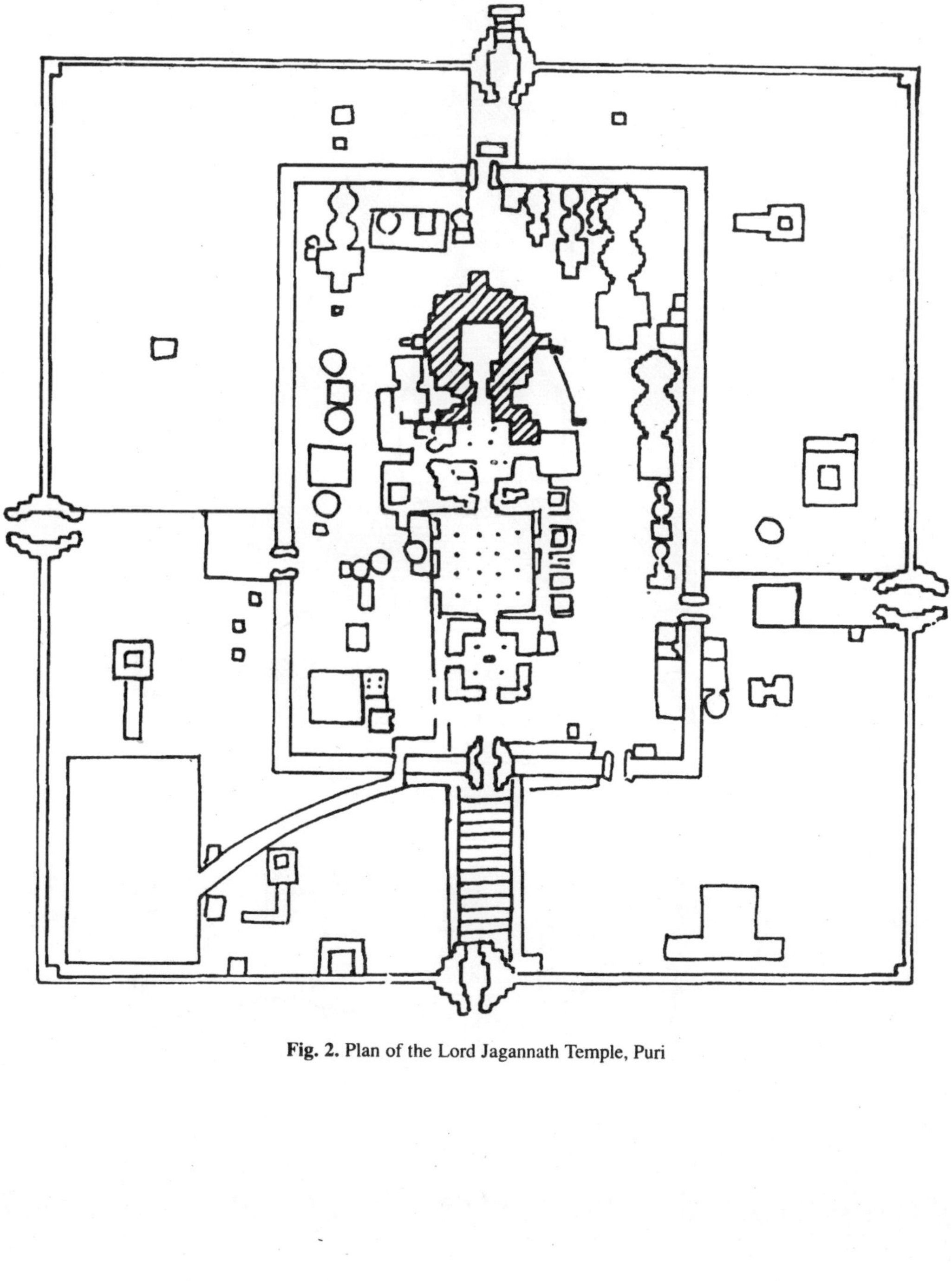

Fig. 2. Plan of the Lord Jagannath Temple, Puri

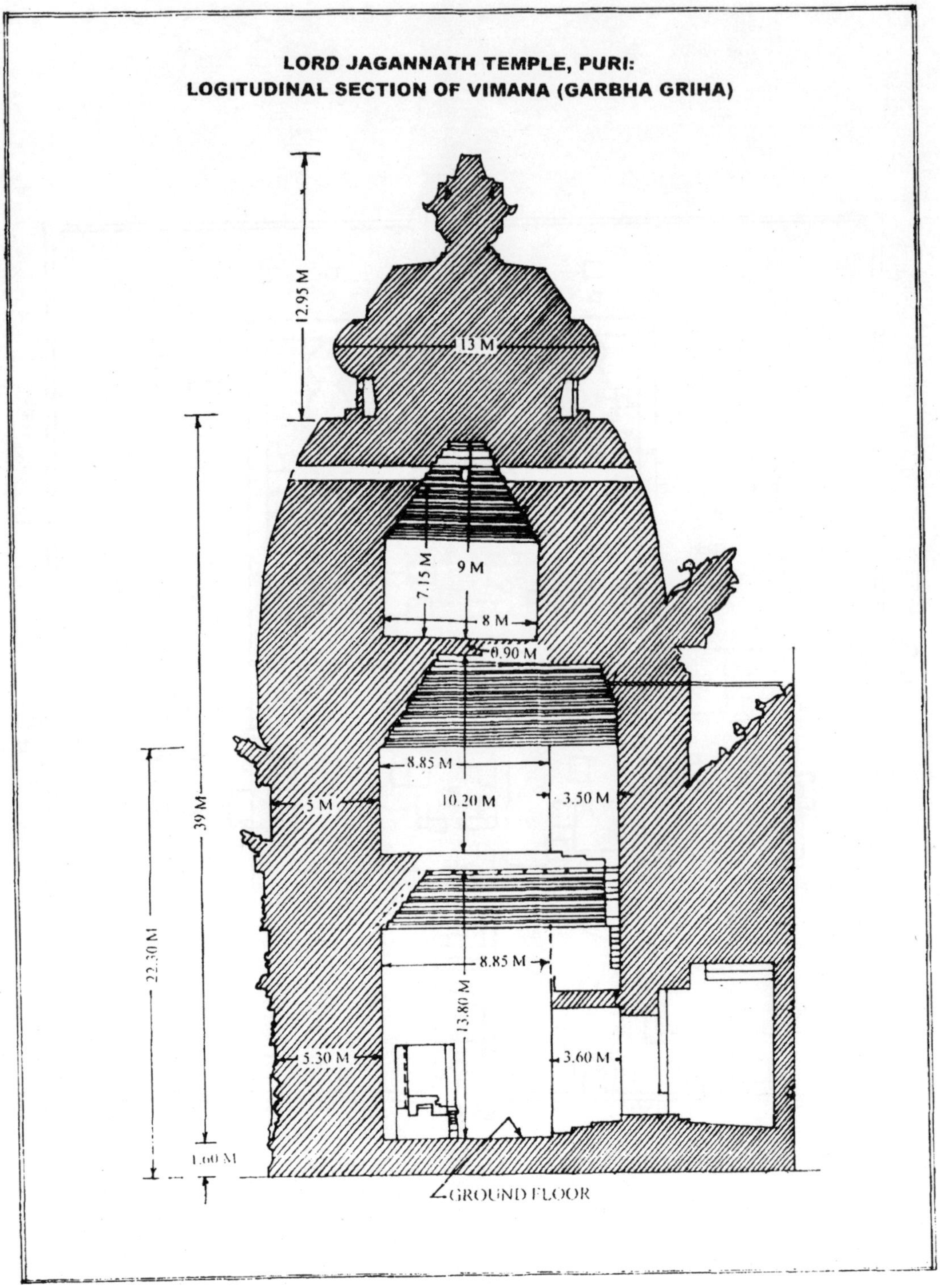
LORD JAGANNATH TEMPLE, PURI:
LOGITUDINAL SECTION OF VIMANA (GARBHA GRIHA)
12.95 M
13 M
9 M
7.15 M
8 M
0.90 M
39 M
8.85 M
10.20 M
3.50 M
5 M
22.30 M
8.85 M
13.80 M
5.30 M
3.60 M
1.60 M
GROUND FLOOR

Fig. 3.

A Study of Group-Information of the Temples of Orissa

D.K. NAYAK*

Orissa is as a land of religions. In the pre-Christian era Jainism and Buddhism were prominent. However, in the early centuries of the Christian era Brahminism began to flourish in Orissa. With the emergence of the 'cult of devotion' and the concept of 'personal God', images were made for worship and temples were built. Initially these were known as *devagriha, devalaya,* and *devakula* (Bhattacharya 1963: 264). The earliest reference is to be found in the Hathigumpha inscription of Kharavela as *Devayatana* (Sircar 1965: 213-221). The terms like *gopura* and *sikhara* are noticed for the first time in Orissa in this lithic record of Kharavela (Sircar 1965: L.17). A long piece of stone found from the Bhadrakali temple of Bhadrak contains an inscription of Sri Gana (Sircar 1965: 99-100) where reference to three devas occurs. It is dated in the 3rd century A.D. and presumed to be a lintel of a temple. The Asanpat inscription, dated in 4th century A.D., records the construction of a temple (Dash 1965: 01-08). Afterwards, *Devakula* and *Devalaya* are found in later inscriptions of Soma and Ganga dynasties (Rajguru 1960, 1966, 1975). The much familiar word *'Mandira'* was used as a substitute for *Devalaya* or *Devayatana* in the 7th century A.D. The first appearance of the term is traced in Banabhatta's *Kadambari* (Bhattacharya 1963: 265).

With the formulation of canons of architecture, temples were being constructed as per the norms laid down by them. The Indian *Shilpashastras* (Saraswati 1953: 233-34) categorised temples into three broad group- *Nagara, Dravida* and *Vesara* on the basis of their location. Nagara belongs to the area stretching from the Himalayas to the Vindhyas, *Vesara* to the area between the Vindhyas and the river Krishna, and Dravida from river Krishna to Kanyakumari. On the other hand, Fergusson divided temples into three groups based on geographical distribution, such as 'Indo-Aryan', Dravidian' and 'Chalukyan' which is the same as *Nagara, Dravida and Vesara. Manasara* however, refers to the formation of four groups of temples taking into account of the ground-plan divided into angles or circles. Those are *Nagara, Dravida, Vesara* and *Andhra* which are quadrangular (*Vedasra*), octagonal (*vasvasra*), circular (*vyasra*) and six angled (*Sadasra*) (Acharya 1946: 381). R.D. Banerjee (1931: 235) has drawn the attention of scholars to an inscription found at the temple of Amritesvara at Holal in Bellary district where it is mentioned that Bammoja, son of Paddoja, was proficient in four kinds of temple architecture, namely, *Nagara, Dravida, Vesara and Kalinga.* The Sorab Taluq inscription refers to *Nagara, Dravida* and *Bhumija* temples (Bhattacharya 1963:157). The Amritesvar temple of Halal in Bellary district of Karnataka mentions Kalinga type which according to Panigrahi, is a subsection of *Nagara* type.

But the Orissan architects devised a novel division

*Reader, Dept. of History, Sambalpur University, Orissa

based on the elevation of the temples. The *Shilpashastras* of Orissa classified temples into three divisions, i.e., *Rekha, Bhadra, and Khakhara* (Bose 1932). *Rekha* has a curvelinear superstructure which is called *vimana and sikhara.* The Bhadra temple contains a pyramidal elevation composed of receding platforms (*pidhas*) piled upward. It serves as the frontal hall (*Mukhamandapa* or *Jagamohana*) of the main temple (*vimana*) of *Rekha* order. The *Khakhara* temple is distinguished by its wagon-vault roof. It is generally rectangular, though square is not unknown. The Vaital temple, Gauri temple of Bhubaneswar, Varahi temple of Charurasi, etc., fall in this category. It is said to have been derived from the *Chaitya*-hall. These groups were formed on stylistic ground.

In the medieval period, temples were formed into groups based on number of temples. This system of numerical division pertains mainly to Saiva temples. The famous place of the twin temples of Gandharadi is called Chari Sambhu. The main twin temples are dedicated to Siddhasvara Siva and Nilamadhava. On the four corners of the big platform are noticed holes where once lingas were implanted. Probably, small shades were over there. Due to the presence of four lingas, the place was called Chari-Sambhu.

The next variety is *Panchayatana* temple the earliest example of which is at Deogarh near Jhansi. It is a Vishnu temple of 5th century. It is a group of five temples where the main temple occupies the central position and is surrounded by four smaller temples on the four corners. The small temples also house the lingas if it is a Saiva temple. In some late Saiva temples of the *panchayatana* type the four subsidiary temples, i.e., Ganesa on the south. Karttikeya on the west, Durga on the north, and Nandi in the east are located. Such an example is available at Suvarnapura (Sonepur) in western Orissa. In the *Panchayatana* group the temples are in the enclosure or in the premises. The Kanakesvara temple at Kualo, Manikesvara temple at Sukleswar, *Panchayatana* temple at Ganesvarpur, *Panchayatana* temple at Sorda near Bolangir and Brahmesvara temple at Bhuvaneswar are some of the examples. The *Panchayatana* temple is normally named after the central shrine. The group of five temples are dedicated to five gods-Vishnu, Siva, Ganesa, Surya and Devi (Durga). The sequence of the Gods in Panchayatana puja is detailed below (Chaturvedi 1981):

Centre	*Agneya*	*Vayavya*	*Nairitta*	*Aisanya*
Vishnu	Ganesa	Sakti	Ravi	Siva
Ganesa	Siva	Ravi	Sakti	Vishnu
Ravi	Ganesa	Sakti	Visnu	Siva
Sakti	Siva	Ravi	Ganesa	Vishnu
Siva	Ravi	Sakti	Ganesa	Vishnu.

The layout of the *Panchayatana* temple should be as per the *Panchayatana puja vidhi.* This is named after the central shrine. For instance, if the central shrine is dedicated to Siva, the complex is called Siva *panchyatana;* if it enshrines Visnu, it is known as Vishnu *panchayatana*; if Ganesa presides in the central temple, it becomes Ganesa *panchayatana* and so on. Thus there are five types of temples. In Orissa, only Siva *panchayatana* temples are found except one. But all five temples of the complex enshrine only lingam, not other deities as prescribed. In Ganesvarpur *panchayatana* complex, the main temple is dedicated to Vishnu and four corner temples are empty. It may be presumed that all the corner temples either had Vishnu as their presiding deities or Siva, Surya, Ganesa and Durga. The *panchayatana* variety was adopted at an early date perhaps with the beginning of the *panchayatana upasana* (worship of five deities).

Much closer to the concept of *panchayatana*, another group evolved as *ashtaparivara* category. In this variety, in place of five, eight temples are built within the premises of the main temple. Though it is named as *parivara* temple, the temples are not occupied by the family members of Siva. In some *ashtaparivara* complex all the temples are found enshrined with Siva lingas only. The Paikpada temple-complex and the temple-complex of Mukhalingam are good examples of *ashtaparivara* variety. The Madhukesvara temple at Mukhalingam comprises central shrine and four temples at the four corners, and three temples having barrel-vaulted roof on the three sides. Dehejia is of the view that the barrel-vaulted temples for Ganesa, Karttikeya and Parvati, the *parsvadevatas* of Siva temples (Dehejia, 1979:35). The other four shrines have *lingas*. The Patalesvara temple at Paikpada also is an eight-shrine temple. In the four corner-shrines are *lingas*. Two other temples also enshrine *lingas*. But the last one is a Saptamatrika temple. If Beglar is to be believed, then Baudh Ramnath temple also belonged to the eight-shrine variety.

In this category there is another group of temples, which is known as Ashtasambu. Like wise there are Dvadasasambhu, Shodasasambhu temples. The Charisambhu formation has already been discussed. Dvadasasambhu temples are found in Prachivalley as described by *Prachi Mahatmya* (Panda 1969). *Isanasivagurudeva paddhati* refers to Shodasasambhus (Mishra 1987). The Ashtasambhu temples are noticed in Kualo, Puri town, Prachivalley, Bhubaneswar in coastal Orissa and the former state of Sambalpur, Sambalpur town (Naik 1993) and Sonepur town (Dorjee 1987) of the western part of Orissa. Sometimes the eight *lingas* enshrined in one temple like Kanakesvara temple earns the name Ashtasambhu. The Ashtasambhu temples do not maintain uniformity in their nomenclature. The names of the Ashtasambhu of Sambalpur town do not tally with the names of the Ashtasambhu found in the ex-state of Sambalpur neither the Sambalpur group of temples bear the similar names of those of Sonepur group. These names do not have the phonetic similarities with the names of Astasambhus of Kualo or of Pachi valley. In Sonepur group, the eight temples belonging to the same group are not contemporaneous. They are not built in the same span of time. They are not even constructed by the same king or a single person.

As the temples belong to different periods and are built by various architects, the homogeneity in architectural details could not be maintained though the general broad components like *vimana* and *jagamohana* with their four essential parts like *pista, bada, gandi* and *mastaka* are found in most of the temples under discussion. Some temples are built on the bank of the river and some are on the border of the tank. Kedarnath temple is constructed in the middle of the tank, Budharaja temple stands on the summit of a mountain. Thus, the location of the temples also varies widely. Different legends are found regarding the manifestation of the lord in *Linga* form. The *Lingas* of Bimalesvara of Huma, Svapneswara of Sorna and Nilakantheswara of Niljee are said to have been found by cows. Cow showering milk on the *Linga* is a common legend not only in Orissa but all over India. The establishment of some *lingas* has been attributed to Lord Rama. In this category fall Ramesvara of Sonepur and Kedarnath of Amvabhana. Lord Gudesvara on the bank of Mahanadi near Durgapalu has a peculiar legend regarding its origin. It is said that the Lord revealed Himself in the form of the linga made of molasses for which he was named so.

In many examples the first to find the *linga* is non-brahmin. Brahmin association with the revelation of the *linga* is not found in these temples. Divergence in style, placement time and builders suggests that they do not belong to a cognate group. Now the question arises that why they are termed as Ashtasambhu. Does it reflect some sub-sectarian association on the group of temples? In some situation religious architecture develops as result of the influence of ascetics or *acharyas* of a particular sect. As these temples are called 'Sambhu' temples, one is tempted to search for a sect which is associated with the term 'Sambhu', one among many names of Siva.One such branch of Saivism was flourishing in the Kalachuri kingdom of Dahala and Daksina Kosala. That branch is known as *Mattamayuri* sect of Saivism. The Ranod Inscription (Kielhorn 1892), the Bilhari Inscription (Mirashi 1995: No.44), the Chandrehe Inscription (Mirashi 1995: No.45), the Gurgi Inscription (Mirashi 1995: No. 46), the Jabalpur Inscription (Mirashi 1995: No.63), the Gwalior Museum Inscription (Mirashi 1955: CL1) and the Malkapuram Inscription (Ramayya Pantula 1929: 156-62) contain lists of a succession of *acharyas* of *Mattamayuri* sect. Almost all the names of the *acharyas* bear the suffix 'Siva' or 'Sambhu' like Kavacha Siva, Sadasiva, Hridayasiva, Chudasiva, Prabhavasiva, Prasanta Siva etc. and Rudra Sambhu, Dharma Sambhu, Isana Sambhu, Patanga Sambhu, Kirtti Sambhu, Soma Sambhu, Visvesvara Sambhu, etc. The *Mattamayurikas* accepted the appellations 'Siva' and 'Sambhu' as a cognomen of their religious order. The centres of the sect were at Mattamayura, Madhumati and Golaki Matha (Mishra 1987). The *acharyas* of these places were undertaking religious journey to distant places for propagation of their faith. The sages of *Mattamayuri* lineage were settled at different places as evidenced from the Inscriptions found in Malwa, Konkan, Orissa, Dahala south Kosala (Shastri 1971:170). The Saiva pontifs of this faith came to Sonepur-Bolangir-Sambalpur area which tract of land was conquered and ruled by the Kalachuris. As there was no infights or sectarian hatred between *Pasupatas* and *Mattamayurikas* they flourished simultaneously (Sahu 1987:310-17). The Pasupata had no special inclination for assuming Sambhu-ending names (Mirashi 1955:CL1). So Siva temples might have been named as Sambhu temples due to predominant influence of the *Mattamayurikas*. But it is not understood why they made a group of eight

(Ashta Sambhu). They could have grouped ten, eleven, or thirteen temples in a set. The *'Isanasivagurudeva paddhati'*, (Shastri 1925: 415-16) refers to sixteen forms of Siva out of which the Kalachuri inscriptios repeatedly mention Uma-Mahesvara, Gangadhara and Natesh forms (Mishra 1987:26). Isana Siva was an acharya of Saiva Siddhanta system of which *Mattamayuri* is a sub-sect. The Mattamayurikas worship Siva associated with Uma, the celestial river Ganga, snakes, Moon and Matted hair (Sahu 1987: 310-17). So sixteen forms (Shodasa Sambhu) may be taken as *Mattamayura* conception but not of Ashta Sambhus. There may be two propositions for the emphasis on number EIGHT. It is, not improbably that the number 'eight' was considered auspicious by the *Sivacharyas* or Siva worshipers at that time. Because the number eight is known to have been used in forming groups of various types (Sircar 1965:232) like *Ashta Siddhi, Ashta Vasu, Ashta Naga, Ashta Takshan, Ashta Mangala, Ashta Dikpala, Ashta Bhuti, Ashta Murti, Ashtanga Yoga, Ashta Yama, Asha Prahara*, etc., even in the early period *stotras* or prayers to gods and goddesses were composed in eight verses which became famous as *ashtakas* (octave) such as *Govindashtaka Mahalakshmiashtaka, Suryashtaka, Sivashtaka*, etc. On this ground the group of eight might have been formed and termed as Ashsta Sambhu. The second possibility may be that there were eight forms of Siva. The Tewar Inscription of Gayakarna opens with an invocation to the eight forms of Siva (Misrashi 1955: 306-07). The Kausitaki Brahmana mentions all the eight names of Rudra Siva (Goyal 1986:241). Those names are Rudra, Sarva, Ugra, Asani, Mahadeva, Isana, Bhava and Pasupati. Among these the first four represent his terrific aspect and the latter four of the pacific character. The pantheon of Pasupata Saiva consists of Siva Ashtamurtis, i.e., Sarva, Ugra, Bhava, Isana, Rudra, Bhima, Pasupati and Mahadeva (Mishra 1987:27). Though little difference is found in the eight names mentioned in the *Kauitaki Brahmana* and those of the Pasupata Pantheon, it is apparent that both the lists point to the ashtamurti or eight forms of Siva. So there is no denying the fact that the Pasupatas were the worshipers of eight forms of Siva. They worship these eight forms of Siva with *Ashta Pushpika* as evidenced from a number of epigraphs. The Pasupati Temple Inscription of Jayadeva in Nepal (Pathak 1980:18) (A, IX, 178) describes the royal gift of an eight petalled silver lotus to the god so that eight forms may be accommodated on its petals. The Sdok Kak Thom Inscription of Udayaditya Varman (Pathak 1980. 18) mentions that an *ashta pushpika* was being offered to Ashtatanu daily by the royal priest. Bana (Pathak 1980) also refers to the worship of eight forms by *ashtapushpika*. The number eight was an auspicious number for the *Pasupatas*. They consider the eight forms of Siva as the guardians of *ashtasiddhis* as revealed by the Harsha Stone Inscription. According to *Vayaviya Samhita* of *Siva Mahapurana*, the eight-fold forms (ashtamurti) are earth, water, fire, air, the *akasa* (space), the soul, the Sun and the Moon (Dasgupta 1965:119). The lord is called by different names such as Sarvi, Bhavi, Raudra, etc., in correspondence with his performance of different functions.

Pasupatas have already gained ground in Puri-Bhubaneswar since 6th–7th century A.D. It is evidenced by the representation of Lakulisa images on the walls of the Bharatesvara and Parasuramesvara temples at Bhubaneswar (Panigrahi 1961:134-35). The Bharatesvara temple is dated to 6th–7th century A.D. (Fabri, 1974:121). Lakulisa is considered to be the founder of the *Pasupata* Saivism. But the inscription (Rajguru 1960) of the Sailodbhava kings belonging to the same period contain the descriptions of the god Siva which resemble the desctiptions of the lord found in the Chandrehe Inscription of Prabodha Siva, an *acharya* of Mattamayuri sect. This suggests the co-existence of the two cults since the time of Sailodbahavas. In western Orissa, the presence of these cults is felt in the 9th–10th century A.D. The *Mattamayuri* cult gained momentum with the advent of Gagana Siva in the Somavamsi kingdom. He established a centre for the cult in Ranipur-Jharial as revealed from the Somesvara temple inscription (Senapati 1968:40) of the same place. The depiction of Lakulisa images in the Baudh temples (Panigrahi 1961:159) and Somesvara temple (Kosalesvara temple) of Patnagarh indicate the prevalence of the Pasupata-Lakulisa cult in this area. As there was peaceful coexistence and close association between these two cults for a considerably long time there must have been mutual exchange of thoughts which helped develop a syncretic religious trend between them in course of time. It is well nigh possible that the *Mattamayurikas* accepted and included the worship of eight forms of Siva in their cultic religious observances. Therefore, the grouping of 'eight' may be taken as a Pasupata influence. This is more convincing. As the naming of the temple as 'Sambhu' is a clear impact of *Mattamayuri* cult, the compound 'Ashta Sambhu' may be a product of composite thought-process of both the sects.

Thus, the temples of Orissa besides being religious edifices are a conglomeration of numerous groups formed on the basis of regional distribution, angular consideration, stylistic variation and quantitative representation.

REFERENCES

Acharya, P.K. (ed.) 1946, *Manasara: Hindu Architecture in India and Abroad*.

Bhattacharya, T.P. 1963, *The Canons of Indian Art*, Calcutta.381

Banerjee, R.D. 1930-1931. *History of Orissa*, I & II, Calcutta.

Bose, N.K. 1932. *Canon of Orissan Architecture*, Calcutta.

Chaturvedi, S. (Trans.) 1981. *Mantra Mahodadhi by Mahedhara*, Varanasi.

Dasgupta, S.N. 1965, *A History of Indian Philosophy*, V, Delhi:119.

Dash, A. 1965. 'Asanapat Inscription', *Orissa Historical Research Journal* (OHRS). XII. 1-8.

Darjee, K.C. 1987. *Temples of Sonepur*, M.Phil (unpublished) dissertation, Sambalpur University.

Fabri, Charles L. 1974. *History of the Art of Orissa*, Calcutta.

Goyal, S.R. 1986, *Religious History of India*, I, Kusumanjali Prakashan, Meerut.

Kiabhorn, F. 1982. A Stone Inscription from Ranod, *Epigraphia Indica*, I, Calcutta.

Mirashi, V.V. 1955. *Inscriptions of Kalachuri Chedi Era*, C.I.I., IV Pts. I & II. Delhi.

Mishra, R.N. 1987. *Sculptures from Dahala and South Kosala*, Delhi.

Naik, D.S. 1993. *Asta Shambhu Temples of Western Orissa*, M. Phil thesis (unpublished), Sambalpur University.

Nayak, P.M. 1981. *Sonepura*, Souvenir, All Orissa Writers Conference, Sonepur, Orissa.

Panda, R.C. 1969. *Prachinadira Aitihasika Vibhava*, Odisa Sahitya Academy, Bhubaneswar.

Panigrahi, K.C. 1961. *Archaeological Remains at Bhubaneswara*, Cuttack.

Pathak, V.S. 1980. *History of Saiva Cult in Northern India*, Allahabad.

Ramagye Pantula, 1929. J. Malkapuram Stone Pillar Inscription of Padrasiva. *Journal of the Andhra Historical Research* Society. IV:1-2.

Rajaguru, S.N. 1960, 1975. *Inscriptions of Orissa*, Orissa, Vols. IV & V, State Museum, Bhubaneswar.

Sahu, J.K. 1987. *History of Orissa*, I, Cuttack.

Saraswati, S.K. 1953. Temples of Orissa, I, *O.H.R.J.*, I, 4: 233-53.

Shastri, A.M. 1971. *Tripuri* (Hindi) Hindu Granth Akademy, Bhopal.

Senapati, N.M. 1951. *Orissa District Gazetteer, Sambalpur*, Orissa Government Press, Cuttack.

Sircar, D.C. 1965. *Indian Epigraphy*, Delhi.

Excavations at Abhaipur – A Painted Grey Ware Site

U.P. Arora*, R.K. Verma**, Anup Mishra*

The Site

The prehistoric site of Abhaipur is locally known as Abhaipur-Chenna-Nakatikhera. It is situated about a kilometre west of the village of Abhaipur in the Bisalpur tehsil of Pilibhit District, Uttar Pradesh. The river Deoha, also known as Garra, is flowing about one-and-half kilometres east of the site at present. A *nala* branch of this river surrounds the site on three sides, except of the north.

A large part of the site has been destroyed and brought under cultivation by the villagers. About 130m x 100m of the site is spared for the Lord Shiva temple present atop the mound. However, only the south-eastern part of the mound has remained fairly intact. The surface of the site is full of tall grasses; the roots of which have disturbed to a depth of about one metre. (fig.1 to 4).

Aims of the Excavations

Aims of the excavation are the following:

(1) To a certain a problems relating to Painted Ware culture as pointed out several scholars (Joshi 1978, Sinha 1982, Tripathi 1990-91, Nigam 1997).

(2) The surface exploration revealed that Abhaipur is a purely PGW site from the beginning.

(3) The major aims of the excavations at Abhaipur were to understand -(a) the beginning of the process of urbanization in this region and (b) the cultural sequences of this region.

The Excavations

The site was divided into five metre-grids for excavation. A contour map of the south-eastern part of the site was also made. One quadrant (2m x 2m) each of three trenches were excavated; one (B7) at the highest point of the south-eastern part of the mound; two (E7) down to the east on the slope and the third trench (E12) to the south of second trench further down to the slope of mound. In order to understand the cultural sequence the trenches were dug up to the natural soil. The cultural deposit of trench B7 is about 3.84 m comprising a total of 12 layers. Other two trenches (E7 and E12) are about 1.5 m deep comprising six layers each. The trench B7 was found extremely disturbed. There were three large pits successively dug one above the other by the people at different times right from the beginning. The trenches E7 and E12 were less disturbed. (fig. 4).

Cultural Sequence

Due to the limited nature of excavations in the south-eastern periphery of the mound the cultural sequences

* Department of Ancient History and Culture, M.J.P. Rohilkhand University, Bareilly, (U.P.)
** Visiting Professor of Department of Ancient History and Culture, M.J.P. Rohilkhand University, Bareilly, (U.P.)

cannot be made in the present juncture with any precision. The presence of a few Ochre ware fragments along with Black-and-Red ware and other associated wares in the lowest level of all three trenches indicate a similar cultural sequence as found at Ahichchatra. The Painted Grey ware arrives after a deposit of about 70 centimetres from the bottom of trenches E7 and E12. Northern Black Polished ware was not found at the site. Some of the Black slipped ware sherds have a lustrous surface like the NBPW which had been wrongly considered as NBPW during the surface survey.

Owing to the limited finding of Ochre ware sherds, the cultural deposit has been divided into two periods-I. Black-and-Red ware and II. Painted Grey ware.

Structural Remains.

The trench B7 yielded two mud-walls and a circular wattle-and-daub house with post- holes. A large number of burnt reed impressed mud plasters are collected from all the trenches. Besides, a number of rammed mud floors, burnt patches were noticed in all the trenches. A hearth was encountered in the trench B7.

Ceramics

The ceramics can broadly be divided into two groups on the basis of their fabric, viz. fine and coarse groups. The fine group constitutes the majority of the ceramic assemblage. It is made of well-levigated clay, turned on fast wheel and baked at a high temperature. This group constitutes four types of wares, such as Ochre ware, Black-and-Red ware, Black slipped ware and fine Red ware. However, the fine Red ware has a number of sakes and fabrics as shown in the flow chart given below. The coarse group comprises two types of wares-Sturdy Red and Coarse Red wares. The pottery of this group is either wheel made or handmade. All these wares are found right from the beginning of the culture at this site, in south-eastern part of the mound in particular, but the hardness and colour of the fabric have changed time to time.

Period I—Black-and-Red ware Culture

Fine Group

Ochre ware: Some potsherds of this ware are obtained from the lowest level of all trenches. The potsherds are highly weathered and therefore, no trace of surface feature can be made out. Jars of medium and small sizes are the shapes.

Black-and-Red ware: The ware has medium fine fabric and shapes are bowls and dishes. The vessels are slipped on either side and are unpainted.

Black Slipped ware: Dishes of various kinds and basins are the shapes in this ware. Made of fine clay this is well baked under reduced condition. The vessels are wheel thrown, slipped in black colour and have lustrous surface. Very often the slip is rubbed off.

Fine Red ware: There are two fabrics, such as soapy and sturdy. Four wares present in soapy fabric- Brown slipped, Brown-and-black slipped, Tan slipped and Black slipped. In all these the fabric remains soapy, porous and brick red or orange red in colour and are painted in different colours. Mostly monochrome and rarely bichrome designs are found. The sturdy group has two variants-fine Red slipped and Black slipped. The fabric of these is very fine and sturdy. The former is plain while latter is decorated in black paintings.

Fine Red ware comprises largely table-wares. However, basins, vases and small jars are also encountered.

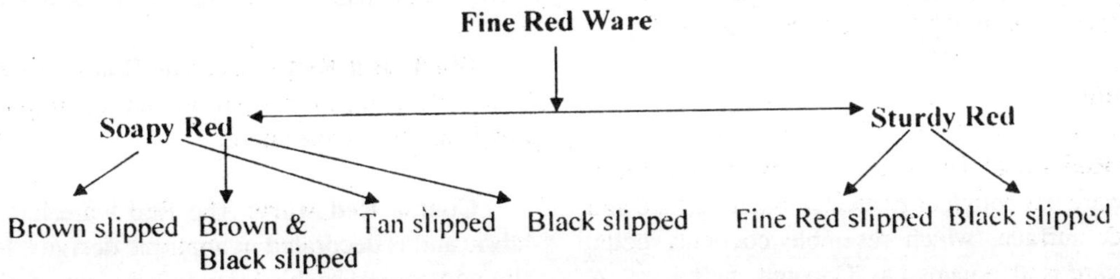

Soapy Red ware

In the Brown slipped ware shapes are dishes, dish-on-stand, basins and jars. Dishes are found in large number. This ware is painted in black or pink colour.

The Brown and Black slipped ware has been slipped in brown colour on outer surface and black on inner surface over which paintings of linear designs are made in black pigment. This ware comprises different types of dishes.

The Tan slipped ware is painted in red or black colour. The designs are linear. It comprises dishes of various shapes and sizes including deep bowls and jars.

The Black slipped Red ware comprises bowls and dishes. The rim portions of these vessels are red in colour on both sides, while rest of the vessels are black/grey in colour. Possibly, continuous use of the vessels has rendered the slip rubbing out of the rim portion. The vessels are decorated with vertical lines in black colour either on inner or on both sides. The ware is made of well-levigated clay and potted on fast wheel. The sturdy and metallic fabric indicates that it is baked at a very high temperature. The colour of the core is red at the rim and grey at the bottom.

Sturdy Red ware

Fine Red Slipped ware has medium to very fine fabric. It comprises deep bowls with flat bases and featureless or rudimentary rim. Some potsherds with carinations are found which could be fragments of dishes. The vessels are slipped on both sides.

The Black slipped ware is same as the previous ware with a black slip applied over it. The slip is washed out in all most all the cases leaving back traces in patches. This ware is painted in black pigment. The designs are linear. Shapes are dishes and bowls of different varieties.

Coarse Group

Sturdy Red ware: This is a coarse ware with sturdy fabric. The ware has rough or rusticated outer surface and smooth inner surface, which resemble coconut shells. Hence, the ware is also named as 'Coconut shell ware'. A lot of white mica could be seen on the surface of potsherds. The surface of the vessels is deliberately rusticated before firing. Some potsherds bear finger marks on the outer surface. Jars of different sizes are found in this ware. One sherd of neck portion of a jar bears a wide painted band of black colour. The vessels are not well baked. The uniform thickness of potsherds indicates that the vessels are made on fast wheel.

Coarse Red ware: This ware has a very coarse fabric with lot of husk impressions. It comprises jars of different sizes. Since the number of potsherds is less, it is difficult to enunciate whether the vessels are wheel made or handmade.

Period II—Painted Grey ware Culture

All the wares of Black-and-Red ware culture continue in this period along with introduction of Painted Grey and Plain Grey wares. However, the fabric of all the previous wares changes to lesser fine stage, except for the Black slipped ware. A technological degeneration in this period may be postulated.

Painted Grey ware: The Painted Grey ware has the usual well-baked, sturdy fabric and grey core. It is painted in black colour either on one side or on both sides. The designs noted so far comprise linear patterns. The common shape is dishes with flat or saggar base. Some bowls and jars are also seen in this ware. Besides, a few miniature vessels are noteworthy.

Plain Grey ware: The plain Grey ware has more sturdier but less fine fabric than the PGW. It comprises similar types of shapes as in PGW. There is no painted design on it and the ware looks dull in colour.

Black slipped ware: The Black slipped ware has a fine, soapy but sturdy fabric. It is as lustrous as the NBPW and shapes are basins, bowls and dishes.

Black-and-Red ware: The Black-and-Red ware has become coarser in this period and has thin cross section; bowls are the shapes here.

Coarse Red ware: The Red ware has improved in fabric and is decorated in applique designs. It is devoid of slip and comprises big storage jars, jars of different types and basin.

Antiquities

The antiquities obtained from the excavations are objects made of bone, terracotta and iron. The bone objects consists of finely polished, delicate bone points of various sizes and decorated arrowheads. All these equipments have hafting facilities either in the form of a hole on tanged part or a pointed tanged part. Among these arrowhead is worth mentioning a barbed and tanged specimen. There are two circular incised designs one on each side. The tanged part is hexagonal and has a hole for hafting. It is about four centimetres in length. Besides these a few antlers are also obtained. One of them is sharply cut and fluted at one end. An unfinished bone pendant is noteworthy, in which perforations have been tried from both ends. It is finely polished and thicker at one end.

The terracotta objects comprise disks of perforated and un-perforated types made of potsherds, decorated clay disks, rounded and *matka* beads. The disks made of potsherds are sometimes perforated. The specially prepared disks are found in a number of sizes, which call for special attention. Some of them are beautifully decorated with incised designs. These are so elegantly made. It is likely that they were used as weights. The weight of these disks varies from 10 gms to 50 gms. A partially broken terracotta dabber is worth mentioning here, which is obtained from the trench B7 and belongs to PGW period. Besides, birdshots, sling balls, stoppers and cylindrical objects of terracotta are obtained from the excavations.

The iron objects are in a highly corroded condition. They comprise arrowheads, knives, chisels, nails and rods. Only the upper half-a-metre deposit of PGW period in trenches E7 and E12 has yielded iron objects. Trench B7 is found highly disturbed; so it is difficult to ascertain the exact location of the iron objects found in this trench.

Other than a few bone points and terracotta disks, most of the antiquities belong to the PGW period.

Economy and Subsistence

The economy of the people of both these periods revolved around agriculture and stockbreeding. Hunting, fowling, fishing and gathering of jungle products have played subsidiary role in the subsistence. The faunal assemblage indicates both domesticated and wild animals. A large number of bones bear sharp cut-marks and some are charred. Splitting of bones, may be for the bone marrow. Presence of terracotta net sinkers indicates use of net for fishing. A large number of charred fish bones and carapace of crab and turtle have been collected from the excavations. The collection is yet to be studied. The charred grains from the excavated soil comprise rice, wheat, barley and some sort of lentils. Besides, jujube seeds are also found.

The industrial activity comprises pottery manufacturing, metallurgy, terracotta and bone objects making. Pottery making was certainly one of the biggest industries.

Discussion

As noted before, the trenches were laid in the peripheral area of the site and the layers have either narrowed down or suddenly deepened down making the chance of intermixing of ceramics more feasible. However, as it is believed, no stratigraphical disturbance occurs in this condition unless there is any interference of external forces. At the same time, the narrowing down of the layers brings the antiquities closer to each other and makes the picture nebulous. With this background an in-depth study of the ceramics has been carried out and is still in progress.

It is interesting to note that similar types of ceramics have been obtained from Ahichchatra (IAR 1963-64), Hastinapur (Lal 1954-55) and Jakhera (Sahi 1978). At Jakhera, the Period IIIA has yielded Black-and-Red ware, Black slipped ware bearing paintings in black pigment and Red ware of various hues. The orange red variety is painted in black colour. A few Painted Grey ware sherds are also found in this level, which the excavator calls as "Proto-PGW" phase. There are copper and iron objects obtained along with other antiquities in this level. In Period III B, PGW appears along with plain Grey ware. Other wares continue in this phase.

The Red ware in different hues and painted designs in red, black and pink colours are also seen at Hastinapur Period II (Lal 1954-55:32).

At Abhaipur, no cultural break or hiatus is encountered between the cultural periods. Although no copper or iron objects are noted in Period I, the ceramics have similar features. A lot of experimentation with various colours of slip and painted decorations by the potters indicates preparation of an antecedent environment for the advent of PGW pottery during this time. Therefore, the Period I, tentatively called as Black-and-Red ware culture, will be closely observed in the future excavations to understand whether the period bears any precursor to the development of a new culture or just a new type of ceramics and if there is any break exists between these periods, which could not be observed due to the limited excavations.

Acknowledgement

The authors are thankful for the help and support of the following staff of the Department: Professors R.P. Yadav, A.K. Sinha, Drs. Abhay Kumar Singh, Shyam Bihari Lal, Pankaj Sharma Sarvashri V.B.S. Yadav, and Gauri Shankar. Dr. S.B. Lal is the man who has brought the site to light along with his students. Thanks are also due to the Abhaipur Excavation team without whose hard work in the scorching summer the first excavation of the University would not have been successful.

REFERENCES

Ghosh, A. and K.C. Panigrahi. 1946. Pottery of Ahichchatra (U.P.). *Ancient India* No.1:37-59.

IAR-Indian Archaeology-A Review.

Joshi, J.P. 1978. Interlocking of Late Harappan culture and Painted Grey ware culture in light of recent excavations, *Man and Environment* Vol. II: 98-101.

Lal, B.B. 1954-55. Excavations at Hastinapura and other Explorations in the Upper Ganga and Sutlej Basin 1950-52, *Ancient India* 10 & 11: 4-151.

————, 1977-78. Chronology of Painted Grey Ware. Did Painted Grey ware continue up to the Mauryan Times? *Puratattva* 9: 64-80.

Lal, S.B. and A. Mishra. 2001. Abhaipur: An Endangered Painted Grey ware Site in District Pilibhit, Uttar Pradesh in U.P. Arora et al. (ed.) *Heritage of Panchal*, Bareilly, pp.121-131.

Nigam, J.S. 1997. The Painted Grey ware Culture: A Fresh Appraisal in J.P. Joshi (ed.) *Facets of Indian Civilization: Recent Perspectives*, New Delhi: 286-304.

Sahi, M.D.N. 1978. New Light on the Painted Grey ware people as revealed from Excavations at Jakhera, *Man and Environment*, Vol. II: 101-03.

Sharma, G.R. 1960. *Excavations at Kausambi* 1957-59, Allahabad.

Sinha, B.P. (ed.) 1969. *Potteries in Ancient India*, Patna.

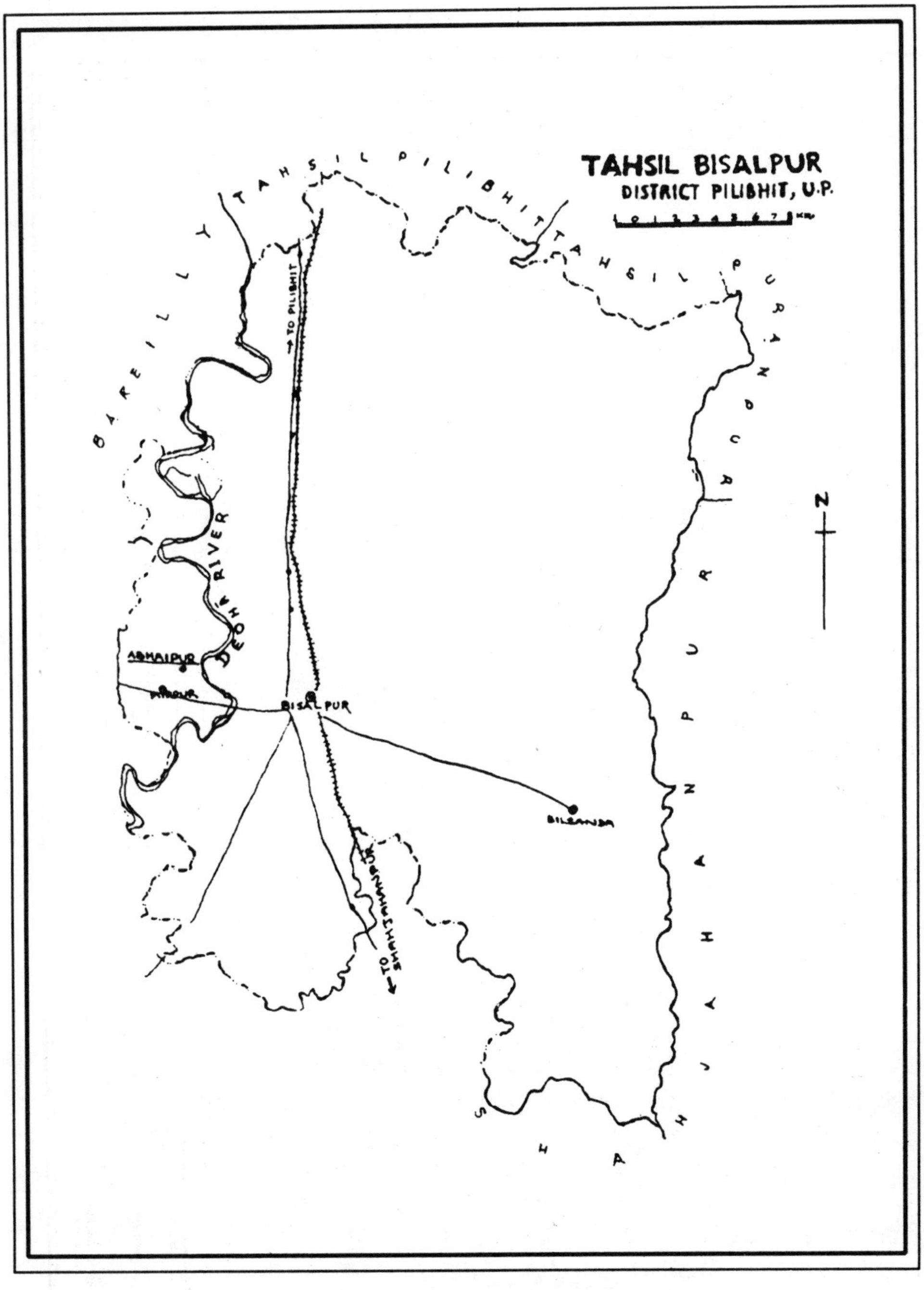

Fig. 1. Map showing location of the site of Abhaipur

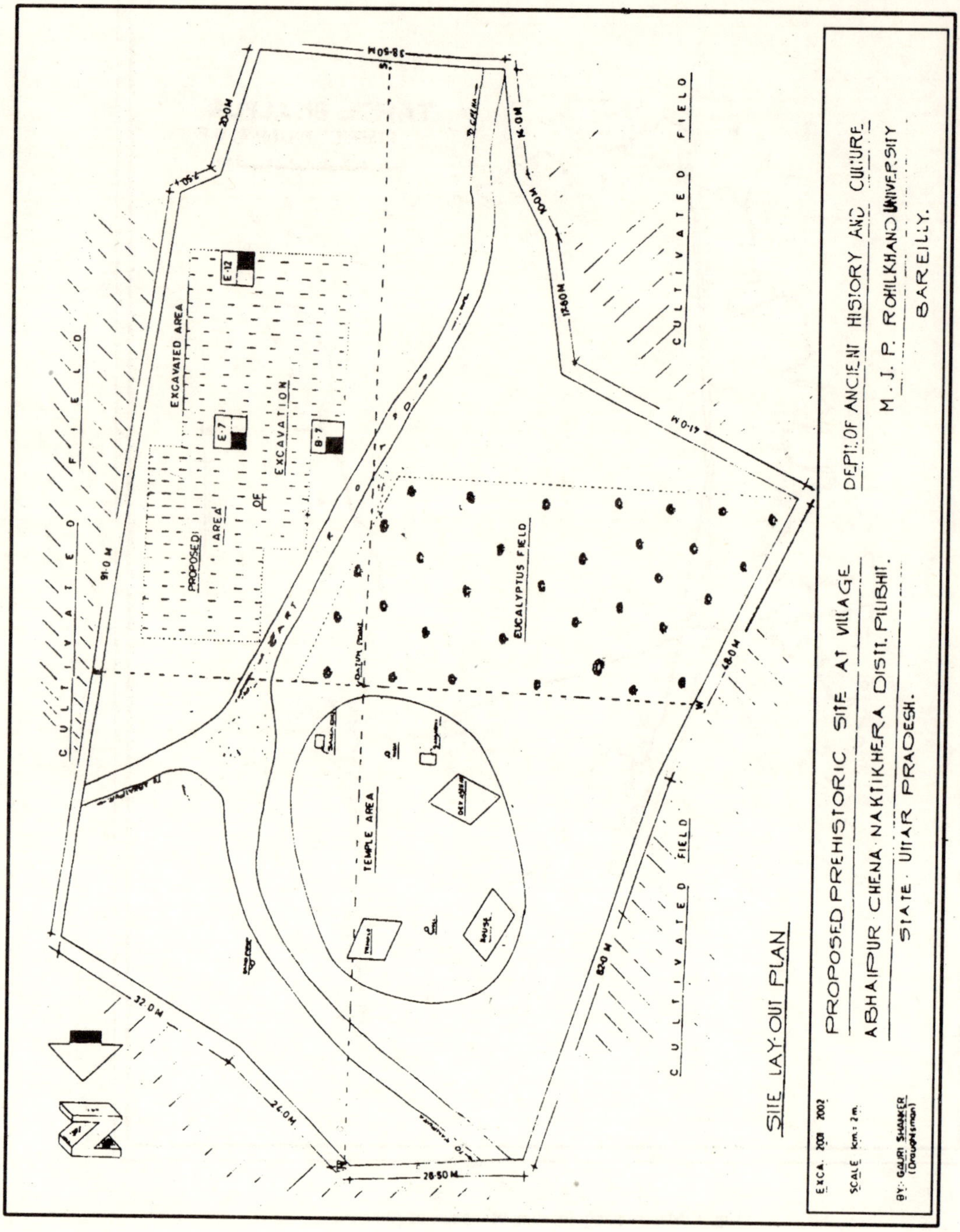

Fig. 2. Site layout plan

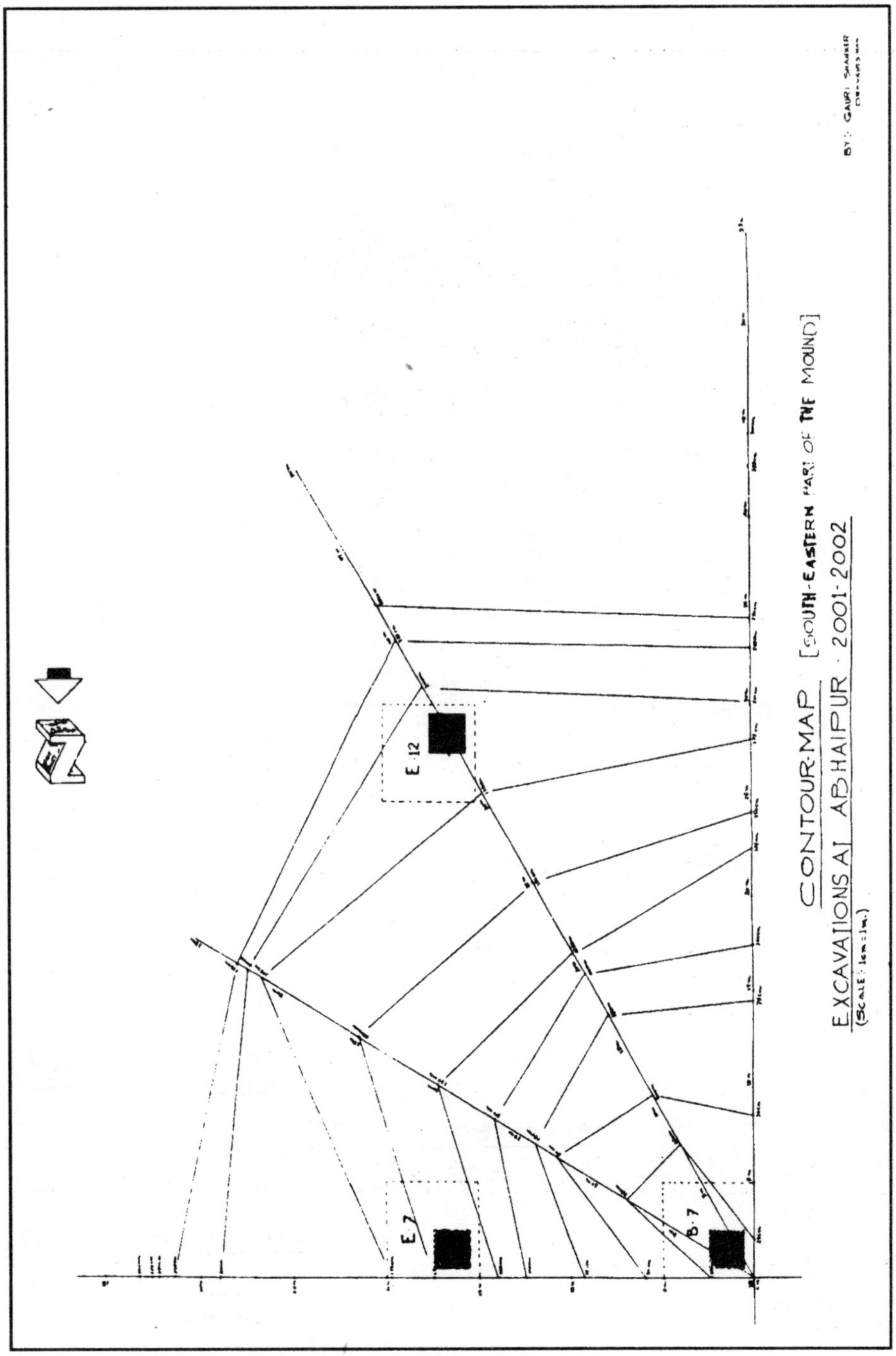

Fig. 3. Contour map of the south-eastern part of the mound

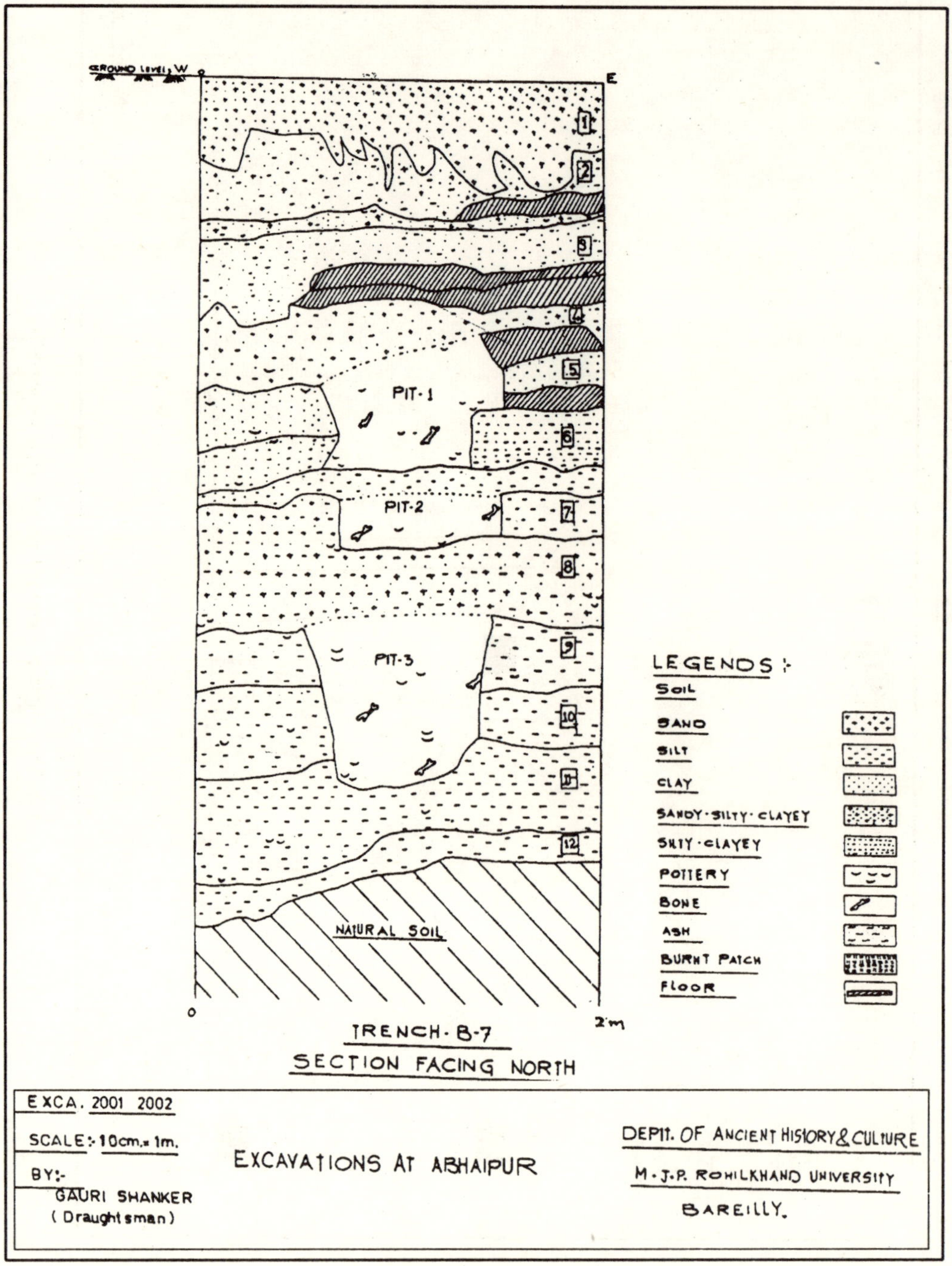

Fig. 4. Section drawing of Trench B7

'Saurashtra Stone Anchors' (Ring-stones) from Dwarka and Somnath, West Coast of India

A.S. GAUR*, SUNDARESH*, SILA TRIPATI*, P. GUDIGAR*, AND S.N. BANDODKAR*

Introduction

Last two decades of marine archaeological research along the Indian coast has brought to light a large number of stone anchors of different types and sizes, indicating that the Indian coast has witnessed brisk maritime activities in the past. Gujarat provides evidence of the earliest such activity in the form of dockyard and stone anchors at Lothal (Rao 1979) and a jetty and stone anchors from Kuntasi (Dhavalikar *et al.* 1996). Each and every Harappan site in Gujarat evidences the use of conch-shells and a variety of marine fishes highlighting the exploitation of marine resources.

Offshore explorations by the Marine Archaeology Centre of the National Institute of Oceanography, Goa, brought to light a large number of stone anchors from Okhamandal region (Sundaresh *et al.* 1999, 28:3:229-52 and Rao *et al.* 2001, 30.1: 95-108) and from Somnath (Rao *et al.* 1992, 3: 13-16) in Gujarat, Vijaydurg (Tripathi *et al.* 1998: 1-8) and Sindhudurg in Maharashtra (Tripathi *et al.* 1997: 51-57). A few grapnel-type stone anchors have been reported from Lakshadweep (Kapitan 1994: 1-6) and from Tamil Nadu coast (Jaykumar *et al.* 1999).

The majority of stone anchors from Gujarat fall in three categories: (i) composite, (ii) grapnel, and (iii) ring stone types. The last mentioned is a very enigmatic type as it is spheroid in shape with an axial hole and has been reported mainly from Gujarat coast (Rao *et al.* 1999: and Gaur *et al.* 2002) and from Oman (Vosmer, 1999 per. Com.). A research paper entitled 'Ring stones from Gujarat coast' is in press. Subsequently, many more ring stones have been found from Dwarka and Somnath waters (NIO: 2001). The presence of these ring-stones in great number in Somnath and Dwarka (Fig. 1) provided an opportunity to discuss further their uses and origin.

The present paper therefore, deals with a detailed description of the ring-stone anchors discovered so far from Dwarka and Somnath and their association with other types. The possible date and various hypotheses on their uses are also discussed here.

Historical background of the sites

1. Dwarka

Dwarka is situated in Okhamandal taluka of Jamnagar district in Gujarat state on the extreme west of the Saurashtra peninsula on the Arabian Sea coast (Lat. 22° 22' N and Long. 60° 05' E). Okhamandal region is separated from the rest of Saurashtra by the *Okha Rann*.

Onshore excavations at Dwarka yielded an undisputed antiquity of the early historical period datable to second

*National Institute of Oceanography, Dona Paula, Goa-403 004, India.

century BC (Ansari *et al.* 1996). Offshore explorations by the Marine Archaeology Centre of the National Institute of Oceanography have been carried out in Dwarka waters since 1983 and have brought to light a number of structures and anchors in water depths ranging between 3 and 15 m. The sea-floor in Dwarka is represented by the occurrence of rocky cliffs, sandy patches and submerged river channel. The offshore contours of Dwarka suggest a gentle slope. Archaeological artefacts have been recovered near the rocky cliffs or found partially buried in sediments. A dense vegetation growth over the artefacts is observed up to 8 m water depth. During fair weather, visibility is excellent for explorations and photography.

2. Somnath

Somnath is situated 5 km east of the famous port town of Veraval in district Junagarh. Onshore excavations yielded evidence of a township of 2000 BC old (IAR 1971-72; 1975-76). Prabhasa-Somnath is situated (Lat. 20° 53' N and Long. 70° 24' E) on the south-west coast of Saurashtra at the mouth of the river Hiranya or Hiran. Somnath-Prabhasa has a nearly straight coastline revealing a vivid manifestation of marine aeolian and fluvial processes that have resulted in a number of important geomorphic land-forms, such as the nearshore zone characterised by the formation of recent alluvium deposits, sand-bars, mud-flats and mangrove swamps. The coastal zone is covered with beach and littoral sands, oyster beds and sand dunes (NIO 1985). The sea-floor off Somnath is represented by uneven rocky patches, flat rocky bottom and sandy sea-bed. A large number of archaeological artefacts are encountered at different depths ranging from 7 to 15 m, near the disturbed rocky patches. A dense vegetation growth is also noticed up to 8 m depth.

Methodology

The offshore exploration comprised two systems such as SCUBA (Self Contained Underwater Breathing Apparatus) and SDDE (Surface Demand Diving Equipment). Each diving team covered an area within 50 m radius. A buoy was tied to each location wherever archaeological objects (structures and anchors) were noticed. Artefacts located underwater were interconnected with rope followed by measurement of distance and orientation. Underwater findings were documented by using u/w still camera and drawings.

Results

Offshore explorations at Dwarka and Somnath brought to light 133 and 43 different types of stone anchors respectively, besides a few stone structures in the Dwarka waters out of which ring-stones from Dwarka are 24 and 35 from Somnath. These ring stones have been collected in various field trips from the respective sites. The basic characteristics of ring-stone anchors are circular in shape with an axial hole. Often the base of ring-stone is flat and top is semi-circular rising to a certain height. The detailed description of ring-stones from each sites is given below.

Dwarka

Offshore exploration during last two decades has yielded a number of ring-stones in the Dwarka area. Important observation that may be mentioned here is that most of the objects have been found at the depth of 8 to 16 m and a few in shallow water and a lone instance is from inter-tidal zone. The position of the ring-stones discovered during last two seasons has been plotted on the map (fig. 2). A total of 24 ring-stones have been recovered from Dwarka waters. The anchor numbered 1 to 11 were recovered up to 2000 and then the remaining 12 to 24 in the season 2001 (figs. 3-4).

Most of the ring-stones were lying exposed on the sea-bed. However, a few, numbers 7, 10, 12, 14 and 22 were partially buried in sediment. Up to a depth of 8 m often the exposed portion of the ring-stones are covered with marine growth such as sea weeds while ring-stones beyond this depth are covered with a thin layer of grayish marine growth. They are lying in a vertical position which is the normal falling position of this anchor on the sea-bed and few ring-stones were marked, for example, number 14. Some ring-stones show chisel marks on the surface, in the hole and on the flat bottom side. On the basis of material and shapes, the ring-stones from Dwarka can be broadly divided into three groups.

Group I: Ring stone numbered 2, 4, 5, 7, 9 and 12 fall in this group. The raw material used for this category is basalt and are heavy. The basic features are low height, flat bottom, semi-curved top with an axial hole; diameter of the hole is same at both ends. Often the chisel marks have been noticed on the surface and in the hole. The average estimated weight of ring-stones is 147 kg. Among them the heaviest one (no. 4) weighs 245 kg and the lightest (no. 12) weighs 80 kg.

Group II: Ring-stone numbered 3, 8, 10, 13-17, 19-21, 23 and 24 fall in this category. The majority of ring-stones of this category are made out of limestone and sandstone. Shape of these ring-stones is the same as of the first category. However, they have often blunt edges and widened axial holes. A few anchors are having smooth surface while a few have very rough surface. Sometimes chisel marks have also been noticed on some of the anchors. The average weight of this group is 98 kg. The heaviest anchor (no. 8) weighs 205 kg and the lightest (no. 14) 64 kg.

Group III: Ring-stone numbers 1, 6, 11, 18 and 22 fall in this last category. They are made out of porous limestone. As usual they are circular in shape with comparatively lesser height and have equal diameter on upper and lower side ends. Often axial holes are wide and irregular. They have blunt edges and rough surfaces. The average estimated weight of these ring-stones is 66 kg. The heaviest anchor (no. 1) is weighing 109 kg and lightest anchor (no. 6) 20 kg.

Somnath

Underwater explorations off Somnath were carried out in three seasons 1991-92, 1999-2000 and 2000-2001 (fig. 5). The explored area in Somnath waters is located at a distance of 400 m south-west of the Somnath temple. The study area comprised rocky out crop, flat rocky sea-bed and sandy patches. The first season yielded 6 objects, and the second 8 objects and in the present season 2001, 21 objects. Somnath yielded the largest number of ring stones (figs. 5–8). Out of 43 discovered stone anchors, 35 belong to ring-stone variety which is more than 80 percent. The water depth varied from 7 m to 15 m. The ring-stone noticed that below 8 m depth, were overgrown sea weeds. However, ring-stones from deeper depths have a layer of grayish marine growth. On the basis of shapes and raw materials the ring-stones have been divided into three groups.

Group I: Ring-stone numbered 25 (Pl. 1), 26, 31-33, 35 and 42 are made of basalt. Most of them were lying exposed on the sea-bed, a few of them lay partially buried, viz., no. 1. This is upside down. The exposed portions of these ring-stones are covered with grayish marine growth. They are spheroid in shape with flat bottom. The upper edge of the axial hole is sharp while the lower edge is blunt. Chisel marks are also noticed on the exterior as well as in the hole. Often they are very heavy and the average estimated weight of a ring-stone of this group is 220 kg. The weight of heaviest ring stone (no. 25) is 392 kg and the lightest (no. 35) is 114 kg.

Group II: Ring-stone numbered 27, 29, 36-40, 43, 45-50, 52-56 and 58 are made out of two types of rock, i.e., limestone and sandstone. They are spheroid in shape with a wide axial hole. Some of the ring-stones of limestone are very rough and have been integrated (?) with the sea-bed. The majority of ring-stones were lying exposed on the sea-bed and a few partially buried in sand. The edge of the upper end of the axial hole is sharp and lower end is blunt. A few ring-stones of sandstone have chisel marks in the axial hole, the average estimated weight of ring-stones of this group is 82 kg. The weight of heaviest ring-stone (no. 29) is 221 and the weight of the smallest ring-stone (no. 39) is 36 kg.

Group III: Remaining ring-stones numbered 28, 30, 34, 41, 51, 57 and 59 are made out of very porous limestone. They are irregular, circular in shape with less height. The axial hole is irregular and wide. Each ring-stone has a rough surface and blunt edges. Most of them are lying exposed on the seabed. One ring stone is broken. The estimated average weight of these ring stones is 54 kg. The weight of the heaviest ring stone (no. 28) is 122 kg and weight of the lightest stone (no. 51) is 16 kg.

Discussion

The above descriptions of the ring-stones from the areas suggest that they are very similar to each other in shape. However, the size and raw material varied. The possible uses, date and probable origin of these ring-stones have been discussed here. Before that, a few facts about these objects given below must be considered.

1. These are man-made objects and have not been found in association with any habitation sites in Somnath or Dwarka.

2. Their association with composite and grapnel stone

anchors indicate that these were used for navigational purposes.

3. These ring-stones were often found in disturbed rocky sea-bed.

4. These anchors have been found in large numbers in the Saurashtra coast which seems to be the place of origin of these ring-stones.

Ring stones from other places

A number of similar type of objects have been reported from Mohenjo-Daro (Marshall 1973 and Mackay 1976) and Harappa (Vats 1975) where they are described as limestone rings, which have very smooth surface and are used for making pillars or for some ritual purposes. Marshall has mentioned that the most typical of them have their upper and lower surface undulating, in some others, the lower surface is flat, and the top takes a quatrefoil form and believes that these objects were used for either ritual or architectural purposes. About the ring-stones from Mohenjo-Daro Mackay (1976) says that 'the height of the ring and the diameter of the central hole increases more or less progressively with the diameter of the ring. The ring stones of Mohenjo-Daro also have dowel holes. On the three rings-stones there were two holes in the top and two in the base, averaging 1/2 inch in dia meter, 1 inch deep and set at equal distances from the edges of the central hole.' However, this phenomenon has not been observed in Dwarka and Somnath. A similar type of stone object is reported from Sri Lanka (Souter 1998) with square axial hole and has been described as a ring-stone anchor. There are examples from Maldives where similar type of objects have been recovered and described as ring-stone anchors (Vosmer 1999, personal communication). Six ring-stones have been discovered off Oman and it is suggested that these objects were used to anchor large fishing nets or traps until the 1950s.

Various views on the uses of ring-stones

Rao (1999) has suggested the use of these objects in combination of door-jamb as they were found along with the stone structure off Dwarka. However, this observation is not tenable as the objects have been found along with other stone anchors also where stone structures were not noticed. The recent explorations off Dwarka have also indicated that the stone structures may be the remains of an ancient jetty or harbour (NIO 2000).

Ethno-archaeological explorations in Oman suggested that these ring-stones could have been used as an anchor for fishnet. The size of the stone used depended on what type of fish was being caught (Vosmer 1999, Per Com). The local fishermen of Oman suggest that 5 to 7 stones were used at a time and they were not more than 40 kg in weight. However, the size and the weight suggested by the fishermen do not match with the present available ring-stones in India as well as in Oman. The weight of ring-stones in India varies from 16 kg to 392 kg and the fishermen would not be using ring-stones weighing so heavy for fishing nets. Another point may be mentioned here is that, if these stones are, as per suggestions made by fishermen of Oman, it should be only for very shallow waters whereas these objects have also been found in 15 m water depth. Out of 59 ring-stones, 14 are below 50 kg, 22 are more than 50 kg, 17 are more than 100 kg and 6 are more than 200 kg. Therefore, these ring-stones may not be suitable as weights for fishing nets. Hence this has to be ruled out.

Recently, Prof. A. Raban of Haifa University suggested that this also could be a lifting device of Grapnel type stone anchors (Raban 2001, Per. Comm.). This suggestion may not hold water in view of findings from Somnath. Of the total 44 anchors reported from Somnath, six are composite type and only 3 are grapnel type and the rest are ring-stones. With this data it can be argued that they may not be lifting devices.

There is a strong possibility that these ring-stones might have been used as anchors for boat. Vosmer (personal communication, 1999) has some information on similar type of objects from Maldives suggesting the use of these as anchoring boats in coral reef areas. It seems that these objects were used as an anchor of a boat in the disturbed rocky bottom. Two objects off Oman, 35 off Somnath and 24 off Dwarka have been noticed in disturbed rocky bottom. There may be apprehension about the uses of ring-stones especially of those ring-stones which have less weight (less than 50 kg) as anchors and that these might be fishing net weights as well. However, the size of anchors always depends on the size of boats. Even today stones weighing less than 15 kg are being used by small out-trigger boats off the Konkan coast and elsewhere in India. Therefore, a few ring-stones having less weight does not indicate that their function would be different from the anchors. It is possible that a single boat might be carrying all types of stone anchors and the same were used depending upon the sea bottom since all of them have been found together in the Dwarka- and Somnath waters. If it were sandy, certainly, composite anchors were more effective and in the rocky area, where there was not much grip, heavy prismatic anchors were in use and in the most disturbed area ring-stones were much effective.

In all probability, it may be said that ring-stones would have been used as anchors for boat. The shape of ring-stone is spheroid and the flat part would serve as the lower end while curved portion would be the upper end. A wooden log would be inserted in the axial hole, and the thickened portion would be on the lower side. Often the lower edge of axial hole is blunt which may be due to the insertion of the thickened part of wood while the upper side of the wooden log will not affect the edges and therefore, the edge of the upper side is sharp. The central wooden log will be further attached to a cross wood which will be tied with a rope, so whenever the ring-stone is thrown in water it would fall with the flat base down and semi-curved at the top and the rope of the boat will be the upper side and would not entangle with any rocky outcrop. The findings also suggest that most of the ring-stones have been found in the same position.

Probable Date

Dating of these ring-stones would be speculative since they have not been found associated with any datable material. Scientific dating may not be possible in the absence of any wood remains in the hole of the rings-stone. However, they have been found with composite and grapnel stone anchors. Therefore, a date ranging between eight century and seventeenth century AD will be more appropriate for other stone anchors. A reference has been made by Schoff (1974) about the visit to Oman by Gemelli Carreri, in 1693-39, and mentions that, for anchors, they have a large stone with a hole. This could be a ring-stone and if the reference is for this type of anchor then this will be a lone authentic record of the seventeenth century about ring-stones. The majority of these objects are made out of locally available rock and a few are of hard rock (may be basalt) indicating that these were made indigenously.

Origin of ring-stones

The largest number of ring-stones have been reported from Somnath waters and followed by Dwarka. As mentioned above, a few instances have come from Maldives and Oman and perhaps, totally absent in Red Sea and Mediterranean (as no nautical archaeological publication has published these type of stones). Perhaps these must have been invented by the Indian sailors after gaining experience of sea-beds, specially in the Gujarat coast where submerged reefs and uneven sea-bed pose problems for lifting heavy grapnel and composite types of anchors. Another important point that may be mentioned here is that these anchors need a very thick wooden stock which will not be easily lost on the sea bed as compared to other types of anchors where a thin wooden log was inserted. The present data suggests that ring-stone anchors are the speciality of the Saurashtra coast of Gujarat, in the medieval period. The sailors of this coast must have visited Oman and Maldives from where similar type of ring-stones has been reported. Therefore, it is proposed a new nomenclature, **'Saurashtra stone anchor'**, for these stone anchors. (pp 90).

Conclusion

Discovery of a large number of ring-stones from Somnath and Dwarka along with other stone anchors indicate that these ring stones are related with navigational requirement. After considering various views on their uses we came to a conclusion that these ring-stones would have been used as stone anchors. This could also be a special contribution by the ancient sailors of the Saurashtra coast in the development of stone anchors. Therefore, it will be appropriate to call the ring-stones as 'Saurashtra stone anchor'. The raw material also indicates indigenous origin. Based on available data these anchors may be linked with other type of stone anchors found along with ring-stones and dated between eighth and seventeenth century AD.

Acknowledgements

Authors are thankful to Dr. Ehirich Desa, Director, National Institute of Oceanography, Goa, for his constant support and encouragement for the preservation of underwater cultural heritage. We are also grateful to Shri K.H. Vora, Scientist-in-Charge, Marine Archaeology Centre for his valuable suggestions and permission to publish this paper. The authors remain thankful to the Department of Ocean Development, New Delhi and the Council of Scientific and Industrial Research, New Delhi for funding this project. We are thankful to Dr. Thomas Vosmer, Western Australian Maritime Museum, Perth and Prof. A. Raban of Haifa University for their valuable suggestions about ring-stones. We also acknowledge the contribution by Shri Yatin Shirodkar, Research Fellow in Ocean Engineering, for providing estimated weights of ring-stones. Thanks are also due to Shri S.B. Chitari for all the line drawings and Shri G.R. Desal for assistance in the field.

REFERENCES

1. Rao, S.R., 1979, *Lothal—A Harappan Port Town*, Memoir of Archaeological Survey of India, New Delhi.

2. Dhavalikar, M.K., Raval, M.R. and Chitalwala, Y.M., 1996, *Kuntasi—A Harappan Emporium on West Coast*, Pune.

3. Sundaresh, Gaur, A.S., Gudigar, P., Sila Tripati, Vora, K.H. and Bandodker, S.N., 1999, 'Stone anchors from Okhamandal region, West coast of India', *International Journal of Nautical Archaeology*, 28.3: 229-52.

4. Gaur, A.S. Sundaresh, Sila Tripati, Vora, K.H. and Bandodkar, S.N., 2001, 'A Group of 20 Stone anchors from Dwarka Waters, West Coast of India', *International Journal of Nautical Archaeology*, 30.1:95-108.

5. Rao, S.R., Tripati, S. and Gaur, A.S., 1992, 'Marine Archaeological exploration of Somnath', *Journal of Marine Archaeology*, 3:13-16.

6. Sila, Tripati., Gaur, A.S. Sundaresh, Gudigar, P. and Bandodker. 1998, 'Historical Stone Anchors from Vijaydurg, Maharashtra, West Coast of India', *Bulletin of Western Australian Museum*, 22 (1&2):1-8.

7. Sila, Tripati and Gaur, A.S., 1997, 'Stone Anchors from Sindhudurg Fort on the West Coast of India', *International Journal of Nautical Archaeology*, 26, (1), 51-57.

8. Kapitan, G., 1994, 'Stone-shank anchors of the Arab-Indian trade period-were they mooring anchors?', *Bulletin of the Australian Institute for Maritime Archaeology*, 18.2:1-6.

9. Jaykumar, P. and Athiyaman, N., 1999, 'Stone anchors of Tamil Nadu Coast', Paper presented in *Second International Conference on Marine Archaeology*, Thane, 8-10 January, 1999.

10. Rao, S.R., 1999, *The Excavation of Lost City of Dvaraka*, Aditya Prakashan, New Delhi.

11. Gaur, A.S., Sundaresh, Sila Tripati and S.N. Bandodkar, 2002 (in press), 'Ring stones from Gujarat Coast, West Coast of India', *Mariner's Mirror.*

12. Technical Report, 2001, *Marine Archaeological Explorations of Dwarka, Bet Dwarka and Somnath*, Phase-II, NIO, Goa.

13. Ansari, Z.D. and Mate, M.S., 1966, *Excavations At Dwarka* (1963), Pune.

14. IAR, *Indian Archaeology—A Review*, 1971-72, Archaeological Survery of India, New Delhi.

15. IAR, *Indian Archaeology—A Review*, 1975-76, Archaeological Survey of India, New Delhi.

16. Technical Report, 1985, *Oceangraphic Studies off Sutrapada*, NIO, R.C. Bombay, pp.7-8.

17. Marshall, John, 1973, *Mohenjo-Daro and the Indus Civilization*, Indological Book House, New Delhi, pp. 61.

18. Mackay, E.J.H., 1976, *Further excavations at Mohenjo-Daro*, Indological Book Corporation, New Delhi, pp. 595-97.

19. Vats, M.S., 1975, *Excavations at Harappa*, Bhartiya Publishing House, Varanasi, pp. 107, 332.

20. Souter, C., 1998, 'Stone anchors near Black Fort, Galle, Sri Lanka', *International Journal of Nautical Archaeology*, 27.4: 331-42.

21. Technical Report, 2000, *Marine Archaeological Explorations Off Dwarka, Bet Dwarka and Somnath*, Phase-II, NIO, Gao.

22. Schoff, W.H., 1974, *The Periplus of the Erythraean Sea*, New Delhi.

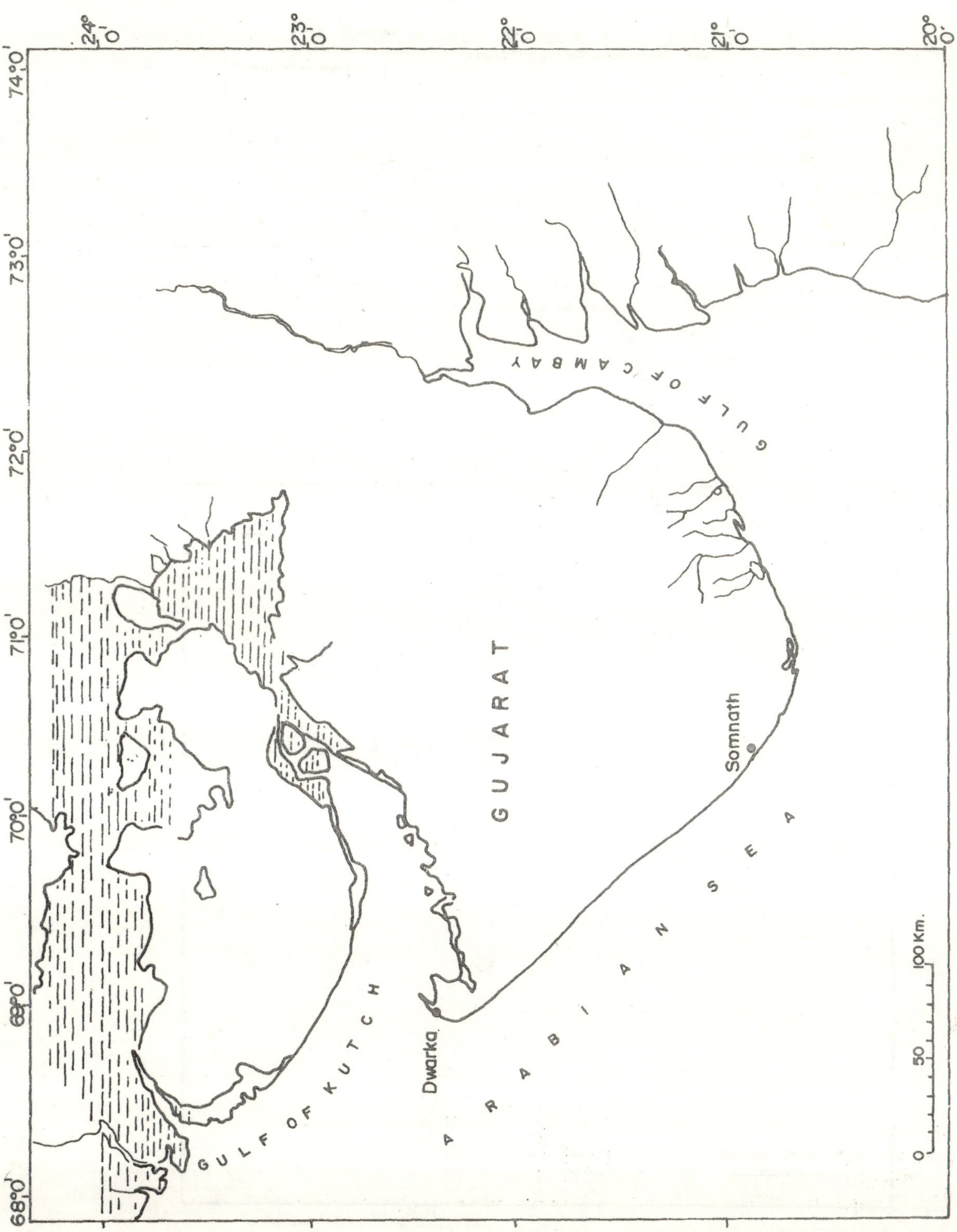

Fig. 1. Location of Ring-Stone Sites in Gujarat.

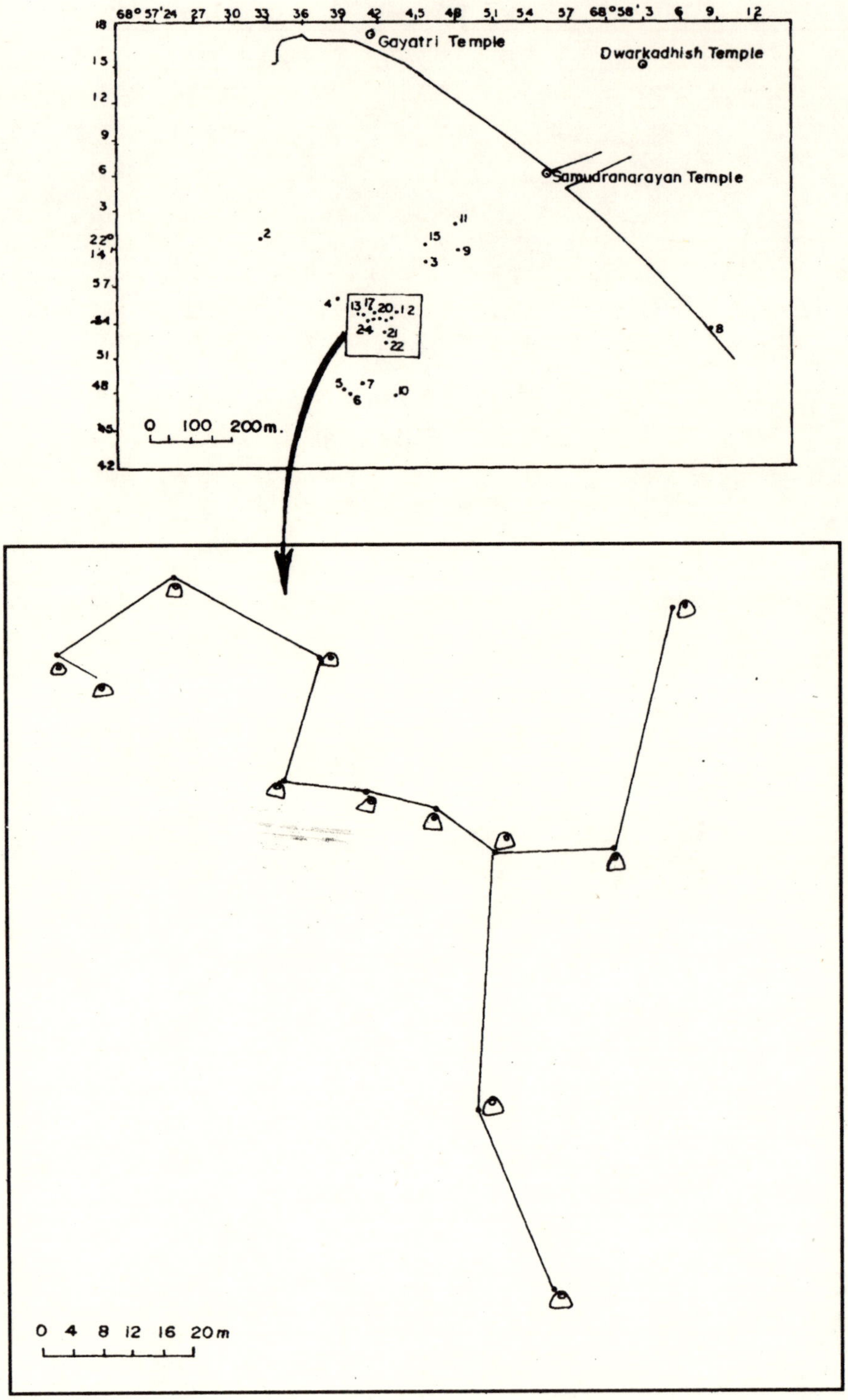

Fig. 2. Ring-stone lying off Dwarka.

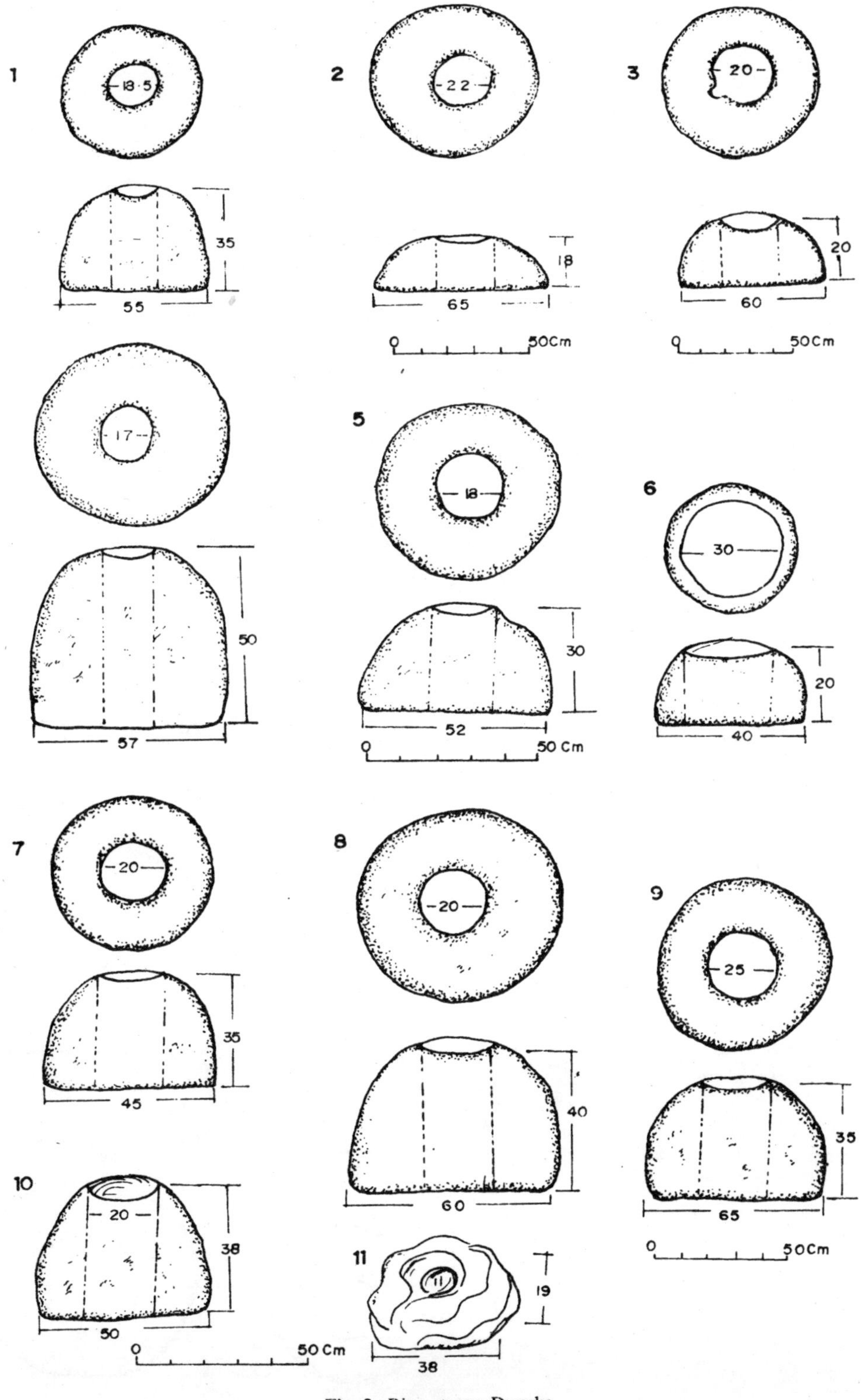

Fig. 3. Ring-stones, Dwarka.

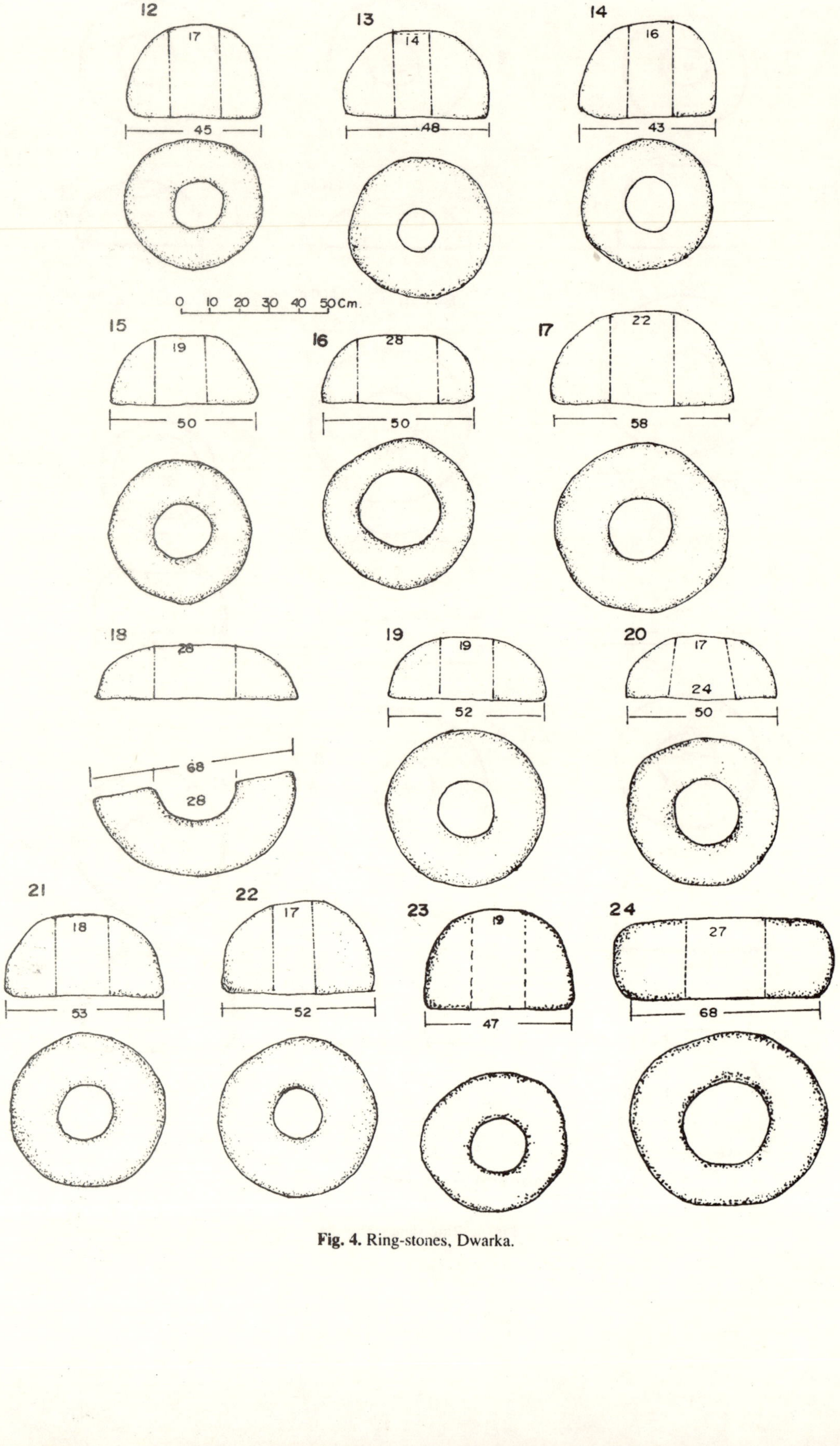

Fig. 4. Ring-stones, Dwarka.

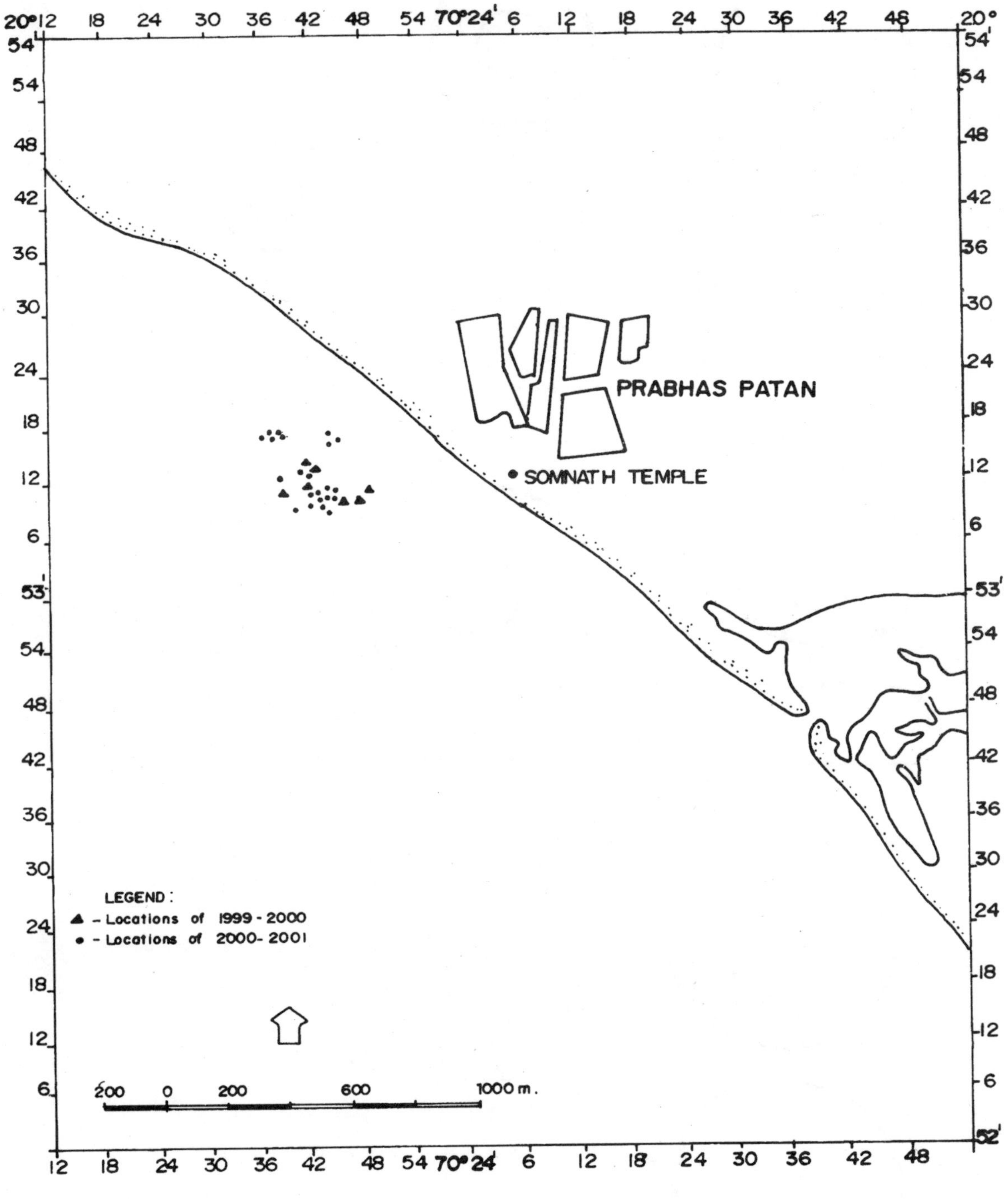

Fig. 5. The location of Archaeological findigns off Somnath.

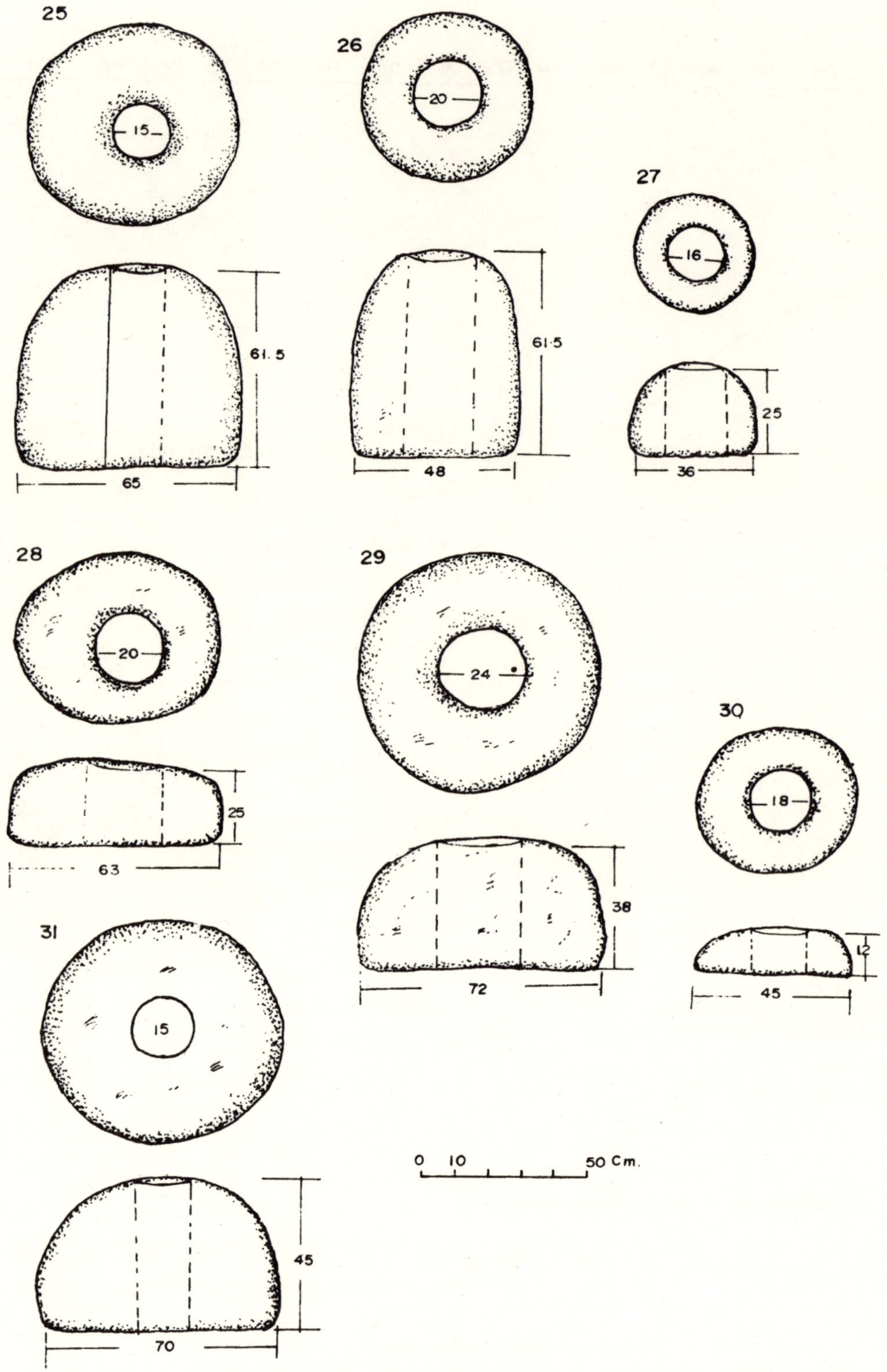

Fig. 6. Ring-stones, Somnath.

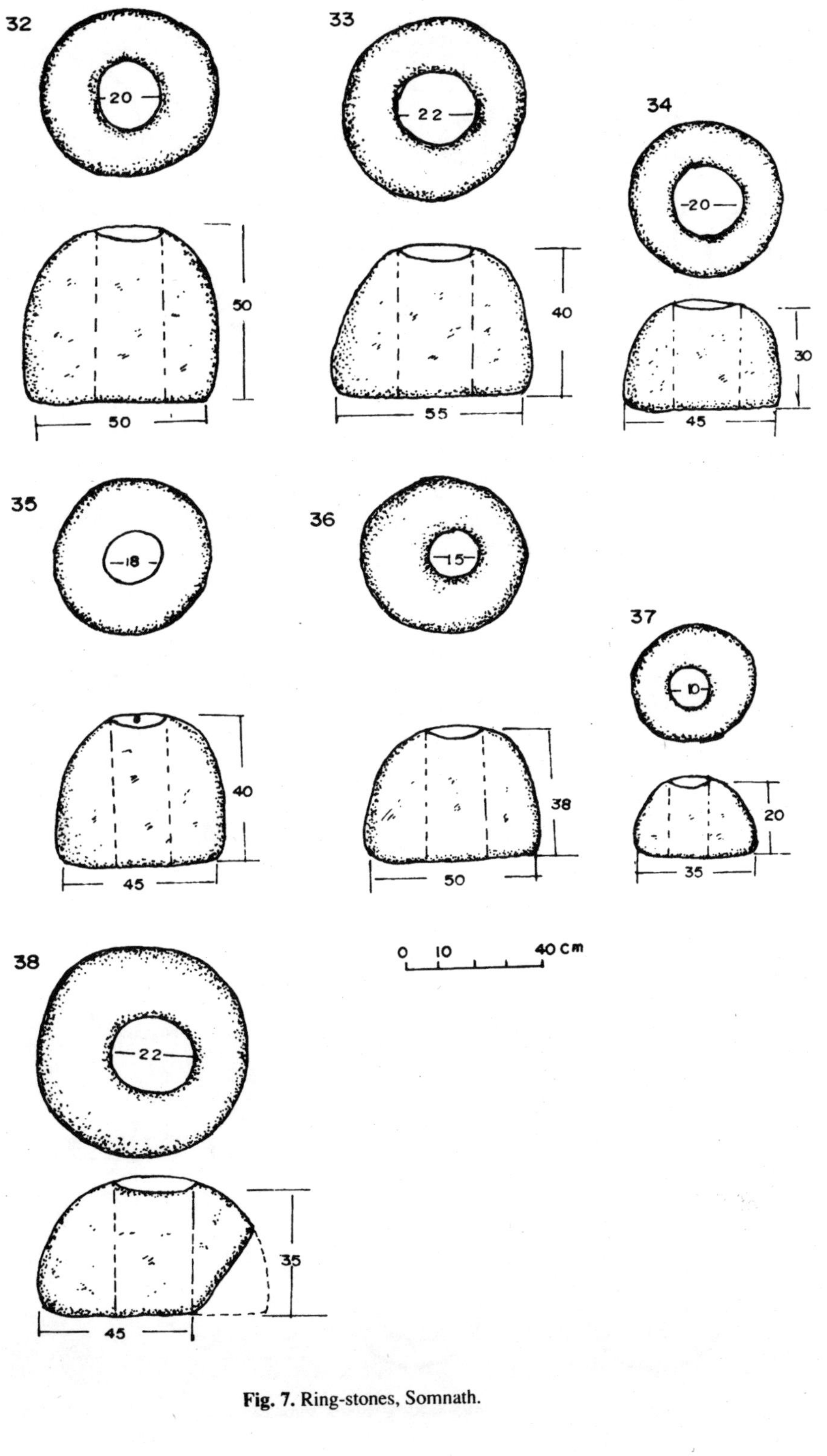

Fig. 7. Ring-stones, Somnath.

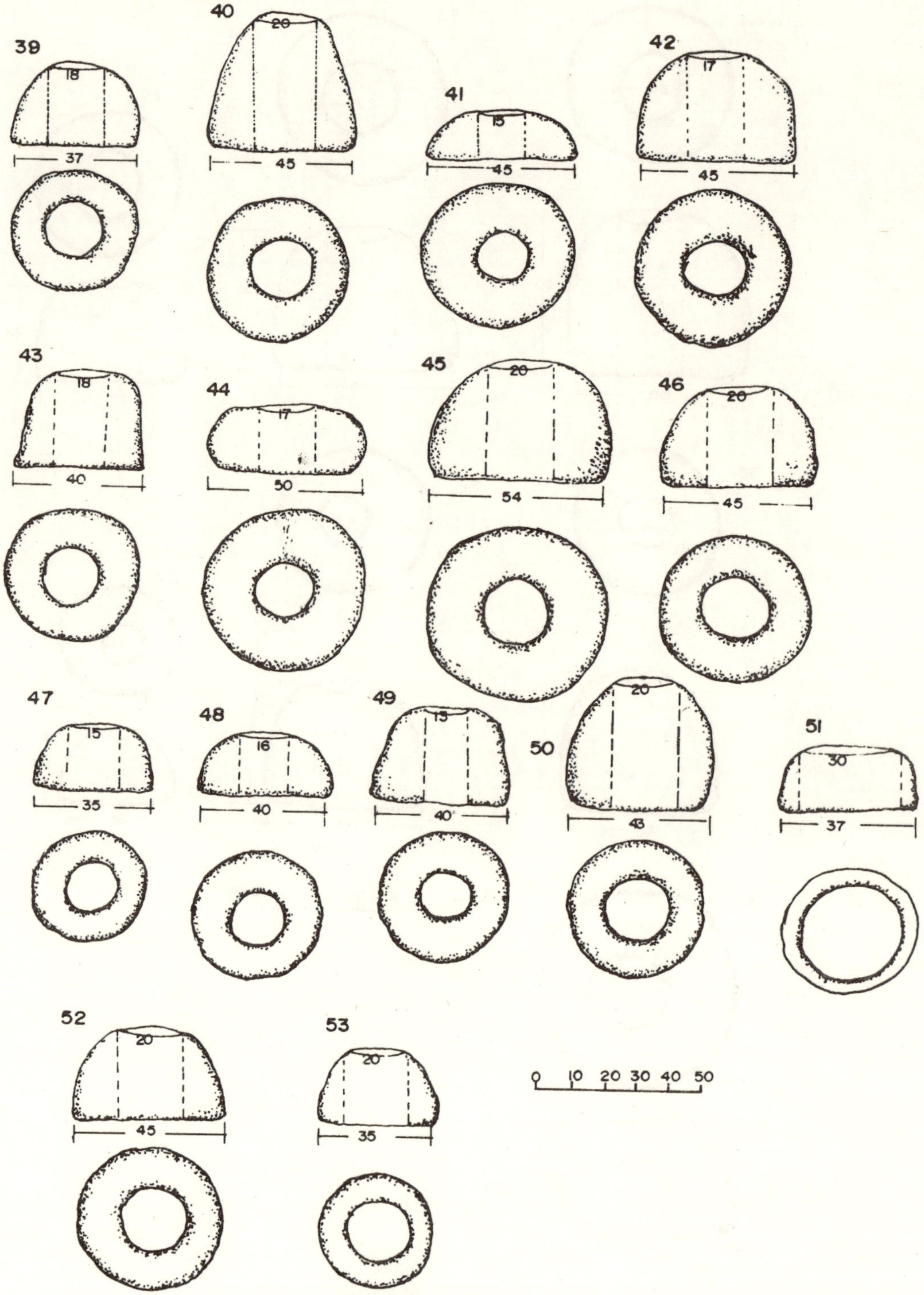

Fig. 8. Ring-stones, Somnath.

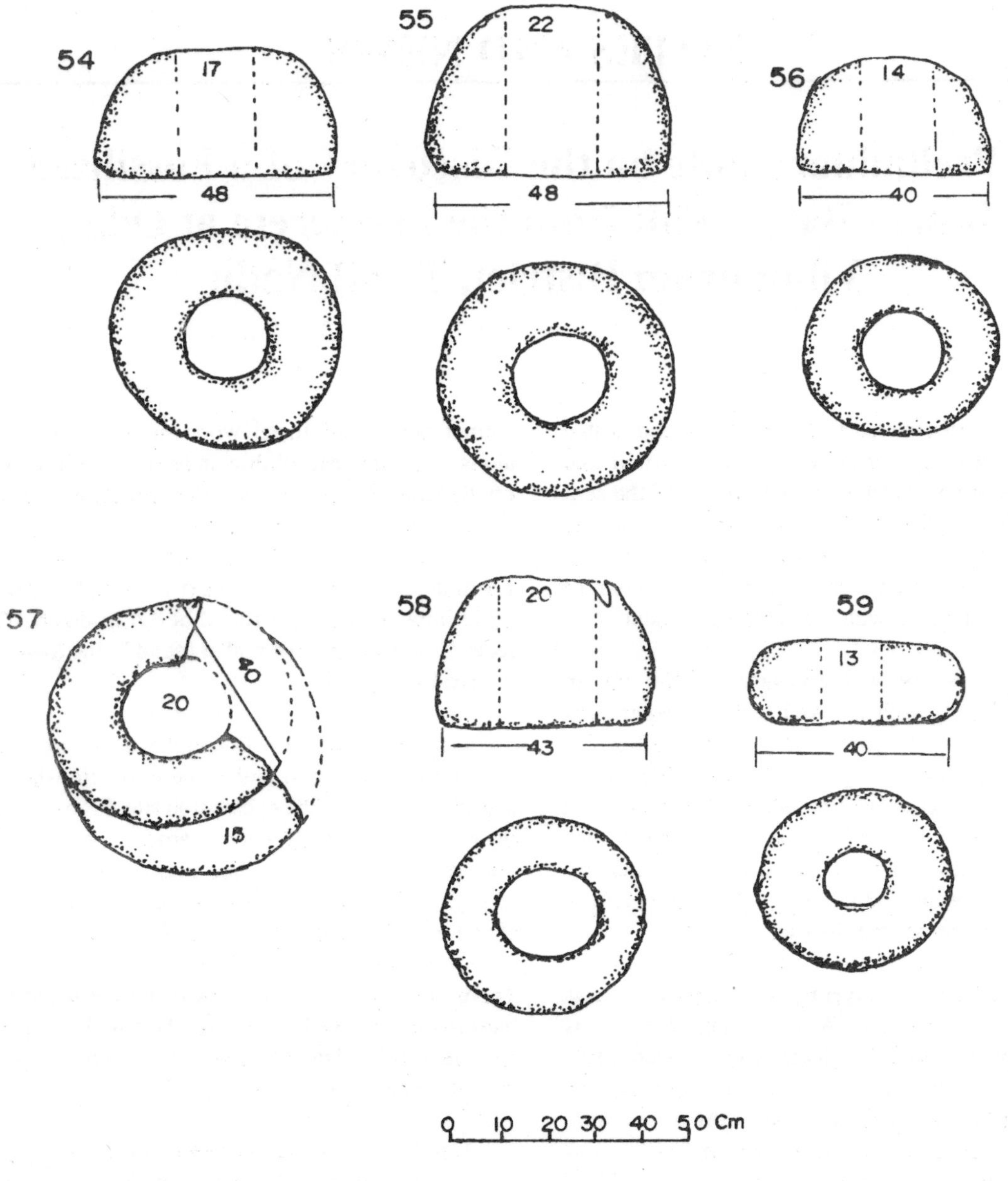

Fig. 9. Ring-stones, Somnath.

NOTES AND NEWS

A Preliminary note on the Discovery of a Fossilised Human Baby Skull from the Ferricrete at Odai, Villupuram District, Tamil Nadu

The site was discovered in March 2000, and at that time several Mesolithic artefacts, fossilised wood and animal bones were collected from the surface of the aeolian deposit. The site lies hardly 1 km inland at an altitude of 12 m above sea level (Pl.1). Several layers of sand and gravel horizons have been seen in the vertical section of the aeolian deposit along with the stone implements.

A small excavation was conducted at the site in October 2001 jointly with the Archaeology Department of the Government of Tamil Nadu represented by S. Krishnamurthy an Archaeological Officer. Besides, I had two other experienced excavators, Mr. George Kutty and Thomas Kunnikal from Kerala. Prof. K.S. Mathew, former H.O.D. of the Deptt. of History in Pondicherry University and present H.O.D. Prof. L.S. Vishwanath of the same department, visited the site.

During the excavation layer by layer step cutting was done for proper examination. A total depth of 6 m was exposed in which up to 5.7 m depth, 9 layers were identified. Within the 9 layers, 5 layers of sand, and 4 layers of sand and gravel are seen alternately. At the bottom, below 6 m, presence of ferricrete was noted. This continued further below reaching the present sea-level.

Two Stone Age industries, viz., Mesolithic and Upper Palaeolithic have been clearly identified. Both the industries consist exclusively of quartz implements. A few Upper Palaeolithic artefacts are made of fossil wood. Besides the stone tools, a large number of semi-fossilised animal bones and fossil wood pieces were also found along with the Mesolithic industry. The nature of the implements clearly indicates the utilisation of river-worn quartz pebbles as the main raw material during the two cultural phases. Mesolithic implements were found at 1.5 m depth in stratified context while the Upper Palaeolithic implements were found at 4.5 m depth. The artefacts of both phases were also found in the lower level in the eroded deposit.

During the work on 14 October 2001. I discovered a fossilised human skull within the ferricrete which is seen slightly away from the excavation site. From the nature of the occurrence of the ferricrete around the fossil, it seems that nearly 2 m ferricrete had been earlier removed from its top. A little part of the fossilised material was exposed at the top. Since it was fully red stained, its difference from the surrounding soil was not so conspicuous. Therefore, I decided not to extricate the fossil from the hard matrix. Instead, I dug out the fossil along with the hard laterite which surrounds it. The fossil was lifted from the site for further studies.

Hundreds of fossilised human skulls ranging from a few lakh to over 5 million years old are known from different parts of the world, and all of them have been found in stratified context. However, none of them has been found within the ferricrete (secondary laterite) and, therefore, they could be retrieved without much damage. It is for the first time that a human fossil has been found entombed in the hard ferricrete.

The normal palaeontological approach to this sort of discoveries is to extract the fossil in its entirety from the matrix. But in this case it could not be taken out from the matrix, thereby putting greater difficulty in understanding its morphology, identification, orientation, etc. Therefore, I decided to reconstruct its morphology in full by using technologies developed for medical purposes. Imaging of the fossil inside the nodule was done by X-ray Computed Tomography (CT), Scanning (2D & 3D).

These analyses (CT & 2D) have shown several human cranial features at various points. However, certain points on its full morphology, orientation, and position remain inconclusive. In order to extract all such information, 3D scanning facility has been attempted through the Helical CT. Thin Helical run (3 x 4.5 mm) of the entire specimen was done and reconstructed at 2 mm interval. The Scannogram shows a hemi-spherical solid object with a spherical object with in it with a few lucent areas. Serial axial section shows the same hemispherical solid object with a central slightly hypo-dense ovoid-spherical object having air containing clefts within it. The spherical object is covered by a fossilised structure measuring 1-2 mm which has been later identified as the fossilised skull having the CT attenuation of 1192 HU (Hounsfield Unit). The CT attenuation of the ovoid-spherical object ranges from 1,137 to 1,1765 HU while that of the outer rock has the CT attenuation ranging from 1,628 to 2,383 HU. These studies have been repeated on many planes at different angles in order to understand orientation, morphology and state of preservation of the fossil, etc. The morphology and other features of the fossil could be reconstructed through the Helical CT of the specimen in 2 mm spacing, and could see its orientation. The length and breadth of the cranium have been measured as 10.1 cm and 8.6 cm, respectively, and it has a cranial capacity of 312 cc.

These studies have proved beyond doubt that it is a complete human baby skull which got embedded in a fluvial deposit in the geological past. The matrix is fully ferricretised and the skull is well fossilised. These characters amply prove a great antiquity for the skull. It may belong to Middle or Upper Pleistocene times, and probably the *Homo erectus* or *Homo sapiens* (archaic) in the Hominid evolution.

Acknowledgements

This discovery is one of the greatest achievements in my research carrier since 1974 and it has become possible due to the continuous help and encouragement I have been receiving from the University Grants Commission, and therefore, I am highly indebted to the Commission. My sincere thanks are due to the former Prof. & Head, Dr. K.S. Mathew of the History Deptt. in Pondicherry University for the help. I also acknowledge S. Kulasekharan's help during the fieldwork.

U.G.C. Research Scientist-C, Archaeologist,
Deptt. of History, Kerala University,
Kariavattom-695 581

P. Rajendran

Recent Exploration in Meghalaya

Not much work has been carried out to know the archaeological potential of the north-eastern states, viz., Assam, Meghalaya, Mizoram, Nagaland, Arunachal Pradesh, etc. In this paper an attempt has been made to highlight the recent discoveries made in the state of Meghalaya.

Exploration in Meghalaya was started as early as in 1857 when Godwin Austin discovered polished and ground stone tools in the Khasi Hills. It was Cockburn in 1879, who found similar tools in the vicinity of Shillong. Coggin Brown (1917) has incorporated details of tools in his *Catalogue Raisonne of the Prehistoric Antiquities in Indian Museum*, Calcutta. Subsequenty it was in 1931 and 1937 that G.D. Walker and J.P. Mills collected polished stone tools from Rogjeng, Fakhre Adap, Adingiri, Molmegiri, Dilmagiri, and Rangkahongiri, all in the District Garo Hills. These finds show that in the Garo Hills had a well-advanced Neolithic culture.

M.C. Goswami of the Gauhati University made a large collection of flaked and ground stone tools. The Department of Anthropology of the Gauhati University under T.C. Sharma collected a large number of pre-Neolithic tools during their explorations in the Ganol, Rangram and Simsang river valleys. The main objective of the exploration was to examine the Pleistocene geo-morphological formations and to locate sites that may yield tools of prehistoric times. Sharma (*IAR* 1971-72: 72) has discovered a number of archaeological sites such as Rongram Alagiri, Waram Thebrongiri, Selbalgiri, Michimagiri and Rambhagiri. Sankalia (1974: 42) feels that Rongram is the only Palaeolithic site in the Garo Hills amongst the reported sites of Prof. Sharma.

A small-scale excavation was carried out at Selbalgiri (*IAR* 1967-68: 8). A cursory look at the bibliography on Meghalaya indicates that a large number of Neolithic sites/tools have been located/collected from the Garo Hills. Prof. T.C. Sharma and H.C. Sharma have collected hand-axes, cleavers, choppers, scrapers, points, blade-tools, microliths, etc., from the Garo Hills.

During 1978-79 (*IAR* 1978-79: 30) R.V. Joshi, S.N. Rajguru, R.S. Pappu of the Deccan College, Poona and T.C. Sharma and others of the Department of Anthropology, Gauhati University and D.K. Medhi of the Arya Vidyapeeth, Gauhati jointly carried out geo-archaeological investigations in the Garo Hills. They opine that 'all the tools of these Stone Age as well as Neolithic cultures are exclusively made on basalt or dolerite'. As far as Neolithic culture is concerned this is the richest area having several factory sites and numerous clusters of implements. The Stone Age cultures contain a few standardised Lower Palaeolithic forms like hand-axe and cleavers; however, the scrapers and points as also choppers are numerous. Many of these are clearly bifacial but on the whole these pre-Neolithic industries are typical. In this respect they are comparable to similar tool kits from Konkan and Kerala on the West Coast. A factory site, situated in the Michimagiri Hills, has yielded, large number of blades and a few burins recalling Upper Palaeolithic traits. The Meghalaya and the West Coast region constitutes two contrasting geographical zones of the Indian sub-tropical zone; the similarity in prehistoric cultural development is, therefore, interesting.

This in brief is the story of prehistoric investigation in the Garo Hills. But in district Jaintia it is the Prehistory Branch of the Archaeological Survey of India, under L.S.

Rao (1992-93: 75) which conducted excavation at Pynthorlangthen and discovered Neolithic adzes, axes, chisels, points, blades and scrapers. The excavation yielded a cultural deposit of one metre comprising neolithic milieu. This site is considered to be a factory site.

In respect of East Khasi district, the recent work carried out by the present author along the Umaim river near Barapani dam site (P. 1) has yielded hand axes and chopper. The former is made of schist and are in a rolled condition. The latter is made of sandstone, which is of a fine-grained variety and is fresh. Further work along this river will definitely yield the tools of the Lower Palaeolithic period. In addition to the above discovery, the Prehistory Branch discovered several megalithic sites in the east Khasi Hills and Jaintia districts. The sites are: Jowai, Mukhla, Mukandar, menhirs: Tuber Kmai Shong, Mawlyn Gkneng, Menhirs and dolmens in cluster, Natural cave (Pl. 2 & 3)—all in District Jaintia Hills, Soryugkham, group of menhirs; Mawlyndep, menhirs; Mawlynged, Laitkor, menhirs and dolmens—all in District East Khasi Hills.

It is believed that the megalithism is still in vogue in the north-east. But the recent explorations in the East Khasi and Jaintia hill districts do clarify that the practice of erecting a menhir in memory of a dead person is not in vogue at least in these two districts and none of the people know what these menhirs are. Enquiries made by the author in the above villages where menhirs and dolmens were discovered, the local people were not aware of the significance of these edifices. Therefore it is not correct to say that megalithism is still in vogue in the north-east. The present explorations do indicate that it is not a living tradition at least in North Khasi and Jaintia hill districts of Meghalaya. Further work on this line is urgently needed here.

Acknowledgements

I am highly thankful to the Director General, Archaeological Survey of India, New Delhi, New Delhi and Director (Explorations and Excavations), Archaeological Survey of India, New Delhi for allowing me to undertake this tour to Meghalaya. My thanks are also due to other team members Smt. Nandini Bhattacharya-Sahu, Dr. K.M. Girhe and Shri R.K. Dwivedi, Draftsmen Gr. I, Sarvashri Ghayasuddin, Photographer Gr. I and T.B. Thapa of the Prehistory Branch, Nagpur.

REFERENCES

Coggin Brown, 1917, *Catalogue Raisonne of the Prehistoric Antiquities in Indian Museum*, Calcutta.

H.D. Sankalia, 1974, *Pre and Protohistory of India and Pakistan*, p. 42.

I.A.R., 1967-68, p. 8

I.A.R., 1971-72, p. 72.

I.A.R., 1978-79, p. 30.

I.A.R., 1992-93, p. 75.

V. Shivananda

Prehistory Branch,
Archaeological Survey of India, Nagpur

Atlas Motif in Indian art

Atlas, in ancient Greek architecture, is shown supporting columns and is carved in the form of standing or kneeling male figures. In Greek mythology, one of the Titans, who revolted against the gods, was punished and compelled to support the heavens on his head and shoulders. Growing weary, he asked Perseus to turn him into stone who, who readily obliged and turned him into a mountain and was henceforth known as Mount Atlas. (*Encyclo.*1995:152) Atlantes are males used in architecture instead of as pillars. Females figures are known as caryatides (Encyclo.1995)

Columns in the form of standing women were used in the Treasuries at Delphi in the sixth century BC (Collin's 1992). Six such figures formed a porch on the Erechtheum (the porch of the Maidens) (Collin's). Each seems to have held an *oinochoe and phialale*, vessels used for libation to the gods (Collin's). The motifs were made in the Roman period for Hadrian's Villa at Trivol (Collin's). Legend is that the maidens represented are captives from Carya condemned to stand in this position for ever (Hillyer and Huey 1966:5). The name Caryatid is derived from the karyatides who were priestesses at the temple of Artemis at Karyai (Wodsworath: 401) .

In India vestiges of a Buddhist monastic establishment at Devnimori, is yielded sculptures reminiscent of the Gandhara School (Lal: 1964:34). An interesting object discovered from the bed of the nearby Meshvo River is a bronze figure of Atlas (Lal). This is an import from the Mediterranean world, possibly via Barygaza (Modern Baruch) of classical geographers (Lal). Such figures of Graeco-Buddhis affiliation come from Jamalgarhi, Peshawar District (Coomaraswamy). It is now in the Lahore Museum.

The Atlantes and Caryatid motifs are well known features of Greek architecture. Though prototypes of Caryatids are not seen in Indian architecture, *gana* or *yaksha* appears in the role of Atlas. The Indian artists found in the *yaksha* statues an opportunity to incorporate this motif. The puranas describe them as creatures of great strength. They, thus appear in Indian art as prototypes of Atlantes, bearing or supporting heavy structures on their hands. They are called *bharavahaka yakshas*. It is not known if the Greek motif had any direct influence on Indian art in this respect. Probably, the motif developed independently in India and Greece, but in Gandhara art it certainly is a direct import.

Yakshas (*guhyas*) as Atlantes formed part of Bharhut stupa (*c.* 175 BC) (Coomaraswamy). The specimen is now in Indian Museum, Kolkatta. *Yakshas* (*guhyas*) as Atlantes appear on the west *torana*, at *Sanchi*.[15] On the same *torana* appear dwarfs. Winged *yakshas* (*guhyas*) as Atlantes can be seen on a railing pillar at Bodh-Gaya, about 100 BC (Coomaraswamy). *Yakshas* occur as Atlantes, bearing or supporting some edifice or vase on their hands in Amaravati art (Sivaramamurti). A four-armed image of a *bharavahaka yaksa* (eleventh century AD) is known from Bhojapur in Sihore district of Madhya Pradesh (Misra 1981:137-38). With his upper hands he supports a ledge above Readaer and Head (Retd)., Deptt. of History, S.C.College, Halra, Dist. North 24 Parganas, West Bengal.

Rao Bahadur K.N. Dikshit discovered a panel at Mahasthan (ancient city of Pundravardhana), now in Bangaladesh (Bogra District). The panel shows a pot-belled dwarfish *yaksha* seated on his haunches, supporting a ledge on both his upraised hands (Misra). A male figurine (in the round) from Tamluk (ancient Tamralipti) seems to possess an extraordinary power that is concealed in massive body of an Atlas or a *yaksha* (tentatively classed as a Maryan Yaksha).

The ruins of Chandraketugarh (in the North 24-Paraganas District, West Bengal) have proved to be a prolific source of early terracottas surprising variety and artistic excellence (Pl. 1 & 2). A particular class of terracotta plaques, comparatively large, show a female deity, precisely *Panhcachuda yakshini* or *Dasachuda yakshini*, (a form of mother goddesses or fertility goddesses) enshrined in a pillared *mandapa* accompanied by attendants with fans and umbrellas and devotees with bowls into which the goddess bestows her blessings. The present writer has collected several fragments of this type of plaque from there. On a fragmented plaque we see a pot-bellied *yaksha* on the capital of an ornamented pillar supporting with two upraised hands the roof of the shrine. Though done as a miniature, the massive and muscular body of the *yaksha* has been delineated with high skill in realistic manner. Stylistically, the specimen belongs to the Shunga period.

A plaque from Chandraketugarh, assigned to second century AD, in the State Archaeological Gallery, represents the scene of adoration of Lakshmi. Here, a hefty male, a *yaksha*, is shown by the side of the deity with raised hands indicating perhaps that he is carrying offering for the divinity. The male with its look of sheer strength recalls the sculptures of Atlantes in Greek art (Biswas 1981: 158). The present writer has collected a tiny figure of the same type (fragment of plaque). The *yaksha* here resembles the figure on the first plaque, but here it supports with raised hands a tray with flowers instead of the roof of an edifice.

Chandraketugarh has yielded an interesting toy cart portraying two *yakshas* supporting with their hands the throne or altar of a deity (only the feet are visible). The twin *yakshas* are seated on clouds, artistically done, indicating that they are carrying the deity through air.

The concept of the *yakshas* probably crystallised from primitive religion (Misra) and the cult of *yakshas* arose from the woods and from the legends of sea-faring merchants (Misra). But, during the Vedic period, they were elevated to the higher philosophic or intellectual planes (Misra). Indeed, they enjoyed a sublime and unique place in the Vedic pantheon (Misra). Later, the votaries of *yakshas* included kings and commoners, recluses, ascetics, the sea-faring and forest-tracking traders (Misra). The exalted character of the Vedic *yakshas* was subdued in the subsequent periods. The epics portray them as semi-divine beings (Misra). The Puranas, in their mythological narrations, have ranked them as secondary deities (Misra). Later, in the Shunga-Kushana period, we find the *yakshas* as decorative motifs (Misra). They occur as Atlantes as well.

REFERENCES

Biswas, S.S., *Terracotta Art of Bengal*, New Delhi, 1981, p. 158.

Coomaraswamy, A.K., *Yaksas*.

Collin's Dictionary of Archaeology, edi. by Paul Bahn, Glasgow, 1992, p. 83. Lal, B.B., *Indian Archaeology since Independence*, Delhi, 1964, p. 34.

Hillyer and Huey, *The Story of Architecture* (3000 BC - Gothic Period), New York, 1996. *The Wordsworth Encyclopaedia*, vol. 1, Ware, 1995, p.152.

R.N. Misra, *Yaksa Cult and Iconography*, Delhi, 1981, pp. 137-138.

Sivaramamurti, C., *Amaravati Sculptures*, Pl. XXII, XIX, 3. (Supporting a vase).

Wordsworth Encyclopaedia, Vol. I, p. 401.

Gourishankar De

A Unique Seal from Budhigarh, Orissa

Introduction

The present paper discusses the seal obtained from Budhigarh in 1982. It is now in the personal museum of the second author. Already, another seal-*cum*-pendant was unearthed at the same site in 2000, which was deciphered by B.N. Mukherjee and a paper was published on it in the *Puratattva* (Mohanty and Mishra 2000, pp. 158-60). The primary aim of this paper is not only to discuss the present seal, which is unreported, but also to correlate it with the former reported seal-*cum*-pendant.

Budhigarh is situated in the M. Rampur Tahsil, near the village Madanpur, district Kalahandi, Orissa. The extensive mound of Budhigarh covers an area of 1000 x 500 m (Mohanty and Mishra 2000). The site has revealed a wide spectrum of antiquities comprising ceramics including North Black Polished Ware, punch-marked coins, gold coins (pre-medieval), copper and iron objects, terracotta figurines, ornament mould, carved stone plaques, brick structure, copper beads, semi-precious stone beads, gold ornaments apart from faunal remains, etc.

Utility of seal was widespread in ancient India as in present time. The earlier use of seal in archaeological parameter is, however, evident from the Indus-Saraswati civilization especially from its mature phase (Gupta 1996: fig.-D, 116-122). The '*Mudra*' is also mentioned in the *Ramayana* and the *Mahabharata* in the sense of 'Identity card' of individual (Chakravarti 1991: 15-16). Marshall, however, equates '*Mudra*' with seal (Marshall 1973: 382). *Dharmakosha* and *Arthashastra* further deals on the 'Authenticated marks' (Seal) (Jana 1998: 242). Seal or *mudra*, in the ancient Indian context has been classified into two main categories, viz. (1) *Abhijnana Mudra*, (2) *Dharma Mudra* (Jana 1998). The former represents authentication, recognition or identification, whereas the latter type stands for religious import (Jana 1998).

Description of the Seal

This seal form Budhigarh was collected from the surface. It is made of red Jasper, measuring 3.5 x $5^{1/2}$ cm and has a cylindrical top, which expands and takes a bulbous form towards its reverse. Circular bands are carved respectively on proximal top and on the middle of the seal, apparently both for aesthetic and functional reason. There is a hole on the top. Highly polished and aesthetically enchanting, the seal on its reverse contains two distinguished symbols. At present however, the seal is partly broken on its reverse side.

Identification of Symbols

The significance of the seal lies in its reverse impression, which displays two symbols such as:

(1) Tree-in-railing with recurved top, which is embodied with three leafy branches in trident form.

(2) Parasol or umbrella (*chhatra*) stands straight on a pedestal, with a concave surface (probably a bowl).

Curved object raising from a rectangular railing is discerned in the Yaudheya coin dated second and first century BC (Allan 1936). It has been identified as sacrificial-post (Mishra 1975: 218). Cunningham, however, considers it as '*Bodhi Tree*' (Cunningham 1891: 75). But the bending top of the object (Tree) in railing of

Budhigarh Seal differs from the above Yaudheya symbol. Three leaf branches on the recurved top of the object conspicuously shows its flora-aspects. In the tree-in-railing type of symbol of coin device, we often notice the stylised representation of either single or double leafy branch (Chattopadhyay 1977: 34) or leafy branches three in number in the form of a trident. It is heartening to note that the tree-in-railing having three leafy branches in trident form is found on the obverse of the copper punch-marked coin of Kharligarh (second century AD to fifth century AD), i.e. Kharligarh is located in Bolangir district of Orissa. It was an early urban centre and is in close proximity to Budhigarh site. Thus, the curved object in railing of Budhigarh Seal is indeed a tree-in-railing, which can be further identified as *kalpavriksha* or *kalpadruma* (all bestowing celestial tree) or *chaityavriksha* of Brahmanical tradition. But at the same time, it can be also presumed as *'bodhi tree'*

The second symbol of the seal impression seems to be a parasol or umbrella affixed straight on a concave form of platform. Similar concave shape platform on which a tree is rising is discerned on the obverse of the punch-marked coin of Asurgarh hoard (Deo 1995: 56). Parasol/umbrella symbol is invariably found not only on the punch-marked coins as in the case of Asurgarh hoard, i.e., but also on the tribal coin (Kuninda coin) (Mishra 1975: 206) and on the *chhatra* type of Gold Coin of the Gupta period (Chhabra 1986, Plate XX, 1-6). Umbrella, however, bears Buddhist characteristics. It also stands for Royalty or Sovereignty of Hindu Polity. Symbol of single umbrella, moreover, vouchsafes the political concept of *ekachhatradhipatya* or paramount sovereign.

Dating of the Seal

Since the symbols and its artistic trend are akin to the signs and coin devices, found on the punch-marked and Tribal coins of early historic India, we are inclined to place the seal between first century AD to second century AD.

Interpretation

The seal from Budhigah falls within the category of *Abhijnana Mudra,* which to be used for authentication, recognition or identification by the king, high official and trader. Official letters, proclamations and documents in ancient India, as in modern times used to be authenticated by official seals (Jana 1998: 243). Chinese pilgrim Hieun-Tsang during his return journey from India obtained a letter from king Harsha, which had been authenticated with the seal of the king. The said letter was addressed to the rulers of those countries through which Hieun-Tsang had planned to pass (Beal 1911: 189-91).

The hole on the top of the seal shows its functional aspect, It can be worn around the neck through a string by an individual or officer, when affixing the impression on any object for authentication. Lack of script or legend on the Budhigarh seal deters proper interpretation. Possible interpretation of the seal can only be made on the basis of the two symbols. It is to be noted further that these symbols could be Buddhist as well as Brahmanical. In Buddhist art of the earlier period, Lord Buddha used to be symbolically represented by the devices like tree, wheel and umbrella, etc. (Chattopadhyay 1977: 273). Similarly, in Brahmanical art, literature, epigraph and tradition, often emphasis is given on tree, flower, leaf, umbrella, kunda and other objects. If we accept a Buddhist affiliation of these symbols, no cognitive interpretation is possible. Consequently, we have accepted Brahmanical characteristic of these symbols for interpretation, which is further substantiated by the earlier seal matrix of Budhigarh.

Budhigarh Seal seems to be the royal insignia and vouchsafes political concept of ancient India. Symbol No.1 tree-in-railing stands for *kalpavriksa*. It was a common motif in ancient Indian art and culture. Liberality of king is always likened to the *kalpavriksa* (Kuvalayananda: 22). Analogy can be drawn in this context from one of the early silver tribal coin (Kuninda Coin) of king Amoghabhuti (first century BC), where we come across *kalpavriksa* besides other symbols (Sivarammurti 1997: 45-47).

Symbol No. 2 representing single umbrella (*chhatra*) suggests sovereignty. The idea of single parasol or *ekachchhatra* or *ekachhatradhipatya* betokens the subjugation of all other kings and chieftains. But the political idea of *ekachhatradhipati* or *ekarata*, although materialised by the Mauryas in ancient Indian history, its popularity was seen only from the Gupta period. The symbol umbrella thus can be construed in the ordinary sense of Royalty.

The two symbols delineated on the seal of Budhigarh, therefore, seem to be royal insignia, adopted from the punch-marked and the Tribal Coins. The symbolical meaning of these two motifs suggests *Benevolent Kingship* or *Ideal Administration*.

The ideal of the king in ancient India was not to live for himself, but for the will and welfare of his peoples (Sivaramamurti 1997: 66). The ideal was executed by Ashoka during the third century BC and the Satavahana, the Chedis and other republican governments also championed this lofty ideal of kingship after the Mauryas. This interpretation is further substantiated by the reported seal legend of Budhigarh, which is already mentioned in this paper. The legend is of mixed script of *Kharoshthi-Brahmi*, dated second century A.D. The language is *Prakrit*. The reading of the matrix is '*Jana Dhapeta*'. Its Sanskrit rendering is thus '*Jajna Sthapayita*' or founder or establisher of sacrifice or a person patronising and performing Brahmanical sacrifice (Mohanty and Mishra 2000: 30. Unfortunately, this name is not given in the inscription. Thus, the question is who was this sacrificer or founder of Brahmanical sacrifice in the interior tribal region of Orissa during the second century AD? In ancient Indian culture and polity, the king (*rajan*), often treated as sacrificer, performing sacrifice mainly for the good of the people. This aspect of kingship is best illustrated in the coin type of the Kushana kings such as Kanishka, Huvishaka and Vasudeva (Sivaramamurti 1997: 46). This aspect of king, moreover, is indicated in the *chhatra* type of coin of Chandragupta II (Chhabra 1986: Plate XX, 1-6), where the king is making offerings in the fire with three flames leaping up from the fire altar such as *dakshinagani, ahavaniyagni* and *garhapatyagni*.

Apparently, the seal matrix of Budhigarh relate to the king who often acted as sacrificer or who had performed the first sacrifice for the welfare of his subject and thereby, earned the title '*Founder of Sacrifice*'.

It appears, therefore, that the two seals of Budhigarh belong to one stock. Still remains unanswered whether there was monarchical form of Government with Budhigarh as its headquarter or a republican form of Government or city-state type of administration with elected chief (also called *rajan, maharaja*) operated at Budhigarh? (Rahul river valley of modern Kalahandi district). As the Kharoshthi-Brahmi script, Prakrit language, symbol 'tree-in-railing' and parasol, etc., enshrined on the Budhigarh seals and also are seen in the tribal coins and seals especially of the tribal republics of north-west India, it tends to support the hypothesis of expansion or migration of one or other republican tribal people into the interior region of Orissa like Budhigarh. It cannot be averred without context that the tribal republican peoples like the Kunindas, the Yaudheyas and the Malavas, etc., professed and championed Brahmanical faith and tradition. Future research and discoveries will shed light on this aspect.

REFERENCES

Allan, J., 1936, *Catalogue of the coins of Ancient India in the British Museum*, PCXLVII-CLII, London.

Beal, S., 1911, *The life of Hieun-Tsang*, pp.189-90, London.

Chhabra, B.C., 1986, *Catalogue of the Gupta Gold Coins of the Bayana Hoard in the National Museum*, Plate-XX, 1-6, National Museum, New Delhi.

Chakravorty, B.B., 1991, *Indus Script-The Artistic Version of Brahmi*, pp. 15-16, Bhartiya Itihas Sankalan Samiti, Calcutta.

Chattopadhyay, B., 1977, *Coins and Icon—A Study of Myths and Symbols in Indian Numismatic Art*, p. 34, Calcutta.

Cunningham, A., 1891, *Coins of Ancient India (From the Earliest Times Down to the Seventh Century A.D.)*, p. 75, London.

Deo, P.K., 1995, 'Forgotten Forts of Kalahandi (Part-I) Asurgarh Fort and a Hoard of Punch-Marked Coins', p. 56, Symbol-5 in the *Orissa Historical Research Journal*, Vol. XIVI, No. 3-4, Bhubaneswar.

Dikshita, A. (ed.), 1903, *Kuvalayananda* 22, Bombay.

Gupta, S.P., 1996, *The Indus-Saraswati Civilization (Origins, Problems and Issues)*, Fig. D, pp. 116-122, Pratibha Prakashan, Delhi.

Jana, R.K., 1998, *Ships on Seals from Chandraketugarh in History and Archaeology of Eastern India*, ed., A. Dutta, p. 242, Books & Books, New Delhi.

Marshall, J., 1973, *Mohenjodaro and the Indus Civilization*, p. 382, Indo, B.K. House.

Mishra, S.N., 1975, *Ancient Indian Republics*, p.18, S. Chand & Company, New Delhi.

Mohanty, P. & B. Mishra, 2000, 'A Note on a Seal Matrix from Budhigarh, District Kalahandi, Orissa', *Puratattva*, pp. 158-60, vol. 30, New Delhi.

Murty, C.S.R., 1997, *Sources of History, Illuminated by Leterature*, p. 45-47, New Delhi

Baba Mishra*
Mihirendra Pratap Singhdeo**

Temporary Shelter in the Sub-Himalayas: An Ethno-Archaeological Observation

Location

The site is situated near the village of Dharmasala (31° 31' N: 76° 36' E) in the Bilaspur district of Himachal Pradesh. The general landscape is a pine-forest cover, undulating topography with an altitude of 780 m above Mean Sea Level (MSL). The hilly terrain consists of eroded gullies of Middle Siwalik deposits, intermittently capped by Holocene sediments. These sediments are covered thickly with grass, plants, bushes, shrubs, and predominantly, pine-trees (often exceeding 20 m in height), interspersed with seasonal streams and a small river (*Makan Khad*).

Introduction

A prime reason for oversimplified conjectures in archaeological interpretations about ancient shelter-design and function, is principally due to the absence of perishable materials in the archaeological context (e.g., wood, leather, bone, grass, reeds, straw, leaves). Only in rare conditions, does such material survive. This frustrating limitation forces us to make most inferences about pre-historic shelters based on the three factors: (a) from what does survive in archaeological context (post-holes, stone-structures, etc.); (b) interpretations by other archaeologists from sites with similar (but more complete) archaeological content; and (c) observations of innovative shelter resources from contemporary hunter-gatherers (in this case, Himanchali villagers). Since caves form in unique and rare geological conditions, the majority of pre-historic group relied on open-air locations, for habitation near fresh water and game sources. The example described in this paper is one such possibility of shelter design and raw material exploitation, for temporary habitation purposes.

In January of 2001, the author participated with an Indian-Australian research team in the vicinity of Hari Taliyangar to search for vertebrate fossils. Less than two days prior to departing from Dharmasala village, the author encountered a modern forest-shelter cluster, which was immediately plotted and photographed the following day. From the evidence at the site (i.e., charred and distinctively cut tree stumps, shelter residue, broken branches, straw), the cluster seemed to have been abandoned (only within two days) by villagers (not local) who extracted pine-tree resin for production of turpentine oil. Unfortunately, due to time constraints, the unavailability of the builders for interviewing, and general site disturbance, this paper has its obvious limitations and is only descriptive in nature. On the other hand, the potential for reconstruction for archaeological relevance should not be completely overlooked. This site basically provides an illustration of how provisional cover might have been erected by pre-historic hunting or travelling group by utilising a few basic raw materials in a similar palaeo-ecological setting (medium altitude, pine forest, hilly topography, and cold winter conditions).

General Dimensions

The shelter cluster consists of three separate features, each an individual unit of accommodation. Although similar in structural morphology and spatial distribution, there is noticeable variation in size. Due to the time restrictions mentioned earlier, only the most prominent shelter feature was recorded (Feature 'A'). This large feature (fig. 1) would have accommodated eight people, whereas the two remaining features would have housed two additional people each, respectively (total accommodation: 12 people). The height of the features (from ground to roof) upon reconstruction, is debatable and probably did not exceed one-and-one-half metres (inferred from post-hole size and straw-roof remnants). The measurement of Feature 'A' are approximately 17 m in length by 6 m in width. It consists of four sub-features (SF-A1 to SF-A4) which in turn, housed two people each, respectively. These sub-features further include such associated components as hearths, 'beds', stone platforms, pegs, post-holes, and grooves. These components are grouped accordingly and discussed in more detail below.

Hearths and Beds

From the clear evidence of purposely-shaped rocks from Siwalik sandstone cobbles around the fireplaces, and their specific arrangement (to support pots), the four hearths inside Feature 'A' seem to have been utilised exclusively for cooking, in addition to being a source of warmth at night. Besides these, four additional fireplaces were noted outside Feature 'A' (not illustrated here). Since the individual placement of rocks at each of these external hearths was irregular and too scattered to support cooking pots, they (probably) served the purpose of heating pine resin and/or bathing-water in larger pots. Interestingly, the hearth in SF-A4 was constructed in a different manner from the other hearths. Basically, it is hollow in the ground and utilises a minimum number of modified sandstone.

All the beds are made of loose pine-needles, layered to a thickness of approximately 2 cm and are generally similar in measurement, profile and orientation. Thick layers of pine-needles combined with the close proximity of a hearth between two beds, probably supplied a generous amount of warmth.

Other Components and Interpretations

All the sub-features are similar in structural morphology excepting certain key traits (Table 1). For instance, SF-A2 is the only sub-feature with a platform made of numerous sandstone cobbles, near the top. This might have been employed to deposit cooking utensils and other necessary tools. In addition, SF-A1 has a large slab (Table 1) between the two beds and exhibits complete absence of

Sub-Feature	Postholes	Pegs	Beds	Hearths
SF-A1	0	26	2	1
SF-A2	5	17	2	1
SF-A3	2	22	2	1
SF-A4	7	15	2	1

post-holes. SF-A3 contains only two post-holes, when compared with sub-features A2 and A4, which have five and seven post-holes (of varying size), respectively. This is probably due to the closeness of a tree-line (along the north side of Feature 'A') which had a sufficient number of branches to secure the straw roof, perhaps with strings (post-holes would then be unwarranted).

There seems to be no evidence of whether the sub-features were physically separated from each other by makeshift walls of straw, straw-domes (roofs), or nothing at all. The only attribute marking each sub-feature as distinct units, is shallow grooves or furrows in the ground each feature, probably to drain rainwater. This is rather perplexing since the amount of rainfall during winter would have been insignificant, unless the furrows served only as a precaution against (occasional) light rainfall. In addition, more slender grooves are also located along and between most of the beds, the purpose or function of which is unknown.

Individual preference seems to have affected the construction of SF-A3 and SF-A4 mutually, in contrast to SF-A1 and SF-A2 individually. For instance, SF-A3 and SF-A4 are strikingly similar in construction and pattern, whereas the other two remaining sub-features are of a random and unique design. The scattered rocks in between the sub-features might have been placed to anchor branches and straw roofs. The only direction that remained for entering and exiting the sub-features, therefore, is located on the southern side. Given that this camp was freshly abandoned, certain artefacts noted prior to plotting, were missing the following day (taken by villagers). For example, a small table made of cut branches was noted (approximate dimensions of 1 m cube) the platform made from thinner branches and pine-tree bark (not illustrated here). Whether it sustained a container of stored resin or served another purpose, is unknown. The bark was also utilised as kindling fire as surmised from ash and strips of burnt bark, found in and around the hearths.

Archaeological Implications and Conclusion

Despite nearby sources of fresh water (*Makan Khad*) and abundant game, this kind of shelter should be interpreted solely as *temporary* in nature, for two fundamental reasons: (a) the delicate character of construction, and (b) the nature of the raw materials exploited. In other words, since this shelter cluster is neither resilient, water-resistant nor perpetually warm, it can never be utilised on a regular basis as a permanent camp or a 'home-base' (Binford 1983; Isaac 1989). Examples for comparison with this shelter comes from contemporary communities as well as from excavated Palaeolithic sites, and both are provided below.

One example of high-altitude adaptation and the *required* resources needed for permanent occupation, is provided by the peasants of the Andean Highlands. These people have conventionally built their dwellings of sod and adobe block. Due to the lack of wood, these mud structures withstand freezing night and driving rains of the weather at 4,000 m above MSL (Moran 1982). However, another type built by pastoralists of the same community involves piled stones with a grass roof, which is a more provisional shelter. As expected, the latter shelter is less warmer than the former mud structures and forfeits durability for ease and speed of construction.

A more regional (and archaeological) comparison to the contemporary shelter at Dharmasala can be seen at the Neolithic sites of Burzahom, Gufkral, and Martand in Kashmir (Sankalia 1974). Instead of exploiting such raw materials as mud, stone, or clay, the ancient inhabitants of these sites built (the now hallmark) 'pit dwellings' by scraping out a major portion of the structure-floor. That aspect is remotely similar to the furrowing observed at Dharmasala, but occurs on a more diminutive scale and with a discrete and different function than the Neolithic. Apparently, the only *shared* structural features between the Kashmiri Neolithic sites and Dharmasala are the postholes.

A more productive comparison, however, can be made with the Magdalenian site of Pincevent (northern France), excavated in the 1960s by Andre Leroi-Gourhan and M. Brezillon (Gowlett 1992). The evidence in cultural layer 'Habitation I' is characteristic of Magdalenian homes and bears some resemblance to the forest shelter at Dharmasala. Three hearths, arranged in a row, surrounded by occupation debris, are in a clear pattern suggesting that they were situated between tents. Bones of reindeer and tiny flakes of flint (for butchering) are strewn around these campfires, and the lack of tidying up at 'Habitation I' is suggestive of a short term occupation (Gowlett 1992). Besides being a pre-historic environmental adaptation, the type of shelter at Dharmasala might also have been employed during Chalcolithic and Historic periods as well apparently continuing right up to modern-day times. Although the design of the shelter might essentially be a static attribute, its function through time can be of a dynamic nature-dependent on aim, duration of stay, and the size of the human groups. For instance, the shelter described in this paper temporarily accommodated local resin-extractors. During ancient times however, human groups might have built a similar shelter for use as a transitory hunting or itinerant camp (as shown through the above examples). In terms of the resin-extraction, turpentine oil was most certainly an unknown and unnecessary resource during pre-historic times. However, (plant) resin, an extremely strong adhesive, has been previously applied to haft lithic blades or flakes in wooden handles during ancient Egyptian times (Whittaker 1994). According to Whittaker (1994: 255), who has conducted hafting experiments, pine resin is the most common and easiest to find. To apply it, one should warm it until it is runny, although overheating will make it brittle after it has hardened. Besides securing the lithic flake, blade, or point in the handle, a thin coat of resin on the bindings also serves as a waterproofing agent.

At Dharmasala, the innovative exploitation of simple and easily available raw material is clearly evident, the shelter cluster is simple, adequate, and fairly easy to construct. Considering that only three raw material sources were available at any given time, the amount of resulting components and their subsequent, are remarkable (fig. 2). As mentioned earlier, the description above can only serve as a potential example of pre-historic structures and demonstrates a resourcefulness with a limited amount of available raw materials in a (pine) forest environment. Indeed, this type of observation should not encourage direct relation with evidence found at archaeological sites, *regardless* of similarity, but should only induce broad comparisons, at the very most.

Acknowledgements

I would like to thank Rajeev Patnaik and David Cameron for providing accommodation and a memorable and valuable introduction to the Hari Talyangar area. I am also thankful to Martin A.J. Williams for the initial suggestion of documenting the shelter area.

REFERENCES

Binford, L.R., 1993, *In Pursuit of the Past-Decoding the Archaeological Record*, London: Thames and Hudson.

Gowlett, J.A.J., 1992, *Ascent to Civilization-The Archaeology of Early Humans*, 2nd edn., New York: McGraw-Hill, Inc.

Isaac, B., 1989, *The Archaeology of Human Origins—Papers by Glynn Isaac*, Cambridge: Cambridge University Press.

Moran, E.F., 1982, *Human Adaptability—An Introduction to Ecological Anthropology*, Boulder: Westview Press.

Sankalia, H.D., 1974, *The Prehistory and Protohistory of India and Pakistan*, Pune: Deccan College Post-Graduate and Research Institute.

Whittaker, J.C., 1994, *Flintknapping-Making and Understanding Stone Tool*, Austin: University of Texas Press.

Research School of Archaeology
& Archaeological Science
(Department of Archaeology & Prehistory)
University of Sheffield

Parth R. Chauhan

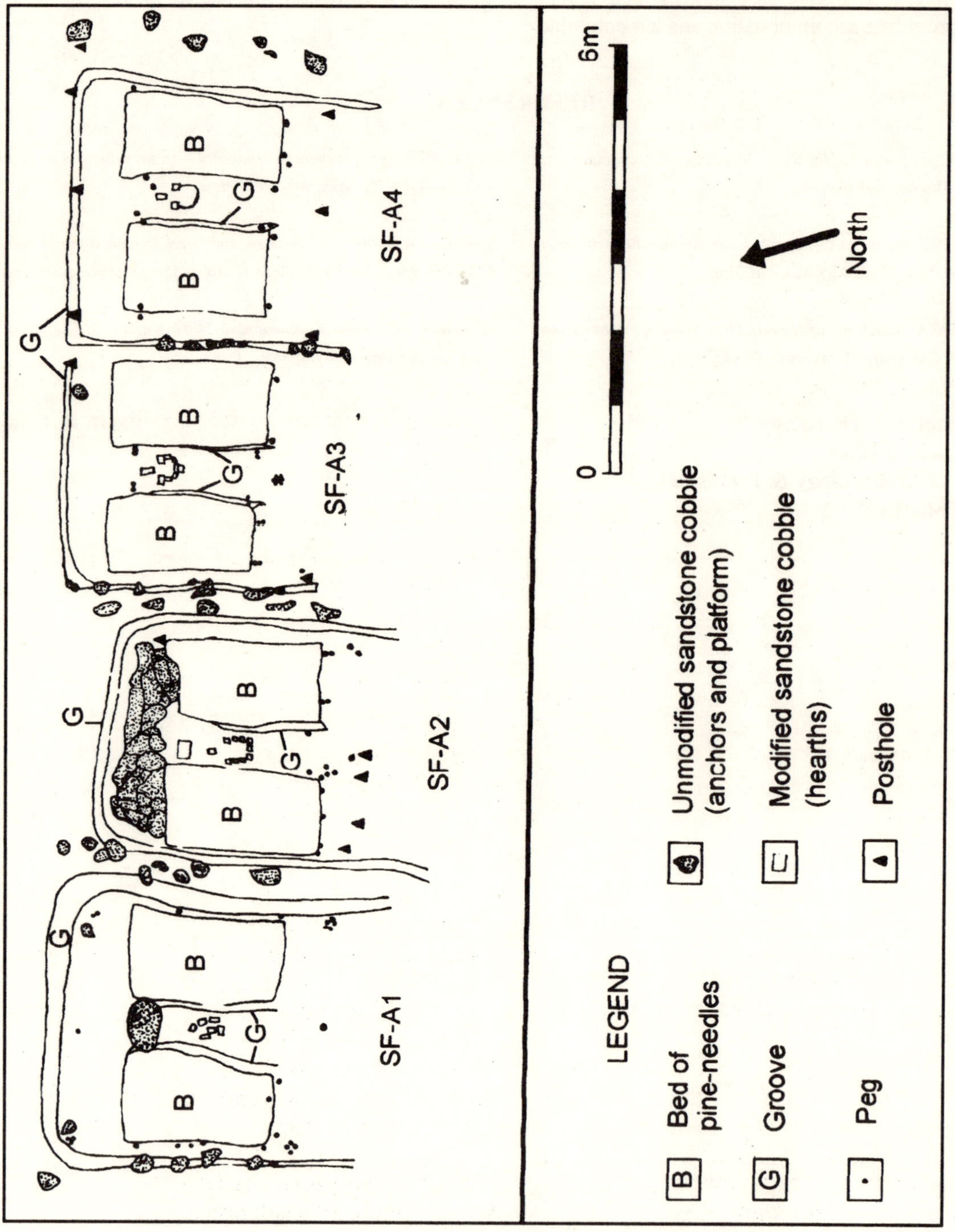
SF-A1
SF-A2
SF-A3
SF-A4
B
G
0
6m
North
LEGEND
B Bed of pine-needles
G Groove
Peg
Unmodified sandstone cobble (anchors and platform)
Modified sandstone cobble (hearths)
Posthole

Fig. 1.

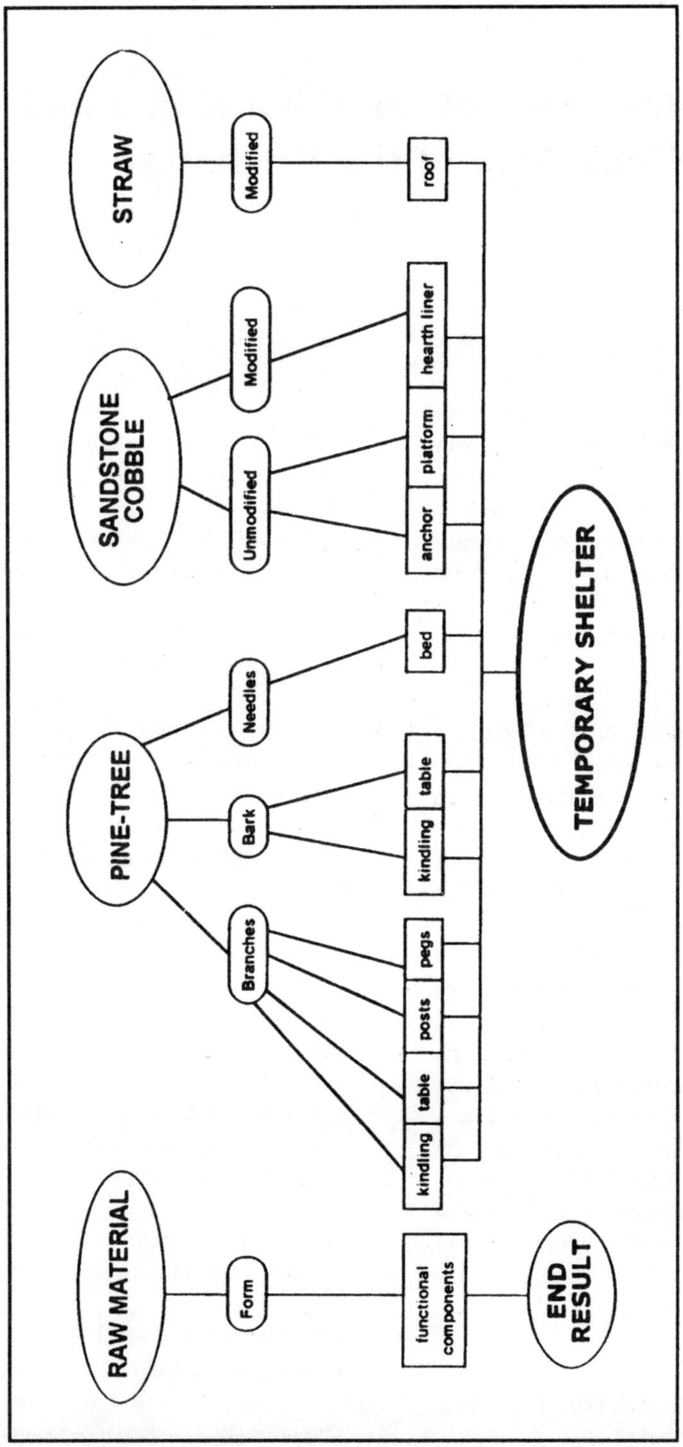
RAW MATERIAL
Form
functional components
END RESULT
PINE-TREE
Branches
Bark
Needles
kindling
table
posts
pegs
kindling
table
bed
SANDSTONE COBBLE
Unmodified
Modified
anchor
platform
hearth liner
STRAW
Modified
roof
TEMPORARY SHELTER

Fig. 2.

Rabatak Inscription of Kanishka and Genealogy of the Kushanas

The chance discovery of a new Bactrian inscription of Kanishka, at a hill known as Kafir's Castle in the region called Rabatak, 40 km north of Pul-i-Khumri in the Baghlan province of Afghanistan, has proved to be very significant in view of fresh information it provides on the genealogy of the early Kushana emperors, foundation of a new era of Kanishka, extent of the empire of Kanishka, discontinuation of official use of Greek language, which was replaced by the *arya-bhasha* (Bactrian or Tokharian language) and further understanding of Kushana religion and dynastic shrines.

The inscription was first noticed by Tim Porter, a British charity worker, engaged on behalf of the Halo Trust, organising the removal of land mines in the Afghan province of Baghlan. He took photographs of some stone objects at the request of Sayyid Jafar, Governor of Baghlan. He sent a photograph through his colleague, Ian Clark, to the British Museum, London for further study as he noticed a similarity of the inscription with the Kushana inscription from Surkh Kotal. The rectangular piece of limestone on which the present inscription was engraved, seems to be 90 cm wide, 50 cm high and 25 cm thick. The inscription in Greek characters was engraved all over one face of the stone block and has twenty-three lines. It was studied and published along with detailed notes by Nicholas Sims-Williams and Joe Cribb in 1995-96 (1995-96) the latter very kindly provided a copy of the photograph to me in October 2000 in London which is being reproduced here (Pl. 1).

TEXT

1. (*ca*.10) NO BWGO STORGD KANESHKE KOSHAND RASHTOGO LADEIGO XOAZADARGO BAGO

2. EZNOGO KIDI AS (O) NANA ODO ASO OISPONAND MI BAGAND I SHAODANI ABORDO KIDI TWGO XSHONO

3. NOBASTO S (A) GWNDI BAGANDO SINDADO OTEIA I IWNAGGO OASO OZOAGTO TADEIA ARIAO WS

4. TADO ABO IWGO XSHON (O) ABO (I) IUNDO PHROAGDAZO ABO SHATRIAGGE SHADRE AGITA KOO

5. ADEAND ODO I WZOPO OD (O) (IZ) AGEDOODOI KWZ (AM) BO ODO I PALABOTRO OIDRA ADA ABOI ZIRIT

6. (AM) BO SIDEIAND PROBAO ODO MANDAR (O) I STORAND ABO I SINDO WSTADO OTE (I) A AROU (G) O

7. IUNDO (ABO) I SINDO WSTADO TADI SHAI KANESHKE ABO SHAPHARG KARALARAGGO PHROMADO

8. (A) BEINA (*ca* 4) O BAGOLAGGO KARDI SIDI B . . . . . ABO RIZDI ABO MA KA.. BARA PHAREIMOANO B—

9. (A) GA (N) O (K) IDI MARO KIRDAN (B) I MA . . .O (PH) ARRO OMMA OOELDI IA AMSA NANA ODO IA AM—

10. S A OMMA AOROMOZDO MAZDO O (A) NO SROSHARDO NARASAO MIIRO OODO MAASEN (O) RIZ (OI) ODO BIZA (G) O.RIZDI OTEIA OUDOA

11. NO PI (DO) GIRBO PHROMADO KIRDI EIMOAND BAGAND KIDI MASKA NIBIXTIGENDI OR—

12. EIA PHROMADO ABEIMO AND SHAONAND KIRDI ABO KOZOULO KADPHISO SHAO BAOI PHR—

13. ONIAGO (O) DO A (BO O) OEMO (T) AKTOO SHAO A (B) (O)

I NIA (G) O ODO ABO OOEMO KADPHISO SHAO ABO

14. (I) PIDA ODO ABO I XOBGO ABO KANESHKO SHAO TA SAGWNDI SHAONANO SHAO I BAGOPOO—

15. (RO) A (*ca.* 7) PHR (O) MADO KIRDI TADI SHAPHARE KAR-ALRAGGE KIRDO EIO BAGOLAGGO

16. (*ca.* 8) O KARALRAGGO ODO SHAPHARO KARALRAGGO ODO NOKONZOKO IASHTO O—

17. A (S TO PI) DO IAPHROMAND EIMIDBA BAGE KIDI MARO NIBIXTIGENDI TADANO ABO SHAON—

18. AN (O) SHAO ABO KANESHKE KOSHAND ABO IADEOANI ZORRIGI LROU (G) O AGGA (O) (A) GGO OANIND—

19. O P (*ca.* 4) I (N) DI OD (..) (D) I BA (G) OPOORO ASQ IWGO XSHONO ABO IO (A) X (X) SHONO IUNDO AROUGO P—

20. ADA (XSHANO) I B (A) GOLAGGO ABO IWGO XSHONO ASPADO TADI ABO I ARIAMOSO (X) SHONO AGGAR (. . .)

21. (*ca.* 10 p) IDO SHAO PHROMANA ABISO I PASHENA LADO ABIGO I BA (ca.5) LADO ABISO (*ca.* 3)

22. (*ca.* 13) SHA I MAD . . . . A (A) BO BAGAND LADO ODO (ca. 4) O (*ca.* 3) AXAD (*ca.* 8) BAGO (*ca.* 4)

23. (Traces only)

TRANSLATION

1. . . . of the great salvation, Kanishka the Kushana, the righteous, the just, the autocrat, the god

2. worthy of worship, who has obtained the kingship from Nana and from all the gods, who has inaugurated the year one

3. as the gods pleased. And he issued a Greek edict (and) then he put it into Aryan

4. In the year it has been proclaimed unto India, unto the whole of the realm of the kshatriyas, that (as for)

5. them—both the (city of) . . . and the (city of) Saketa, and the (city of) Kausambi, and the (city of) Pataliputra, as far as the (city of) Sri-Ç̣hampa—

6. Whatever rulers and other important persons (the might have) he had submitted to (his) will, and he had submitted all

7. India to (his) will. Then King Kanishka gave orders to Shafar the Karalrang

8. At this . . . to make the sanctuary which is called B . . . ab, in the p lain of Ka . . . for these

9. gods, (of whom the . . . . Glorious Umma leads the service here, (namely): the lady Nana and the

10. lady Umma, Aurmuzd, the Gracious one, Sroshard, Narasa, (and) Mihr. And he likewise

11. gave orders to make images of these gods who are written above, and

12. he gave orders to make (them) for these kings: for King Kujula Kadphises (his) great

13. grandfather, and for King Vima Taktu (his) grandfather, and for King Vima Kadphises

14. (his) father, and also for himself, King Kanishka. Then, as the king of kings, the devaputra

15. had given orders to do, Shafar the Karalrang made this sanctuary.

16. (Then . . .) the karalrang, and Shafar the karalrang, and Nukunzuk (led) the worship

17. (according to) the (king's) command. (As for) these gods who are written here—may they (keep) the

18. king of kings, Kanishka the Kushana, for ever healthy, secure, (and) victorious

19. And (when) the devaputra, the ruler of all India from the year one to the year one thousand

20. had founded the sanctuary in the year one, then also to the . . . year. . .

21. according to the king's command, (and) it was given also to the (and) it was given also to the ... (and also to . . .)

22. the king gave an endowment to the gods, and. . . .

23. (traces only)

The above version of the inscription clearly suggests the following genealogy of the early Kushana emperors—Kujula Kadphises followed by his son Vima Tak(to) who was followed by his son Vima Kadphises who was succeeded by his son Kanishka.

A controversy on the second ruler mentioned in the inscription was created by B.N. Mukherjee in 1998 when his monograph (Mukherjee 1995) appeared, based on the information already published earlier by Nicholas Sims-Williams and Joe Cribb. In place of the part of line 13 having the words "(O) E M O (T) AKTOO SHAO A (B) (O) I NIA (G) O" Mukherjee seems to have purposefully read "IMO N (I) AKO (?) OOM (ORK) I (or Y ?) SA (DD) A SHKAND".

Although letters in this particular part of the inscription are no doubt not very clear, but a closer look at this part of the inscription suggests that the earlier reading is more correct where the name is mentioned as Vima Takto and in finding the name of his merely intentional in order to fix the genealogical position of Sadashkana about whom B.N. Mukherjee has remained confused throughout these years since this scion of the Kushanas came to light after the publication of the Kharoshthi gold plate inscription of Senavarma, the ruler of Odi (Udyana in Swat) which mentions the name of Sadashkana Devaputra as son of Maharaja Rajatirya Kuyula Katphsa (Kujula Kadphises) (Bailey, 1980: 21-22). Commenting upon this discovery and publication of the inscription, B.N. Mukherjee, thought first Sadashkana to be a brother of Vima Kadphises and then making the things have been an epithet (or a second name) of Vima (Mukherjee 1981: 752-59 and 1988).

Even if the name of Sadashkana is read in place of Vima Takto in the present inscription, the contention of B.N. Mukherjee after his study of the Kharoshthi gold plate inscription mentioned above that Sadashkana was either a brother of Vima Kadphises or one of his own epithets proves to be wrong as he is mentioned as father of Vima Kadphises in the present inscription.

The name Vima Tak(to) can be traced in Dasht-e-Nawur inscription, Mat inscription on the royal image of Vima Takshuma and several coins including those of Soter Megas (Nicholas Sims-Williams *et al.* 1956-96; Michael Alram *et al.* 1999: 177-206) and as such it should be accepted as the name of second emperor mentioned in the present record and not the one suggested wrongly by B.N. Mukherjee.

The Rabatak inscription belonging to the year 1 of Kanishka throw light on the commencement of a new era which can be equated with the Saka era. The proclamation of his rule in the year one in the cities of Saketa, Kaushambi, Pataliputra, Siri-Tambo (Champa in Bihar or Tamralipti on the eastern coast) suggests the extent of Kushana empire at the beginning of the rule of Kanishka. The extent of his empire in the east as far as Saketa and Pataliputra is also mentioned in Chinese and Tibetan sources (Mani 1987). B.N. Mukherjee has further deciphered the names of the cities of Koonadiano (Kaundinya) and Ozeno (Ujjayini) in this inscription (Mukherjee 1997-98). The record gives a vivid description of the royal belief of the Kushanas in worshipping Nana and various deities and construction of temples and bagolaggo (*devakula*).

REFERENCES

1. Nicholas Sims-Williams and Joe Cribb, 'A New Bactrian Insctiption of Kanishka the Great', *Silk Road Art and Archaeology*, 4, 1995-96, Kamakura.

2. B.N. Mukherjee, 'The Great Kushana Testament', *Indian Museum Bulletin*, 1995, Calcutta (published in 1997-98).

3. H.W. Bailey, 'A Kharostri Inscription of Senavarma, King of Odi', *Journal of the Royal Asiatic Society*, 1980, pp. 21-29.

4. B.N. Mukherjee, 'New light on the History of the Kushana Period', *Journal of the Asiatic Society*, 1981, vol. XXIII, nos. 1-2, pp. 152-59; *The Rise and Fall of the Kushana Empire*, Calcutta,

1988, pp. 665-66.

5. Nicholas Sims-Williams and Joe Cribb, *op.cit.*, p. 97; Joe Cribb, 'The Early Kushan Kings: New Evidence for Chronology (Evidence from the Rabatak Inscription of Kanishka I)', *Coins, Art and Chronology, Essays on the pre-Islamic History of the Indo-Iranian Borderlands*, edited by Michael Alarm and Deborah E. Klimburg-Salter, Wien, 1999, pp. 177-206.

6. B.R. Mani, *The Kushan Civilization*, New Delhi, 1987, pp.16-17.

7. B.N. Mukherjee, 'The Great Kushana Testament', *op. cit.*, p.16.

Archaeological Survey of India,
New Delhi-110 011

B.R. Mani

Historicity of Casting Technology in Nepal

In the whole of Indian sub-continent metal has been used from the very ancient times as evidenced by the findings of Indus Valley Civilization (Marshall 1931; Vats 1940) and number of sites throughout northern India mainly in the Gangetic Basin, where hoards of copper objects of certain types were deposited (Lal 1951). But the history of casting in Nepal is not yet adequately known, while the excavations show the development of this art from many centuries before Christ. The recent archaeological excavations carried out by Nepal-Genman Archaeological Project in 1992 at the caves of Mustang have revealed many copper hoards, viz., arrowheads with a tang strip made of bronze, iron blades (Simon 1992-1993:1-19 figs. 4:2, 9:1), iron ritual objects, embossed bronze or copper sheets (Simons, A. *et al.* 1994:51-75 figs. 16,10) also called anthropomorphic object by Tiwari (1984-85: 1-12), bronze objects like cross-shaped, copper bangles (Simons, A. *et al.* 1994: 51-75 fig. 9), likewise iron spatula (blade?), metal jewellery, long tubules made of brass and of copper, brass bell and iron belt buckle (Simons, A. *et al.* 1994: 93-129 figs. 2:1, 3: 2-5, 21:1,2) and anthropomorphic figure of copper also have come to light from Jagatpur village of Kailali District (Darnal 2002: 39-48 fig. V). The findings of Mustang have been called Megalithic and Neolithic by Mr. Tiwari (1984-85:6 and 9), Dr. Schuh (1992-1993: c-m) named them as Neolithic and Megalithic. According to Angela Simons (1992–1993: 8), this was the Prehistoric and Iron Age Culture. T.N. Mishra (1994: 151) is of the opinion that the findings from Mustang are comparable to be Neolithic, Chalcolithic and the Megalithic sites found in the south Asian region. Besides, the successive excavations at Tilaurakot, the ancient Kapilvastu, in the western Tarai region of Nepal during 1962, have yielded nearly three thousand silver and copper coins, dating from fifth to second centuries BC (Mitra 1972: 84-99). Mitra is of the opinion that these coins were issued locally at ancient Kapilavastu when it was a sovereign state. Besides, melting furnace along with it, metal pieces and slag have been excavated at Kapilavastu (Rajil 1979:37). These evidences suggest the possibility of having the knowledge of casting metal art objects at Kapilavastu during the said period. However, no other places from the Kathmandu Valley, has so far yielded similar contemporary evidence. But the art of casting is still being practised in Nepal. It is, therefore, possible to have a direct access to the technology of image casting which has its roots in the ancient tradition.

By the end of the first century AD the Lichhavis migrated to Nepal from India (Regmi 1969:64). The ornaments and *mukutas* (coronets) used in the so-called Kirata images suggest that the technique of image casting in metal had already been developed in Nepal before the arrival of the Lichhavis (Marie Laure de' Labriffe 1973: 185). According to R.J. Mehta (1971:22), however, the art of image casting was introduced in Nepal only during the regime of the Imperial Gupta in India. There is no doubt that the artistic vision of the Gupta indeed had a strong influence on Nepal's Lichhavi artists. The influence is apparent in the bronze Buddha dated to AD 591 preserved in the Cleveland Museum of Art (Schroeder 1981 Fig. 74E; Ray, N.R. *et al.* 1986, Fig. 26) for which Czuma (1970:55) describes as *Gupta style Bronzes Buddha.*

At a later date, Pala and Sena schools (eighth to twelfth centuries AD) influenced Nepalese sculpture. Because of this influence, it helped Nepalese image casting to assume the stutus of a major art form in the Kathmandu Valley. However, when the art was waning in

India under the swords of Muslim invaders, it found refuge in Nepal. It further got matured and flowered here in Nepal. Nepalese art began to take its own shape and direction, and, ultimately, it evolved as an unmistakably independent Nepalese style (Alsop and Charlton 1973:23). Nepal proved itself to be more than a mere transit point for the exchange of art ideology and style between India. Tibet and China, but in its own right became a cradle of sculptural art. Newar artists became renowned and were highly acknowledged in Tibet and China for their artistic skills and they were in demand in these countries. They were honoured as masters of their craft and they imparted their knowledge to local people (Schroeder 1981:333). The Tibetans and the Chinese in their turn learnt from their Newar teachers and gradually evolved them into distinctly local styles. The circle was complete when, the Tibetan and Chinese styles exerted great influence on the art of Nepal (Alsop and Charlton 1973: 23). At this juncture, A.K. Coomaraswamy (1921:1) suggests that the history of Nepalese art is one of flux and change by way of adoption and transmutation of neighbouring styles. In the scheme of Asian art history, Nepal remained at the centre of exchange of techniques and styles of her neighbouring countries, which surrounded her.

While the tradition of Indian image casting was given a mortal blow in eastern India because of the waves of Muslim invaders who swept the sub-continent periodically and signaled the end of the Pala and Sena traditions (French 1928:20). The art and craft of metal sculpture and casting reached the perfection of excellence in south India under the Cholas (Sivaramamurti 1977:41). As Khandalavala has said, "the best south Indian bronzes are amongst the finest achievement of metal sculpture in the world" (quoted by Mehta 1971: 29). But with the end of the Pala and Sena styles in eastern India and the decay of the great Chola dynastic tradition in the south, the Indian art of image casting was lost into oblivion and thereafter it never recovered the past glory. With the modern period of Indian history, beginning with the takeover by the British distanced India from her heritage of philosophy and art and concentrated her energies on the forging of a modern state. The result has been thinning of interest in the great heritage of arts. Mehta (1971: 32) writes, "Made in large numbers the images of the eighteenth century till this day are poor specimens of a decadent style, a hollow mockery of the great traditions of the past, the one-time skill and aesthetic vigour of the image-makers of old. It seems as if today they are no longer inspired but are just the uninterested producers of what is demanded of them. The Sthapatis are now no more creative artists but mere artisans. The once great art of metal sculpture and casting in India is dead."

Casting metal images is still being done in India, but they are largely copies of pieces which can hardly considered works of art, for they are not sculptured, but copied through the use of moulds. So great has been decline of Indian artistry that most of these pieces are no longer made through the process of *madhuchhistavidhana* or Lost-Wax but produced in halves and then welded together. But the tradition, which Indian artists had begun, was still being continued in Nepal, China and Tibet. But just as medieval history saw the undoing of the great India tradition, similarly trends of modern times put an end to the indigenous tradition of the religious art in China and Tibet as religion and religious arts have no place within communism (Alsop and Charlton 1973:23). The advent of communism in China sounded the death-knell for her religious art forms, and as it expanded from its base within China and eventually swallowed Tibet by 1959, another tradition of art faced destruction. Although many of the Chinese occupation over Tibet were artists of the first rank, it seems that image casters were not among them. That leaves Nepal, Nepal alone among her neighbours has managed to preserve the art of image casting. The reasons for this remarkable survival are multiple (Alsop and Charlton 1973: 24-25). One reason is grographical. Nepal's isolation from the plains of India spared her the sword of the Muslim invaders who devastated India in medieval times. As Mehta (1971:4) opines, "fortunately for the culture of India, the iconoclastic invaders did not penetrate every nook and corner of this vast sub-continent and in isolated regions like Nepal and Tibet, the ancient art of metal sculpture and casting continued to exist". Had the civilization of the Valley of Kathmandu been situated in the Taraì, the art of Nepal would no doubt have died with that of India.

Just as Nepal's geographical isolation from India protected her from Muslim invasion many centuries ago, so her historical and cultural ties with India and the Himalayas separating the Valley of Kathmandu from Tibet in the north, protected her from invasions from the north. China's takeover of Tibet in 1959 was based on the claim that Tibet was essentially under the political sovereignty of China although it is customary to call it as Tibetan Autonomous Republic of China. No such claim could be made on Nepal whose status as a sovereign state was more firmly established than that of Tibet and whose cultural and historical ties with India were more ancient than those she has had with China and of course, reverse was the case with Tibet.

Although the casting of metal images continued without hindrance in Nepal, it was not without changes over the centuries. In religious art, the style, quality and quantity of production depend not only upon the artists but also to a great extent upon the patrons as well. Asian countries whenever witnesses a period of great artistic creativity, it was under the patronage of a pious ruler who maintained peace and provided security in his kingdom. Thus in Nepalese art history, as in India and China, periods are named after the ruler or rulers who oversaw and patronised the rise of a particular style. Until the rise of the Gorkhas, there were five such periods between the Lichhavis and the Mallas: Transitional period, marked most probably by the rule of Thankuries (ninth to twelfth centuries) followed by early medieval period, also called late Malla period (fifteenth century to AD 1769). During the medieval period, Newar artists received state patronage and also achieved great fame in the court of China (Kramrisch 1964:11). The temples, shrines, images, both in metal and stone as well as in wood, that are strewn in and around the Kathmandu Valley even at present, are the handwork of the Newar artists of the medieval periods. When the three kingdoms of the Newar Malla kings were captured and united under the Gorkha king, Prithvi Narayana Shah in 1768, the Newar artists of the Kathmandu Valley found themselves in a precarious position. For, as Gopal Singh Nepali (1965: 77) writes: "With the overthrow of the royal Mallas, the patrons of fine arts, the Newar artisans ceased to receive encouragement from the Gorkhas who idealized a different branch of human excellence-the art of chivalry".

Thus the Gorkha period had been a difficult one for the artists of the Valley. State patronages had all but disappeared; and image casters as well as other artists, had to fall back upon private patronage (Nepali 1965: 77). This sudden drop in royal patronage caused the fall of several of the art forms for which Newars were most famous, but even under these conditions the art of casting images in metal, however, survived, for there has always been a demand among religious Newars for icons for the purpose of worship and for household uses. Thus, throughout the reign of the the Gorkhas, until the modern time, the tradition of image casting has managed to survive though in a small measure through private patronage. So the art could maintain itself during this period, and this is largely due to the cultural solidarity and religious spirit of the Newar people. The tradition has received a renewed impetus due to the influx of pious Tibetans from their homeland and also the rise of tourism in the Kathmandu Valley.

After the Chinese occupation of Tibet, Tibetan refugees entered into and settled in India and Nepal. They brought with them their characteristic religious devotion, but not their temple nor the images of their gods. Soon after settling in their new homeland, they began to rebuild their religious establishments. In this they sought the help of the Newar artists of Patan. Almost all the images in modern Tibetan monasteries and temples in Nepal have been sculpted and created by the image casters of Patan. The large image of Padmasambhava in the Kargyutpa Gompa at Kathmandu;s Svayambhunath (Alsop and Charlton 1973:26) and the large and gilt image of Bodhisattva Maitreya of Tashilumpa Monastery at Shigatse (Tibet) (Schroeder 1981:412) are the typical examples of their art.

Over the past ten to fifteen years another source of patronage, namely, tourism, has opened up as the Valley of Kathmandu has been transformed from its traditional isolation to a metropolitan city. As more and more Western visitors come to Kathmandu Valley, a lucrative business in curio objects has bloomed. The demand for bulk supply has had a bad effect on the overall quality on most of the items produced, and images are no exception. Most of the items available today in the curio shops seem to have been cast poorly and finished hurriedly. Even some of the best artists turn out poor pieces for the average tourists. This helps them to earn some profit and devote more time on finely made status.

REFERENCES

Alsop, I. and J. Charlton, 1973, 'Image Casting in Oku Bahal', *Contibutions to Nepalese Studies* 1 (1): 22-49.

Coomaraswamy, A.K., 1921, 'A Nepalese Tara', *Rupam* 6: 1-2.

Czuma, S, 1970, 'A Gupta Style Bronze Buddha', *Bulletin of Cleveland Museum of Art*, LVII (2): 55-56.

Darnal, P. 2002, 'Archaeological Activities in Nepal since 1983 A.D. to 2002 A.D.', *Ancient Nepal* (Journal of the Department of Archaeology) 150: 39-48.

French, J.C., 1928, *The Art of the Pala Empire of Bengal*, London: Oxford University Press.

Karamrisch, S, 1964, *The Art of Nepal*, New York: Asia House Gallery Publications.

Lal, B.B., 1974, 'Further Copper Hards from Gangetic Basin and Review of the Problem', *Ancient India* 7:37.

Marshall, J., 1931, *Mohenjo-daro and Indus Civilization*, London: Aurther Probsthain.

Mehta, R.J., 1971, *Masterpieces of Indian Bronzes and Metal Sculptures*, Bombay: D.B. Taraporevala Sons & Com. Pvt. Ltd.

Mishra, T.N., 1994, 'The Archaeological Research in the High Mountains of Mustang District', *Ancient Nepal* (Journal of the Department of Archaeology) 136: 141-61.

Mitra, D., 1972, *Excavation at Tilaurakot and Exploration in the Nepalese Tarai*, Kathmandu: Department of Archaeology/His Majesty's Government.

Nepali, G.S., 1965., *The Newars, as Ethno-Sociological Study of a Himalyan Community*, Bombay: United Asia Publications.

Ray, N.R., K. Khandalavala and S. Gorakshkar, 1986, *Eastern Indian Bronzes*, India: Lalit-Kala Academy.

Regmi, D.R., 1969, *Ancient Nepal*, Calcutta: Firma K.L. Mukhopadhayay.

Rijal, B.K., 1970, *Archaeological Remains of Kapilvastu, Lumbini and Devadaha*, Kathmandu: Education Enterprises (Pvt.) Ltd.

Schroeder, U.V., 1981, *Indo-Tibetan Bronzes*, Hong Kong: Visual Dharma Publications.

Simons, A., 1992–93, 'Trial Excavation of a Cave System in Muktinath Valley', *Ancient Nepal* (Journal of the Department of Archaeology) 130-133:1-19.

Simons, A., W. Schon and S.S. Shrestha, 1994, 'Preliminary Report on the 1992 campaing of the Team of the Institute of Prehistory, University of Cologne', *Ancient Nepal* (Journal of the Department of Archaeology) 136: 51-75.

Sivaramamurti, C., 1977, *The Art of India*, New York: Narry N. Abrams, N.C. Publisheres.

Schuh, D., 1992-93, 'Introduction', *Ancient Nepal* (Journal of the Department of Archaeology) 130-133: c-m.

Tiwari, D.N., 1984-85, 'Burials from Western Nepal, Mustang', *Ancient Nepal* (Journal of the Department of Archaeology) 85: 1-12.

Vats, M.S., 1940, *Excavations at Harappa Being an Account of Archaeological Excavations at Harappa Carried out in Between the Years 1920-21 and 1933-34*, Delhi: Published by Manager of Publications.

Mala Malla

Central Deptt. of Culture,
Kirtipur, Tribhuvan University

Early Jaina Women Teachers and their Contribution in Tamil Region

Introduction

Jainism was a powerful religion that influenced the religious and cultural life of Tamils during the early historical times; and lost its importance in the medieval period. It was *bhakti* cult with which Jainism came into direct conflict and that eventually destroyed the progress of Jainism in south India although it could not completely wipe it off from the region. Jainism survives in small pockets in Tamil Nadu. Noteworthy feature in the Jaina monasticism in the Tamil region is the prosperous institution of women teachers and their wide circle of female disciples. There is also a reference to a University run by them.

This paper focuses attention on the magnificent role played by Jainas who played courageous, crucial and decisive role in brining out the essential thought of Jainism particularly in the field of education.

Early Evidences

Mahavira made no distinction between men and women. He was in his own lifetime followed and accompanied by male as well as female recluses. It is recorded that his followers included 14000 monks and 36000 nuns. Jaina Church provides evidence for the leadership of some of Jaina monks and nuns who played the role of teachers and preceptors. Thus we come to know of nuns like Chandana, the first female disciple of Mahavira, Jayanthi, sister of king Sayani of Kosambi (Deo, 1956: 491) and Yakin' who is said to have converted the famous author Haribhadra (a learned brahmana) to Jainism and made him her pupil. But an exclusive organisation of nuns does not appear to be quite popular in the history of the Jaina church. However, the practice of renouncing the world and taking to the life of a nun has no doubt survived to this day among the followers of Jainism (Desai 1957: 76).

Turning to south India many women who were lay followers of the faith and some who had renounced the world figure in the inscriptions of Karnataka and a few in Andhra Pradesh. This is as should be; for women are well known as devout supporters of the faith in all religions. But it is only when we study the epigraphs of the Tamil region that we come across, for the first time, a large number of ladies who were not merely the lay followers of the faith or even solitary recluses and nuns, but also who played the role of teachers and preceptors guiding the religious activities of the creed (Desai 1967:77). Regarding the antiquity of Jaina nuns in Tamil region, Tamil Brahmi inscription provide some references to nuns like Mathavirai and Sbhamitha (Sabhamitra), and their religious services (Mahadevan No. 4, 5-13). Even in *Silappadikaram* (a post Sangam work), we have the references to nuns and their services to the people (Ekambaranathan 1998: 206).

The lady teachers are generally referred to as *kurattiyar* (or) *kuratti adigal*, both are honorific forms derived from Sanskrit *guru*. These *kurattiyars* of the Tamil region have to be distinguished from the *shravikas* or lay disciples who are found in all parts and from the *kantis ajjis* (Sanskrit *'arya'*), signifying nuns and female recluses who are mentioned in the inscription of Karnataka, or from the *sadhvis* of north India (Desai 1967:76).

The *kurattiyars* (Lady Teachers) of the Tamil Land constitute a surprisingly unique class by themselves.

According to the Digambara School, women are not entitled to attain *moksha* in this life. The *yapaniyas*, a well known sect of Jainism in the south and having some *Svetambaras* are characteristically distinguished for their view which advocates liberation or *mukti* for women in this life: *Strinam tad-bhave mokshah* (Desai 1967: 77).

Jaina Pallis

The centres of learning are called *Pallis*. Even today the school in Tamil Nadu is known as *palli*. From this one can judge the influence in the field of education. This type of *pallis* existed in Thirupanmalai, Vedal both in Tondainadu (modern northern Tamil Nadu) region and Thiruchchanattamalai in Pandya (modern southern Tamil Nadu) region. Thirupanmalai, another Jaina centre is located 5km south-west of Arcot. Here a seventh century rock-cut cave served as jain *palli*. During tenth century a women teacher named Pattini Kuratti (a disciple of male teacher Arista Nemipattaragar) resided here. She taught jaina *sastras* to students and even dug a well in the same *palli* area for drinking water for these students (Ekambaranathan 1991: 43). Whereas the other jaina Palli in Vedal in Tondai Nadu contained two caves for teaching as well as for residing purpose of women teachers. A renowned lady teacher named Kanakavira Kurattiyar headed it. She was the pupil and follower of the teacher Gunakirti Bhatara of Vidal. When a dispute arose between the lady teacher and her five hundred lady pupils and the four hundred nuns of a different school the inhabitations of the locality who were lay disciples of the school to which Kanakavira Kurattiyar belonged, came forward with an assurance that they would protect the lady preceptor and her pupils and provide for their maintenance (ARE, 84/ 1908).

Regarding the existence of a unique University managed by lady teachers (around ninth century A.D.), a place called Thiruchchanattmalai gives an interesting detail. It is a small craggy hill near Chitral in the Vilavangod taluk of the Kanyakumari district. On the top of the hill is a natural cave, which has been subsequently transformed into a Hindu temple by suitable alteration. Jaina lady teachers of renown resided here and conducted classes. It was visited by adherents of the jaina doctrine from distant parts, who hailed from such places as are now included in the districts of South Arcot (modern Thiruvannamalai) and Thanjavur. This is confirmed by a ninth century A.D. votive inscription from Kalugumalai, another famous place of Jaina pantheon in Tamil Nadu.

Inscriptional Evidence

Some of the lady teachers mentioned in the Kalugumalai epigraphs seems to have been fairly important personalities. We may illustrate these by citing the following instances. The references are to the number of the inscriptions in the South Indian Inscriptions, Volume Vol 1. Tiruchcharanam *Kurattigal*: figures in two epigraphs Nos. 324 and 326. *Tiruchcharanam* is the name of the hill in the Travancore area. 2. Pichchai *Kuratti* of Chirupolal (No. 319): *Pichchai*, we may note with interest, is a nickname conveying sense of soliciting alms. Compare Sanskrit *bhiksha*. 3. Sangakkurattigal: Her lady disciple was named Srivisaiyakkurattiyar possibly, the leader of a jaina *Samgha*. 4. Mammai Kuratti: she had a lady disciple named Arattenemi Kuratti (No. 371). The male name of the latter is noteworthy. *Mammai* sounds like a nickname. 5. *Tiruparutti* Kuratti: she was the pupil of the teacher Pattni Bhatara (No.372). Tiruparutti may be an abbreviation Tirupparuttikkunram. 6. Nalkur Kuratti: she was the pupil of Nalkur Amalanemi Bhatara and had of lady disciple named Nattikappatarar (Nos. 355-56). Nlakur is a place name. 7. Mialur Kuratti: she was a disciple of Perur Kuratti and daughter of Mingaikuman of Karai Pidankudkkana Nadu (No. 394). 8. *Tirumalai Kuratti*: She had a male disciple in Enadi Kuttanan (No. 370).

Lady teachers who became Jaina educators were women of mature age as a rule; and consequently, they were thoroughly fit for their task, being well versed both in secular and sacred learning. They had a sound knowledge of child and adolescent psychology and they taught all people without caste or sex difference. They taught children in all aspects of education. They as a rule had ladies for their teachers as well as for pupils. But instances are not rare to show that men also had their share in both the roles as evidenced by Kalugumali inscriptions.

Unfortunately the factors that contributed to the growth of the institution of lady teachers in the Tamil land and the function of these institutions on such a large scale are not fully known. This subject requires further study and research.

REFERENCES

Chakravarti, A., 1974, *Jaina Literature in Tamil*, (ed. K.V. Ramesh), New Delhi, 50-55.

Champakalakshmi, R., 1958, *Jainism in South India* (M. Litt. thesis), Madras University.

Deo, S.B., 1956, *The History of Jaina Monchism from inscriptions and Literature* in Bulletin of the Deccan College Research Institute, Poona. 491-492.

Desai, P.B., 1957, *Jainism in South India and some Jaina epigraphs*, Sholapur, 46-80.

Ekambranathan, A., 1998, *Cholar Kalathil camana Samaya Valarchi* (in Tamil), Chennai, 206-09.

Nilakanatasastri, K.A., 1975, *The Colas*. Reprint, University of Madras, 1975.

Mahadevan, I., 1970, *Corpus of Tamil-Brahmi inscription*, Alagarmali, No.4, *South Indian Inscriptions* (*SII*), vol. V.

Sivaramamurti, C., 1983, *Panorama of Jaina Art-South India*, New Delhi.

Indian Archaeological Society,
New Delhi-110 016

T. Arunraj

Terracotta Figurines of Chebrolu, District Guntur, Andhra Pradesh

Chebrolu (16°,13"N; 80°, 30"E) a small town is located 14 km south-east of Guntur city. The ancient Buddhist site at Dharanikota, is only 45 km from Chebrolu. The present-day town Chebrolu stands on the ancient mound which rises to about ten metres from the surrounding plains. The earliest occupation here is neolithic period. The other important finds at the site include several Satavahana, Ikshavaku, and a few Roman coins made on tin, copper and one on gold (Hanumantha Rao 1964); pottery of various types like Northern Black Polished Ware, Arretine and Rouletted wares, Black and Red Ware and other types; beads, pendants, also large number of votive pots, inscribed terracotta sealings (Hanumantha Rao, 1987), several limestone slabs and pillars, and limestone rings with lotus motifs, probably belonging to Buddhist establishment (Rama Rao 1939). In the early inscriptions Chebrolu is mentioned as Tambrapa (E.I.X.V.). It is probable that Tambrapa was on the highway connecting Dhanyakataka, the later Satavahana capital with Kanchi (Hanumantha Rao 1987). Most part of the mound has been disturbed by the villagers in the process of procuring earth for construction, plastering the wall of their houses and also for manuring their fields.

Exposed sections have yielded one complete female terracotta figurine with one leg and few fragments. A few terracotta figures which were used for the present study are the private collection of local teacher and other residents of Chebrolu town. A few terracottas are also found in Kothanandayapalli Village near Chebrolu.

Besides Chebrolu other important terracotta find spots in Andhra Pradesh are Amaravati, Nagarjunakonda, Kondapur, Peddabankur, Dhulikatta, Yeleswaram and others.

Terracottas of Chebrolu are made of hallow, double-mould technique. Moulds used for making terracotta figures have been recovered during the excavations at Yeleswaram (Waheed khan 1963). A thin layer of clay was pressed in these moulds and the casts are joined together with the same material. Some terracottas have holes in the body which are useful in letting out air during firing. This type of technique was adopted in the Deccan as a fully developed one in about the first-second centuries AD (Amarendranath 1999).

Typologically the Chebrolu terracottas can be classified into human and animal figures. Six human (Women) figurines with missing head or legs or both; three animals and birds, numerous votive pots were collected during the digging of the mound by local people for earth. Out of the six terracotta human figurines two women figures look alive and they are mother goddesses. They are having *makara* type headdress secured with a band and wearing four rows of small beaded ornaments on the forehead. The flowing hair is gathered in back knot. One of them is wearing two rows of small bead necklace. Below the naval two rows of threads and one big beaded ornament are present. Her arms are resting or holding the large protuded belly which looks like that of a pregnant lady. The legs are outstretched and the genitals is prominent. Interesting feature in this type is below the beaded necklace and above the navel is a design. The same design also looks like two snakes with connected tails.

Remaining four women terracotta figures belong to the second type one is with broken head, three are broken busts, one figure without head and legs. One is having prominent breasts and is wearing a fillet over the forehead and beautifully coursed hair towards top as a *shikhara* and with prominent nose ornament. All the figures are having beaded necklaces. Common feature in all the above four figures are having raised empty hands above the shoulder and the nudity is not depicted. In one of the figures, even though the head is broken, the raised hands above the shoulders are intact.

Thirteen broken heads are found and most of them look like women heads. Two kaolin made heads are also found. The animal and bird collection includes one elephant head with raised trunk, goat with curved hornes, wearing a necklace like ornament and the legs are missing. A horse head and a bird are also found. All the above animals and birds are cast out of double mould.

The first type of mother goddess figurines can be placed under the Lajjagauri type 4 of the Janssen (1991) and type 1r of Bolon (1997). The hands on the swollen abdomen, prominent genital and snake hood symbol affirm that these are associated with fertility cult. This type of mother goddesses with minor differences are found in other sites in early Andhradesha, viz., Nagarjunakonda (IAR 1956-57), Yeleswaram (Waheed Khan 1963) and Vaddamanu (Sastri, T.V.G. *et al.* 1992) as also from contemporary Satavahana sites such as Paithon (Dhavalikhar 1976), Ter (Deshpande 1999), etc.

The second type of figurines are with upraised hands are reported from Nagarjunakonda (IAR 1955-56), Peddabankur (Krishna Sastry 1979, 1983) and Nelakondapalli (Krishna Sastry 1983). Some are torsos and a few are busts with raised hands while some are with fillets over their foreheads and with beautifully combed hair gathered at the in a *shikhara* fashion and display prominent nose ornament. Most of the figurines are having beaded necklaces. As said earlier all these figures are with upraised hands above the shoulder and these are not nude.

Animal figurines were also recovered from other sites in Andhradesha such as Kondapur, Peddabankur, Yeleswaram, Nagarjunakonda, Vaddamanu, Salihundam, Veerapuram, etc. Besides archaic animal types double-mould animal figures are also found at the above sites. Common animals represented are horses, elephants, bulls, lions, rams, dogs and birds like hens and cocks; the most popular bird is the parrot. Some times, figures of horses, bulls, elephants are found decorated with ornaments.

The female figurines discussed in this paper seem to be related in one way or other with the fertility cult. The first type of figurines are nude sitting figures holding swollen bellies appear to be a Lajjagauri type, while the second type with upraised hands type represents most probably a developed form of *shrivatsa*, an auspicious symbol denoting 'Sri' in course of time assumed human form. *Srivatsa* found on the breast of Chunde (Agrawal P.K. 1974) and the occurrence puppet-like motif in the centre of the necklace of the female terrocotta (200-100 BC) in Ahichchhatra proves that it is an archaic mother goddess, a divinity of the class of fertility goddesses (V.S. Agarwal 1948). This has also been interpreted as a secularised Lajjagauri type in the process of evolution, because we find naked Lajjaguri type figures with upraised empty hands in other parts of India (Tiwari 1985, Kala 1980, Bolon 1997).

It may be presumed that the terracotta figurines might have been used for worship, as votive offerings or simple decorative pieces (Sircar 1980). The number fragments of heads recovered from majority of sites out number the headless and complete specimens. At sites like Chebrolu and Nagarjunakonda which have yielded intact upraised handed female figurines without heads, suggesting that the heads were broken intentionally and not accidentally; this presumption has also been observed by Uhlen Brok (1992). In southern Italy a deep well, fallen in to disuse contained tens of thousands of female heads chopped off from figurines. It may be presumed that beheading was part of intentional mutilation that took place when the figure was offered so that it could not be reused by any one else and this is perhaps a form of ri-tual head offering, a substitution for actual human sacrifice.

Even today worship of terracotta figures of Mansa (the snake goodess) Ghat horse, are prevalent in Bengal's Bauri community (Bhattacharya 1991). Terracotta votive offering is also common in the same community. Near Ahmedabad (Gujarat) in a village-shrine childless couples perform rituals and offer small round faced clay idols, which are placed in a line near the wall of the compound (Mitra 1984). In front of Ayyanar in Tamil Nadu terracotta horses and elephants are installed. Worship of terracotta elephants is prevalent in the present in Anantapur District of Andhra Pradesh.

Presence of so many double-mould animal figurines,

with or without heads or broken limbs can be explained as votive sacrifices; or they were perhaps toys. Excavations in Jordan at the neolithic site of Ain Ghazal (*c.* 8300-6000 BC) yielded large number of clay animal figurines, the most interesting are two animals each stabbed with three flint bladelets in the throat, the abdomen, the chest to the eyes (Denise Schamandt 1997). This indicates that the practice of animal sacrifices as ritual was prevalent.

REFERENCES

Agrawala, P.K., 1974, *Srivatsa, the Babe of Goddess*, Varanasi, Sri Prithivi Prakasan.

Agarawala, V.S., 1948,.' Terracotta figurines of Ahichchhatra, District Bareilly, U.P.', *Ancient India* 4; pp.

Amarendra Nath, 1999, 'Satavahana Antiquities from Adam' in *The Age of the Satavahanas* (Ajay Mitra Shastri, ed.), New Delhi: Publication.

Bhattacharya, D.K., 1991, 'Terracotta worship in fringes of Bengal,' I. Hodder, eds., *In the meaning of Things*.

Bolon, C.R., 1999, *Forms of the Goddess Lajja Gauri in Indian*, Motilal Banarsidas Publishers, Delhi.

Denise Schmandt, B., 1997, *Animal symbols at 'Ain Ghazali, Expedition* 39 (1).

Deshpande, 1999, 'Satavahana Terracotta Art with special Reference to Ter' in Ajay Mitra Sastri (ed.), *In the Age of the Satavahanas*, New Delhi.

Dhavalikar, M.K., 1976, 'Paithan Terracottas', *Journal of the Indian Society of Oriental Art*, VII, Calcutta.

E.I. XV., *Epigraphy Indica*, vol. XV.

Hanumantha Rao, B.S.L., 1964, *Traces of Roman contact at Chebrolu Andhra Pradesh*, 1987, Inscribed sealing from Chebrolu proceedings of AP. History Congress.

Indian Archeological Review, 1955-56, 1956-57.

Janssen, FHP.M., 1991, *On the origin and development of the So-called Lajjagauri*, Proceedings of the 11th International conference of the association of south Asian Archaeologists in western Europe.

Kala, S.C., 1950, *Terracotta figurines from Kausambi, the Municipal Museum Allahabad;*

————, 1980, *Terracottas in the Allhabad Museum*, Abhinav publications, New Delhi.

Krishna Sastry, V.V., 1979, *Terracottas from Pedabankur and Dhulikatta*, The A.P. Journal of Archaeology I, (I).

————, 1983, *The Proto and Early historical cultures of Andhra Pradesh*, Govt. of A.P. Hyderabad.

Mitra, N., 1984, 'Bahuchare Mata and her rooster'. *The India Magazine*, 4 (5).

Rama Rao M., 1939, Antiquities of Chebrolu Proceedings of all India oriental conference.

Sastri, T.V.G., M. Kasturibai, M. Veerender, 1992, *Vaddamanu Excavations*, Hyderabad.

Sastri, T.V.G., M. Kasturibai and J.V.P. Rao, 1984, *Veerapuram a type site for cultural Study in the Krishnavalley*, Hyderabad.

Sircar, D.C., 1980, 'Aspects of the cult of the Indian Mother Goddess', *Journal of Indian Museums*, 36,9-20.

Tiwari J.N., 1985, *Goddess cults in Ancient India*, Sundeep Prakashan, Delhi.

Uhlenbrock, J.P., 1992, 'History, Trade, and the terracottas', *Expedition* 34(1-2).

Waheed Khan, M.D., 1963, *A Monograph on Yeleswaram Excavation*, The Govt. of A.P., Hyderabad.

S. Murali Mohan

Dept. of History & Archaeology,
Nagarjuna University,
Nagarjuna Nagar-522510. A.P.

Interesting Sealings from Mansar

Mansar in the Nagpur district of Maharashtra is a site of great antiquarian interest and has yielded quite a lot of interesting antiquities including some short shell-script inscriptions and a few Vakataka records from time to time. It is situated some 45 km to the north-east of Nagpur and about 5 km west of the well-known Vaishnava religious centre of Ramtek representing ancient Ramagiri. In early 1930s in connection with his survey of the rich Manganese-yielding area T.A. Wellsted visited the site and from the configuration of the lower mound he felt that underneath it probably lay a Buddhist Stupa, (JPASB) and since then it is commonly known as the 'Stupa Mound'. However, nothing much of real Buddhistic importance has yet been reported from the site. On the contrary it yielded in 1972 an exquisite image, variously identified as Batuka Bhairva or Shiva[1] dating from the Vakataka period and now adorning the porch gallery of the National Museum, New Delhi[2]. The small-scale excavations conducted by the Department of Ancient Indian History, Culture and Archaeology, Nagpur University (1989), and by the Excavation branch of the Archaeological Survey of India located at Nagpur a few years later on Wellsted's so-called Stupa mound also yielded non-descript remains of small and big temples dating from the Vakataka period. The ongoing excavations on the top of the hillock locally called Hidimba Tekdi under the auspices of the local Bodhisattva Nagarjuna Research Foundation have, during last three seasons, yielded a rich haul of valuable antiquities; but, despite the excavators' claims, nothing of really Buddhistic interest has been unearthed as yet, while quite a lot of objects and sculptures (including *Shiva-lingas)* relating to Vedic-Pauranic religion is there for everyone to see and decide for one self. And all this cultural equipment is clearly datable to the Vakataka cultural horizons (third-fifth centuries A.D.).

In this course of the ongoing archaeological diggings a very large hoard of clay sealings has been found, and Shri A.K. Sharma, the excavator, was kind enough to show me these sealings with a view to deciphering their legends and give me the photographs of a couple of these sealings and allow me to publish the same. Some of these show clear cord impressions on their back indicating that they were attached as a mark of identity to some consignment sent some locality or localities to Mansar. The two sealings published here may be taken to represent the whole lot as only these inscriptions with only some minor variations are found on them.

Both these sealings are baked red and are oval in shape.[3] The seals were impressed on them with the result that the portion bearing the seal-impression in somewhat depressed. The legends, positive on the sealings, are in relief and beautifully engraved in the box-headed variety of the southern class of Brahmi of the fourth-fifth century AD and composed in chaste Sanskrit.

The legend on one of these sealings reads *Pravareshvarasya* meaning 'it belongs to (god) Pravareshvara'. On some of the sealings the honorific *sri* is prefixed. Obviously it was attached to some consignment sent from the shrine of god Pravareshvara Shiva which was situated somewhere else[4]. Its exact location is not possible in the present state of uncertainly enveloping its identification, but it is not unlikely that it may have been situated at Paunar (Wardha district, Maharashtra).

The other sealing has the legend *yavriddhi* which would stand for *jayavriddhi* which is found on several other sealings from the same site. This reminds us of the legends on a few Vakataka or Vakataka like coins hailing from the Wardha region and more especially from Paunar commonly identified with Pravarapura, the capital of the later members (Pravara Sena II onwards) of the Padmapur-Nandivardhana-Pravarapur branch of the Vakatakas[5]. Some of these coins bear on the obverse the legend *Jaya* and on the reverse a retrograde *svastika.* Some other coins have the legend *vriddhi*, again in box-headed alphabets, on the obverse and on the reverse a device consisting of a circle with a smaller circle attached to its lower portion and the whole within a beaded circle as seen on a unique coin of Prithivi Sena, probably second king of this name. There are some other coins with the legend *vriddhah* on the obverse and the same device on the reverse (Shastri 1992, pp. 140-41). Since the device found on the *vriddhi* and *vriddhah* coins is identical with that met with on the coin of Vakataka Prithivi Shena[6] (Shastri 1992, 286–87), it is likely that these coins, too, belong to some Vakataka kings who might have, following the practice prevailing in the Deccan and south India, issued coins not with their proper names, but with their *virudas* or titles. In this connection it is pertinent to remember that the word *vriddha* formed the terminal of their *gotra* name, Vishnuvriddha.

In view of the sameness of the legends it is almost certain that the sealings with this inscription did in reality belong to a member of the Padmapura Nandivardhana Pravarapura branch of the Vakatakas though his identity still remains uncertain.

NOTES

1. Hans T. Bakker is inclined to identify it as Pravareshvara Shiva and to regard the Ramtek-Mansar region to represent the Pravarapur complex. *Vide* his *The Vakatakas: An Essay in Hindu Iconology*, Edgert Forsten, Groningen, 1997, pp. 87-88.

2. For a Beautiful illustration of this image, see *ibid.*, pl. XXXVII.

3. The two sealings measure 2 x 2.2 cm and 1.3 x 1.90 cm respectively.

4. Shri Sharma is of the view that the sealings were prepared locally for presenting or sealing as mementoes to the visitors to Mansar which represented the site of the shrine of god Pravaresvara and some evidence in the form of ashes is cited as an evidence of their local production in mass.

5. For the latest account of the history of this branch of the Vakarakas, see Ajay Mitra Shastri, *Vakatakas: Sources and History*, Aryan Books International, New Delhi, 1997.

6. *JPASB*, NS, XXIX (1933), pp. 159-66 (a).

7. For the coin of Prathivi Shena, *vide, ibid.*, pp. 138-39; *The Age of the Vakatakas*, pp. 286-87.

Nagpur University, Nagpur

Ajay Mitra Shastri

Copper Bronze Objects from Jakhera

Jakhera (27° 50' and 78° 41' E) situated in Etah district of Uttar Pradesh (Sahi 1994; 139) was subjected to horizontal excavation; a site mainly of Painted Grey Ware (PGW) levels, to obtain more information about the material life and techno-cultural activities of the users of PGW pottery. The results of excavations were found more rewarding than was expected. A cultural sequence from Ochre Coloured Pottery (OCP) to Northern Black Polished Ware (NBPW) period was found here.

During the course of excavation an early PGW phase, called Proto-PGW (Pd. IIIA), was detected. The ceramic complex of proto-PGW phase is similar to that of the earlier Period II characterised by unpainted Black-and-Red ware, Red ware, both slipped and coarse, and Black-slipped wares. What is most important, is the introduction of painting tradition comprising black painting on Black-and-Red ware, Black slipped wares and slipped Red Wares. Red slipped wares range in colour from deep brown to orange red. Paintings, which have been executed on the inside as well as outside of the pots are mostly in linear patterns in groups of strokes, verticals as also obliques. Groups of horizontal strokes also occur but are rare. The pottery could be easily distinguished from the preceding and succeeding periods at the site.

In the upper levels of PGW it tends to occur with an increasing frequency and in the succeeding mature PGW, i.e., Period IIIB.

PGW of period IIIB forms a homogeneous group belonging to a well-defined industry (Lal 1954-55: 32) and is witnessed by a rich variety of painted designs which comprise horizontal rim band both inside and outside, group of vertical, oblique and crisscross lines, chain spirals, concentric circles, concentric semi-circles, sigma, swastika, rows of dots and dashes, hooked pattern intersecting U-shaped designs, sun motifs as well as floral patterns. PGW has been described as a 'deluxe ware' (Agrawal 1971: 48). Other ceramics associated with the PGW include Red ware, Plain Grey ware, Black slipped and Black-and-Red wares. However, the frequency of grey ware is much greater.

Regarding the introduction of iron in northern India, Jakhera has become a key site. It is also significant for the study of the impact of iron on socio-economic life (Sahi 1989), agricultural production and cultural development of the people in northern India, particularly in the Ganga-Yamuna doab (Sahi 1982). Iron is introduced in Period II which is characterised by the Black-and-Red ware. The objects were tanged arrowheads and a few indeterminate pieces found during the excavation in 1992-93. It is a very significant evidence because earlier it was believed that iron was introduced in the Ganga Valley in the PGW levels dateable to *c.*1100 BC. The earliest calibrated date for iron from PGW levels at Atranjikhera, TF-191 is 1165± 110 BC (Gaur 1983: 18). Now iron found the from Black and Red ware levels at Jakhera has pushed back the date by about a century or more. From Noh (*IAR* 1971-72; 42) and at Kausambi (Sharma 1960; 13) iron was reported in fragment from the Pre-PGW (BRW levels) but with no recognisable object.

About 150 copper objects were found from various cultural deposits which include ornaments, toiletry, crafts objects, household items, smelted lumps, slags and unidentifiable objects/pieces and crucibles. The distribution of objects is given below.

Period I (OCP) None

Period II (Black and Red Ware) copper is evidence

Period IIIA (Proto PGW levels) 2

Period IIIB (Mature PGW levels) 82

Period IV (NBP and PGW phase) 66

No copper objects was found from Period II, but its occurrence cannot be ruled out because copper objects (3 beads and 1 ring) have been reported from the similar level from Atranjikhera, located just 16 km downstream of the Kalinadi in district Etah (Gaur 1983; Plate XVII). With the expansion of settlement area, a remarkable change started taking place from Period IIIA (Proto-PGW levels). Objects recovered from this deposit indicate well-developed industries, such as of bone, semi-precious stones and terracotta (Sahi 1989; 55-56). Iron objects recovered from these levels are mainly agricultural tools (hoe, sickle), ring, rod, and lumps of smelted iron. While copper objects from this level are only bangles and a small rod which, however, indicate that proto-PGW people were familiar with metallurgical skills and the copper objects were fashioned locally.

The mature PGW phase (Period IIIB) is marked by further technological development at the site and throws new light on industrial activities of both iron and copper, besides bone, semi-precious stones and terracotta. Prolific use of iron and occurrence of raw material in the form of ore, smelted lumps and variety of objects and their quantity is itself an indication of advanced technology. Production of craftsmen's tools supplemented by production of finer and more luxurious ornamental items of copper, gold, ivory and semi-precious stones. Nine gold objects, six ivory buttons and one comb, 25 copper ornaments (Chart 1) and quite a large number of semi-precious stones beads are the noteworthy finds from the mature PGW levels (Pd. IIIB).

Besides the above-mentioned copper objects, as many as 15 crucibles were also recovered. Of these one belonged to Pd. IIIA and 11 to period IIIB and 3 to period IV.

The maximum number of artifacts and crucibles comes from the mature PGW levels. Occurrence of five smelted lumps and slag pieces indicates that smelting and manufacturing of objects was done at the site. However, it is difficult to say that copper was smelted from copper ore at the site. The nearest sources of copper ore are Kumaon, Dilwara, Kirovli, Debari (Udaipur District) Agrawal 1971: 146-47). The other source of the metal may be chalcopyrite copper ore deposit in the Aravalli region. (Sankalia 1961-62; 225-28), particularly the Khetri belt. In the absence of metallographic data of copper specimens it is not be possible to say anything about the methods of production. The nature of copper objects, which have been recovered from the PGW levels, shows both that they are pure and alloyed copper. The evidence indicates that alloying was done to produce lustre and to harden the metal, and then the various types of objects were fashioned.

On the basis of typology, the specimens have been classified into seven groups (Chart 1)

A. Ornaments

In all nine types of ornaments were found from different levels. The maximum number comes from the mature PGW levels which indicates the artistic taste of the PGW people and also throws light on their craftsmanship and includes bracelet, bangles, ear-rings, nose-pin/stud, nose rings, finger rings, pendant, amulet and beads. Besides, nine gold objects (Ramjit 2001: 72-175), six buttons and a comb of ivory were also found from the PGW levels.

B. Toiletry

These includes antimony rods, nail parers, antimony rod-cum nail parers and tooth-pick; which is unique and not found elsewhere in the PGW level.

C. Craftsmen tools

There are six specimens which include borers, pins, awls, crescent, and chisel and bunk-nar(?) Probably awls were used for making holes in semi-precious stone beads. Chisel is noteworthy find which were used by goldsmiths and bunk-nar to concentrate the heat in smelting small bits of gold as well copper in the desired shape and for soldering and fusing the joints of ornaments.

D. Household objects

Besides ornaments and craft tools, household objects were also found. These include vessels, nail and needle. Copper vessels, dishes and decorated PGW pottery were used by the prosperous people. Copper dish is also reported from the middle phase of the PGW levels at Atranjikhera (Gaur 1983: 232-233; Plate LII, No.10).

E. Seals and Sealings

Sealing(?) is a rare specimen of bronze, not reported from any PGW site. Depiction of concentric circles/spiral is significant: the upper part has been damaged. It is quite heavy and appears to be a seal. Probably, an impression of circles was trademark of the PGW people.

F. Other objects

Four specimens of fish-hooks were recovered from the PGW levels. Similar specimens were also found from PGW levels at Atranjikhera.

In the absence of hunting objects except a small arrow-head from Hastinapura, it may be concluded that copper being precious and having flexible property was used for manufacturing ornamental or luxury items and not for any other purposes. Probably iron objects were more suitable for hunting purposes.

Some specimens are either fragmentary or in brittle condition or unfinished or in the form of melted lumps and slag. It is very significant because it provides a clue about the process by which the objects were fashioned from melted ore. The occurrence of thin copper sheets and beaten rods and wire pieces is clear indication of it.

G. Copper Coins

From Period IV (NBP), six specimens of copper coins, including two thin flat, rectangular pieces, were found. Most probably these were Punch-marked coins. Out of these two were silver coated copper coins, bearing punch-marked symbols were also found which are yet to be identified. The rest were disintegrated and damaged, therefore, unidentifiable.

To conclude, it may be observed that at Jakhera the evidence indicates that during Period II, for a rural settlement, copper was not easily procurable in the absence of well-knit trade contacts. But during the Mature PGW Period IIIB, it appears that trade contacts became well developed. With the growth of economic prosperity, copper was very much in demand for various purpose and therefore, we find a developed copper, as also other industries at the site.

Acknowledgement

The author is very grateful to Prof. Suraj Bhan, Kurukshetra University, Kurukshetra for useful discussion and valuable suggestions.

REFERENCES

Agrawal, D.P., 1971, '*The Copper Bronze Age in India*, Munshiram Manoharlal, New Delhi, pp. 48, 146-47.

Gaur, R.C., 1983, *Excavations At Atranjikhera, Early civilization of the Upper Ganga Basin*, Motilal Banarsidas, New Delhi, pp.18, 116, 232-33, fig: 69, Pl. LII, No. 10.

Kumar, Vijai, 1971-72, Excavation At Noh District, Bharatpur', *Indian Archaeology-A Review*, p. 42.

Lal, B.B., 1954-55, 'Excavation at Hantinapur and Other Explorations in Upper Ganga and Satlej Basin', *Ancient India* No. 10-11, p.32, p.97, fig. 30.

Ramjit, 2001, 'Gold Object from Painted Grey Ware Levels at Jakhera', *Puratattva*, Bullatin of the Indian Archaeological Society, New Delhi, No. 31, pp. 172-75.

Sahi, M.D.N., 1994, *Aspects of Indian Archaeology*, Jaipur, pp. 139, 142.

Sahi, M.D.N., 1989, 'Role of Iron in Socio-Economic Change in Northern India-Jakhera A Case Study', *Dimensions in Indian Archaeology and History*, New Delhi, pp. 55-56.

Sahi, M.D.N., 1982, 'Agricultural Production during Early Iron Age in Northern India', *Proceedings of the Indian History Congress, Kurukshetra Session* 1982, pp. 95-101.

Sharma, G.R., 1960, *Excavations at Kausambi*, p.13.

Sankalia, H.D., 1961-62, *Excavation at Ahar*, pp.225-28.

Department of History
Aligarh Muslim University, Aligarh
(Uttar Pradesh)

Ramjit Singh

A Preliminary Report on the Excavations at Sanjan (2002)

S.P. Gupta, Kurush F. Dalal, Abhijit Dandekar, Rhea Mitra,
Rukshana Nanji and Rohini Pandey

(The excavation at Sanjan was conducted with the permission granted, and financial assistance offered by the Archaeological Survey of India, under the overall direction of Dr. S.P. Gupta, Chairman, The Indian Archaeo-logical Society. This is a part of the Indian Council of Historical Research's project entitled, "Historical and Archaeological Study of Parsi/Zoroastrian Religious Places of Importance in Western India with Special Reference to Bahrot Caves", given to Dr. (Mrs.) Mani Kamerkar and Dr. Homi Dhalla of the World Zarathusti Cultural Foundation.)

As per the oral traditions of the Parsi community (a group of Zoroastrian refugees who fled Islamic persecution in Iran in the 7th century A.D.), their ancestors first made landfall on the Indian mainland at a place they named Sanjan. They built here a city and prospered as merchants, traders, craftsmen and farmers. It was from here that they spread to other parts of Gujarat and, later in the rest of India. The Parsis have no written history of their flight and subsequent rehabilitation in India. The only semi-historical document is a Persian poem, the '*Kisseh-i-Sanjan*' written in approximately A.D. 1600 (Edulji 1991).

The *Kisseh-i-Sanjan* says the Parsis landed here and made a pact with the local ruler, Jadi Rana, to abide by the customs of the land in exchange for asylum (Edulji 1991: 1). The king granted this and he demarcated a place for them to settle and to erect a place of worship (Edulji 1991: 2). This town founded by the Parsis was named Sanjan, supposedly, in memory of a town in Iran bearing the same name. The fire-temple they built here was called the Iranshah and enshrined their most sacred icon, a fire bearing the same name (Edulji 1991: 2). According to the *Kisseh-i-Sanjan* the Parsis flourished and spread to all parts of Gujarat until the conquest of Sanjan around A.D. 1399 by the forces of Sultan Mohammed (Kamerkar and Dhanjisha [In press]). After this, Sanjan was deserted. Sadly none of the dates or people mentioned in the *Kisseh-i-Sanjan* can be identified with any degree of certainty. The location of Sanjan was ambiguous and presumed to be near the modern town, which was established around A.D. 1850 with the advent of the railways.

The ancient site of Sanjan (20° 11' 59"N; 72° 48' E) is situated 2.5km from the Sanjan Railway Station, Taluka Umargaon, District Valsad, Gujarat (fig. 1). The site is located on the northern bank of the Varoli river/creek. The area is locally known as the *bandar* or port (Pl. 1).

The five main aims of the excavations were:

To establish the existence and location of the ancient settlement of Sanjan;

To establish the date of the founding of the settlement;

To establish the nature of occupation;

To establish the date of desertion: and

To ascertain the role of Sanjan in the East - West trade in the Indian Ocean.

The Stratigraphy (fig. 2)

A total of seven layers were encountered. Of these layer 1 was a thin layer directly under the humus and, therefore, heavily disturbed. Layers 2 - 6 were habitational layers, layer 7 was the natural soil, which rests on the bedrock. Excavations ceased at a depth of 5.35m (Pl. 2).

Layer 1: This layer is heavily disturbed and the upper 5 cm (humus) were removed prior to excavation. The humus was full of plastic bag pieces, a few un-corroded iron fragments, heavily fragmented potsherds and some pieces of plastic rope.

The succeeding deposit was more compact and also disturbed with a few modern intrusions. These included small brickbats, scraps of plastic and a few pieces of modern glass. The layer slopes and thins towards the north-west. The layer has of an average thickness of 15 cm.

Layer 2: At the base of layer 1 were encountered an amazingly large number of brickbats. Under these brickbats were encountered the collapsed remains of brick walls. Layer 2, is similar to layer 1 but has a higher concentration of brickbats. It is also much denser and brickbats seems to have been rammed into a sticky black clayey matrix. This layer resembles a burnt platform of rammed rubble.

Layer 3: This was a thin layer of dark brown sticky claylike material and was first encountered in Tr. TT 1 (SE and NE). It is devoid of brick-bats. This layer rests on a brickbat floor and was rich in artefacts and ceramics. In the southeastern and northeastern quadrants of tr. TT 1 at the base of layer 3, at a depth of 1 m, were noticed the tops of two ring-wells. These are separated from the rammed brick bat floor by a brick wall. The ring-wells, wall and brick bat floor form the terminal occupational phase at the site.

Layer 4: This layer is lighter in colour than the preceding one and made up of soil intermingled with potsherds and small brickbats. It is a silty, sandy, greyish-brown layer interspersed with tiny calcrete nodules. This layer is exposed clearly only in Tr. TT 2 (SE).

Layer 5: Layer 5 was encountered at approximately 2.4 m and is similar in appearance to layer 4; the main exception being that it is slightly darker and more clayey compared to the former layer.

Layer 6: This layer was noticed only in a small area between Ringwells I and II and between Ringwell I and the southern section (facing north) of tr. TT 1. It is dark brown with what appears to be bands of decomposed organic materials. These may be the residues of the adjoining wells.

Layer 7: This layer is the natural soil over which the settlement was established. It is a sandy siity yellowish layer, which appears to be a fluvial deposit. Only the upper 15 cm of this layer has any artefactual or ceramic material. The lower portion of this layer is progressively sandier and is interspersed with small pieces of *murum*. At the base of this layer was encountered the weathered crust of the local bedrock. The bedrock was met at a depth of 5.35 m.

The Structural Phases (fig. 3)

The excavations yielded a number of structural remains. These were divided into two phases.

The first structural phase (Structural Phase I) lay upon layer 7 and is represented by a large, structure made of burnt bricks. The bricks measure between 35 and 40cm in length, 21 and 25cm in breadth and 6 and 7cm in thickness. Only parts of the northern and western walls are seen in the excavated area. The walls are made up of 15 courses of bricks under which is seen the foundation of three courses of cobbles interspersed with clay. The later inhabitants have robbed a large portion of the western wall of the structure off its bricks. This was seen very clearly in the form of a ghost wall in the southern section of the excavated area. To the west of the structure lay a deep ringwell made up of nine rings. The rings are straight sided and are between 33 and 39 cm in height. The rings have everted rims and very slightly splayed in the lower two centimetres. The four upper rings have collapsed upon one another but the lower rings are in good condition and are preserved *in situ*. The ringwell was excavated 1.5m into the sandy *murum* represented by layer 7. The complete depth of the ringwell is 3.2m. To the north-west of Structure I was seen the base of a rammed cobble floor.

To the north-west of the structure in Tr. TT 2 (SW) was a flimsy one-brick thick 'S' shaped extension of five courses this was designated Structural Phase IA.

The second structural phase, Structural Phase II, was situated at a depth of 1.05 - 1.10 m from the extant surface of the mound. It was made up of a small wall of burnt bricks, one course thick and two courses high and running north-south. To its east was a floor made of horizontally placed brickbats and cobbles. This floor was covered with a 10 cm thick layer of rammed sticky clay. To the west of the wall were two large ringwells both with an average diameter of 80 cm. They are in the same alignment as the wall. The southern one was designated Ringwell I and the northern one Ringwell II. These are made up of five and seven rings respectively. The rings are rimmed and flare downwards. Each ring is approximately 20cm tall. At the base of both the ringwells was seen, in a pit, a thick deposit of charcoal, potsherds and clay. This was done in all probability to filter the contents, as they were absorbed into the ground and also to prevent the upward movement of gases as charcoal absorbs gases. This is done even today when building septic tanks in the region. Lying above these ringwells were a large numbers of vertical bricks and brickbats, probably denoting the collapsed walls of an adjacent structure. This collapsed debris had severely damaged the upper rings of both the ringwells. A large number of artefacts were found associated with the wall and floor of Structural Phase II. Prominent amongst these were two complete glass bottles, an iron ladle, two silver coins and one copper coin. The first of the silver coins bears on its obverse an elephant walking towards the right in a circle of dots; on its reverse are a number of letters in the Brahmi script. The second is a broken fragment of a Sassanian silver issue. The copper coin is a corroded highly debased Indo-Sassanian or Gadhiya coin.

The Ceramics (figs. 4 to 8)

A surface survey undertaken prior to excavations revealed a range of wares going from coarse wares to fine porcelains. Many of the wares found at the site had never been previously reported in India in regular excavations. It was decided to adopt a methodology that would encompass this wide range. A system of identification has therefore been devised which is both descriptive as well as distinctive. The nomenclature indicates the fabric and subsequent surface treatment. For example - Pink Ware, Glazed Pink Ware, Red Slipped Pink Ware, etc. The coarseness or fineness of the core has not been used as a criterion, with the exception of Coarse Red Ware and Coarse Grey Ware, where the term has been used loosely for fabrics lacking any surface treatment.

The wares identified so far are: Porcelain, Glazed Grey/ Stone Ware, Glazed Pink Ware, Pink Ware, Red Slipped Pink Ware, Glazed Buff Ware, Mica Washed Red Ware, Slipped Grey Ware, Coarse Grey Ware, Slipped Red Ware, Coarse Red Ware and Red Polished Ware. (The nomenclature used in this study is liable to change in the light of new information that may emerge from further study.)

PORCELAIN: The porcelain found at this site is very fine and well made, ranging in colour from white and cream to grey and light green and pale blue. Some of the sherds appear to be Chinese Qingbai and Yueh wares (Ian Glover, Pers. Comm.). There are very few sherds in this category. The thickness of the core varies from 0.7cm to 0.4cm. The predominant shapes in this ware appear to be bowls and dishes. The rims are mainly everted and at least two types of bases are represented. None of the sherds have any decorations on them.

GLAZED GREY/STONE WARE: The fabric of this ware is grey in colour, very well levigated and appears to stop one step short of porcelain. The colours in this ware are mainly shades of green and greyish-green. The most important feature of this pottery is the presence of spur marks on the inside surface of the bases of bowls. These Spur marks are evenly spaced and are white in colour. Most are squarish in shape. These could be of great relevance in establishing the provenance and chronology of this pottery. Similar spur marks have been observed on vessels at the site of Mantai, Sri Lanka (Carswell and Prickett 1984). Some of the body sherds have incised designs. The shapes in this ware are jars, bowls and dishes, although the rim fragment of a vase-like vessel has also been found. The bases are ringed. This ware has a very compact fabric like porcelain. Some of these sherds have a mottled effect on the surface either due to glaze, firing or a deliberate effort. Some sherds are quite thick in section. A few of these sherds may be of South Chinese origin (Ian Glover, Pers. Comm.) (Pl. 10).

GLAZED PINK WARE: This is an unusual type of pottery the provenance and identity of which is yet to be established with certainty. The predominant shapes in this ware are convex - sided bowls and dishes. The colour of the core ranges from a pale creamy pink to a darker reddish/orange shade. The fabric has a fine, soft kaolin-like texture and is in some cases very chalky. None of the sherds show any signs of over firing. The clay is well levigated. There is profusion of elaborate decoration in this ware. A pearly glaze is used to coat the incised and painted designs. The glaze coating seems to be thin and much of it is eroded or worn out. The designs are mainly freehand curved lines forming abstract, floral or stylised motifs. A remarkable feature of this incised decoration is the use of hatched oblique lines as 'fillers' in background spaces so as to highlight the main design. Unfortunately due to the fragmentary nature of the pottery found, no complete designs can be studied. The designs are elaborate and almost completely cover the inner and occasion ally the outer surface of the vessels. The exterior of the vessel frequently has either a plain glaze or no glaze at all. The rim is usually highlighted with plain bands or a border. Green, yellow, brown and white blotches of colour can be seen on the surface. Some painted designs have also been recovered. Base types identified are discoid, ring type and contiguous flat with variations within each. The general impression received is that this ware was mainly for table use (Pl. 8–9).

PINK WARE: The fabric of this ware is similar to Glazed Pink Ware, but is devoid of any surface treatment. The colour of the core ranges from pale creamy pink to reddish pink. The sherds are mainly thick in section and sturdy, indicating storage and transportation uses. It should be mentioned that a large number of handles have been found in this ware. Some of the sherds have a chalky texture while some are medium-coarse and cement-like. Storage jars seem to be mostly high-necked. A large number of sherds in this category had a black residual coating on the inner surface and these have been kept aside for residual analysis. The handles are mainly large and show versatility, indicating the variety of uses. Contiguous ring bases and contiguous flat bases have been found. With the exception of one incised sample and one fragment of an appliquè design, there is almost a total absence of decoration.

RED SLIPPED PINK WARE: The shapes in this ware appear to be predominantly pots and jars. The core is greyish pink and in some cases pink. The texture is medium-coarse. The surface is treated to a slip that varies in colour from a bright red to dark red and brown. One handle fragment and a spout with serrated design have also been found. Only one base has been retrieved and this is of a concave discoid type. Decoration in this ware is limited and the few sherds found with any attempt to decorate show incised lines and dots.

GLAZED BUFF WARE: This is a very dramatic and interesting ware showing imagination and versatility in treatment, decoration and shapes. The fabric is fine, chalky, soft and, in some cases, medium-coarse depending upon the purity of the kaolin used. The colour of the core ranges from milk white to yellow. The surface treatment shows great versatility. The smaller vessels have white and cream glaze. Some sherds have a greyish-brown matt glaze. The larger vessels have green, blue green and turquoise glaze. These have been identified as Turquoise Glazed Ware or South Mesopotamian Islamic TGW (Glover, personal communication). This is also variously termed by different scholars as 'Hib' (Mason 1991), Sassanian-Islamic Blue Glazed pottery (Rougeulle 1996: 162) etc. There is evidence of over-firing and vitrification on some sherds. This vitrification may also be due to the vessel's repeated use for preparing glazes or melting of glass. The glazes themselves appear to have been treated differently in order to achieve certain effects, e.g. crackle effect, mirror finish, etc. On a few sherds the glaze is almost half a centimetre thick. However, some of the smaller sherds have neither surface treatment nor glaze. There is one sherd with no surface treatment, but glaze has been used to paint a design on it (Pls. 1A, 2B, 3, 4, 5, 6).

The shapes vary from storage jars and globular pots to large and small bowls, dishes and cups. There is a range of rims within each category - from the everted external projecting to the inverted and the bilateral projecting. High-necked jars, convex-sided bowls and bowls with flaring sides are present in this collection. Special mention should be made here of a high-necked vase in Turquoise Glazed Ware with four handles, two of which are extant. A similar kind of vessel is reported from Nishapur in Iran (This reference is from the Internet, Re: The Rietze Collection).

A large number of handles have been retrieved. These

are of three types viz. oval or elliptical in section, round section and small, unglazed handles probably belonging to cups. The base types found in this ware include contiguous flat, discoid, ring, pedestal and stand types.

The designs are very interesting and unusual. The decorations are done by techniques such as appliquè, painting, incision, impression and stamping. One design resembles very closely one of the vessels found at Susa, which has been dated to the ninth century A.D. (Lane 1947: 9, fig. 5). Floral designs, zigzags, horizontal and curved bands, dots, etc. are also noticed. The unglazed samples have some incised and intricate patterns, which are very well executed. None of the designs in this ware are seen on the coarse wares.

MICA-WASHED RED WARE: The fabric of this ware is well-levigated, medium-coarse clay. The surface has been treated to a mica wash. No other attempt has been made at decoration or design, though a few sherds do have ridges below the rim. The shapes most represented are carinated *handis*. These sherds do not appear as eroded and rolled as the other wares.

SLIPPED GREY WARE: This ware has a medium-coarse grey fabric with a slip applied to the outer surface and sometimes on the inner surface as well. Predominant shapes include pots with wide mouths and constricted necks, carinated pots, cooking pots / *handis*, a few high-necked pots, some carinated and convex-sided bowls and small pots. An interesting observation in the case of some high-necked pots is the resemblance of some rims to those found in Glazed Buff Ware. There is not much effort at decoration.

COARSE GREY WARE: This ware has been designated as a coarse ware only because there is no surface treatment and because the fabric ranges from medium coarse to coarse. The predominant shapes are wide-mouthed pots, bowls, carinated and convex-sided bowls, and some finials of lids. Some spouts have also been retrieved.

SLIPPED RED WARE: This ware has a fabric, which is medium-coarse to coarse and is treated to a slip/wash that varies in colour from bright red and brown to grey and, in some cases even black. The firing appears quite uneven and a large number of sherds show signs of weathering and rolling. The shapes represented in this ware are mainly utilitarian and range from large and heavy-set storage jars and pots to bowls, cooking pots/*handis*, plates, a ring stand and a basin. A large number of spouts have also been found.

COARSE RED WARE: This ware is medium coarse to very coarse in fabric and while most sherds appear to be wheel-made, some storage jar fragments and a few other pieces appear crude and hand-made. The shapes suggest a utilitarian function and range from large storage jars, globular pots and carinated pots to carinated bowls, small pots, dishes and plates. There is no surface treatment and the firing appears uneven. The colours of the vessels vary from red to brown and grey to black. Some of the vessels show evidence of over-firing and burning. A large number of spouts of different kinds are also present. The finials found are flat knob-like and some are bell-shaped. Some lugs have also been found. There is a certain type of fabric found in this category that has a medium coarse, but compact fabric with well-levigated clay. This pottery goes from a dark pinkish purple to grey and even maroon to deep red. Sometimes cream coloured bands or incised designs can be seen. This has been treated as a sub-category in this analysis as it is distinctive in nature. Its identity is yet to be established.

RED POLISHED WARE: Three fragments of this ware have been found. The first is a spout with six perforations at its base and the second is part of a sprinkler. The third sherd is a small non-diagnostic fragment. These have been retrieved from a ringwell pit. Hence no stratigraphic context can be attributed to them. These fragments appear fresh and show no evidence of rolling. These sherds are of great significance considering that Red Polished Ware has been reported from various sites in association with Early Islamic Pottery and sometimes also with Chinese wares. Sites such as Mantai in Sri Lanka (Carswell and Prickett 1984), Siraf in Iran, Suhar in Oman (Kervran 1996: 38) and Qana' in Yemen (Sedov 1996: 16) amongst others in the Persian Gulf and the Indian Ocean have yielded all three wares. Archaeologists have used Red Polished Ware as a chronological marker to establish trade contacts between these sites and the Indian subcontinent. The earliest date of Red Polished Ware in India with types like sprinklers goes back to the 1st century A.D. in northern India.

The Artefacts

A large number of artefacts in iron, copper, terracotta, stone, glass and shell were recovered from the excavations.

GLASS OBJECTS: The single largest group of artefacts from the excavations consist of glass objects. These include: vessel fragments, bangle fragments, ring fragments and other miscellaneous objects. Many of the glass objects display an iridescent patination. For purposes of streamlining the artefactual analysis the corpus of glass objects has been split up into: Glass Vessels and Other Glass Objects.

GLASS VESSELS: In the course of the excavations, an unusually large quantity of glass vessels and vessel fragments was encountered. These range in size from large fragments to very tiny chips that are often difficult to hold. The fragments range in colour, surface treatment, shape and decoration. It is also very significant that a few intact/nearly intact glass bottles/vessels were also found (Pl. 11).

COLOUR: The glass fragments show a wide variety in colour, thickness and shape. Colours range from light and dark green, pale blue, dark blue, clear, yellow, and one or two specimens of an opaque white.

Patination and Sub-soil Weathering of Glass: In a majority of cases, the fragments are covered with multiple layers of patination. This patina varies in colour and durability. The patina also shows a range of textures and colours. Sometimes it is matte, and in many cases it has a 'mother of pearl-like' iridescent smooth finish. The colour of this patina ranges from an iridescent blue or green, and in some instances an iridescent white; to a dark brown/black muddy 'lumpy' coating that is firmly stuck to the surface of the glass fragment. In most cases the iridescent patina flakes off quite easily, and is very fragile, reducing to almost nothing as soon as it comes off the artefact. This patina is the result of a chemical reaction of the soil on the surface of the glass, a weathering effect. 'Patination' is not an addition to the existing piece of glass but is, in fact, the degenerated outermost layer of the fragment itself. This, however, seriously limits the study of the glass fragments as the mildest handling of the glass loosens this patina and, as such, results in its destruction.

The thin layers that remain on a piece of weathered glass are called 'iridescence'. These layers are actually colourless. The thin layers take on a play of iridescent colours by an effect known as thin-film interference. This weathering pattern is visible on a majority of glass fragments excavated at Sanjan.

The bulk of the glass fragments recovered, however, is composed of fragments, most of which are too tiny to categorise.

Rims: A significantly large number of rim fragments have been found in the course of the excavations at Sanjan. The majority of the rims are plain featureless rims showing no distinct shaping or decoration.

A unique case is a complete disc-like rim attached to a neck flaring gently downwards. An identical rim/neck is seen in the Al Sabah Collection of the Kuwait National Museum, where it has been described as a cylindrical neck (with) a large splayed opening. It has been dated 9th-10th century A.D. and the reported probable provenance is the Mesopotamian region. (Carboni 2001: 202)

Bases: The majority of the bases seen in the collection are circular. They are mainly flat or hemispherical. A few exceptions are ringed with a small rounded ridge or ledge. Two of the intact bottles are exceptions; one has a square base whilst the second has an eleven-sided polygonal multifaceted base (Pl. 12).

The only other exception is the rim fragment of a dish with a 'L-shaped' foot. It is of course a matter of debate as to whether this artefact should be categorised as a base or as a rim fragment.

Other diagnostic objects include bases, finials (Pl. 13), a thick stopper like object and a disc reminiscent of 'marvered' glass objects produced by Medieval Near-eastern glass manufacturers in the 8th to 12th centuries A.D. (Carboni 2001: 291-93).

OTHER GLASS OBJECTS: This category includes bangle fragments, ring fragments and a few miscellaneous objects.

BANGLE FRAGMENTS: The Bangle fragments from Sanjan are similar to such objects seen at most Early

Historical and Early Medieval excavations in India. They are mainly plain and a few bear appliquè dots in white. They are mainly opaque black in colour with a few examples of transparent green. It is interesting to note here that whilst three probable bangle fragments in copper have been recovered from the excavation, not a single example of a terracotta bangle fragment was recovered.

RINGS: The glass finger ring fragments are fewer in number and are essentially smaller versions of the bangles. The rings are plain and show no evidence of a boss or other decorative devices.

MISCELLANEOUS: This category is made up mainly of lumps, fused fragments, and an inlay piece. The only artefact of note is a small flat bevelled glass object reminiscent of a ring inlay. It is octagonal in shape and yellowish in colour.

Iron Objects:

NAILS, RODS AND POINTS: This is the largest sub category. It is made up mainly of nails and what are most probably broken parts thereof. The nails are of two kinds; square sectioned and round sectioned.

ARROWHEADS: Four arrowheads were recovered from the excavations. These vary in length from 4 cm to 8.5 cm in length and from 1.5 to 2.4 cm in breadth.

KNIVES/BLADES: Three such artefacts were encountered. Two are probably blade fragments whilst the third is a small knife, complete, with tang and blade intact.

ANGLES: These are flat 'L' shaped iron strips, which were probably used in woodworking.

AXE: This is a unique example. It is a small short narrow, rectangular adze-like axe.

LADLE: This is also a one of a kind artefact from the site. It consists of a long rod-like handle ending in a thin hemispherical bowl.

SPIKE ON RING: This is a typical device used today to secure the chains of a swing to the wooden board. It consists of a thick iron ring on which is added an equally thick short spike.

Terracotta Objects:

DISCS: This is the single largest sub-category with 133 individuals represented. The discs are made on a variety of potsherds belonging mainly to the red and grey ceramics found at the site. They have ground sides and are not always round; some examples from Sanjan are triangular and/or squarish

LAMPS: These form the next largest sub category. They are essentially plain, shallow and circular with featureless everted rims. Whilst the majority are examples in unglazed red ware there is one exception (No. 622) in glazed ware of a lamp rim fragment with what appears to be part of a wick-channel.

FIGURINES: There are three objects in this sub category. Two are cylindrical stubs reminiscent of toy animal limbs. The third (No. 1069) appears to be a stylised elephant head and is unique to the site. It was found in the pit dug to hold Ringwell I.

MISCELLANEOUS: This category includes a small ball, a wattle and daub fragment (burnt), a triangular cake (?), a round cake, a pellet, a small crucible (No. 357) (?), and, a small toy stool (No. 495) with its corners rounded and legs broken off.

COPPER OBJECTS: These included three intact antimony rods, two needles (both with flattened eyes), a small copper bell, a tiny bowl-like object, broken pieces of wire and ring fragments.

STONE OBJECTS: Only 14 stone artefacts were recovered from the excavations. Two are hammer stones. One is a small menhir-shaped pestle (No. 99) with a height of 5.5 cm and a basal width of 2.5 cm. there is also one half (vertical) of a round deep quern. This was found close to the surface and may be of recent origin as similar examples are used today. There is also one muller and half of a sling-ball. The excavations also yielded three pieces of what can only be described as worked stone.

COWRIES: Three cowrie shells (*Moneta moneta* sp.) were recovered from the excavations. Their dorsal portions have been modified by grinding so as to facilitate attachment to garments.

COINS: Of the 32 coins collected from the excavation and first studied by Ms. Rohini Pande, 21 are of copper, 4 are probably of lead and 7 are silver coins. Twelve coins with any discernable features were given to Dr. (Ms.) S. Gokhale, Pune for decipherment. She has identified five of these. They are:

A small silver coin with elephant on obverse and lion on reverse. This coin is attributed to the 2nd century A.D. The lion was the mintmark of the Satavahana mint at Nasik. The combination of the two symbols on such a small issue shows remarkable craftsmanship.

A fragment of a silver Sassanian coin with traces of a fire altar on the reverse. The coin is attributable to the 7th - 8th century A.D.

A small silver coin with an elephant facing right on the obverse and a Brahmi legend on the reverse. The legend reads, *Amavalisa*, and can be attributed on palaeographical grounds to the 8th - 9th century A.D.

A silver coin of the Sultan of Sind, dated to A.D. 900. It bears Arabic legends on both faces: the obverse bears a legend, *Allah Yathig umar wafah an nasr,* whilst the reverse bears the legend, *Allah Muhammad Rasulallah.*

The fifth is a highly corroded Indo-Sassanian copper coin. The obverse depicts the bust of a king and the reverse bears faint traces of a fire-altar. It is ascribable to the 10th - 11th century A.D.

BEADS: In all 113 beads were recovered from the excavations and the site. The dominant material is glass with 91 beads, followed by terracotta with nine, carnelian with four, garnet, chalcedony, paste and copper are represented by a single specimen each. Two of the beads may be made of agate or a glass mimicking it known as agate glass. Of the last two beads one is made of an as yet unidentified material whilst the other is made of an unidentified white stone.

Dating:

In the absence of absolute dates the tentative dating of the site on the basis of historical, ceramic, numismatic and artefactual data is between the 8th and 11th centuries A.D.

Conclusion

The tentative and preliminary conclusions suggest a thriving site, economically strong and involved in trade both local and foreign. Thus gives rise to what is probably a vital link in better understanding Indian Ocean trade during the 8th and 11th centuries A.D.

This is a preliminary study and these conclusions are thus of a preliminary nature.

Acknowledgements

Prof. V.N. Misra, former Director, Deccan College, Pune and Shri K.N. Dikshit, General Secretary of the Indian Archaeological Society, gave their matured guidance, we are deeply grateful for the same. Our thanks are also due to Dr. Nivedita Mehta of the Alpaiwala Museum, Mumbai for the storage of the materials from the site. The authors thank Mr. Feroze H. Dalal, Mumbai, for his help in personally transporting the team and equipment to Sanjan. The authors would also like to thank Dr. Sunil Gupta, Deputy Keeper of the Allahabad Museum, for his intensive and extensive survey of the Varoli River/Creek and its environs. The authors are also very grateful to Drs. Brill and Koob and Ms. Shana Wilson of the Corning Museum of Glass, Corning, New York, without whom it would have been very difficult to study the glass objects. The authors would also like to thank Dr. Ian Glover for his invaluable help in identifying the ceramics and his guidance for further study of the same. The authors also thank the staff of the Indian Archaeological Society, Delhi, Mr. M.S. Mani, Mr. Laxminarayan, Mr. Jassu Ram, Mr. Rakesh Datta, Mr. Himanshu Joshi, Mr. Tejas Garge and Mrs. Anuja Geetali. The authors would also like to thank Mr. and Mrs. Davierwala and family, of Sanjan, for all the help they have rendered to the excavation team. We deeply appreciate the kindness of Mr. Dawood Patel, the owner of the field in which the excavation took place. Lastly we thank the labourers who worked for us and the helpful citizens of Sanjan without whom this study would have been impossible.

REFERENCES

Carboni, S 2001. *Glass from Islamic Lands*. Thames and Hudson: London.

Carswell, J. and M. Prickett. 1984. Mantai 1980: A Preliminary Investigation. *Ancient Ceylon* No. 5: 7-69.

Edulji, H 1991. *Kisseh-I-Sanjan*. K.R. Cama Oriental Institute: Bombay.

Glover, Ian 2002. West Asian Sassanian-Islamic Ceramics in the Indian Ocean, South Southeast and East Asia: *Man and Environment* XXVII (1): 165-77.

Kamerkar, M and S. Dhanjisha [In Press]. From the Iranian Plateau to the Shores of India. Allied Publishers: Mumbai.

Kervran, M. 1996. Indian Ceramics in Southern Iran and Eastern Arabia Repertory, Classification and Chronology, in (H.P. Ray and Jean-François Salles eds.) *Tradition and Archaeology Early Maritime Contacts in the Indian Ocean*, pp. 37-58. New Delhi: Manohar.

Lane, Arthur 1947. *Early Islamic Pottery*. London: Faber and Faber.

Mason, R.E. 1991. The Abbasid Glazed Wares of Siraf and the Basara Connection: Petrographic Analysis. *Iran* 29: 51-66.

Rougeulle, A. 1996. Medieval Trade Networks in the Western Indian Ocean (8th - 14th cent.): Some Reflections from the distribution Pattern of Chinese Imports in the Islamic World, in (H.P. Ray and Jean-François Salles eds.) *Tradition and Archaeology Early Maritime Contacts in the Indian Ocean*, pp. 159-180. New Delhi: Manohar.

Sedov, A.V. 1996. Qana' (Yemen) and the Indian Ocean: The Archaeological Evidence, in (H.P. Ray and Jean-François Salles eds.) *Tradition and Archaeology Early Maritime Contacts in the Indian Ocean*, pp. 11-36. New Delhi: Manohar.

MAP SHOWING SANJAN AND ITS ENVIRONMENT, VALSAD DISTRICT, GUJARAT STATE

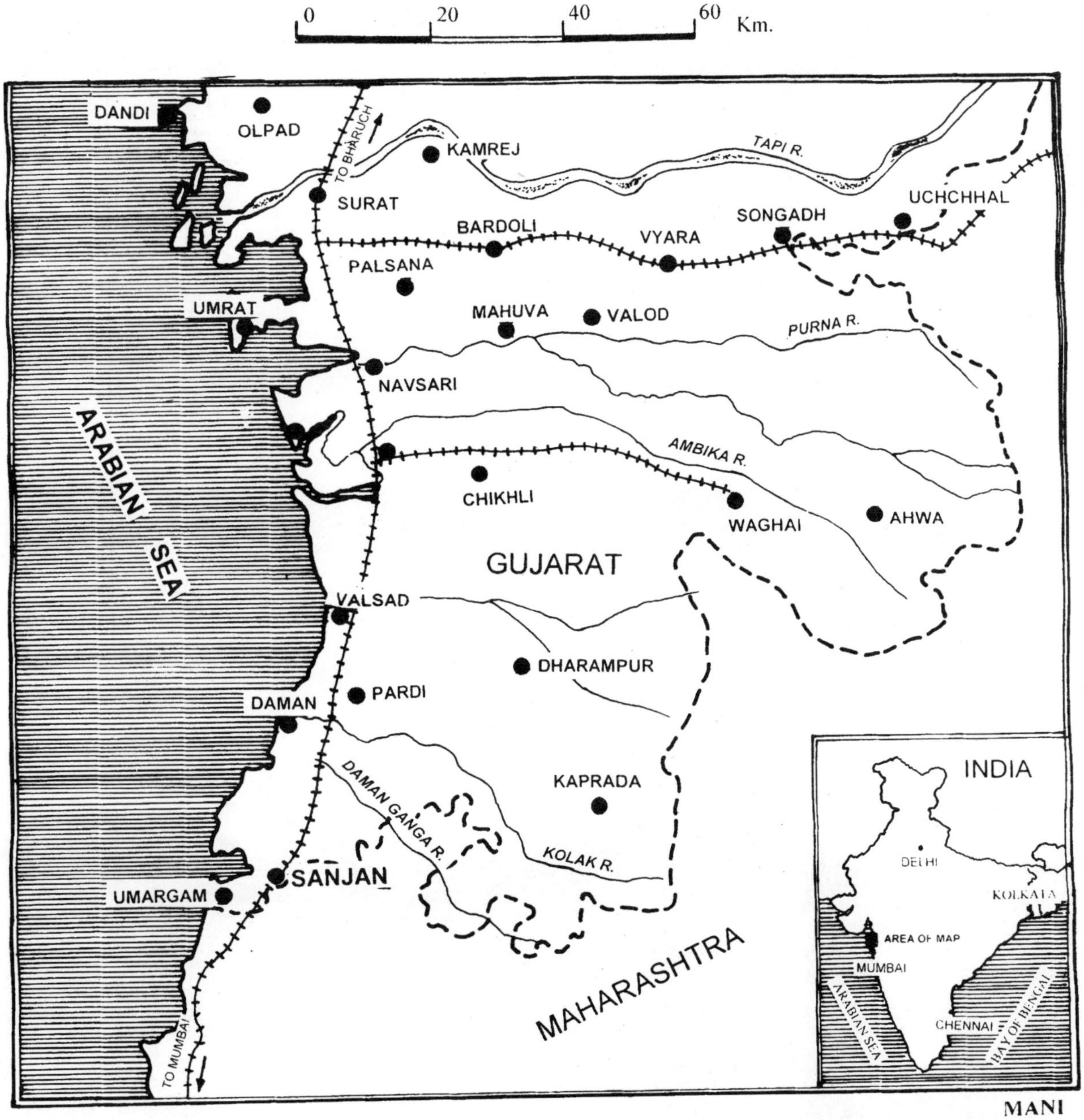

Fig. 1.

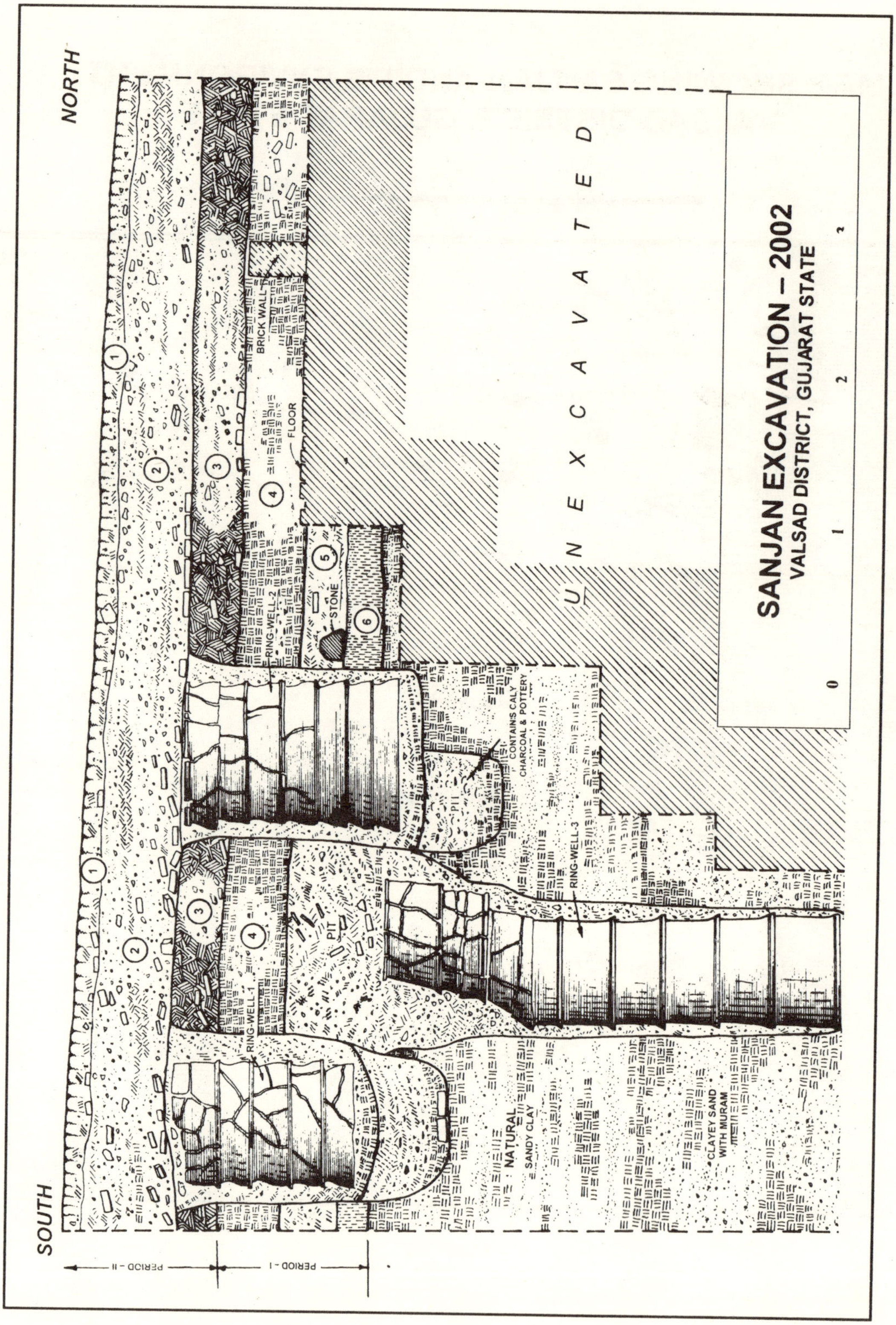
NORTH
SOUTH
UNEXCAVATED
SANJAN EXCAVATION – 2002
VALSAD DISTRICT, GUJARAT STATE
0
1
2
BRICK WALL
FLOOR
RING-WELL-2
STONE
CONTAINS CALY CHARCOAL & POTTERY
PIT
RING-WELL-3
RING-WELL-1
NATURAL SANDY CLAY
CLAYEY SAND WITH MURAM
PERIOD - II
PERIOD - I

Fig. 2.

SANJAN EXCAVATION – 2002
VALSAD DISTRICT, GUJARAT STATE
0
1
2
3
METRE
A
B
FLOOR
BRICK WALL PHASE-II
STONES
RAMP (BRICK BATS)
FLOOR
STONES
RING-WELL-2
RING-WELL-3
RING-WELL-1
BRICK WALL
STONES
RAMP (BRICK BATS)
DRAIN
SOAK-PIT (BRICK BATS)
BRICK WALL PHASE-I
BRICK WALL PHASE-III
FLOOR PHASE-II
PLAN
MANI, KURUSH & RHEA

Fig. 3.

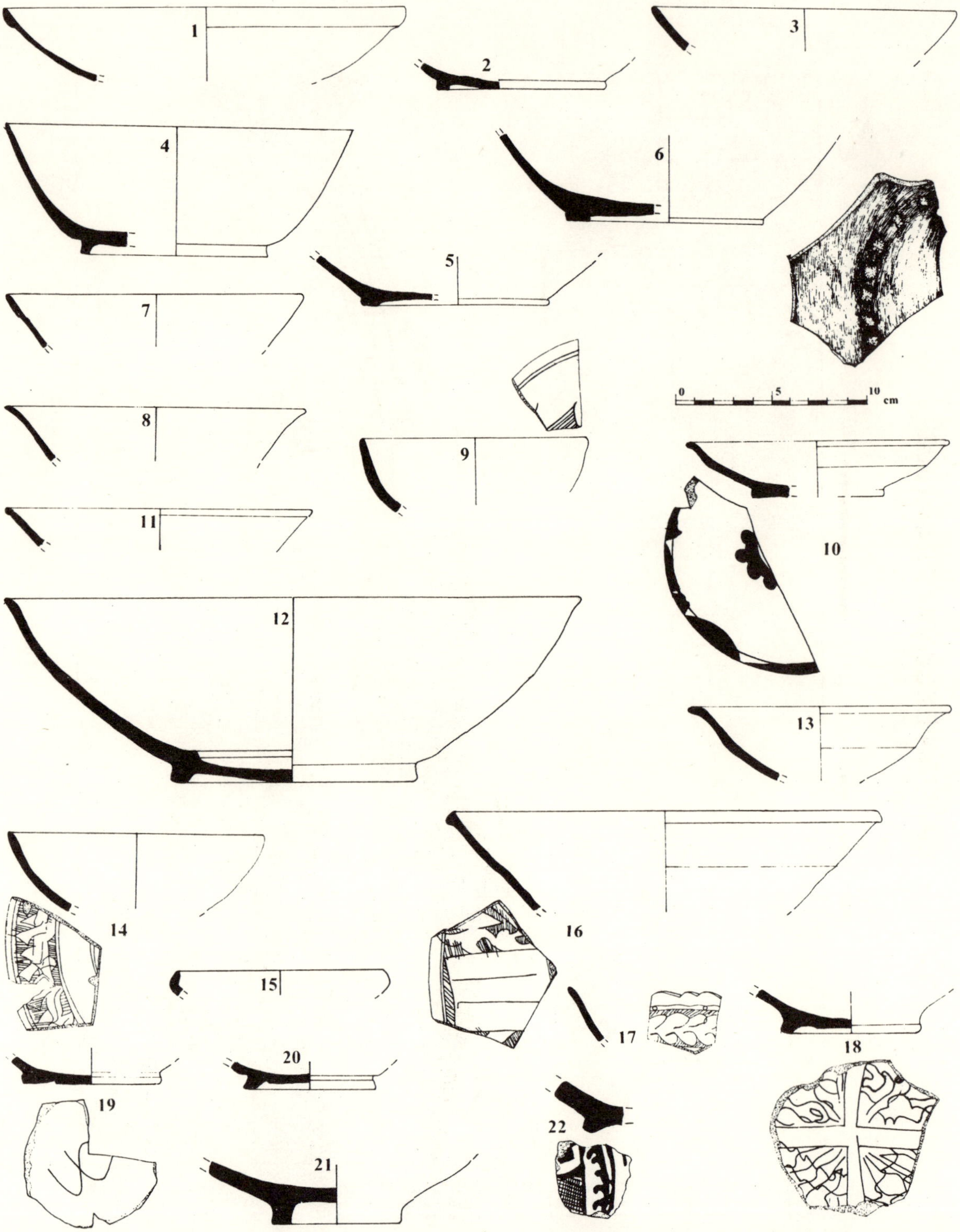

Fig. 4. Sanjan Pottery No. 1. to 3, Porcelain, No. 4 to 8, Glazed Grey/Stone Ware No. 9 to 22 Glazed Pink ware

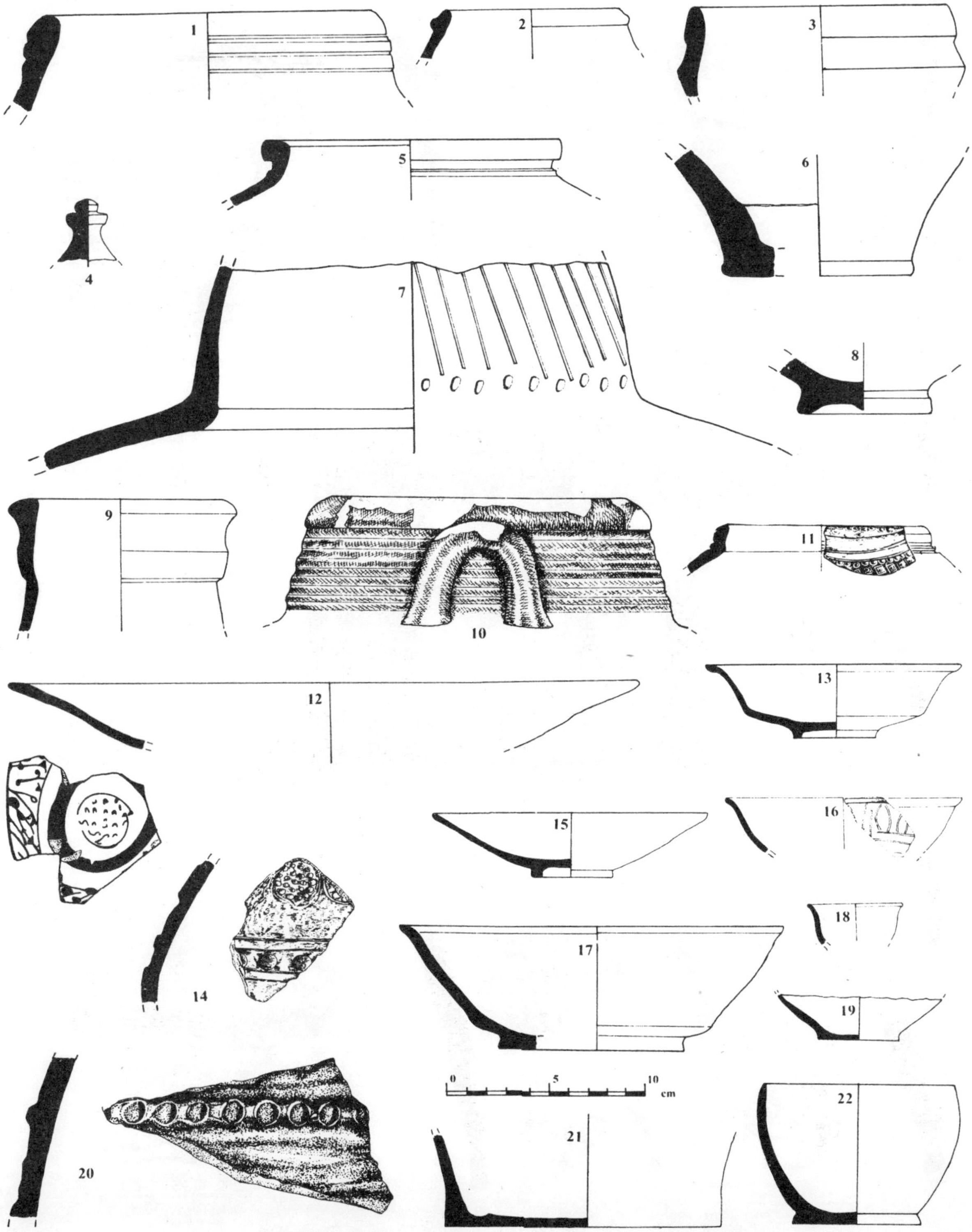

Fig. 5. Sanjan Pottery No. 1. to No. 8, Pink Ware No. 9 to No. 22 Glazed Buff Ware

Fig. 6. Sanjan Pottery No. 1 to 14 Glazed Buff/Tuquoise Glazed Ware

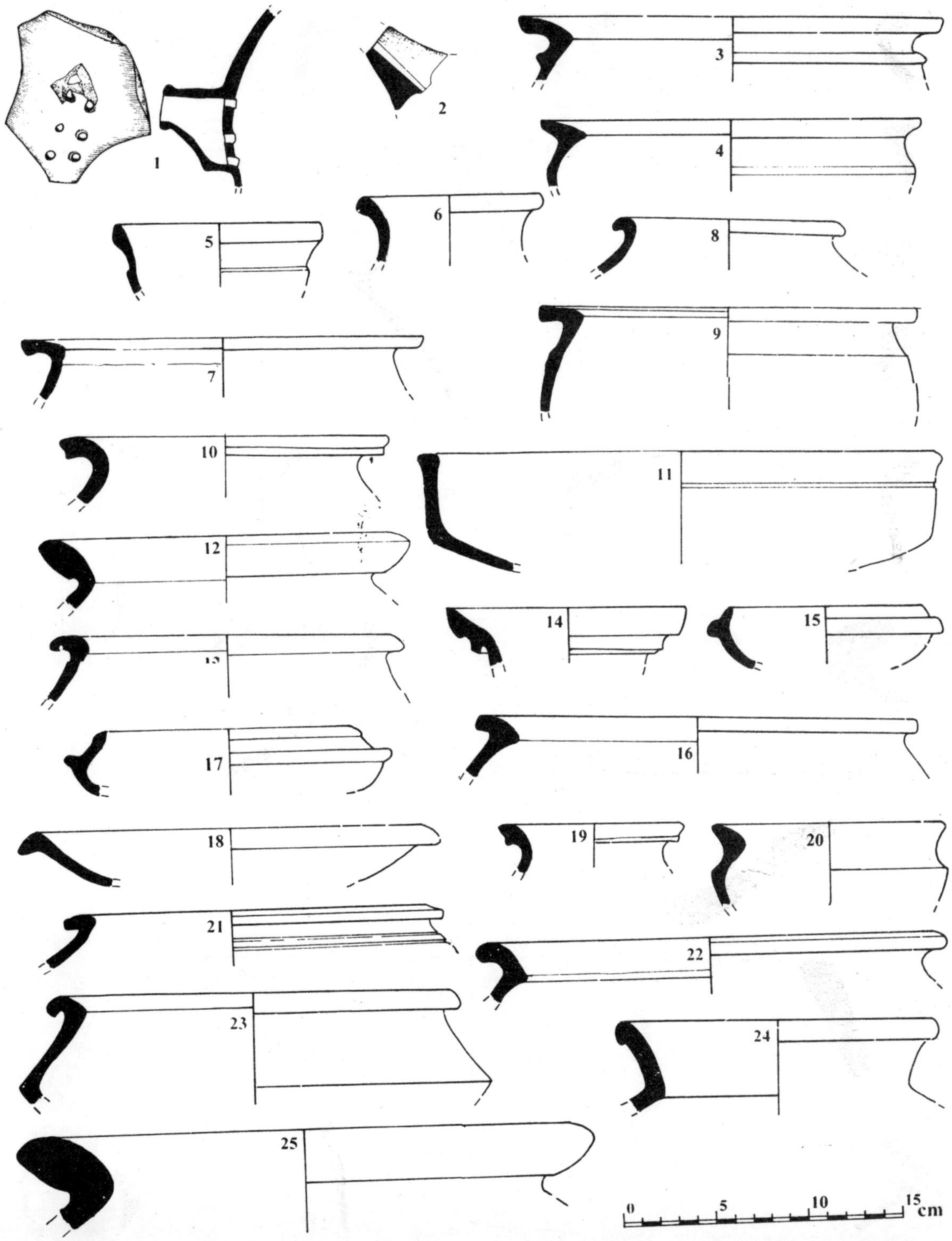

Fig. 7. Sanjan Pottery No. 1 and No. 2 Red Polished Ware, No. 3 and No. 4 Mica Washed Red Ware, No. 5 to No. 7 Red Slipped Pink Ware, No. 8 and NO. 9 Slipped Grey Ware, No. 10 to No. 16 Course Grey Ware, No. 17 to No. 25 Slipped Red Ware

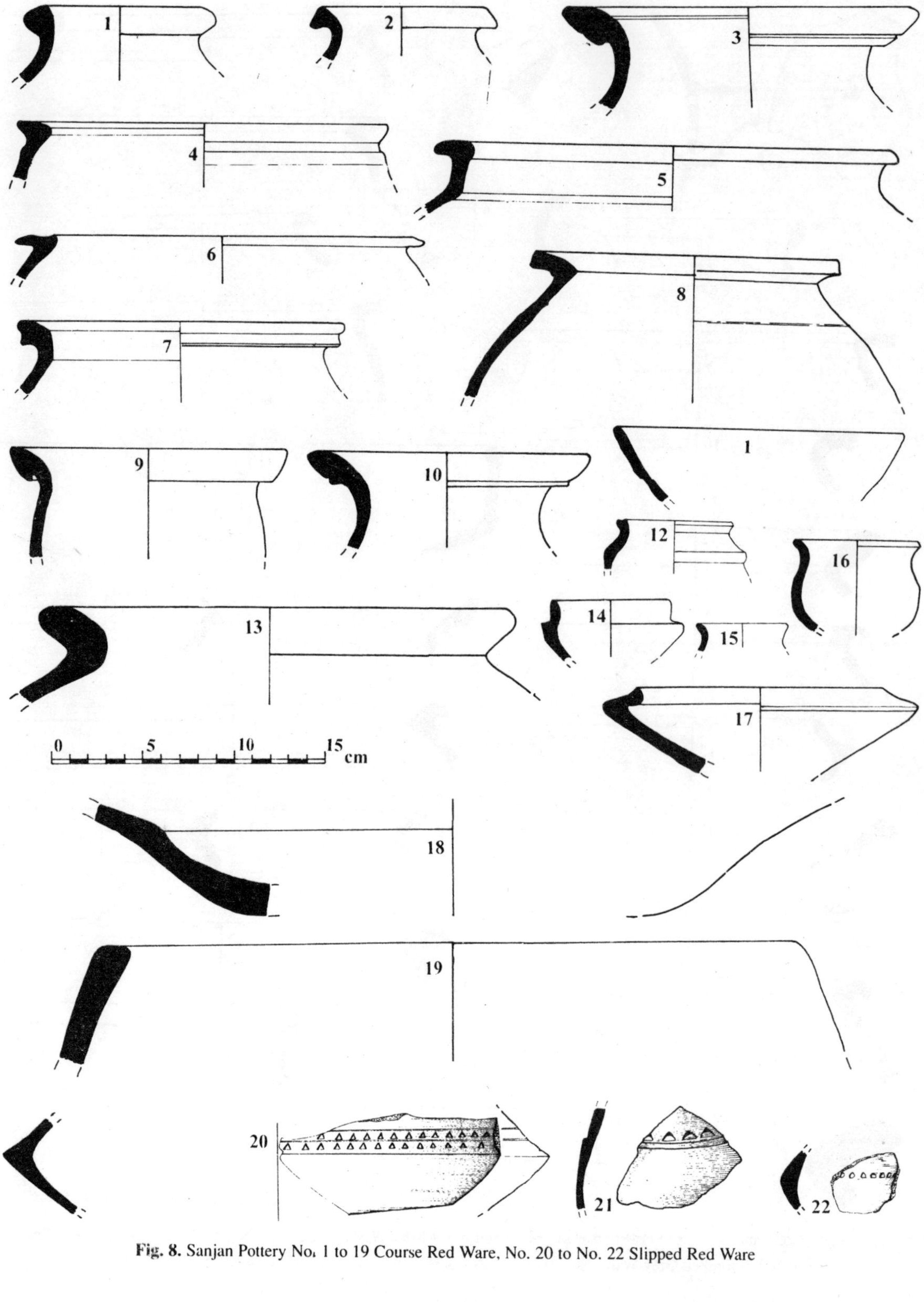

Fig. 8. Sanjan Pottery No. 1 to 19 Course Red Ware, No. 20 to No. 22 Slipped Red Ware

BOOK REVIEWS

Raghunath S. Pappu: *Acheulian Culture in Peninsular India: An Ecological Perspective*, D.K. Printworld (P) Ltd. New Delhi, 2001, Pages 170, Price: Rs. 455/-.

An astounding achievement of humankind in the Pleistocene world was that of *homo* becoming *erectus.* This erect upright posture gave the species not only superior vision but made them excellent *homo fabor*, a skilful fabricator of tools in a regular and set pattern. The first humans were crude fabricator of artifacts, but in India we still have no evidence by which it can be suggested that we have manufactured tools and artifacts belonging to the first humans. The first humans, perhaps, did not venture out of Africa. *Homo erectus* certainly did. Between about 1.5 and 0.1 million years, the Old World belonged to them, but it cannot be said that they were great colonizers. Nevertheless incontrovertible evidence for their colonisation comes from lands in Africa, Europe and Asia, from Spain and Britain in the west and north, to India in the east. *Homo erectus*' characteristic stone artifacts were first recognized at Saint Acheul, a Lower Palaeolithic site in the Somme Valley of northern France. In many parts of the Old World, the Acheulian industries are the oldest known manifestation of material culture and human settlement. But more importantly in the evolutionary history of humankind, the time-span between about 1.5 million years and 100,000 years ago was singularly significant in understanding many of our behavioural development in the conceptual, linguistic, social and organizational fields.

Despite notable improvements in research designs and excavations in as many as twenty primary context sites in the peninsular India in the last three decades, there has been no attempt to present in a single volume a pan-India picture of the earliest manifestation of human settlement in the Indian subcontinent. The publication of the *Acheulian Culture in Peninsular India -An Ecological perspective* by Dr. Raghunath S. Pappu fulfils a need long felt in the field of Prehistory in India.

This book, under review, gives an account in detail in four chapters covering aspects of a brief history of Acheulian research and various research methodology adopted to tackle primary context Acheulian sites in India found in varied situations, viz., open stations, rock-shelters and channel beds.

The first Chapter of the book introduces in brief the Acheulian tradition as is currently known from the three continents of Africa, Europe and Asia.

The second Chapter, which presents a detailed account of the twenty-two excavated primary context Acheulian sites in India and an outline of four sites notable for hominid remains, association of implementiferous alluvial deposits with volcanic ash, miliolite formation and a rich cluster of open-air occupation, forms the core chapter of the book.

The salient features of the Acheulian culture in peninsular India have been delineated in Chapter three with emphasis an understanding of the early hominids from geographical, cultural, biological and behavioural patterns. The Acheulian in the peninsular India as an industry and culture does reflect diverse adaptive mechanisms in colonizing various ecological zones and it is this dynamism that gave the Acheulian hunter-gatherers a distinctive niche in the history of evolution of humankind.

Finally, the author deals with the Acheulian cultural system in the concluding Chapter of the book by piecing together the data presented in earlier chapters and incorporating additional data by integrating and synthesizing them in a comprehensive way focusing upon interrelationship between human culture and environment. It is indeed a difficult arena of research in Lower Palaeolithic archaeology, notably so in Acheulian hunter-gatherer societies of the peninsular India.

This is a book authored by a scholar who has behind him more than three decades of field-research experience and, also, first hand knowledge of excavating primary context Acheulian sites in India. With this book now we have the advantage of recommending to the students and scholars alike a single monograph on a subject which is truly multidisciplinary.

Subrata Chakrabarti

S. Pradhan (ed.) *Orissan History, Culture and Archaeology-In Felicitation of Prof. P. K. Misra.* New Delhi: D.K. Printworld (P) Ltd. 1999. Price: Rs.1200/-.

Dr. S. Pradhan's edited volume on Orissa is outstanding since first for the time the articles project Orissa's archaeological records, various aspects of history both, ancient and modern periods, besides religions, education, etc. Beginning with a rich tribute to Prof. P. K. Misra, to whom the volume is dedicated, it has twenty-nine well-researched papers, authored by eminent scholars, majority of whom have received their doctoral degrees under Prof. P. K. Misra.

The volume is divided chronologically. The first seven chapters deal with the various facets of archaeological records, ranging from prehistory to rock-art, and state formation to maritime heritage. Another interesting piece is about the Jaina heritage of southern Orissa, of which little was known earlier. The archaeological section is followed by the political, social and religious sects of medieval Orissa, covering major and minor religions, Sun and Vishnu worship, etc. An interesting paper is on stellate temples of Orissa. At the end the some the papers are devoted to modern history.

To sum up, the volume is undoubtedly a significant contribution to Orissan study in particular and India in general. Neatly printed in good quality paper, with colour and black-and-white plates and maps, illustrations, the volume can be easily recommended for scholars evincing interest on the fascinating past of Orissa.

Jitu Mishra

B.R. Mani, *Delhi-Threshold of the Orient (Studies in Archaeological Investigations)*, Aryan Books International, New Delhi, 1997, pp.162, 56 line drawings, 120 plates including 42 in colour, Price: Rs.1500/-.

Delhi, the capital city of many kingdoms and empires, is well known for its monuments dating from the Mauryan period to recent past. Founding of the city of Indraprastha by the Pandavas during the period of Mahabharata is well known. During historic period Delhi shifted several times to cope with the unpredictable vicissitudes of the time and rulers' attempts to protect the city and make it more resourceful and majestic.

The present book deals with archaeological studies, particularly explorations and excavations in and around Delhi. It also takes into account the vast information since

16th century when official writers of contemporary history in the Mughal court wrote biographies of emperors, including the account of the people and culture and monuments of Delhi.

The book is divided into seven chapters with a bibliography and an index.The first chapter traces the early history of Delhi based on inscriptional and literary sources. Lalkot and the surrounding city came to be known as Dhilli or Dhillika after it was founded by the Tomars. During Gupta, post-Gupta and Pratihara periods, the area comprised a temple-complex and was called Yoganipura (Yoginipura) and later became famous as Dhilli, Dhillipura or Dillika. The earliest inscription mentioning Dhillika is the Bijolia inscription of AD 1170. It also includes information about physical features, early work on history, art architecture and monuments of Delhi from biographies of Mughal emperors up to the times of independence. The founding of the city and local traditions connecting the various names of Delhi are also included here.

The second chapter traces the earliest evidence of man's activity in the region in the form of stone tools. Forty-three Stone Age sites have been discovered around Delhi with main concentration around Anangpur, a large factory site. Based on prehistoric investigation, it is found that the southern slope of the Aravalli was better suited for early habitation, which can be taken to Lower Palaeolithic period, which appears to be a late Acheulian. This chapter also includes geology, history of discoveries of prehistoric tools in the region in brief and shifting of Palaeo-channels of Yamuna from west to east.

The third chapter deals with protohistoric and early historic vestiges. Late Harappan and Painted Grey Ware settlements in the area are datable from the first half of second millennium B.C. to mid first millennium B.C. During protohistoric period a cultural shift towards north, west and north-east in adjoining plains of Yamuna is clearly visible from southern hilly area. These areas were more suitable for agriculture farming and river trade and transport. The author concludes that the occurrence of Late Harappan elements and PGW degenerate Siswal ware culture provide sufficient evidence of protohistoric activities in the area.

The excavation at Bhorgarh by Dr. Babu of the Delhi State Deptt. of Archaeology at the lowest level revealed two parallel-extended burials assignable to Late Harappan period. Here are given the results of the excavation. He further discusses the results and wherever there is some difference of opinion about dating. Other excavated sites mentioned in the book are Mandoli and Salimgarh. Salimgarh is among those very few sites in India where GPR survey is done. More details of GPR (Ground Penetrating Radar) survey would have been of great interest to archaeologist. Details of Khera Kalan, Kharkhari Nahar, mound at Gordon Highlanders column, Loni, Bankner, Jhatikara are also included.

Chapter four gives the account of the excavation conducted at Purana Qila during the 1954-55 and again in 1969-73. Chronological information along with photographs of excavated trenches, structures of different periods and antiquities of this very important excavation makes the book very useful.

Chapter five gives a detailed report on the excavations at Lal Kot and Anang Tal, which the author conducted during 1992-95. This report with a number of measured drawings, plans and sections provides very significant information about the first city of the Delhi, which was founded by the Tomar King Anang Pal II in the middle of the eleventh century.

The chapter six describes the finds of archaeological investigations on medieval sites like Anangapur fort, Qila Rai Pithora, Kilokhari, Siri fort, Bijai Mandal, Jahanpanah and Adilabad. The last chapter, entitled Monuments of Delhi, gives a chronological account of human activities in the area covering a vast span of time from Lower Palaeolithic to the recent times.

The author, who worked for over a decade in the area, is not only familiar with the region but also has been closely associated with conservation of monuments, explorations and excavations conducted in Delhi. Reproduction of old drawings, plan and elevation of some of the monuments, old pictures and conjectural drawings makes this look more interesting and useful not only for the archaeologists and historians but also for a common reader.

Alok Tripathi

Om Prakash Pandey, *Sarnath Ki Kala* (Hindi), Bharati Prakashan, Varanasi, 2000,vi+161, line drawings 7, black and white photographs 63, Price: Rs. 750/-

Sarnath, near Varanasi in Uttar Pradesh, is the place mentioned in the Pali Būddhist literature as *Isipatana Migadaya* (*Risipattana* mrigadaya) where the Buddha turned the Wheel of Law in motion and preached his first sermon to the five fellow ascētics who had left him earlier, but who became his first five disciples. Sarnath became a centre of Buddhist pilgrimage when commemorative constructions were made by Asoka, the great, in the third century B.C. He constructed *stupas, chaityas* and perhaps *viharas* for monks to stay, and erected a pillar with his edicts and a beautiful lion capital over it. A large number of art objects of Maurya, Sunga and Kushana periods have been found from Sarnath in the excavations conducted during the British era. Sarnath became famous for a particular school of art where elegant Buddha sculptures were carved during the Guptas and the tradition continued for several centuries following the Gupta rule. A need has been felt by art historians since long for a comprehensive research work on the topic.

The present work seems to be an attempt in this direction. It gives a generalized overview of the art and architecture at Sarnath during the fifteen hundred years of creative activities at this important Buddhist centre. The book is divided into nine chapters followed by a bibliography and an index. Relevant drawings and photographs have been incorporated, though the printing quality could have been improved further.

The first chapter of the book describes the geographical background in the light of identification of nearby Buddhist sites. The second chapter deals with the political set-up under which Sarnath remained a centre of creative activities. The third describes the Buddhist architecture with special reference to Sarnath. The fourth contains information regarding sculptural art of Maurya and Sunga periods while the fifth chapter describes Kushana sculptural art. The sixth chapter is dedicated to the sculptural art of the Gupta period when art reached its climax in Sarnath. The seventh chapter relates to the sculptural art of the pre-medieval period. The eighth chapter deals with ornamentation in art, and the ninth contains the concluding remarks.

The present book is a welcome attempt towards study of the Sarnath School of art, particularly in view of the less number of books in Hindi on such topics of art. The author would do well to remove some grammatical mistakes and printing errors in the next edition. The book may prove to be very useful for both researchers and students interested in the study of art and architecture of Sarnath.

B.R. Mani

Sanyukta Koshal, *Ploughshares of Gods, Ladakh* vol.1, Om Publications, New Delhi, 2001- xxiv+643, colour plates 22, Price: Rs.2000/-

Amidst a vast desert of rock and sand, Ladakh, located in the northernmost region of India, with barren mountain ranges capped with snow, stretch through the area from south-east to north-west determining the courses of rivers as well as natural boundaries. Ladakh is one of the most elevated regions of the earth where the extreme dryness of the air, where temperature falls much below the freezing point, often throughout the year, except during summers. Besides rivers Indus, Zanskar, Shyok and Lakes, the main source of water remains the winter snowfall which feeds the glaciers whose melted waters carried down by streams, irrigate the fields in summer, particularly in Zanskar and Sunu Valleys.

As claimed, the present work no doubt provides detailed personalised description of the land and people, contemporary study of the region, including environment, agrarian and pastoral life, associated customs, based on careful field observation and thorough knowledge of the language and dialects possessed by the author.

The book is divided into seven chapters which deal with topography of the Region; Bounties of Nature; Thang, Spang, Nang, Tok-po Deserts; Pastures and Streams; Agriculture; Ownership Pattern of land and Property, and Labour; Trade and Development; and Folk Traditions. Besides above, there are two appendices -1) containing information about insects found in the region and 2) carrying excerpts from interviews of various local population. This is followed by a bibliography and an index. While describing the land, people, customs or economic activities of the people, the author has made the subject authentic and interesting by putting the essence of traditional inputs and folk material.

In the first two chapters, the striking physical features and landscape of Ladakh has been described giving short notes on its history, topography and geography. Chapter three not only describes the *thang* (deserts), *spang*, (pastures) and *tok-po* (streams) besides mountains and lakes of this high altitude moon-land, but also provides graphic narration of life attached to them and how the people of the land have exploited them for economic gains in the past.

The fourth chapter is dedicated to agriculture of the region and gives vivid picture of agricultural land, Cultivation, traditions, calculation of time for agriculture, pre-sowing and harvesting ceremonies, preparation for cultivation, making of iron tools, cutting, pruning and planting trees, selection of village official and village head, irrigation system, the curious job of Lo-ra-pa or the protector of the village crop who is empowered to fix fines upon the owner of the animal for damaging the crops, preparation of fields for sowing, including details of manure and watering and *sa-ka* ceremony, ploughing and sowing, weeding and details of harvesting along with ceremonies involved, measurements, coins and flora and fauna.

The fifth chapter contains details in connection with ownership of land and property including the powers of the king and the monastery, the middle class and the labour.

The sixth chapter deals with trade and development and traces in brief the history of exchange of commodities and formation of trade routes centuries ago which led to the establishment of trade centres like Leh Bazar. The chapter mentions both internal and external trade but it lacks in tracing out the nomadic movements in ancient times when it helped in connecting the land with the Silk Route through exchange of commodities and developed the trade links as evidenced by the Kushan inscriptions in the Indus and Karakorum valleys which gradually gave birth to the sub-routes which were frequented by the cultural entrepreneurs and plunderers in later times. The chapter, however, describes the present-day scenario of development and tourism. The seventh chapter is very interesting as it focuses on the folk traditions related to various occasions and festivities. The book contains just 22 colour photographs depicting life and scene of Ladakh which is too short a number in view of the vast scenic beauty of the land and material dealt upon.

Although the book is limited in time and space, yet it provides the results of thorough field work, deep observation and exhaustive investigation of research work required for a region which was till recently a forbidden land. The input of folk and traditional material helpful in understanding the land and the people has made this volume a useful reference book. The next volume of the series is expected to contain much more information of this kind.

B.R. Mani

Shashi Kant, *Hatigumpha Inscription of Kharavela, and the Bhabru Edict of Asoka*, xxiv+ 136 pages, two maps and eighteen plates, 2000, second edition, D.K. Printworld (P) Ltd., New Delhi, hardback, Price: Rs. 295/-

The book has three sections, which have six, four and two chapters respectively. The Hatigumpha inscription, though chronologically later, has been dealt with in section I, whereas Bhabru edict of Asoka, which is an earlier inscription in the next, Section II. The general issues like the genesis of the Prakrit dialect, origin of writing, and general discussions on Brahmi and Devanagari scripts are the subject matter of Section III.

The six appendices pertain to the text of the inscriptions in Nagari characters and render their translation in Hindi. The symbols in the Hatigumpha inscription as well as transcription chart of Brahmi script along with additional notes on the history of Jainism, date of *parinirvana* of Buddha and Mahavira, and Jaina religion with reference to Kalinga, Nanda and Mauryan kings are the subjects of other appendices. Appendix IV on chronology records useful absolute dates from Buddha's *parinirvana* (544 B.C.) till the incision of Hatigumpha inscription in 172 B.C.

The inscription has been compared with *prasasti* of Harisena of Samudra Gupta, popularly known as Allahabad stone pillar inscription of Samudra Gupta. (c. A.D. 335 - 76.). He has also fairly dealt with circumstances of the discovery of the inscriptions, the sites, text, Pali and Sanskrit renderings of the inscrintions and chronology thereof.

The campaigns and conquests of Maharaja Mahameghavahana Kharavela are discussed along with political alliances with confederacy of Tamil countries and Rathikas and Bhojokas. Festivals and fairs were organized to entertain people, some distinction was made between towns-men and villages-fold with regard to taxes, caste system, and polygamy. Temples were constructed and images were installed and worshipped. Primacy was given to Jainism, which appeared to be the state religion. Inscription of Kharavela begins with obeisance to Arahamtanam and Siddanam, showing royal inclination towards Jainism. The date of the inscription is 172 B.C.

The other inscription taken up by the author for study is Bhabru Edict of Asoka, which was found near Bairat on the Old Delhi - Jaipur Road, and is named after a camping station known as Bhabra or Bhabru, 6 *kos* (16 km) to the west of Bairat in the year A.D.1840. It is a well-preserved epigraph comprising eight lines. The main purpose of inscription was to exhibit the devotion of Asoka to *Buddha, Dhamma* and *Sangha.* He addresses himself as king of Magadha, an empire which included at least twelve *janapadas* viz. Anga, Magadha, Kasi, Kosala, Vajji, Malla, Vatsa, Chedi, Kuru, Panchala, Surasena and Matsya. Broadly, this is the Madhyadesa. Bairat, the capital of Matsya *janapada,* fell well within the empire of Asoka and within the core province of the empire. The chief contribution of the inscription is that line six of the inscription mentions the six-scriptures namely Vinaya-Samukasa, the Aliya-Vasas (*Vamsa*), Anagata-bhayas, Munigathas, Moneya-suta, Upatisa Pasina, and Laghulavada. The king exhorts the *bhiksus* and the laymen aiike that they should read, and follow these scriptures, which contain the commandments of Buddha. The author has identified properly these scriptures.

The author has utilized not only epigraphical and literary data, but also archaeological data revealed by the excavations at Udayagiri (*IAR 1961-62* - pp. 36-37 and *IAR 1958-59* pp. 38-40), district Puri, Orissa. He cites "That the shrine over Hatigumha, the ramp in front of it and the cave to which dexter wall leads were the product of single building activity. It thus confirms the epigraphic evidence as interpreted above about the location of the shrines of Kharavela and Sindhula as well as of the site for assembly of monks" (p. 70).

The author has given a rightful place to the technical part; but has mainly delved into the data to construct the political, social, and religious history of Orissa, as well as the then religious history of India.

R.P. Sharma

Amarendra Kumar Singh, *Temples of the Kalachuri Period*, Pratibha Prakashan, Delhi, 2002, xvi+ 118, Fig.16, Plates 90, Price: Rs. 1650/-.

The present book on the Kalachuri art and architecture comprises a comprehensive description of the temples, monasteries and sculptural wealth of Central India.

The book is divided into four chapters. The first chapter briefly introduces the need to study Kalachuri monuments, their chronology, three phases of evolution of the temple architecture, the decorative motifs used in the temples, influence of the Pratihara temples on the Kalachuri architecture and how Shaivism had influenced on the Kalachuri dynasty. The second chapter is entirely devoted to the political, geographical and dynastic history of the Kalachuries. The third chapter is an overview of the architectural developments which are discussed in terms of plans and elevation with the help of suitable illustrations. The last chapter describes thirty-five temples which are architecturally and sculpturally important, including monolithic temple of Manda, group of temples of Bandhogarh, Devi temple of Deorkothar, Shiva temple, monastery of Chandrehe, Siva temple of Khajuha and Chaturmukha Mahadeva temple of Nachna. The book is well supplemented by bibliography, glossary, and index and with ninety black and white plates.

The book is a welcome addition to the existing literature, as it deals with the temples which are less sophisticated and are more archaic in form and style compared to the other temples in Central India. It is also important to the students of temple architecture as it provides new data on this period. This is quite useful to study the pre-medieval and medieval architecture under the Chedis and Kalachuris in the *Dahaladesa,* including its major as well as minor-centres of architectural splendours. Though the author has discussed each temple with the help of ground plan and elevation, he has not dealt with the other features like the sculptural art and decorative motifs, etc. They are referred to only in brief. However, it is a very useful look for everyone interested in the subject.

Deccan College, Pune **Anuja Geetali**

Romano Mastromattei and Antonio Rigopoulos (ed), *Shamanic Cosmos, From India to the North Pole Star*, Venentian Academy of Indian Studies Series, No.1, D.K.Printworld (p) Ltd., New Delhi, 1999, pp.i-x + 252, colour photographs 10, line drawings 2, Price: Rs.320/-

The present work is a collection of 14 papers presented by various scholars in the First International Conference on Shamanism, which was held in Venice, Italy at the Auditorium Santa Margherita of the "Ca' Foscari", Venice University on October 11-12, 1996, organised by the Department of East Asian Studies of the University together with the Venetian Academy of Indian Studies and the Inter-University Centre for Research on Eurasian Shamanism. The symposium was prompted by the results of the field research conducted by the first editor and his team in Nepal and the adjoining Himalayan regions and by Prof. Gian Giuseppe Filippi and other Indologists of the Venice University. These scholars have contributed to the symposium and their field results comprising new data providing scientific interpretations on Shamanic conceptions present in Asian civilizations focusing upon the central issue of spatial organization.

Besides the two editors, contributors to this volume include V.N. Basilov, Benedicte Brac dela Perriers, Augusto Cacopardo, Gian Giuseppe Filippi, Giovanni Giuriati, Mihaly Hoppal, I .M. Lewis, Marcello Massenzio, Martino Nicoletti, Galina Ogudina, Valerio Sestini and Giovanni Torcinovich. Thus, the present Volume represents the proceedings of the symposium.

The editor of the work is correct in his assertion that in spite of much publications and discussions on the subject we are still discussing what shamanism is. V.N. Basilov in his paper gives the latest definition of Shamanism as it "is an early form of Polytheism, a special stage in the development of the religious beliefs of mankind which emerged in the period when hunting and gathering were the main means to support life". Shamanistic world-view suggests that the world is animated and inhabited by the spirits who can influence man's life, and human beings can acquire some qualities of a spirit and visit the other worlds as human society is one form of life which is closely connected with the cosmos. A shaman is assisted by spirits and he possesses some supernatural qualities and knowledge and can penetrate into the other world to communicate with the gods and spirits.

While Benedicte Brac de la Perriers gives the details of Naq cult of Burma, which became a component of the local Buddhism, Cacopardo gives an account of his field-work in 1973,1977 and 1989 in the Chitral district in Pakistan tracing the shamans and the sphere of the 'pure' among the Kalasha tribe of the Hindukush. In the shamanic symbols of riding and hunting, Filippi traces their origin in Indian ethnic tribes and in the Vedic cults. Lewis, Massenzio and Mastromattei discuss about shamamic cosmology and shamanic quality of space. While Giuriati traces shamanism in Khmer, Hoppal discusses about the same in Siberia to day.

Martino Nicoletti describes an interesting therapeutical ritual practiced by the Kulunge Rai of eastern Nepal which is known as say Pom or 'the rite for raising say'. This is practiced whenever the 'vital force' of an individual deteriorates or falls below its customary level of intensity.

The shamanic ideologies in question and answer form with reference to modern shamanism in Russian social life has been given by Ogudiana. Antonio Rigopoulor has given details of his field research in Maharashtra in 1991 with special reference to forms of possession in the Marathi cultural area describing the cases of Khandoba, the most important folk god and Dattātreya whose function as a healer has been associated with the Sufism, recognising the incarnations of him in the *pirs*. Sestini has traced the association of water bodies with Newan architecture based on mythological tales and legends, which were regarded as sacred places in Kathmandu valley right from the Licchavi period when the area witnessed the syncretic integration and amalgamation of ancient Buddhist and Hindu religious practices. The symbolism of horse associated with Sun and celestial journey to heaven of the shaman and the Vedic sacrifices is discussed by Giovanni Torcinovich. Collection of such thematic articles in this volume opens a new chapter in the investigative studies of the traditional shamanism and neo-shamanism in the Asiatic regions and depicts the concept of shamanism in understanding the cosmos and movement among the dead, spirits and gods. It would attract the readers who are interested in knowing more about the religious history, ethnology and socio-cultural and anthropological studies.

B.R. Mani

Arun Kesarwani, *Excavations at Balu (Distt. Kaithal -Haryana)*, Nirmal Book Agency, Kurukshetra, 2002, pp vi + 60, Maps 2, Figures 4, Plates 42, Price: Rs. 100/-

The present work is an excavation report of the site Balu, District Kaithal, Haryana. Balu is a Harappan settlement situated in the greater Saraswati valley, possibly along Apaga, a tributary of Saraswati. It is proved to be a very potential site excavated by the Kurukshetra University. The site was excavated, back in 1977 and in 1996-97 but only short reports were published. It is now somewhat more detailed report.

The report is divided into five chapters, starting with introduction informing readers about the history of archaeological research in the Haryana plains with special emphasis on the Protohistoric period. The second chapter is about the Early Harappan period in general and Early Harappan period at Balu informing us about the structures, ceramics, antiquities and botanical remains. The third chapter is also structured in the similar manner giving information about the Mature Harappan period. First the author gives the background of the First Urbanization with views of several scholars. The second part of this chapter gives details of the structural remains, their special features, pottery, antiquities and botanical remains. Similarly, the fourth chapter is devoted to the Late Harappan period with description of structures and features like drains, *bhattis* and ceramics. In the final and fifth chapter, the author surmises the entire excavation and appropriately assigns the function of the settlement as the agricultural village which was supplying food-grains to the major Harappan towns. The report is supplemented with list of a antiquities, bibliography and index.

The monograph is, however, too sketchy to take it as the full-fledged excavation report on Balu. If the printing of the photographs been on art paper, the details would have been better. Similarly, had the list of antiquities given the details about its period, locus, etc. it would have made it more useful. Still it is good effort on the part of the author to gather scattered data and publish them. This will help the researchers in Harappan archaeology to understand the dynamics of this culture in the eastern domain of the Harappan Civilization.

Tejas Garge

K.V. Raman and Srinivasan Srinivasan, *Studies in South Indian Coins* (eds.), New Era Publications, Chennai. 2001, pages 167 .

This volume on the *Studies of South Indian Coins* was released in Kerala in the XI Annual Conference of South Indian Numismatic Society. The current volume contains thirty-seven articles on south Indian coins and other cognate items, such as rings, religious tokens, Persian dinars and terracotta seals, covering a period from the Satavahanas to Cheras, Rashtrakutas, Kadambas, Vijayanagara, Venad kings, Mysore Sultans, Chanda Sahib, Wodeyars of Mysore and Rajahs of Travancore. Some of the important papers in the volume include Satavahana coins from the *Mahastupa* excavation at Kanganhalli in Karnataka, a lead coin of Chuttu-Anandas from Uttar Kannada, an unique identity ring from Karur, a terracotta seal of Krishnadevaraya from excavation at Bekal in Kerala. The ancient Greek coins by R. Krishnamurthy, is worth reading. The silver punch-marked coins from Karur establish the sway of the Cheras over it. The rest of the articles in the book are descriptive but well illustrated with photographs. The editors Dr. K.V. Raman and Srinivasan Srinivasan are doing yeoman service for bringing to light coins of south India and have ably edited this volume. The volume is a welcome addition for those who are interested in South Indian numismatic researches.

M. Rajesh

Parmeshwari Lal Gupta and Ajay Mitra Shastri (eds.), *Numismatic Digest* Vol. 21-22 (1997-1998), IIRNS Publications, Nasik, 2002 pp. ii + 179, Price: Rs. 350/-

This small book contains as many as nineten articles on coins of almost all the major dynasties like the Satavahanas, Kushanas, Western Kshatrapas, Yadavas, Vijayanagara kings, Bahmani sultans, Haider Ali and Tipu Sultan who ruled over Mysore region, besides articles dealing with coins, inscription, amulets, seal and sealing and their scientific analysis. Among the articles mention must made to B.N. Mukherjee's Vima Taktu,an alleged Kushana king, Ajay Mitra Sastri and Sanjay Godbole's 'A Silver coin of Yadava King Seunadeva', Michael Mitchiner's 'Some early Vijaya Silver Taras' belonging to three geographically separate series, K. Ganesh and Girijapathy's 'Some Rare coins of Haider Ali and Tipu Sultan' and Joe Cribb's 'Representations of Hindu epic Heroes on Javanese and Balinese coin- shaped amulets'.

Apart from 19 Articles, this volume contains two book reviews also.

This volume has been copiously and tastefully illustrated with photographs and line-drawings.

T. Arunraj

M.K. Dhavalikar, *Ellora-Monumental Legacy.* Oxford University Press, New Delhi. pp. 100+5, Illustrations 46, Price: Rs. 395/-

The Oxford University Press embarked into publishing a series of brief notes titled "Monumental Legacy", which describe cultural sites situated in India forming part of the World Heritage Sites. The author is an exponent in his field and brings *'Ellora'* to the readers with utmost simplicity. The historical background forms the base from where the author builds up in the rest of the chapters.

The work is concise and takes the readers on a journey into the evolution of Indian sculptural art. The author initiates his discussion with the development of cave temples in western India wherein cave making activity is glanced upon.

The influence of the three religions namely Hinduism, Buddhism and Jainism had a deep impact on the way cave-temple activity took its form and evolved. The author concentrates on each religion in different chapters by giving a brief backdrop and the corresponding influence in cave art and architecture. Each, of the caves described are supported by illustrations, drawing plans, maps and photographs. Coupled with this information, the author also discusses myths associated with the religions and their effective implementation in sculptural representations.

Rock-cutting activity has by no means been an ordinary feat achieved by our ancestors. The author's vivid description of this activity has enabled the readers to view the cave temples as a moving picture of life. It is a 'must' read for general readers as well as tourists.

Sonali Gupta

S.P. Gupta, Krishna Lal & Mahua Bhattacharyya, *Cultural Tourism in India-Museums, Monuments and Arts.* D.K. Printworld, New Delhi, 2002: Price: Rs. 390/- (Paperback)

In the promotion of Tourist industry in India Cultural Tourism alone has the vital role to play. India is very distinctive in presenting a vast panorama of grand cultural mosaic-diverse ethnic groups, languages faiths, dress and ornaments, social customs and practices, art and architecture, music and dance, pilgrim centres and holy spots. Each region has contributed its mite to this multifaceted cultural pattern that has made even the western scholars like Prof. A.L. Basham to exclaim "The wonder that is India". If one takes even a single item like the Buddhist, Hindu and Islamic architecture one can see the remarkable variety and stylistic patterns. The richness and the continuity of many traditional and institutions have been the hallmark of Indian civilization, rightly ranked as one of the major civilizations of the world. For one who wishes to undertake a cultural tour of our country and enjoy the beauties of this mosaic, this volume provides excellent introduction. The thoughtfully prepared and lucidly written by experienced authors, the book presents a highly informative account of all the important historical places, pilgrim- centres, festivals, state-wise monuments, cultural institutions, handicrafts and museums- major and minor-which display the treasures of our cultural heritage.

Now that a regular degree course or Tourism has come up in several universities in India, this book would serve as an ideal text book for students and teachers alike. For professionals, it provides valuable data on the organization of package tours, tour circuits and planning, training guides and marketing of tourism, tourist information centres in India and abroad. The appendices give detailed accounts of latest cultural policy in India (2002) as well as several national and international conventions and their resolutions. Excellent colour photographs, maps and plans add to the utility of the volume.

The book is recommended to all, students, professionals and visitors to our country.

K.V. Raman

S.P. Gupta and Shashi Prabha Asthana: *Elements of Indian Art*, Published by Indraprastha Museum of Art and Archaeology, B-17, Qutab Institutional Area, New Delhi-110 016 and D.K. Printworld (P) Ltd., New Delhi 2002. Price: Rs. 200/- (Paperback)

Hindustan has recognized the validity of conceiving of god both as the abstact *Nirguna-Brahman* and formless *(arupa)* as well as *Saguna-Brahman;* full of auspicious qualities and with myriad forms *(rupa and vyakta).* The abstract Vedic deities like Aditya Agni, Rudra, Varuna who were invoked and propitiated in the Vedic fine-altars were later on given iconic forms and worshiped in temples. The Agamas and the Bhakti ideology expounded the validity of the temple *(sthala)* and the icon *(murti)* and the latter was revered as the *archa-avatara* (idol incarnation). The temple was not only the home of god but also his form *Vastu-Purusha.*

The *Vastu* and the *Silpa* texts explain in great detail the different forms of the temples like *Nagara, Dravida* and *Vasara* and their numerous expanded regional variations. They also tell us about the concepts and symbolisms of the temple as miniature universe (cosmos); *Meru* symbolism, etc. The authors have done well to explain the various conceptual symbolism of the temple.

The *Agamic* and *Silpa* texts elaborately deal with the iconographic features *(pratima-lakshanas)* of the Hindu deities-*asanas,* hand gestures *(hastas and mudras)*, ornaments, weapons mounts *(vaharas).* Similarly, the Buddhist architectural forms like the *stupa chaitya* and vihara and their symbolisms have their own interesting story to tell. The Buddhists also have numerous iconomic representations like the Bodhishatvas Dhyani Buddhas and goddesses like Tara while the Jains have their own distinctive temples and icons.

The authors of this volume, well-known archaeologists and art-historians of our country, have taken great pains and presented this complex subject in simple language and suitable illustrations for easy understanding of the subject by the common man. All the important technical terms used in architectural and iconographic texts are explained in great detail. The authors have also cleared some of the misconceptions regarding idol-worship by focusing on the principles of visualization of symbols and signs. All the important schools and styles in Indian temple forms and sculptures are described with more than 300 illustrations and line-drawing. The authors have to be complimented for presenting a handy reference book on Indian Art-highly informative.

K.V. Raman

T. Padmaja: *Temples of Krishna in South India (History, Art and Traditions in Tamil Nadu)*, pages 198, photographs 105, Abinav Publications, New Delhi, 2002. Price: Rs. 900/-

The Bhakti movement in India concentrated on Siva

and Vaishavana *devatas* of his *parivara* propagated by the *nayanmars* and *alvars*. However, it is a fascinating story as to how the various individual *devatas*, worshipped in India independent of each other, were brought together to form the *parivaras*. One powerful mechanism evolved in Vaishnavism was that of *Avataravada* or Incarnations of Vishnu. Through this mechanism even Buddha was incorporated in Vaishnavism.

It is common knowledge that out of the ten or more *avataras*, Krishna and Rama became the prominent ones, although in the beginning both appear to be the centres of their own cults. For example, the Krishna cult had its roots in the 'Panchvira' worship in the *vyuha* format at places like Mathura in the early centuries of the Common Era (C.E). In Tamil Nadu it continued up to 8th century. In many parts of south India, from the 9th century the Krishna cult replaced it and inspired poets, devotees, kings, courtiers and common men to come forward and get monumental images and temples built in different parts of Tamil Nadu. The present work deals with these subjects. The author has made a complete survey of the Krishna temples in Tamil Nadu according to different regions. The author has not only given details of the temples but also of the deities and sculptures therein besides going into the details of the history of these temples, their art forms, themes, the traditions underlying them. She has also taken care to study all the inscriptions which throw light on them. She has gone deep into the literature enlightening the subject of Krishna-bhakti and the specific temples.

In one of the chapters, the fifth, the author deals with the beautiful Krishna themes portrayed in bronzes, woodcarvings, stone sculptures also. It is significant to note that she has included the temple-paintings also which are no less significant than the bronzes and stone sculptures.

It is a beautifully designed and produced work of great research value.

S.P. Gupta

S.L. Shali, *Settlement Pattern in Relation to Climatic Changes in Kashmir*, Om Publications, New Delhi, 2001, pp xxi + 383, Figures and Plates 48. Price: Rs. 500/-

The valley of Kashmir has witnessed a rich past which is reflected in its cultural, literary, archaeological and oral traditions. Geographical settings and the environmental conditions of the Kashmir valley has been a major factor influencing the human settlements since the early times. Settlement pattern study in Indian archaeology is still in the preliminary stage and the present work is the only and the first attempt to study the settlement systems in the Kashmir valley.

The first chapter is an introduction to the background, aims and objectives of the present book. Basic theme remains that settlement patterns changed with the change in the environment and climate. The study also involves wide range of socio-economic problems which affected settlement patterns in relation to climatic changes in the Kashmir valley.

The second chapter deals with the geological events that led to the development of the landform in the valley with changes in the palaeoclimate. These changes are also reflected in the literature and oral traditions. The literary records and the legends indicating these geological and climatic changes are successfully traced by the author here. A brief review of the material cultures which prevailed in the valley also appears in this chapter.

The third chapter is about the Prehistoric period of the Kashmir valley. It begins with the literary records regarding the Prehistoric period and references in relation to original settlers of Kashmir in Vedas and Puranas. The second part deals with archaeological remains from Palaeolithic period to Historical times in terms of technology, settlement patterns, ethnography of the (modern parallels) settlements, rituals and means of subsistence and economy.

The fourth chapter is entirely devoted to the Early Historical period and the main focus of discussion is Iron Age and Megalithic cultures with their physical distribution. The settlement and subsistence pattern remains the main key of this chapter. A small account of the Indo-Greek settlements is also given here.

The fifth chapter entitled 'Cultural Expansions' is about the Historical period with favourable climatic conditions which witnessed development under Kushanas in trade, agriculture, art and architecture. Again, the settlement patterns, social structure within the settlements, subsistence pattern, religion, literature, art and architecture are the main components of this chapter.

The post- Kushana period is the theme of discussion of the sixth chapter. Political history of this period is given in detail. Social structure, administrative organization, religion, ceramics, coinage, literature, art and architecture, subsistence and finally their impact on the settlement pattern form the main premise of this chapter. Though the author has discussed the political, social and economic developments of each period in detail, still the main factor affecting the settlement pattern remains the natural settings of the Kashmir valley. For example, decline of the Kushans in the Kashmir valley was due to excessive snowfall and the prosperity in the post-Kushana period is ascribed to the favourable climatic conditions.

Each chapter is supported with detailed notes and references which are quite useful for further reading. In the end, a detailed bibliography and index are given. The author has provided as many as 48 illustrations and plates to support the text.

Generally, settlement pattern studies involve application of various theory models and numerical data related with environment as well size, function and extent of the settlements. The layout of data in numerical and tabular form would have made this book more useful. Still, the most important contribution of this book is the application of the historical data to study the climatic changes in relation to the settlement pattern. The book is recommended to specialists as well as the common readers.

Tejas Garge

Laxman S. Thakur, *Buddhism in the Western Himalaya*, (A Study of the Tabo Monastery) Oxford University Press, New Delhi, 2001, pp. xxii+332; 21 figures, 80 plates, price not given.

The western Himalayas was a centre of attraction for the Buddhists who developed the Lama form of Buddhism which can be described as Tantrik Mahayana. Here they remained safe and did not face the persecution in the hands of Muslim invaders who destroyed Nalanda, Odantpuri and other great centres of Buddhist studies in Bihar and Bengal.

At a place called 'Tabo', located in the Spiti basin of Himachal Pradesh in the Lahul-Spiti District, the Buddhists established a temple in the year AD 996 which later on developed a complex of as many as nine structural units. The temples here are full of beautiful wall paintings, sculptures and architectural beauties, datable to two periods: AD 996-1050 and 1450-1974. There are also epigraphical records of great historical value.

Dr. Laxman S. Thakur, a scholar who has studied the great wealth of there works of art, has re-drawn the plans and elevations of these monuments and corrected the defects he found in the earlier works of A.H. Francke, G.Tucci and Romi Khosla. Hence, the documentation is now accurate and complete for all those interested in the subject.

The book has been divided into eight chapters : (i) Ecological and Economic Setting, (ii) Historical and Cultural Perspective, (iii) Architectural Emplacements, (iv) Sculpture and Iconography, (v and vi), The Vanishing Murals, (vii) Epigraphical Evidence, (viii) Tabo Monastery Today and its Future.

The treatment of the subject, therefore, is exhaustive. The art and iconography, influences on them—Persian, Central Asian, Tibetan and Chinese—names of artists and patrons, etc. make the work extremely valuable for the art historians all over the world. The bibliography is exhaustive but the book lacks index. However, it is recommended to all individuals and institutions devoted to Buddhist studies. It is indeed a monumental work.

S.P. Gupta

Dilip K. Chakrabarti, *Archaeological Geography of the Ganga Plain:The Lower and the Middle Ganga*. Permanent Black, Delhi, 2001. 307 pp. maps, plates, index. Rs.1095/-

This book discusses the ancient historical geography of the lower and middle sections of the Ganga plain consisting of the areas covered by the Chotanagpur plateau which borders the area on the west and the Bangladesh section of the Ganga delta which lies to its east. The eastern limit of the study-area is the Sagar island south of Kolkata and its western border is an irregular line running through the trans-Sarayu plain in Bahraich and adjoining Faizabad, Sultanpur, Pratapgarh and Allahabad districts. Further, south of the Yamuna in Allahabad traverses have been taken up to Chitrakut and Kalinjar and south of the Ganga between Banaras and Mirzapur. Similar traverses were taken upto Robertsganj and the border of Surguja in Madhya Pradesh to understand the nature of the middle Ganga plain's links with central India. The major hill range which flanks the valley on the west between Bhagalpur and Munger and sends outliers right up to the river bank is the Kharagpur range. Westward from Maldaha and west Dinajpur in West Bengal, the northern bank of the Ganga provides a broad and uninterrupted sweep of alluvium which is fringed far to the north by the line of the Siwaliks in Nepal.

First the study proposes to establish the proto-historic perspective extending well back into the third millennium BC Secondly, the importance of exploration is given a proper recognition as well.

The base line of the study is the sites which have already been published in different areas. The main geographical issues of this study are the locations of sites, the historical linkages of different areas, the problems of ancient political geography and finally the major routes passing through these areas.

In the context of the Mahananda plain the abiding significance of Varendra as a geo-political unit in the history of the Ganga plain is being highlighted. A chain of inscriptions from the Maurayas in the third century B.C. to the Palas and Senas till the twelfth-thirteenth centuries AD are being used for this analysis. According to Chakravarti that such a geo-politically significant area must likely to have had a proto-historic antecedent, although the direct testimony is still not more than a fragment of a Black and Red Ware bowl from the surface of Bangarh.

In conclusion, Chakrabarti draws attention to only two major archaeological tasks ahead in the lower and middle Ganga plain. The first is to determine the origin, character and spread of its neolithic antecedent. The second concerns the region on the western bank of the Bhagirathi in the lower Ganga plain, it is perhaps connected in some way with the newly emergent Orissan neolithic at Golbai Sasan, whereas in the case of the middle Ganga plain, the role of the Vindhyan region has to be considered.

The book rests on extensive cross references from diverse disciplines. It has been able to capably frame the issues relating to topographical connection of Ganga valley with other parts of India.

The statements of archaeological dispersal, however, seem to be mainly conjectural, primarily because Black and Red Ware ceramics like a dominant colour seem to mar variations in the entire region under consideration and exhibit a false uniformity.

Like all other works of Chakrabarti, this work also does not cover any issue in depth. It is also true that covering of such an enormous canvas does not leave any space for an author for deeper probe.

Department of Anthropology
Delhi University-110 007

Sruti Kona Dey

S. Settar and Ravi Korisettar (eds.) *Indian Archaeology in Retrospect (in 4 volumes).* ICHR and Manohar Publishers and Distributors, New Delhi, 2002. Price Rs.1250/- each volume.

Indian Archaeology in Retrospect is the result of a very far-sighted planning made by the Indian Council of Historical Research.

A total of 59 papers have been compiled in 4 volumes. These papers reflect the changing attitudes and methodologies in the field of archaeology and also give direction for future work.

Prehistory- Archaeology of South Asia forms the subject matter of Volume I. The papers discuss the progress made in the fields of Paleolithic, Neolithic, Chalcolithic and Megalithic cultures along with prehistoric art, ceramics and beads. This volume has 4 appendices, which provide detailed information on various sites explored and excavated till date in the upper Paleolithic, Neolithic and Megalithic periods.

The focus of Volume II is on Protohistory, the archaeology of the Indus-Saraswati Civilisation and the progresses made in its study in the post-independence period. The papers are contributed by scholars of repute and deal with topics like the Indus script, Harappan technology, religion, pastoralism, social organisation, symbolism, etc. The year to year advent made in the study of this civilization is clearly reflected in the papers presented. The scholars have discussed the fundamentals of this great civilization from its origin to its zenith and subsequent end. With the help of multidisciplinary investigation, a broad framework of this civilization has been brought forth and allows us to view it from a better perspective.

Volume III- Archaeology and Interactive Disciplines', gives a whole picture of South Asian Archaeology. Themes include Ethnography, Palaeoclimate, Palynology, Pedology, Archaeozoology, Archaebotany , Bioanthropology of the living and prehistoric communities, dating, preservation and conservation methods. The importance of archaeology and its relationship with geology and natural sciences is discussed.

'Archaeology and Historiography' - History, theory and methods, is the final volume of the series. This volume around theoretical and methodological developments in Indian archaeology.

Details of the progress made in chronological sequences, the study of the inter-relationship of prehistory with the Quaternary science, the history of the great epics, the *Ramayana* and the *Mahabharata*, have been examined in an archaeological framework, the review of the work of the Archaeological Survey of India and the latest techniques in the field of archaeology amongst others have been marine The papers highlight the paradigm shifts in Indian archaeology along with our changing perceptions.

It is a very fine publication and is recommended for individuals as well as institutions.

Sonali Gupta

Dilip K. Chakrabarti, *Archaeology in the Third World-A History of Indian Archaeology since 1947*, D.K. Printworld (P) Ltd., New Delhi, 2003, pp.281.

The book is arranged into five chapters with bibliography, index and an appendix 'Towards a nationalist archaeology in India'. In the first chapter the author outlined the main compulsive issues facing the Indian archaeology during 1947-52. The archaeologists in India realized in 1947 that the main sites of the Harappan Civilization have remained in Pakistan. They also realized that a hiatus exists between the end of the Harappan Civilization and beginning of the Early Historical period. The need for the survey of prehistoric sites was also felt. With the arrival of Sir Mortimer Wheeler in India and the publication of *Ancient India* by Archaeological Survey of India, the archaeology of India took strides in the right direction, especially in the fields of prehistory and protohistory.

In the second chapter the year 1974 has been taken as the most important one due to publication of *Prehistory and Protohistory of India and Pakistan* by H.D. Sankalia. The author also refers to some major books of the period from 1975 to 1981, including the early issues of *Puratattva* and *Man and Environment*. The problem of the beginning of iron, leading to a number of postulates, new trend in prehistoric studies, and concern with history of technology and mediaeval archaeology have also been discussed. The period from 1983 to 1989 is referred to as the time of major discoveries and studies in prehistory, including area-studies. The publications brought out from 1990 to 2000 and their concerns with 'theory' in archaeology have also found place.

The third chapter provides a useful summary of procedures dealing with heritage management, education and nationalism, whereas in chapter four, the problems of the preservation of archaeological heritage in modern India have been explained for our understanding of both individual buildings and building types. The last chapter deals with the 'Common Denominators of Third World Archaeology' with India as an example.

The book is a good attempt for understanding the history of Indian archaeology during the last three decades.

K.N. Dikshit

REPORT OF THE XXXV ANNUAL CONFERENCE

Report of the XXXV Annual Conference of Indian Archaeological Society held at The Maharaja Sayajirao University of Baroda, Vadodara, Gujarat from 22nd - 24th November, 2001

The Annual Conference of the three Societies namely Indian Archaeological Society, Indian Society for Prehistoric and Quaternary Studies and Indian History and Culture was inaugurated by the Hon' able Dr. Mrinalini Devi Puar, Chancellor, Maharaja Sayajirao University of Baroda, Vadodara on the 22nd November, 2001. Ms. Kasturi Gupta Menon, Director General, Archaeological Survey of India was the guest of Honour.

After the inaugural function, Prof. Thimma Reddy delivered the Presidential Address of the Indian Society for Prehistoric and Quaternary Studies followed by Prof. M.G.S. Narayanan of Indian History and Culture Society. As Dr.M.S. Nagarajarao was unable to attend, the Presidential Address of the Indian Archaeological Society could not be read. The closing function was held on the 24th November, 2001 and Prof. V.D. Pathak gave valedictory Address.

23rd November, 2001: Forenoon Session

SEMINAR ON ARCHAEOLOGY OF WESTERN INDIA

The theme was introduced by Prof. B.P. Sinha and Prof. B.B. Lal. Other participants were Prof. A. Sundara, Dr. Viraj Shah and Sri O.N. Chauhan. They discussed the role of recent archaeological discoveries and their implications on the archeology of Western India.

The paper on the Genesis of the Harappan Civilization by Prof. M.D.N. Sahi received varied academic comments. Prof. B.B. Lal, M.K. Dhavalikar, S.P. Gupta, D.V. Sharma, Manoj Kumar, Ashok Singh, Sukanya Sharma, Rajeev Pandey, R.C. Agarwal, Suman Pandeya and K.N. Dikshit participated in the discussion. It was concluded that more data is required for arriving at any definite conclusion.

CONFERENCE PAPERS

A. Sundara

Western India and the Krishna Valley: The Protohistoric Tradition

Viraj Shah

Jaina Caves of Maharashtra: Historical Perspective

O.N. Chauhan

Eighteen Fiftyseven, depicted in wooden architecture at Swaminarain temple in Ahmedabad

M.D.N. Sahi

The Genesis of the Harappan Civilization

D.N. Tripathi

Indian Western Asian Cultural Contact with special reference to Western Indian Archaeology

P. Rajendran

Megalithic Cultural Evidences at Kunnoni in the light of the Oliyani Cist Burial excavation, Kottayam District, Kerala

S.K. Bhatt

The Impact of Tradition on the Coinage of Ujjayani

Sharmi Charkraborty

Wooden Artefacts from Chandraketugarh

D.V. Sharma

Excavation at Madarpur - an OCP site

Alok Tripathi

Underwater Exploration of Mahabalipuram

23rd November, 2001: Afternoon Session

Ravindra Nath Singh

Scientific Examination of Steatite Beads from Imlidih Khurd

Sashi Bala Srivastava

Introduction of Divine Images in Temple Architecture

K.N. Deka

On the Background of the Brahmaputra Civilization

A.K. Singh

Saivite Monastic complex of the Kalachuris at Chunari in Central India

N.R. Patgiri

The Role of the Kamata Kingdom

Subra Pramanik

Exploration in and around Junagadh, Gujarat

Naina Pandey

Buddhakalin Samajik Parivesh-Nagarikaran Me Iska Yogdan

R.P. Sharma

Early Historical Settlement Pattern in Ganga-Yamuna Doab

S.C. Bindra

Computer Aided Design of a Vedic Period Merchant Vessel - A Study

I.S. Vishwakarama

Some Aspects of Archaeology of Saryupar Region

Mr. Homi Dhalla

On Parsi Archaeology

V. Shivananda

Recent Exploration in Meghalaya

D.V. Sharma

Conservation of Anup Talao, Fatehpur Sikri

A.K. Singh

A Spectacular Discovery of metal objects from NBP, Agaibir

24th November, 2001: Forenoon Session

S.K. Aruni

Architecture of Nolambavadi in south India

Manila Rastogi

Prostitute: The Multi-Dimensional figure in Ancient India

Arakhita Pradhan

Archaeology of Asurgarh sites in Western Orissa: A Case study of Asurgarh sites at Badmal Tehsil Rairakhol, District Sambalpur

S. Radhkrishnan

A Peep in the Alwar Tradition of Tamilakkam

Mira Sharma

Bhusparsh Mudra ki Buddh Pratimayae: Ek Vishleshan

Mala Malla

Gilding Technology in Nepal

Bharati Shroti

Gandhrava puri ki Durlabh Haygrive Pratima

Suman Pandaya, et.al.

Rani ki Vav-Their Builders

Subhash Brahmbhatt

The Gujarati Style of Islamic Architecture of Ahmedabad

Nirmala Sharma

Flora in Indian Miniature Painting

24th November, 2001: Afternoon Session

P.B.S. Sengar

Black Taj-Myth in Reality

Punya Baruah

A Study of the Ancient Technology found on a few artifacts on North-East, Jorhat, Assam

Vasant Shinde

Excavations at Gilund

Dhanpat Singh Dhania

Deciphering Harappan Mystery

Rajeev Pandey

Exploration and Antiquities of Shahjahanpur

B.R. Mani

Excavation at Ambaran: Akhnur terracotta heads and discovery of Buddhist relics in the exposed Stupa

Ajit Kumar

Some Terracotta figures from Megalithic Urn burials at Malampuzha, District Palaghat, Kerala

B-17, Qutab Institutional Area,
New Delhi-110 016

K. N. Dikshit
General Secretary
Indian Archaeological Society

THE INDIAN ARCHAEOLOGICAL SOCIETY

BALANCE SHEET AS ON 31.03.2002

LIABILITIES		AMOUNT	ASSETS		AMOUNT
CAPITAL FUND			FIXED ASSETS		
Op. Balance	22,57,216.16		(As per Schedule 'A' attached)		13,897,540.00
Add:L.M.Fees	32,115.00				
:Donation for vehicle-Capitalised	2,00,000.00		Current Assets & Investment		
:Income over Expenditure	5,48,318.41		Fixed Deposits	314,339.00	
	30,37,649.57		Accrued Interest	97,839.00	3,244,168.00
Less: transferred to Corpus Fund	100,000.00	2,937,649.57	Indian Council of Historical Res.		11,000.00
CORPUS FUND	1,500,000.00		Delhi Vidyut Board		86,886.00
Add:- transfer from Capital Fund	100,000.00	1,600,000.00	Tax Deducted at Source	21,251.00	
BUILDING FUND		8,858,263.00	Less: Received	19,388.00	1,863.00
Dr. A.K. Narain (Award) Fund		50,000.00	SUNDRY DEBTORS		
Donation for Cupboards		20,000.00	(As per Annexure 'E' attached		80,775.00
Donation for Podium		25,000.00			
Donation for Books		19,000.00	CASH & BANK BALANCES		
PROJECTS FUND			Indian Bank-460017		82,045.15
(As per Annexure 'B' attached)		454,344.46			
Securities			S.B.I. - 45062		41,205.32
(As per Annexure 'C' attached)		995,976.00			
ADVANCES			S.B.I.-45082		34,241.71
Bharat Sanskrit Parishad		1,500,000.00			
Akhil Bhartiya Itihas Sanklan Yojna		450,000.00	Cash in Hand		17,296.39
Loan:- Dr. S.P. Gupta		400,000.00			
Current Liabilities					
Sundry Creditors					
(As per Annexure 'D' attached)		186,797.54			
		17,497,030.57			17,497.030.57

Sd/ Sd/ Sd/

Chairman Treasurer For Rajan Sharma & Co., Chartered Accountant

Place: New Delhi
Daed: 10.10.2002

(Rajan Kumar Sharma)
Prop.

THE INDIAN ARCHAEOLOGICAL SOCIETY

INCOME EXPENDITURE ACCOUNT FOR THE YEAR ENDED 31.03.2002

PARTICULARS	AMOUNT (RS.)	PARTICULARS	AMOUNT (RS.)
To Honorarium	250,140.00	By Grant from I.C.H.R.-Conf. 35	60,000.00
To Municipal Taxes	400,000.00	By Grant from I.C.H.R.-Conf. 34	5,000.00
To Publication Expenses	123,619.00	By Grant from I.C.H.R.-Pura 30	26,500.00
To News Paper & Periodicals	639.00	By Grant from I.C.H.R.-Pura 31	50,000.00
To Medical Expenses	1,847.00	By Grant for Pura 30-ASI	25,000.00
To Telephone Expenses	52,281.000	By Sale of literature	71,464.00
To Conveyance & Travelling	72,971.00	By Annual Membership Fees	100.00
To Printing & Stationary	32,117.00	By Water Charges	6,915.00
To Electricity Charges	168,061.00	By Electricity Charges	27,550.00
To Generator Running & Maint.	1,150.00	By Bank Interest	349,005.41
To Conference Expenses	63,342.00	By Rent	2,051,659.50
To Computer Rep. & Maintenance	49,528.00		
To Establishment Expenses	76,156.50		
To Repairs & Maintenance	439,385.00		
To Staff Welfare	8,447.00		
To Car Running & Maintenance	77,042.00		
To Car Insurance	12,818.00		
To Postage & Stamps	25,549.00		
To Internet Charges	4,974.00		
To Bank Charges	3,160.00		
To Board Meeting Expenses	1,630.00		
To Diwali Expenses	3,098.00		
To Ground Rent-DDA	23,000.00		
To Heritage Helpmates corpus	2,000.00		
To one Day Seminar-National Mus.	1,300.00		
To Prof. A.K. Narain Award	5,000.00		
To Audit Fees	21,000.00		
To Professional Charges	17,500.00		
To Tender Expenses	2,000.00		
To Short & Excess	1.00		
To Depreciation	185,120.00		
To Excess of Income over expenditure	548,318.41		
	2,673,193.91		2,673,193.91

Sd/
General Secretary

S/-
Treasure

Sd/
For Rajan Sharma & Co.,
Chartered Accountant

(Rajan Kumar Sharma)
Prop.

Place: New Delhi
Dated: 10.10.2002

OFFICE BEARERS OF THE INDIAN ARCHAEOLOGICAL SOCIETY

Headquarter:

INDIAN ARCHAEOLOGICAL SOCIETY
B-17, Qutab Institutional Area, South of IIT, New Delhi - 110 016
Tel.: 2652-3728 Tele-Fax:011-2696-0654
E-mail: ias_newdelhi@yahoo.co.uk
K.N. Dikshit: 2694-8971
K.S. Ramachandran: 2695-5209

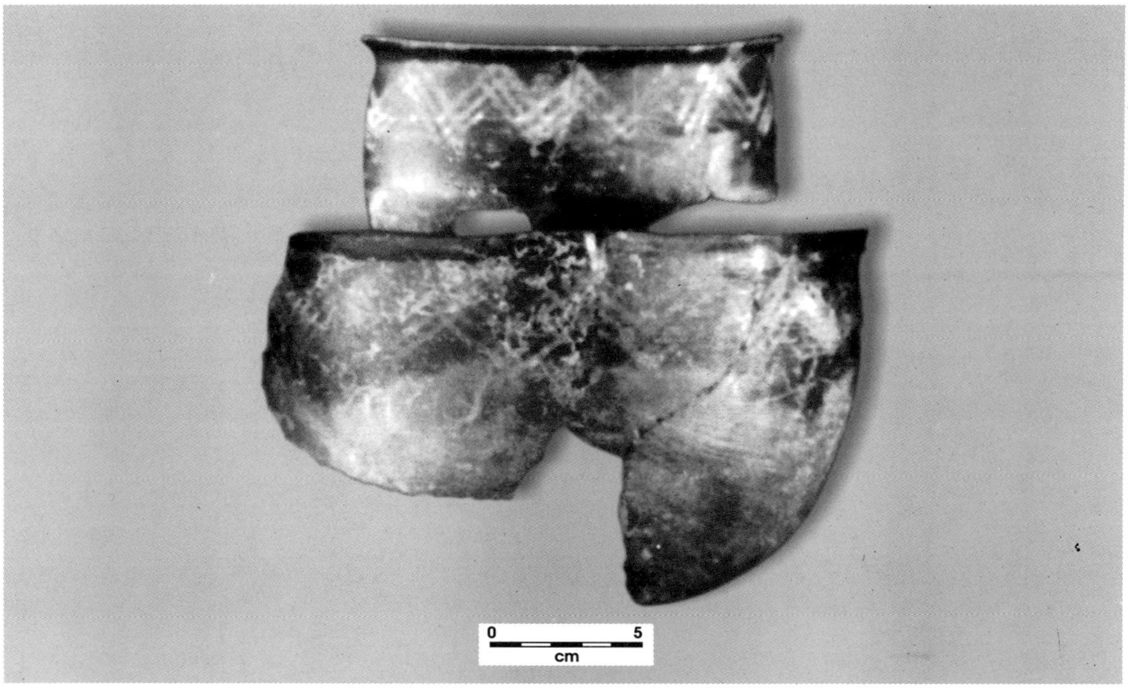

Shinde. P1. 1: Black and Red Ware, Gilund

Shinde. P1. 2: Coarse Grey Ware Globular Pot, Gilund

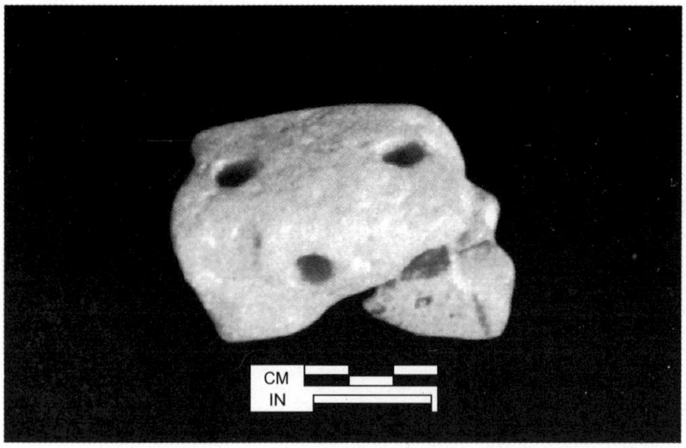

D.V. Sharma. P1. 1: Fragment of terracotta toy cart, Madarpur.

D.V. Sharma. P1. 2: Specimen with graffiti marks, Madarpur.

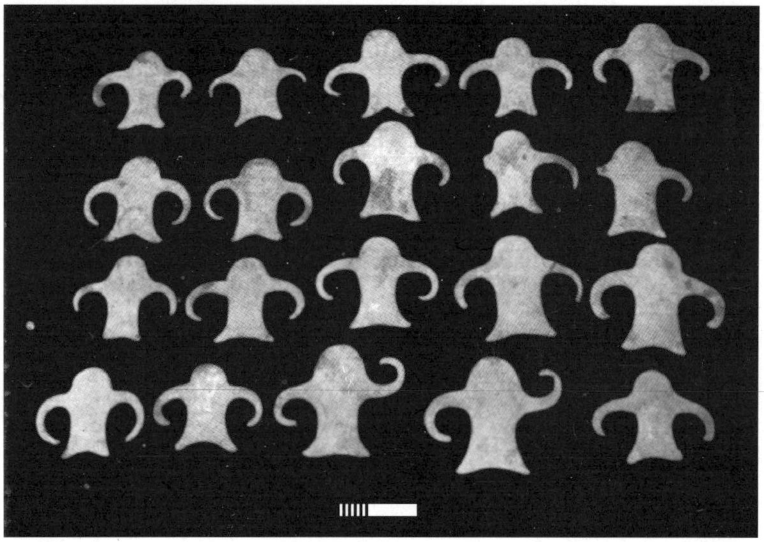

D.V. Sharma. P1. 3: Copper Anthropomorphic figures, Madarpur. (Before chemical cleaning)

D.V. Sharma. P1. 4: Anthropomorphic figure showing right hand upraised.

D.V. Sharma. P1. 5: Another Anthropomorphic figure showing left hand upraised.

Tewari, *et al.* P1. 1: Representative potsherds, Period I B, Lahuradeva.

Tewari, *et al.* P1. 2: White painted black slipped Ware, Period II, Lahuradeva.

Tewari, *et al.* P1. 3: Decorated potsherds, incised patterns, Period II, Lahuradeva.

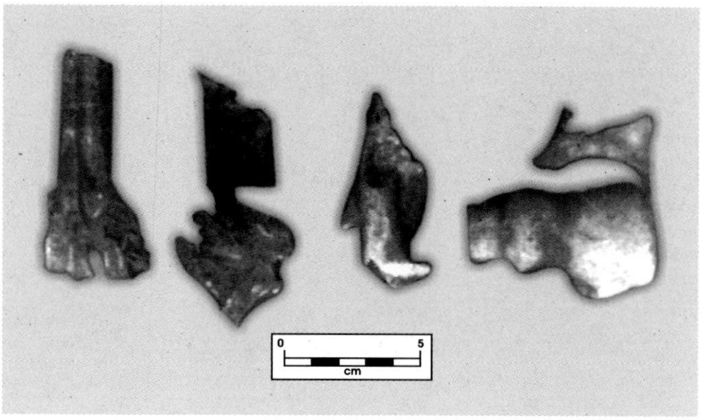

Joglekar. P1. 1: Mamalian bone fragments, Kelshi

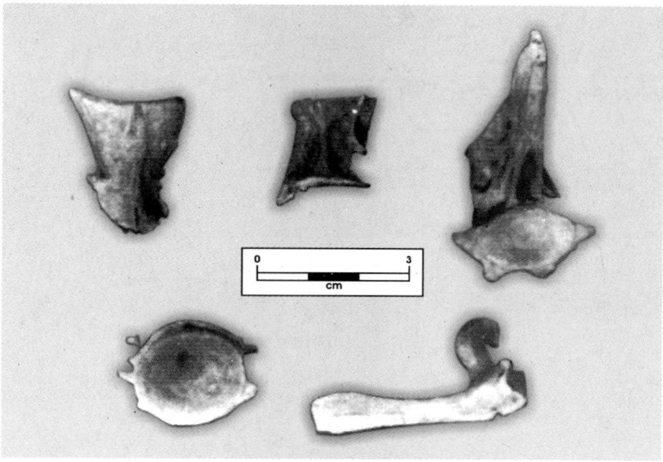

Joglekar. P1. 2: Fragments of vertebrate and spines, Kelshi

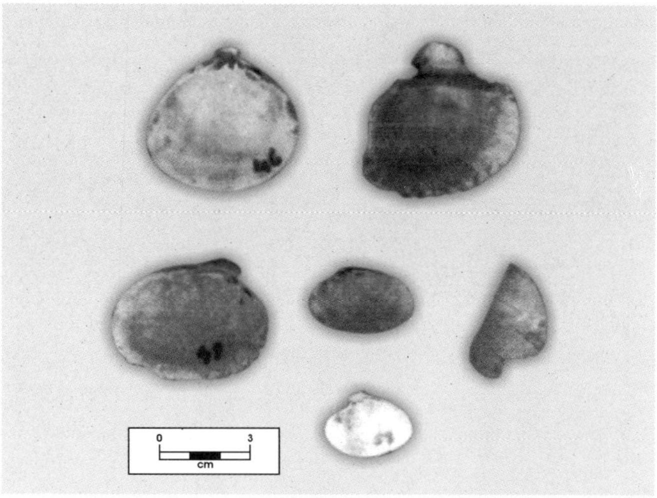

Joglekar. P1. 3: Molluscan shells, Kelshi

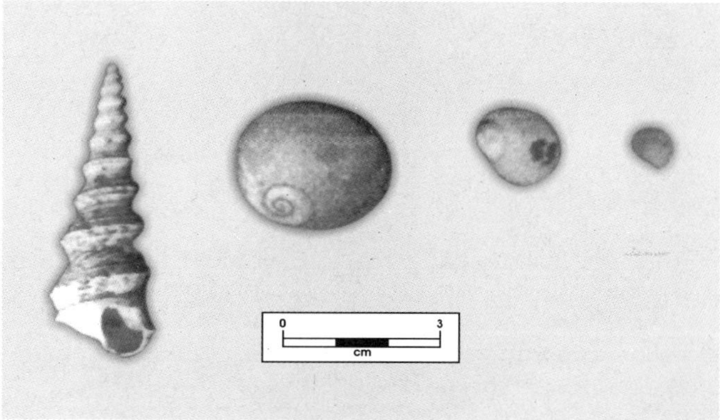

Joglekar. P1. 4: Molluscan shells, Kelshi

Amarendra Nath. P1. 1: Decorated portion of thick trough, period IV, PKD I.

Amarendra Nath. P1. 2: A view of the cuttings showing Menhirs numbered 1 to 4 from left of right, PKD-II

Alok Tripathi. P1. 1: Mahabalipuram: submerged architectural member.

Alok Tripathi. P1. 2: Mahabalipuram: part of a submerged structure.

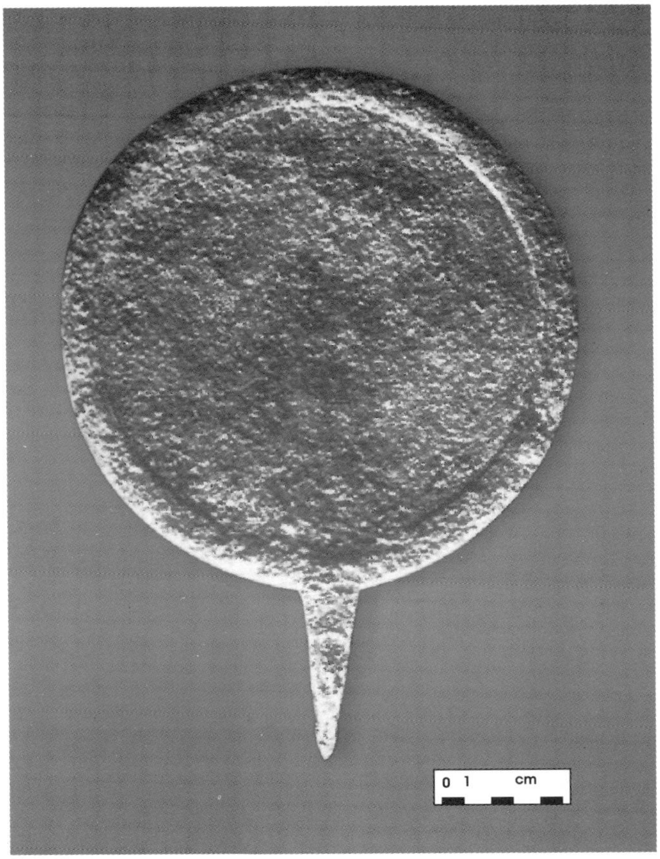

Singh & Chattopadhyay P1. 1: Copper-Bronze mirror, Mahasthangarh.

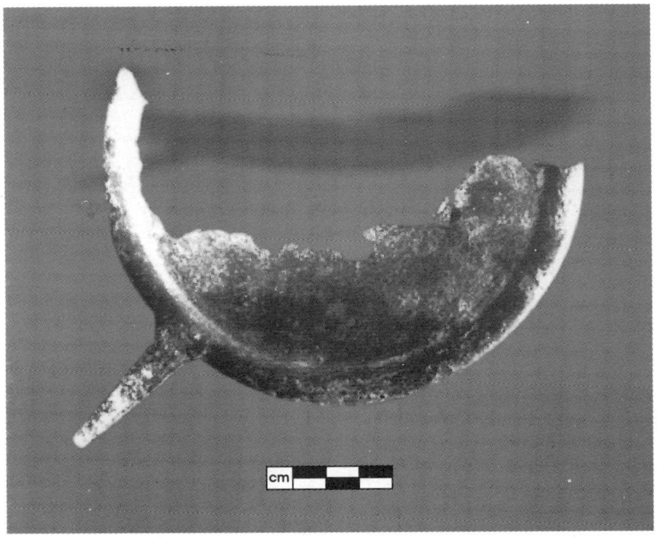

Singh & Chattopadhyay P1. 2: Copper-Bronze mirror, Chandraketugarh.

Singh & Chattopadhyay P1. 3: Copper-Bronze mirror, Agiabir.

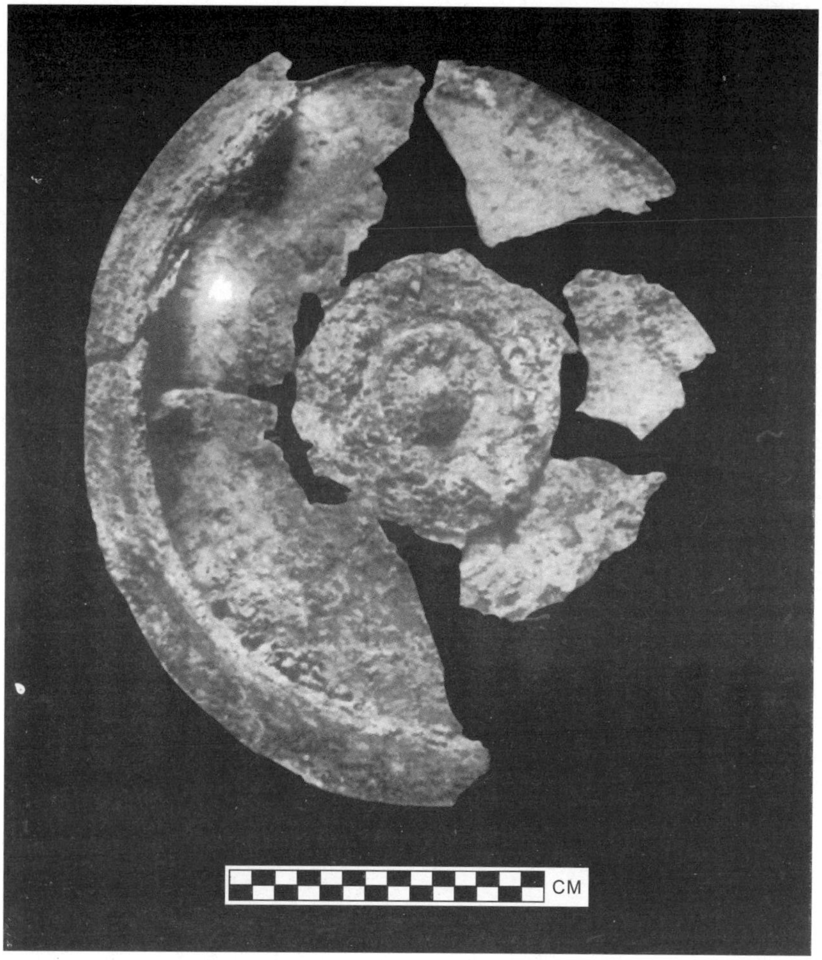

Singh & Chattopadhyay P1. 4: High tin Bronze vessel, Agiabir.

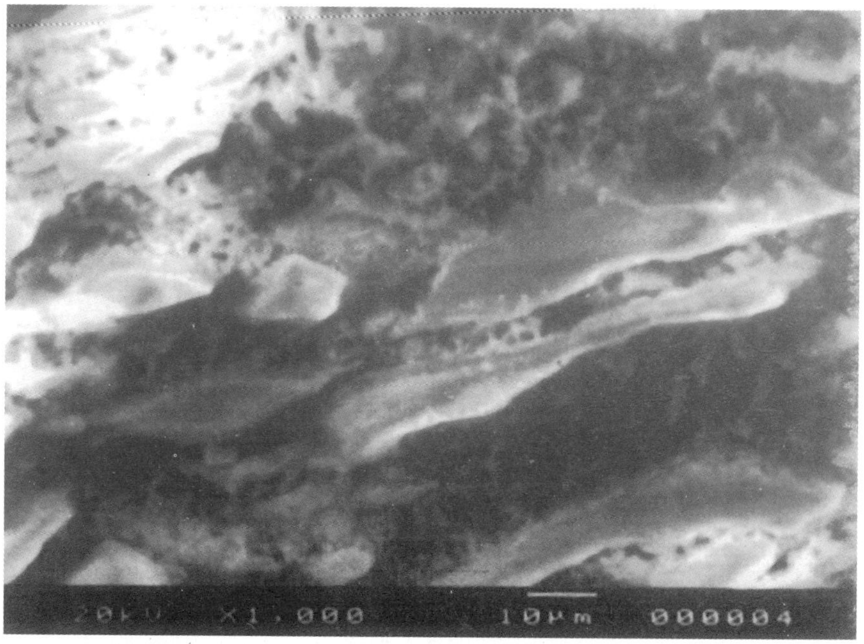

Singh & Chattopadhyay P1. 5: SEM Microstructure of knobbed vessel 1000X, Agiabir.

K.N. Dikshit P1. 1: General view, Lord Jagannath Temple, Puri

K.N. Dikshit P1. 2: Lakshmi temple wall covered under plaster.

K.N. Dikshit P1. 3: Lakshmi temple wall after removal of plaster.

K.N. Dikshit P1. 4: Lakshmi temple during the removal of plaster – part of sculpture noticed.

K.N. Dikshit P1. 5: Lakshmi temple during the removal of plaster – full sculpture visible.

K.N. Dikshit P1. 6: Lakshmi temple after the removal of plaster – sculpture wall noticed.

K.N. Dikshit P1. 7: Deplastering upto springing level, Lord Jagannath temple.

K.N. Dikshit P1. 8: Shikar after removal of plaster, Lord Jagannath temple.

K.N. Dikshit P1. 9: Location of falling stone, Lord Jagannath temple.

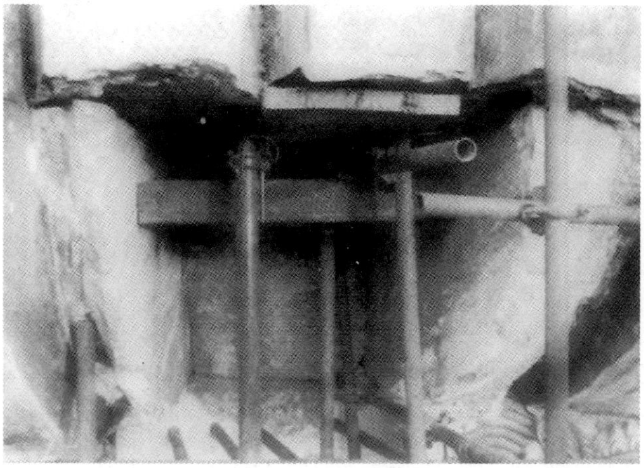

K.N. Dikshit P1. 10: Arrangement during fixing, Lord Jagannath temple.

K.N. Dikshit P1. 11: New stones fixed, Lord Jagannath temple.

K.N. Dikshit P1. 12: Arrangement of stress during fixing, Lord Jagannath temple.

K.N. Dikshit P1. 13: Drilling of holes for PMC grout, first floor, Lord Jagannath temple.

A.S. Gaur *et al.* P1. 1: Partially buried ring stone no. 25 off Somnath (scale: 45 cms with 15 cms divisions).

Rajendran. P1. 1: Panoramic view of the prehistoric and human fossil site at Odai.

Shivnanda. P1. 1: Lower palaeolithic tools from Umiam river: Meghalaya.

Shivnanda. P1. 2: Mawlyn Gkneng, view of Dolmens and Menhir. Meghalaya.

Shivnanda. P1. 3: Tuber Kamai Shong: view showing the Dolmens: Meghalaya.

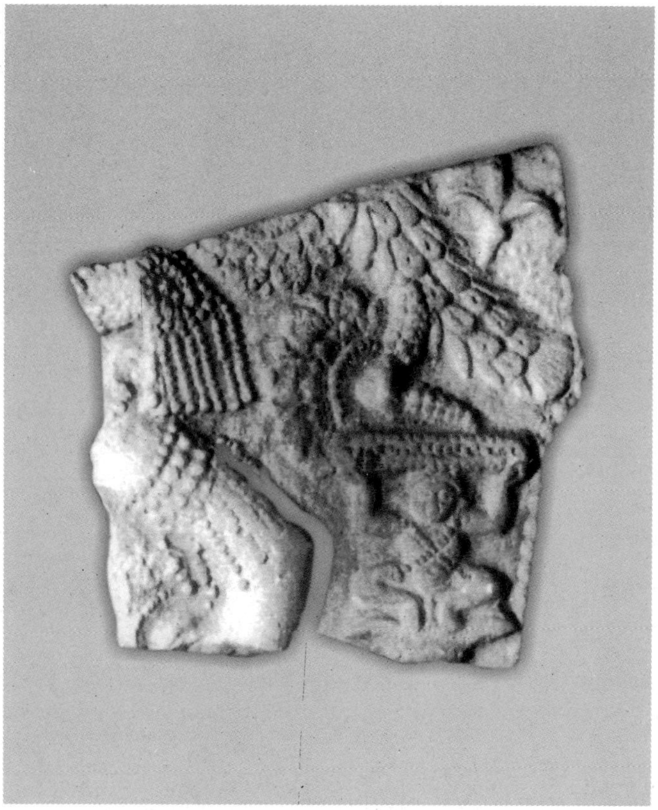

De. P1. 1: Two Yaksa supporting a pedestal (terracotta), Sunga, Chandraketugarh.

De. P1. 2: Two Yaksas supporting the throne of a deity (terracotta) (broken part of a cart), Sunga, Chandraketugarh.

Mani. P1. 1: Rabatak Inscription, Kafir Castle, Baghlan, Afghanistan.

Gupta ***et al.*** **P1. 1:** Vairoh creek and river, at Sanjan.

Gupta ***et al.*** **P1. 2:** Excavations 2002: Sanjan.

Gupta ***et al.*** **P1. 1A:** A three handled, high-necked jar in Glazed Buff Ware/TGW

Gupta ***et al.*** **P1. 2B:** Fragment of a decorated Glazed Buff Ware/TGW vessel

Gupta ***et al.*** **P1. 3:** Two potsherds and a rim fragment with painted designs in Glazed Pink Ware

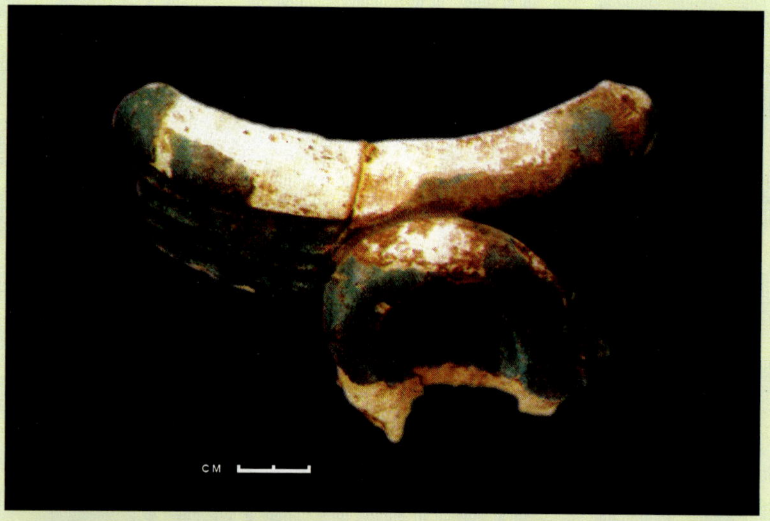

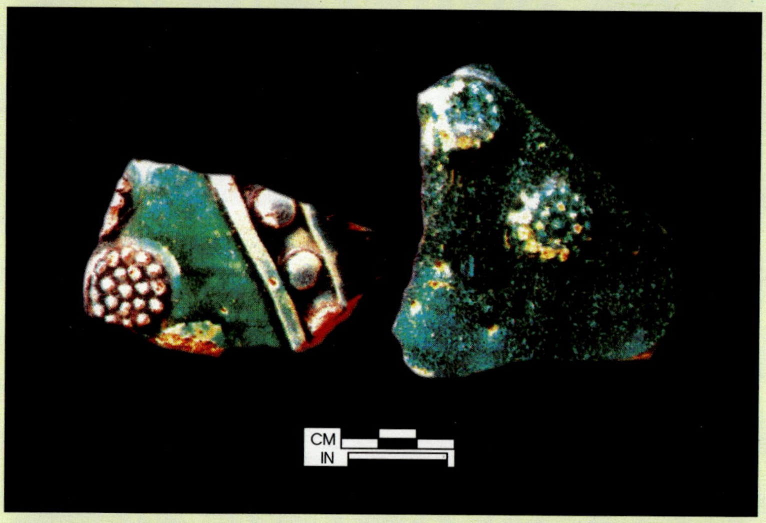

Gupta *et al.* Pl. 4-6: Glazed Buff Ware/TGW, Sanjan

Gupta *et al.* P1. 7: Glazed Buff Ware bowl with painted designs, Sanjan.

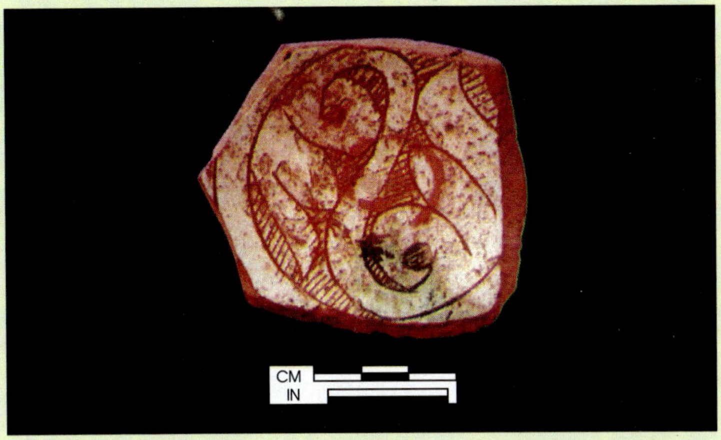

Gupta *et al.* P1. 8: Glazed Pink Ware base bowl with incised and painted designs, Sanjan.

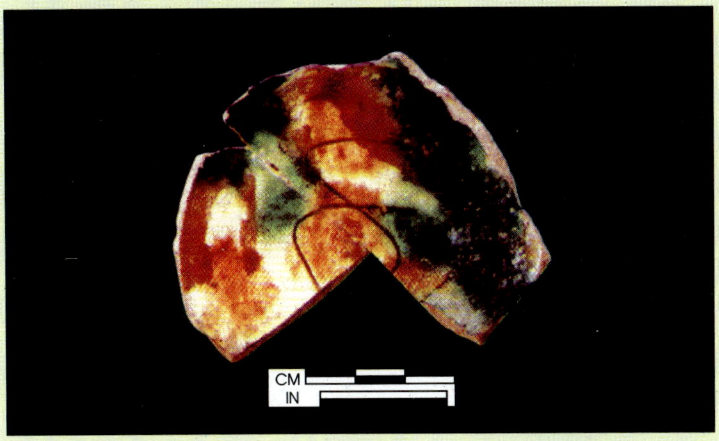

Gupta *et al.* P1. 9: Glazed Pink Ware base bowl with incised and painted designs, Sanjan.

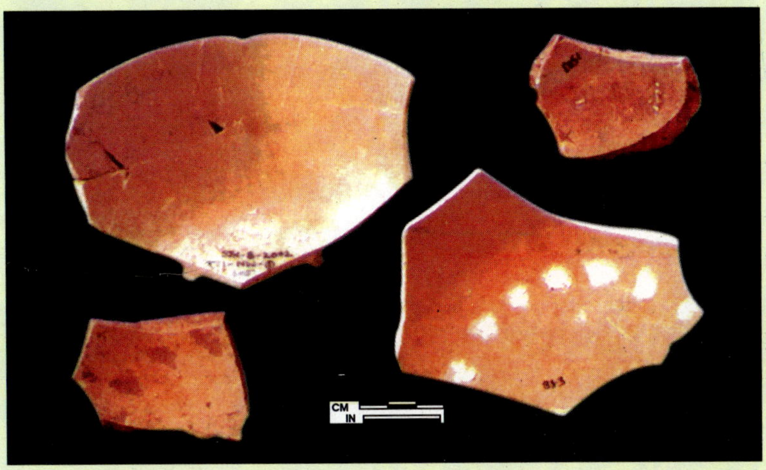

Gupta *et al.* P1. 10: Glazed Grey/stone ware bases, with Spur marks, Sanjan.

Gupta *et al.* P1. 11: Left: Square based rectangular sided bottle (9th-10th century AD)
Right: Eleven sided/facetted bottle (9th-10th century AD), Sanjan.

Gupta *et al.* P1. 13: Neck and shoulders of a long necked globular vessel of blue glass, Sanjan.

Gupta *et al.* P1. 12: Glass vessel bases, Sanjan.